DEBATING RACE
WITH MICHAEL ERIC DYSON

Michael Eric Dyson

BASIC
CIVITAS
BOOKS

A MEMBER OF THE PERSEUS BOOKS GROUP
New York

Books published by Basic Civitas Books are available at special discounts for bulk purchases in
the United States by corporations, institutions, and other organizations. For more information,
please contact the Special Markets Department at the Perseus Books Group, 11 Cambridge Center,
Cambridge, MA 02142, or call (617) 252-5298 or (800) 255-1514, or e-mail
special.markets@perseusbooks.com.

Text set in 10-point Berthold Baskerville

Cataloging-in-Publication Data for this book is available from the Library of Congress.
ISBN-10: 0-465-00206-4
ISBN-13: 978-0-465-00206-1

07 08 09 10 11 / 10 9 8 7 6 5 4 3 2 1

TO THE MEMORY OF THREE
BRILLIANT AND PRECIOUS FRIENDS
GONE TOO SOON

ELIZABETH ANN MAGUIRE
Beloved Editor
1958–2006

VIRGIL JOHN MAUPIN
Cherished Son-in-Law
1975–2006

COACH JOE HOSKINS
Noble Teacher
1944–2006

CONTENTS

PREFACE
A Taste for Talk

Over the past decade and a half, I've had the opportunity to have many public conversations about a wide range of subjects that tickled my intellectual fancy and captured the social imagination, from politics to sports, and religion to rap music. My vocation as a scholar took off just as the phenomenon of the black public intellectual was being celebrated or scorned in august publications and academic circles. Two years out of graduate school, in 1995, I found my face and work featured in a widely circulated *New Yorker* magazine essay that also explored the scholarship of bell hooks, Cornel West, and Derrick Bell. As the youngest member of this group of public intellectuals, I'd written only two books—one a collection of scholarly essays in cultural criticism and the other a study of the cultural renaissance and intellectual appeal of Malcolm X. I was humbled and amazed to be counted in their number, and I have worked eagerly and diligently since to justify my standing as a scholar interested in exploring complex ideas in public.

I learned early that such a desire is often frowned on by many scholars in the academy. Writing in an intelligent but clear fashion for the broad public is seen by many academics as beneath their profession or, much worse, as betraying the scholarly guild. But I didn't become a scholar simply to impress other scholars. Because I hadn't pursued higher education until I was twenty-one—I was a teen father who lived for three years on welfare before enrolling in college—I was much more mature and focused in my academic plans. My intellectual vocation drew from my wish to use learning as a springboard for public conversation that would ultimately make a difference to folk beyond the ivory tower.

Then too, becoming an ordained minister at about the same time that I started my formal studies meant that I never saw the academy as the only means to tell stories, challenge myths, and share learning. The pulpit had been open to me as a means of wrestling with truth and faith, and as a way to express my desire to not only study the world but, in my small way, change it as well. And because I'd been writing speeches and delivering them in public since I was eleven years old—when I entered a local oratorical contest sponsored by the Detroit Optimist Club—I had a keen appreciation for the power of the spoken word to inspire human beings to deeper thought and higher purpose. Beyond the mechanics of good speech and communication, I reveled in the sheer delight of oral expression: the beauty of speech, the sensuousness of words, and the sacred sway of rhetoric in the mouth of a master.

I yearned to grasp hold of both the great poets and writers I encountered—from Alfred Lord Tennyson and Abraham Lincoln, to James Baldwin and Ralph Ellison—and the great oral technicians who lit my path to the majesty of the spoken word, including my pastor, Dr. Frederick Sampson, and the legendary Detroit lawyer, Kenneth Cockrel, to Martin Luther King, Jr., and Malcolm X. From Sampson and King I learned the soaring song of intelligent and passionate sermonizing: speechmaking and homily-giving as the art of rhetorical transaction with God and human beings. From Cockrel and Malcolm X I learned that speech could be forensic and empirical: a means to prove and persuade, to argue a case, and to state facts ordered by reason and morality. In this mode, conversation, debate, and dialogue are supreme means of communication.

It is the latter mode that makes up the book you hold in your hand. I have had the privilege of engaging in stimulating public conversation with a broad range of interlocutors for nearly two decades. A lot of these conversations have taken place in university halls, in religious institutions, in public meeting halls, on lecture stages, and on television and radio. I've had the chance to speak with professors and pundits, spokespersons and leaders, journalists and actors, comics and commissioners, artists and activists, and with Jews, Latinos, and all sorts of black and white folk.

The big issue that unites the conversations, dialogues, and debates presented in these pages is race: how it is conceived; how it is expressed; how it is lived; how it confers power; how it undermines social stability; how it ruins or revives lives; how it is embraced and discarded. As you'll read here, my vocation as a public intellectual has taken me from the halls of the United States Senate to the stage of major political organizations, from sanctuaries to studios. I have had the chance to break bread with political comrades and go to the mat with ideological foes. But I've also disagreed at points with colleagues who share my broad worldview, while striking occasional accord with figures at the opposite end of the political continuum.

These conversations, dialogues, and debates on America's Great Problem are among the most memorable encounters I've had in my public intellectual vocation so far. They are more than the record of speech in search of truth and change; they are the imprint of talk meant to alter perception and sway thinking while illuminating the moral and intellectual paths down which such rhetoric can travel. Some say that talk is cheap; I say that talk is one of the most precious means we have to tap the roots of our democracy while expanding the minds that define its substance. In this spirit, I offer these words as a witness to hope—to the belief that wise words are better than wicked ways. I believe that disagreement in speech and working out our differences in word and in the world are better than hate or war. In the end, talking really is better than killing.

INTRODUCTION

Imani Perry

There is no debate on this: Michael Eric Dyson is riveting. And alongside his oratorical magic is a great depth of intellect and commitment. In his example, we see how the proverbial "fire in the bones" blazes even brighter when stoked with knowledge. This collection of debates that the reverend scholar has participated in for more than a decade displays the arc of his insightful commentaries and conversations with a diverse and impressive group of fellow public figures.

"Public intellectual," unfortunately, has become a hackneyed title. Some professional academics derisively take it to mean someone who spends a lot of time on television rather than writing books or doing research. The general public, on the other hand, often takes it to mean someone who is so smart that we just love to hear him or her talk, even if we don't actually listen to what that person is saying. Michael Eric Dyson, however, is a public intellectual in the best sense of the word. He is a serious writer and scholar, and yet he consistently shares his message beyond the ivory tower. The world listens because he doesn't speak from some high gilded perch. He gets down into the nitty-gritty of life with the rest of us, at once an adored teacher and an everyman.

Michael Eric Dyson, sometimes called a "hip hop scholar" due to his urban poetics and because, as they say in the hood, he "knows what time it is," is the author of more than a dozen books on a range of subjects. This volume, however, is a rare gift. It allows readers to re-visit many of his most important live exchanges over social issues with other leading thinkers, politicians, pundits, and policy makers. It is also somewhat reminiscent of another literary tradition: published sermons. In the history of African American letters, the sermon is both an oral and textual art. The homilist has a live moment, but the very best sermons are often transcribed or taped, and become cherished artifacts that we return to for spiritual sustenance. It is no accident that Dyson, so rooted in this tradition, would understand the usefulness of sharing debate and dialogue in written form. Whether we agree or disagree with Professor Dyson on a given issue, these newly published debates give us something to hold onto beyond the television or radio moment and the opportunity to share those live exchanges with an even wider audience. These debates provide vehicles for reflection and conversation in our daily lives.

The role of the public intellectual is an essential one in times of change, conflict, political confusion, war, and suffering. We need global scholar-citizens to weigh in, to help us make sense of it all. But more than that, we need people who are willing to enter the fray and speak to what is good, humane, and just. Enter Dr. Dyson. He keeps his rhetorical finger on the pulse of our world.

The book is also in a sense a cultural history of the past decade and a half, and is thus a record of the many social challenges we have faced and continue to struggle with. A number of the earlier debates shared here are prescient of issues that have since grown to greater prominence and puzzlement—from the politics of immigration to what the *New York Times* refers to as the "crisis of black men." Hence, this is not just a text version of a public intellectual holding forth. It is a document of a public engagement, in which Dyson shines but also, at times, steps back and becomes simply part of the fabric of the conversation.

In the twenty-first century, academics are increasingly in the public eye. But they are often trotted out only as objective experts on specific details and don't offer moral, ethical, or critical assessments of the issues at hand. Michael Eric Dyson, who arrived as the junior star in the early '90s rise of the black public intellectual, a movement that served to revive the intellectual life of Americans generally, doesn't exist in the narrow box that academic-pundits of today are so often placed. He argues positions as well as facts. Especially important, in this book he doesn't stand alone. This work shows him as part of a community of thinkers. In that way, the life revealed in this book might remind those who are familiar with black history of early twentieth century African American "race men and women" who spent their lives thinking, talking, and acting to address the race problem. For them, as with Dyson, talk was neither cheap nor superfluous.

The impressive array of figures with whom Dyson debates is matched by the venues in which the debates occur: on the outlets helmed by well-respected broadcast journalists such as Mara Tapp, Tavis Smiley, and Juan Williams, in mass media arenas such as the Bill O'Reilly and Bill Maher shows, and in the halls of academe and on the airwaves of NPR.

In these debates, Dyson speaks with people all across the political spectrum; with a diverse body of professionals: academics, commentators, policy makers, and entertainers; and with a multiracial, multigendered group who represent multiple constituencies. The diversity of the conversations is not just about who they include, who they are in front of, and where they take place, but also in the formats. Some are interviews, others are round tables, and still others are adversarial. Each has its own distinct way of showing how critical subjects can be explored.

Although the chapters are thematically arranged, several important ideas cut across all the sections. One is this: Although this book is titled "Debating Race," race in the contemporary world is about much more than the color of one's skin. It is deeply tied to ethnicity, power, class, culture, gender roles, belief systems, institutions, and identity. Hence, debating race is also about debating all these as well as other issues. One cannot speak of race in two-dimensional terms any longer.

Another theme that emerges is the value of the Socratic ideal of learning through conversation. These are not a bunch of public figures standing on soapboxes; these are true conversations.

And a third important, but perhaps more subtle, idea that comes through in this book is that despite the fact of media consolidation, such that now multimedia company ownership is held in a few hands (a phenomenon which has been a cause for alarm in many democratically minded people), and despite the dumbing down of our television and print news media, our media worlds continue to have spaces in which people can address important and complicated issues.

In this book, you'll witness Dyson's measured responses to deeply challenging questions about many events and issues. And it soon becomes clear that although he debates and strongly identifies as a political progressive, he is not stuck in a simplistic or calcified position on anything, nor does he have a knee-jerk reaction to even the most rattling challenges. He takes all ideas seriously, weighs their merits and their limitations, and then illuminates.

Like his many audiences, the reader of this volume will be struck by Dyson's disregard for what or who is considered highbrow or lowbrow. Nothing is too high to be subject to critique, nothing is too low for it not to be taken seriously. He can talk with the same rigor about daytime TV and the philosophy of Martin Buber. There is philosophy, cultural criticism, and good old opinion in these pages. He'll call George Bush out, to his face, and Bill Cosby too. In the words of the hood, "If you don't know, you better ask somebody." In particular, the ongoing face-off between Dyson and Cosby is a public vetting of an ideological conflict over how black people should be seen and see themselves that promises to be of historic importance. President Bush, on the other hand, was rendered to sputtering frustration by Dyson. (When news anchor Brian Williams, in an interview with the president, cited Dyson's characterization of Bush as a "clueless patrician" on Williams's program the previous day, Bush could only manage, "Dyson doesn't know . . . I don't know Dyson, and Dyson doesn't know me . . . the Professor Dysons of the world say things . . .")

But Dyson treats even his heroes with rigor and skepticism. When he talks about Martin Luther King, Jr., for example, and brings up King's infidelity and his "sampling" of others' words, it is a risky road but one taken because Dyson has such a deep love for King despite, or even perhaps in part because of, his human fallibility and frailty.

Because Dr. Dyson rejects treating highbrow and lowbrow subjects with different standards, and because he refuses to think high-status people are immune to critique when it comes to their personal failings, he answers questions with a broader collection of evidence than that generally drawn on by other public intellectuals. For example, in his debate with Shelby Steele, in which the theme of black responsibility for social ills is at issue, Dyson talks about the ubiquitous Sunday morning and sidewalk talk in African American communities in which responsibility is a key cultural tenet, not a flouted social norm. Evidence comes from many quarters.

Although some of these debates were, and still are, hot topics, others are far less likely to garner headlines, although they are no less prescient. The nuanced discussion of black and Latino relations in chapter 5 is one essential example of Dyson's dedication to talk about what matters, even if we don't yet know its importance.

The seriousness with which he takes the range of his subjects is tempered by a good-natured embrace of ideas, a sense of humor, and a love for all the people in his earshot, who he pushes to think hard but never looks down on. We may not understand every word he says, but he isn't saying them so that we don't understand. He's telling us to go to the dictionary. And unlike his other texts, which originated as (elegantly) written documents, the laughter, timing, and grace that are signature features of his oral style jump off the page.

There are conflicts here; some are clearly beefs and others are gentle disagreements. For example, in chapter 15, there appears to be no love lost between Dyson and Joe Klein in their discussion of the Million Man March (or between Dyson and Shelby Steele or Mary Matalin, for that matter, in other chapters). He takes his opponents on in a dignified but incisive fashion. You get the sense that Dyson never thinks about how to stay out of trouble. He meets it head-on. On the other hand, he doesn't attack—he dissects. That's how we know he's not just stubborn when he clashes with ideological opposites; he's on a mission. Part of why so many people in his audiences trust and appreciate him is because he is willing to take unpopular positions. He uses his platform not to be shock jock but to be a "holler scholar" who is both loud and righteous.

On the other hand, some chapters are conversations with like-minded thinkers. These read somewhat like exchanges behind the walls of a think tank or a literary salon, where all involved parties are trying to develop a deeper understanding. Some of the most beautiful exchanges are with Dr. Dyson's intellectual peers and friends, such as in chapter 6, where he sits with others (the lone African American) to talk about whiteness and white identity, or in chapter 10, where he talks to Cornel West, a Princeton professor similarly rooted in the black theological tradition and Western philosophy. In these debates you see amongst all the participants a heartfelt desire to serve humanity.

Likewise, his engagements with politicians are responses to the call to serve. Chapter 14, an excerpt from his Senate testimony in 2000 about youth and violence, is a nuanced rendering of the relationship between rap music, deindustrialization, and the effects of capital and inequality. Meaningfully, he testified in an effort to affect the positions of elected officials, not merely to assert his own. When he talks about contemporary basketball and Latrell Sprewell (chapter 16), you see the same drive to edify us and to help us understand the vulnerability and complexity of black public figures and popular culture.

The great variety of the chapters reminds us of the real point of debate. It is not sensationalism or aggression; it is a way of sharing and arguing many points of view and many aspects of an idea. *Debating Race* is just such a rhetorical and expository delivery of thought.

This volume may help readers garner a deeper understanding of Dyson the public intellectual. Critics will be hard-pressed to claim that his public persona is too much flash, or pomp and circumstance. Read the debates. They are without exception examples of thoughtful interventions on important issues. They are alternately humble, full of bravado, emotional, even personal, but never egotistical or empty.

This is but a small fraction of the debates in which Dr. Dyson has engaged. For mention of Dyson's future public debates and examples of his recorded or transcribed debates not included here, look on his Web site, Michaelericdyson.com.

Readers who are familiar with Dyson the public figure but not Dyson the scholar will find this volume a useful introduction to many of his other works, especially *Come Hell or High Water*, written in the aftermath of Hurricane Katrina; *Is Bill Cosby Right? Or Has Middle Class Black America Lost Its Mind?; I May Not Get There with You: The True Martin Luther King, Jr.*; *Holler If You Hear Me: Searching for Tupac Shakur;* and *Reflecting Black: African-American Cultural Criticism.*

In sum, Professor Dyson guides a public, which is sometimes terribly anti-intellectual, to want to learn, think, and understand. I know that readers will appreciate being able to return to the debates again and again, and to have the time to look up his many and diverse references. Dyson is not a bourgeois intellectual (he rejects bourgie affectations), nor is he an organic intellectual (he has formal training). Instead, he is a sincere, from-the-gut intellectual. And I am honored to introduce this volume, in which he shares that sincerity and passion with the world.

DEBATING RACE

PART I

CIVIL RIGHTS

MOVIN' ON UP?

Segregation, Integration, and Assimilation

with Gary Orfield and Arturo Vargas; moderated by Mara Tapp

In the fall of 1998, several scholars, journalists, activists, artists, and authors gathered in Racine, Wisconsin, at the Johnson Foundation's Wingspread Conference Center to discuss the issue of race and ethnicity. Divided into five panels, each one examined a different aspect of racial and ethnic identity, solidarity, and conflict. Expertly moderated by host Mara Tapp, the programs were taped for later broadcast on "Conversations from Wingspread," a radio show that was originally broadcast from 1972 until 1988 and revived in 1998 for a couple of years. The gathering provided some of the most stimulating conversations about race and ethnicity that I have ever participated in. This conversation, with Harvard educational expert Gary Orfield and Latino activist and advocate Arturo Vargas, offers a wide-ranging exploration of the politics of (re)segregation, integration, and assimilation in the United States, especially as they relate to public schools and bilingual education.

Mara Tapp: I'd like each of you to tell me what you see as the defining issue with regard to race and ethnicity at present.

Michael Eric Dyson: I think that one of the defining issues has to be the tension between memory and identity. We live in what has been termed "the United States of Amnesia" when it comes to race and ethnicity in American society—our inability to acknowledge the social context and the political context that frame debates about what's happening now. We see this in popular culture with issues over slavery—to what degree was the slave past so significant that it continues to cast a long shadow over American life? The recent brouhaha over Thomas Jefferson, and now DNA proves, alas, what people of color have known all along: that is, white slave masters had relationships with people of color, and it had a significant impact upon the construction of American material and social life. And the way it relates to identity, then, is that there has been an enormous array of contests over how we define ourselves as Americans.

People are often posing the questions to people of color and women, "Are you Latino first or are you American? Are you black first or are you an American? Are you a woman first or an American?" And the reality is the simultaneity of our identities; they converge together, they come to us at the same time. And many people have not been trained to think about or to understand the complexity of that convergence. And yet, we must pay attention to the particular ways in which our identities are shaped as a result of race and ethnicity. So the tension between what we have been and where we have come from, and what we are now, continues to express itself, I think, with a lethal intensity, with a ferocity that is indexed in the following: that people simply keep asking the question, "Haven't we been there and done that, and can't we move forward?" But until we wrestle with those demons that have shaped and framed us, we will scarcely be able to embrace the full measure of our humanity as citizens in American society.

Tapp: When you say, "Haven't we been there and done that," I want to ask if color doesn't play a significant role here. Because it strikes me that many of us in this country, particularly people who have fairer complexions are—forgive me—mongrels. They may have some Italian, some Irish, some English, some American Indian. And yet, for some reason, there's not that same kind of query going on, is there?

Dyson: I think there's no question that people are trying to debate now the nature of their roots. And there's a kind of politics of resentment going on. Because when people of color seize the opportunity to announce what their identities have been and how America has, in some sense, leveraged its weight against them in unfair ways, people tend to retreat into their wombs of ethnic piety. So they begin to say, "I'm Italian, I'm Polish," and so on. But you're absolutely right in this sense: many immigrants who arrived here from Europe in the early part of the twentieth century, the latter part of the nineteenth century, and even before certainly have not been honest about the process of their identities being shaped in American culture. And as a result of that, [they] tend to ignore, or at least fail to recognize, the differences between ethnicities and race. And one of the things we have to come to grips with is that there's a profound difference between ethnicity and race. And let me give you one example.

I was recently going to LaGuardia Airport, and a Polish brother picked me up. And he had rage. It was visceral, tangible rage. And I told him, "Sir, if you go down this street and not down that street, you'll get there." He said, "Be quiet. Shut up. Don't say anything to me." I said, "Look, brother, you don't have to speak to me in that tone." And then I said [to myself], "Let me try the Christian route." I said, "Where are you from?" He said, "Poland, where we work hard."

And then he said, "Where are you from?" I said, "I'm from Detroit." He says, "Originally, 99 percent of people in this country are from Europe." And then he went on to tell me how they worked hard and people came to this country because of a free education. And I said, "There are not many black people in Poland." He said, "One percent, and we have to work hard there. That's why they're not there." So we got into this kind of, shall we say, extended consternation, a kind of nasty exchange.

And finally I told him, I said, "You know, what's interesting is you've been here one year. You look at me. I've got a suit on. I'm a black man. You don't know my educational pedigree. You don't have to know that to treat me like a human being. But you don't even realize it. In the context of this country, I can't buy you—but I could certainly rent you for a long time." [*Laughter*] "And what's interesting is that you have the unblushing hubris and pride to assume [you're superior] because of your white skin—whether you learned that in one year in America, or global technology has mediated to you the belief that black people are mongrels, or dogs, or beneath the dignity to be treated like human beings." Whatever, the fact is that he learned that lesson. And he was an immigrant. He failed to acknowledge my fundamental humanity because of the lessons he received from this American soil that were being beamed across the world, or that he learned right there in New York City. So, for me, the tension between ethnicity and race has to be explored in very serious ways before we can come to grips with what America is.

Tapp: We need to come back to that as well, because I think we're going to be running into that in the course of this conversation, how those two butt against each other, and how they create tensions between those groups. But let me try to bring some of the other people into this conversation as well. Gary Orfield, I wouldn't want to follow that, but go ahead—your sense of the defining issue for race and ethnicity at present.

Gary Orfield: Before I answer your question I have to say even us white guys run into trouble with New York City cabdrivers. [*Laughter*] I think that what's going on in the country is we're going through a very big change, and we want to forget about where we're coming from, and we don't have any plans about where we're going to, and we're being polarized in many ways by very short-sighted politicians. We are going through a huge demographic change, the largest of any major democracy. In the next half century we're going to be only about half white, or Anglo as we'll probably be called, or European American, or whatever we will be then. And we will have ninety-five million Latinos if the present trends continue; maybe eighty million African Americans. We're going to be a country of tremendous diversity—forty or fifty million Asians. That's what the Census Bureau is telling us. It'll be only twenty years or so before that begins to happen in our schools on that huge level.

There are tremendous inequalities in our society today, [measured] by race and by poverty. They're growing. We have the most unequal distribution of income and opportunity of any major democracy. In the 1960s and '70s we developed a set of policies to try to make that work better. We're now dismantling them on a very large scale under the leadership of a Supreme Court that was constructed by Ronald Reagan and George H. W. Bush. We do not have an alternate plan. We think it will just work out automatically, and it won't. And we have to face up to that. We have not cured the problems of our history. We have not achieved equality for even one day, in terms of outcomes in the society. We can't deny that, and we have to try to resolve it. And we have to resolve it, those of us who are white, before we become a minority, and minority rights become not just a theory but something that we have to worry about also.

Tapp: Again, I want to come back to some of that, but I do want to bring Arturo Vargas into this conversation, as well.

Arturo Vargas: I think the demographic shifts that Gary described, in fact, are happening now. The defining issue, I would say, is power. And how do we share power? How do we shift power from one group to another? Or do we have to shift? Does somebody have to lose in order to win? How do we share political power, how do we share economic power? I think there's an incredible discomfort today in communities—not just white communities, but African American communities, Latino communities—about this change in demography. And there is conflict that emerges: struggles over economic resources, struggles over jobs, over quality of education, over political power between blacks and whites, and blacks and Latinos, and Asians and Latinos. And all that's in the mix. So when we talk about race and ethnicity, it's not just minorities versus whites, it's everybody debating each other. And we have to realize it. How do we negotiate this?

Tapp: Who, honestly, is going to stand up here and say, "Okay, I'll give up power on behalf of my group? I'm going to relinquish this because I'm just such a nice guy." I mean, that's not about to happen, is it?

Vargas: Well, someone once told me, power isn't given—power is taken. And I think that is exactly where we are today in America. Power is being taken. And we do it peacefully, generally, if we look at political power, through redistricting, through electing people. And of course the Supreme Court has done a very effective job in trying to eliminate those modes of shifting power from one group to another by decimating the Voting Rights Act. But I think that's a very strong question that we will have in the year 2001 when it comes time to redraw congressional and state legislative lines. When we won't have the same law we had in 1991, how are these groups going to share power?

Orfield: One of the dangers of making it [the debate about race] into a conflict over power is that a lot of the goals of each of the groups are exactly the same, and they're all being obscured, and we're being diverted from them by divisions in which people who have power now are playing one group against another, and using wedge issues and other things.

Tapp: Give me an example.

Orfield: Everyone in the United States wants their kids to be able to go to college. A fight is being created over who gets into college, not over whether we have more college, or whether we have adequate financial aid and so forth. It's very important who gets into the existing colleges. But the other part is equally important, and it is a common interest that everybody has. And we need to figure out how to get past these issues of race by admitting that we have racial problems we have to solve—but also recognizing we have class and other problems we have to solve.

Tapp: Michael Eric Dyson, do you agree with Gary Orfield?

Dyson: Yeah. Well, I think to a degree, yes. One theory of power is that it's located in a centralized place and somebody wields it mercilessly against another force that cannot prevail against it. On the other hand, there's a notion of power that says, well, it breaks out everywhere. And it breaks out among people of color, even. And one of the interesting debates, for instance, in California is to what degree can there be coalitions forged among black and brown peoples around issues of enormous import to one particular community as the demographics change? For instance, in South Central L.A., what used to be a predominately black neighborhood is now predominately a Latino neighborhood. And so what's important there is: what issues are crucial to the maintenance and preservation of Latino communities in relationship to African American communities? The issue of bilingual education. The first go around, a lot of black folk voted with their predominantly white colleagues *against* bilingual education, not understanding, I think, the complexities of the issues involved and how they hurt their brown brothers and sisters, buying uncritically into the stereotypes being foisted upon them by the large political machine. So I think that in a sense, it's not simply power, top down, white people against everybody else. It's also about the scampering for scarcer resources among people of color. And if they forge coalitions in crucial and credible ways, they'll certainly be able to deploy them politically.

Tapp: Let's talk about bilingualism a little bit. That's a nice example. Let me go to you first, Arturo Vargas, because there clearly are two poles on this one. I'm sure there's some middle ground. It's hard to hear sometimes. And I want to hear a little bit about research, but I also want to hear a little bit about reality. So let's start with reality with you.

Vargas: Well, I think one of the major issues we have is that when people say bilingualism, or bilingual education, they hear non-English language. They hear, "Oh, you just want to learn Spanish." That it's only important for you to learn Spanish and to not learn English. And they don't get it that when you say *bilingual,* you're talking two languages. You're talking about using a native language to develop literacy, and using that native language to then transfer literacy skills to the child so the child can learn English, looking at your classical model of translation in bilingual education. The interesting thing about Prop 227 in California is that the people who have been crying out the most about how it's affected them have been the middle class, which has been able to send their children to emergent class schools where their English-speaking children can learn Spanish. Now that, in theory, is illegal in California,

Tapp: *See,* this is the part I don't get. We sit here and we talk all the time about how our test scores are so much lower than those of Europeans countries, how our children aren't learning as much. And we sort of conveniently forget sometimes that children learn many languages in European countries; that this is one of the few continents where we speak but one language, and not always well. Now, what do the data actually show us about bilingual education, and is that what this is about?

Orfield: This fight, and all these fights, have mixes of race, of polarization, of actual conflict over substance, and lots of prejudices. And lots of false memories of the past, of what happened to previous groups of immigrants. And lots of bad analogies. What we actually know about bilingualism isn't really a whole lot. The National Academy of Science recently summarized the research. It seems apparent that it takes most children some time to acquire a second language. A recent national study of reading said children should start learning how to read in a language they can speak fluently, which makes sense. Now if, as in California, under this proposition, you're not allowed to have more than one year of bilingualism, the kids probably will not speak English fluently, because they're isolated and segregated away from native English-speaking children, and the conservatives don't want to do anything about that.

So the result of that will be that they'll probably have extra problems learning how to read, which poor kids and high poverty schools have anyway. So these problems will be confounded by the politicization of an issue that's pretty complicated and difficult. And it seems to me this is exactly the kind of issue where we need to understand each other and think about whether there isn't a better outcome where we could use the resource of millions of Spanish-speaking and Chinese-speaking children to help our children—who are English speaking—learn another language, as well as to help them acquire fluent English proficiency. Virtually all immigrant parents wanted their children to be fluently English proficient. And they'd like to maintain their original language as well. And it's an asset for us if they can do both of those things.

Tapp: Michael Eric Dyson?

Dyson: Absolutely right. We can't deny, though, questions of literacy and linguistic ability have always indexed peoples' intelligence level. So it doesn't have to be about different languages—say Spanish versus English. Within African American communities, the whole debate about Ebonics—although not apparently on its face about bilingualism—was a real example of how debates about "proper" or "standard" English have been deployed against people who are powerless to defend themselves, and [how we've] not recognized in this country that we've had all kinds of loose standards when it comes to mainstream white Americans speaking, or not being able to speak, standard English. And when it comes to, say, bilingualism on the one hand, or so-called Ebonics on the others, it is about power. It's about who's able to determine what's proficient in what language. And it's about ignorance, I think. Because both in terms of bilingualism and in terms of Ebonics, the point is not to teach people how to speak "wrongly," how to speak non-English. The point is how do we meet people where they are? If you are dealing with a class of people, and you go into that class and say, "Ce n'est pas difficile d'apprendre Francais—c'est facile," and you know what that means, then you're in the wrong class. Move. If you don't know what that means, somebody's got to translate that for you. So what is the big deal by saying, listen, if we have an immigrant group of people who speak Spanish, if we want to reach them with the possibility of having higher test scores, why are we going to force them to a test of English as a foreign language, a second language, without reaching them in their primary language first and then facilitating a transition from the indigenous linguistic base to the base we want, which is English?

Secondly, it's about power in this sense: we're the only country in the modern West that celebrates its monolinguisticality. We ain't speaking but one language, we proud of it, and don't be messing us up with nothing about nobody else. We're damn proud of being rigid, and we're damn proud of being ignorant. So we go all over the world. We want to force people to speak English, as opposed to involving ourselves in other countries. In Ghana, poor people speak five languages, three dialectics, and two regional understandings of their linguistic derivation just to get around. And here we are in America: we can be *affluent* in any language. Can we be *fluent* in any language is the real question. And that is a question of power, it's a question of region, it's a question of resource, and it's a question of orientation. Because here's the final analysis: it is not simply about language; it's about power, in terms of who gets to come here. Immigration policies are directed against Jose. They are *not* directed against Jurgen. Because we want Jurgen to come over here and help us on the super-information highway, whereas we think Jose comes across the border so he can help us rake our lawn or be a nanny to our children. And I think we have to be honest about that.

Orfield: I've often thought, what would happen if the universities in California and Texas started giving preference to students who could speak fluently two languages?

Vargas: They'd be on financial aid and be able to go to college free. [*Laughter*] But I think the point that was made about bilingual education, at its core, is: do we have a commitment to educate Latino children? Asian children? And I think the answer is no. We don't yet have that commitment. If we talk about does bilingual education work, I think bilingual education largely has been set up to fail, because we have not invested the resources into a good bilingual education program. If you go to, I think, your average bilingual education classroom, when it was legal in California, typically you found a teacher who was not bilingual. You had a part-time teacher's aide who spoke Spanish, who did most of the teaching with no training. And they call that bilingual education. That is not bilingual education. That is the state of education that we're giving children of color in this society today.

Orfield: Arturo, don't you think one of the problems has been that Latinos have been on the defensive on this issue so they've been not criticizing what's wrong with their own programs, because they think that they'll lose it all? And it's gotten very vulnerable to criticism by others.

Vargas: Absolutely. We've been so focused on defending what little we have that we have not been focused on actually insisting on quality education.

Dyson: But you know what's interesting about that debate too? All of a sudden anybody can say anything, halfway sounding intelligent, about people of color issues without any kind of training. We wouldn't stand up and say anything about Heisenberg's Principle of Uncertainty, or Chaos Theory, if we were non-physicists. But everybody feels capable of speaking about people of color issues. And one of the interesting things about Ebonics was all these Negroes who had been trained by people like they mommas and daddies—who spoke Ebonics—all of a sudden were outdone. "Oh my God, we're gonna teach our kids Ebonics." You ain't gonna teach kids what they already know. So the thing is, what is wrong, then, with acknowledging Ebonics, or Black English, as a credible linguistic derivation imposed upon people of color for centuries—when literacy was literally illegal? Second, a lot of people spoke Ebonics [when they] were coming up, and they were bilingual in that sense. You could be at home sayin', "I'm fixin' to go to the sto'." My daddy said, "I'm fittin' to go to the sto'. I'll be back directly." Now, I didn't say to him, "Father, is that a geographical dislocation? [*Laughter*] The point of your departure is significantly different than the point of your return." Because I wanted to live. [*Laughter*] But I understood what he was talking about, right? And so my point is, it's not simply about power in the sense of who owns it, who wields it, and who's able to prevent people from learning English. It's also about the rigid attitudes of some Americans that are so fundamentally racist that we're unable to understand that language is a tool of power. Language becomes a vehicle of self-expression. We love it when it's on a rap album. We love it when it's on TV spoken by Damon Wayans and the *WB* brothers. We think it's a source of enormous economy. But we denigrate it when people themselves choose to commandeer their own English and speak it the way they know how. I think we got to deal with the issues of culture, of racism, of power, *and* of economic inequality to get to the bottom of that.

Tapp: I want to throw assimilation in here for a minute. Because what I think Michael Eric Dyson just described, in a way, is an experience that we've had before. And Gary Orfield, let me go to you. I think you touched on this a moment ago when we talked about this divide between race and ethnicity, which we said we'd come back to. Let's do that now. How many examples can we think of, let's call them European immigrant examples, where people were embarrassed, mortified even, by the way their parents spoke, whether that was with a heavy Polish accent—to go back to your cab driver [Michael]—Russian, Latvian, Swedish, German, and their effort to get away from that? Their very own success involved not speaking that way. And isn't this just a typical experience?

Orfield: Well what's not typical about it at all is the level of isolation that kids have who are African American and Latino. Even in the days of the most ethnically defined neighborhoods, in cities like Chicago, there was never more than half of the people who were from one nationality group, from one language group. And there was never a caste-like barrier between them. So it's a very different thing than anything we've experienced with European immigrants. My grandfather came from Norway. One of his brothers taught Norwegian in Minneapolis, Central High School. None of the kids learned how to speak it. None of the grandchildren learned how to speak it. It was not considered what you do.

Tapp: I want to stay with you a moment and broaden the conversation even beyond bilingualism and into the field of education, which is one that I know you've written a lot about and researched a good deal. And I guess I want you to talk about a phrase that struck me particularly in your writing. You talk about "sleepwalking back to *Plessy*." Now, I think we need to spend just a moment and explain what *Plessy* is. I suspect that most people know what *Brown v. Board of Education* is, but if you could just give us the briefest of senses of education and the legal system, and why you would make such a provocative statement.

Orfield: Many people think that *Brown v. Board of Education* is the defining principle of our race relations. But actually, the defining principle is much more *Plessy v. Ferguson*, 1896, and one of the most disgraceful decisions in the history of the Supreme Court, where the Supreme Court said "separate but equal" was the basic principle of our Constitution. And set in place a process of making "separate" almost absolute in the country and never enforced the "equal" part of it. I say "separate but equal," *Plessy v. Ferguson*, is the most massive social experiment in the history of our country. We tried it for seventy years. It never worked anyplace. Now in the 1990s, the Supreme Court, or the majority that was consolidated by the appointment of Clarence Thomas, is adopting that as its principle again. It's dismantling the desegregation orders in the country. It's pulling back on voting rights. It's cutting back on affirmative action. All of the race-conscious efforts to change the pattern of inequality that was built on generations of discrimination are being taken apart. The Supreme Court's denying history. It's saying, "We solved the problem. We've had civil rights laws, and everybody's got an equal chance," even though everybody's segregated in unequal schools. And they're getting more segregated each year. There's a historic denial of huge proportions going on, and we're betting the future of the country on "separate but equal" working. And there is no enforcement of the "equality" part of it.

Tapp: Let me ask a question I think needs to be answered at this point. What you've presented is a model of integration. And I think the critical thing here is it's not "separate but equal," it's separate and unequal.

Orfield: And what the Supreme Court said in the Brown decision was, "separate" was inherently "unequal" where it's imposed in this country. And it's never been chosen. There's only about one out of ten African Americans who say they want to live in a totally African American world. So it has been imposed historically on groups that are without power to change it.

Tapp: Would you go so far as to say—and I think we should all talk about this for a minute—that we still believe in integration? Because I'm starting to think that as a society, really, honestly, when we go to our separate homes and shut those doors, we don't necessarily.

Orfield: I think the way we've defined our communities in metropolitan America, where over three-quarters of our people live, is by increasing separation by both race and social class, and a huge class separation even within the black and Latino communities. It's a kind of proposition that is untested, and I don't think it's workable. Americans by *huge* majorities say they think integration is better than segregation—of every race. But they're not prepared to do anything much to get it. And they think that they can go along the path they're going and have the society work out. I think that's a really large bet. I don't think it's going to come true.

Dyson: And the question, too, is on whose shoulders is the burden for integration or desegregation placed? And what's interesting, even in a postintegration society after *Brown v. Board of Education* 1954, integrated education has been a disaster for, in this case, say, African American students.

Orfield: I don't agree with that.

Dyson: Well, disaster in this sense. The teachers who are teaching those students, who are black and Latino—largely white teachers—those students are being tracked for special education. They are being taught by teachers who don't feel fundamentally that [black and brown students] have the capacity to perform up to a certain intellectual capacity and level. Who don't demand from their students what they should demand from them. So even under an ideal integrated society, black and Latino students continue to suffer tremendous liabilities as a result of both their class, and their ethnicity and their race. I'm not *against* the ideal of the integrated society. I'm just saying, though, if we're going to be honest about it, as you were asking us earlier to be about the mix of bilingualism, let's be honest about integrationism. There's a difference between old school, 1920s apartheid, imposed from the outside, and neoseparatism that's generated among African Americans. Parents who say, "Look, I'm sending my kids to a white school, they're killing their psyche, they're making them believe they can't perform, and so what's wrong with me now trying to at least organize the possibility that a black school might be the outlet for them, if we can generate enough resources within our own communities? Or to, alternatively, take over the local public school education and make sure that it represents the interest of my child."

Orfield: I would really like to answer a couple of these things. Black students, during this period of integration, had a huge decline in the gap between black and white achievement in this country. There was a huge decline in the difference in high school graduation. It just soared in this period. The biggest gains came in the South, which is the only part of the country which was ever integrated to any significant degree. We never did integrate the Northeast or the Midwest or the West because of the Supreme Court's decision creating an absolute wall between city and suburb. There was always inequality in interracial schools. That's absolutely true. But when we go back to segregated schools, which we've been studying, they are extremely inferior. And not because they're black, because black and Latino students who are in segregated schools are sixteen times as likely to be in schools of concentrated poverty. Those are schools that have enormous social and economic crises, that have problems in every classroom, that are incredibly challenging to the teachers. Black teachers that start teaching in those schools leave the profession twice as fast as those who start teaching in less isolated, less impoverished schools. It's just an overwhelming task. White students never end up in concentrated poverty schools.

Tapp: I think you're also saying, we haven't had integration, so what are we talking about?

Orfield: We certainly haven't had it in this part of the country.

Vargas: Integration's only going to happen when people start living in integrated neighborhoods. And that goes a lot to economic power. If people can *choose* where they want to live, as opposed to living in a place of last resort, where they can only afford to live.

Orfield: The richest group of blacks in the country is as segregated as the poorest group, according to Doug Massey's *American Apartheid.*

Tapp: Let's talk for a minute about trying to put poverty into this equation. I think there's a pretty interesting argument, made by a number of young activists, mostly black, but others as well, that integration was the worst thing in the world. Isolation is now both by race and by class, and the kind of isolation that I think has been alluded to here, but not really talked about, has been exacerbated by this mock integration. Because, as Arturo Vargas just pointed out, it's not really happening. It's happening occasionally in the workplace, occasionally in a university for a brief period of time. Not usually where we live. And Arturo Vargas, let me go back to you for a minute and ask what the poverty factor is here. Particularly with regard to Latinos, where you have a wide range of countries, views, classes, colors.

Vargas: Well, I think poverty has a big role in how race and ethnicity plays out in society today. And if we look at the experience, for example, of Latino immigrants, they are probably the most isolated and segregated of the Latino communities, because they have the fewest resources in which to choose where to live. But you have a huge emerging Latino middle class as well. And if you look at Los Angeles County, which has the largest concentration of Latinos in the United States—there are about four million who are living there—you see this growing integration of Latinos moving eastward into the suburbs of the San Gabriel Valley and integrating what were once predominantly white communities. You also have a large Asian community growing in the San Gabriel Valley. So I think there is some hope.

Dyson: I think that's absolutely right. But as an avowed, hopefully complex integrationist, I want to put forth the claim that America is better, rather than worse, under the notion that we should live out the *E Pluribus Unum*—"out of many, one." But at the same time, I think we have to be honest about the failures of that [creed]. And part of the failure has been the unwillingness of liberal and left thinkers, who support integration, to acknowledge its failures. And to say that we haven't tried integration in one sense means to say, under what present conditions do we detect the possibility that integration, after the enormous amounts of resources that have been put behind it, will succeed in a way that it hasn't in the past?

Orfield: There have not been enormous resources put behind it.

Tapp: Actually, I want you to engage just a bit more on this. Michael Eric Dyson, you say the resources were there. They were applied. Gary Orfield, you said, no, not true.

Dyson: Well, I don't want to say that. I don't want to say "enormous resources" like there were enough. I'm just saying this: In the present climate of American society . . . the shift to the far right has been so complete that now affirmative action looks like the litmus test for our commitment to racial justice, when I believe it's the first step toward a larger project of racial justice in American society. So I'm saying in that climate, when affirmative action can't even be conceded, how are we going to truly integrate American schools to represent the justice that we're aiming at?

Tapp: Wait a second. Last I checked, you were hitting on the left. Don't stop hitting on the left. I want to hear what the left and the liberals did wrong, too.

Dyson: Oh, well I can tell you. First of all, the uncritical valorization of the notion that integrationism is the ideal of American society. Martin Luther King, Jr., ten days before he died, said before the Rabbinical Assembly of America that black people ought to practice "temporary segregation" unless we're going to be "integrated out of power." We associate that with Malcolm X. But King said if we're not going to hold onto the little resources we do have, we cannot trust an American society whose arteries of memory have become clogged with self-interest to really act on our behalf and to defend our interests. So temporarily–he didn't say how long that would be–we have to organize our own interests and defend them as best we can. That's a complex form of solidarity that, of course, goes against the narrow reactionary [drift] of certain forms of racial unity. But I think we have to put something like that forward.

Tapp: Do you want to pick on both the left and right?

Orfield: Yes, I'd like to take both of these things on. One of the most frequent and most inaccurate statements that's being made about integration is that we've invested a lot of resources in it, and they've diverted us from other things. We have invested virtually zero in integration. The only period in which we invested any significant resources in it was for about five years in the '60s. We've had five administrations that have been opposed to integration of any sort, two that have been very tepidly in favor of it since the 1960s. All of the appointments to the Supreme Court for twenty-five years were made to the opponents of integration by conservative presidents. There has been no significant amount of money invested in it by the civil rights movement. There just isn't very much. There's never been more than ten or twelve lawyers for the country working on integration as a serious goal. It's usually been less than that. It just is wrong to say there are huge resources. The huge resources have been invested in segregation. They've been invested in compensatory education. We've invested in segregation and we've been constantly criticized for inputting huge resources into integration. It never happened. That's wrong.

Dyson: That wasn't my argument. Okay, let's concede that point for the sake of brevity. How are we going to redirect the resource allocation so we can support integration as opposed to desegregation, if we can't even support a major vehicle to expand the middle-class to make the argument credible?

Orfield: Oh, I agree with you completely. Right now in the South there are many communities debating whether they should end their school desegregation plan or not. It's an important debate. There *are* millions of kids who are in interracial schools, and the level of segregation's increasing rapidly, and people are choosing to change their policies to increase it more. I think that's a terrible mistake.

Tapp: Forgive me. I'm one of those people who like solid, clear answers. I really want to know, I would like some data that would say integration in education—let's just confine it, okay?—is good for these reasons, and bad for these reasons. And here's my problem. I keep looking for it.

Orfield: It exists.

Tapp: Does it?

Orfield: Yes.

Tapp: And what does it say?

Orfield: Basically it says that if you have a child that goes to an integrated school, they're more likely to go to college and more likely to finish college. Everything else being equal, they're likely to have slightly higher test scores. They're likely to have a different life. They're more likely to live in an interracial setting as an adult, they're more likely to work in an interracial setting. It's not a magic bullet. There are no magic bullets. But it does produce solid benefits.

Tapp: If that's the case, why isn't that printed everywhere, and everyone knows it, and we all are rushing to integrate our schools? Oh, I know Michael Eric Dyson wants to take that question.

Dyson: Well, again, Gary and I are on the same side. But I'm saying, if present strategies have led to the impasse that we presently have endured, what are we going to do strategically to make sure we can get beyond the impasse? Because my point is about a kind of *racialpolitik*. We've got to be real about what we can do.

Tapp: I think you're presuming there's a consensus on these issues, and Arturo Vargas, I would argue that there's not. Everybody will sit here and say, we want our children to be healthy, happy, and well educated. But once you get beyond that, I would suggest, I would just throw it on the table here, there's a real range of opinion.

Vargas: I agree with you. I think people are seeing integration as what they want to see. They want to see a quality education.

Tapp: But let's go whole package, shall we? Because I've heard a pretty good argument increasingly in recent years, that it's not only about schools, that it's about something Arturo just mentioned—family involvement, community, good housing. I noticed with some interest, Gary Orfield, that you suggest that when people put together school reform packages for the future, they throw housing in as part of the deal. That communities say, "We don't want this unless we have decent housing attached to this." There's the issue of health care, there's the issue of job opportunity. Now, I know a lot of what I've just said are terms that are charged now and, in some instances, even buzz words. And I've tried to pick more neutral ones. But the reality is, there's a growing body of scholars—is there not?—who are saying, "It's got to be an organic whole. It can't just be a good school. That won't work alone."

Orfield: The root of our present system of racial inequality is housing and communities. It's illegal in our country now to distribute things unequally on the basis of race. But it's perfectly legal to do it on the basis of residence, and on the basis of community. And we do it in all of our metropolitan areas in a massive way. If we don't create housing opportunity within that system, we're creating lack of access to schools, to jobs, to all kinds of life opportunities. And we really aren't seriously thinking about this at all. There really isn't any significant program of housing construction for low-income families, outside of very impoverished areas. Whenever we subsidize a family, we should think about what kind of school opportunity they'd get. Whenever we put in sewer lines and expensive infrastructure for our suburban communities, we should think about getting some affordable housing in there, and then making sure that it's not given out in a discrimi-natory way. We're building in very systematic polarization of our society, and we aren't thinking about how to get out of it. And to think we can get out of it just with schools, after we do everything wrong in terms of figuring out how our com-munities are going to develop, is a mistake.

Tapp: Sounds to me like doing all that other stuff is extraordinarily costly. It might even be an example of liberal spending. Michael Eric Dyson—big money!

Dyson: Well, yeah. What we're arguing here is that it's all part of a larger whole. Because you can't talk about schooling kids, and having them in the right frame of mind to go out into the world, if they don't have any economic resources to sustain them once they get out there, or more than that, after they go home. More than that, what kind of world are we creating in which these kids will operate? So, for me, education is tied—not only in terms of integrationist versus self-segrega-tionist stuff going on in the private versus public debate—to access to colleges and education, and to affirmative action . . . I keep trying to wedge in affirmative ac-tion, hoping we're going to speak a little bit more about that. Because I think it's important to deal with that issue.

Tapp: We'll talk about affirmative action. I just want to be a little provocative here: GI Bill, affirmative action of a sort. We had, for the first time, all kinds of people serving in the military in World War II, and when they came home we said to them, "Here, we want to educate you and give you homes. You may end up outside cities, by the way, but that's something we'll deal with later." And there are those who are now making the very provocative argument that, in essence, the GI Bill was affirmative action, though we didn't call it that, and it was clearly not targeted to people of color, but rather to these folks who had just returned from the war, many of whom were immigrants. They'd fit into the ethnicity part of this conversation. Is this theory totally off the wall, Gary Orfield?

Orfield: The GI Bill was one of the best investments in American history. It took people who wouldn't have dreamed of going to college and sent them to college, paid for them to live while they were going to college. And another thing we did for the GIs after World War II was to give them the ability to buy a home in sub-urbia, cheaper than renting an apartment in the city, through the VA loans. Vir-tually none of those ever went to any black or Latino family, because they were only given in areas that were designed to be for whites only, because the federal government at that time would not enter mortgages in areas that were racially mixed. That opportunity was given out on a racial basis. It helped to create the racially stratified segregation and unequal distribution of wealth we have in this country now. And the college part of it was brilliant social innovation. And it didn't take from some group and give to others. It made our whole country richer and more capable, internationally, and more scientifically powerful.

Dyson: Are you implying that affirmative action takes from one group and gives to another?

Orfield: No. I'm saying that it's like the GI Bill. We can expand the pool. By educating more people, we don't subtract, we add.

Tapp: And yet you're almost suggesting that the GI Bill was—is racist too strong a word? Discriminatory?

Orfield: The housing part of the package for the GIs after World War II, the VA loans and so forth, was racist and discriminatory—no question about it. Everybody admits it. But I think what it shows us is that we can greatly expand the kind of people who can benefit from [opportunity], and who will serve society well if we give them the opportunity. It goes back to us.

Vargas: It goes back to, are we willing to invest in the children that we have in our classrooms today?

Orfield: And you look at a place like California. They built new campuses all over the state. Now that they have Latinos coming in, they're raising the barrier to get into the existing campuses. And it's a terribly shortsighted view of the future.

Dyson: Martin Luther King, Jr., in *Why We Can't Wait* made this analogy between the GI Bill and affirmative action. He also said, let's have a GI Bill for the socially disadvantaged, the people who are economically unable to compete. But I think that the recent book, *The Shape of the River*, by the former president of Harvard, Derek Bok, and the former president of Princeton, Bill Bowen, has made an important contribution to this debate about affirmative action. Because they claim, when we talk about so-called unfair admissions, 25 percent of college education is about these elite schools. So 75 percent of schools take people pretty much as they are. Then they argue that, well, if affirmative action is destroyed tomorrow, the chances of white Americans getting a better shot at gaining entrance to education has only increased 1.5 percent. On the other hand, black and brown students will be enormously disadvantaged as a result of the destruction of affirmative action.

Orfield: One of the things that has happened with the conservative movement is that somehow we've created the impression that it is a danger to the country if more blacks and Latinos get college degrees, when they're our future population. And we stop thinking about how to expand the pool and we've tried to make whites and Asians afraid that they're going to be shut out. And by huge margins, they're much more likely to fear that they've been affected negatively than actual research shows. Maybe 1 to 2 percent may have been affected in some way by affirmative action. But many, many believe that they have been. So whites start tending to blame whatever happens wrong in their life on affirmative action, even though it's a weak and small policy.

Tapp: Let's go back to that immigrant model and wrap the GI Bill into it. And let's just make the argument that the GI Bill helped a lot of people who were working class, in some cases working poor, children of immigrants—in some cases fairly recent immigrants—to move up that social ladder, to move solidly into the middle class and, in some cases, even higher. Is the idea, to take the good parts of the GI Bill, to take the good parts of affirmative action? How do we stop these trends? How do we stop the move of immigrants, as soon as they're successful, right out of those cities, right out of those few integrated schools? How do we begin to do that? These are a lot of natural human behaviors to put an end to, aren't they, Gary Orfield?

Orfield: I don't think it should be our goal to stop the movement of successful African Americans or Latinos to some community they want to move to. Why should we have that as a goal? Our goal should be to diversify and enrich those communities in the central cities and to open up opportunities for poor people to move out where the jobs and the good schools are, as well. We shouldn't try to confine people. People think we can recreate the period where middle-class blacks were confined to certain neighborhoods. We can't put that back in the box again, and we shouldn't try to. We've got to try to figure out how to upgrade those neighborhoods. Make them diverse in terms of social class, perhaps, and race, and to open up the opportunity for everybody who wants it to have a real broad choice in the housing market, in a choice of communities. And we should try to cut down the concentration of extreme poverty, which only affects black and Latino communities, to a significant degree, by not concentrating our subsidized housing and other things in just a few communities.

Dyson: Right. And some social scientific research, of course, had tried to suggest that the out-migration of blacks and Latinos from the postindustrial urban inner cities left these people bereft of role models. But especially bereft of moral capital—that is, the ability to act right and behave right—that's why we've got all these terribly isolated families. And I think that's ridiculous. There is a kind of nostalgia that suggests, "Well, back in my day, fifty years ago, when segregation happened, we loved each other, we disciplined each others' kids, and we had a great community." As if there was no economic inequality. As if there were not these internal divisions that we have scarcely talked about tonight, which are quite important. So I think we don't have to romanticize the past. But we also have to talk about how we can make equality the principle for these collapsed postindustrial urban centers where people are suffering enormously.

Tapp: Well I think we *do* have to talk a little bit about the past. And I guess I have to ask Gary Orfield . . . I'm a bit shocked, because I heard you make a pretty good argument for integration. I heard you pull out data. And now it sounds to me like what you're suggesting is almost a kind of voluntary, namby-pamby integration. And I don't see how you think that's going to work.

Orfield: But we can't assign people where to live in this country. If we could, maybe we'd have some different possibilities. We can assign people where their kids go to school. We always do that in our public school systems. That's why we can do school integration in a massive way. But doing housing requires us planning, creating incentives, supporting interracial communities, opening up segregated outer-suburban communities, redeveloping inner-city communities. These are really hard and complicated things to do. And I think they're terribly important. They don't happen automatically; they're not a priority in our present political climate. But we do know a lot of things that would move us in that direction. And I think they're very important.

Tapp: I don't even think you can say we can do it in the schools. Because the fact is, what happens, what we've seen, is flight.

Orfield: We have put a million children in metropolitan areas, where the city and the suburbs are together, and they're all desegregated. Those are very stable. And many of those are actually gaining population and gaining middle class; very economically healthy. And many small cities have integrated schools. The places that are really segregated are big central cities. If you do it so it encompasses the housing market, it works very well. If you do it in a little part, it's very unstable and not very successful.

Tapp: Michael Eric Dyson, you look so puzzled.

Dyson: Well, I think my only bewilderment is about how we can have the will. Because I think everything we're hearing here tonight, all of us, in broad strokes, could agree to. But where's the political will to make sure that this happens? And I'm saying that in light of—

Orfield: We don't have the will to do any of the things we're talking about right now.

Dyson: Yeah. And I'm saying to forge forward. You say we don't assign people where to live. Well, we don't do it explicitly; we do it by default. When you force people to live in enclaves of civic terror called slums or ghettos, you assign them where to live. And whether you have white flight, mimicked by black track, or brown track, from the inner city to the suburbs, what's involved there is not simply about: should we assign people where to live? There's a larger debate here, and it's about the ecology of the culture, the ecology of the race. Debates about, "But are we really being real Latinos? Are we being real blacks?" That question is provoked by saying, on the other hand, "Well, we can't assign people where to live; we have to allow the laissez-faire law of social ecology to determine where they will end up." When, in fact, we are forcing them, we are coercing them, to live and inhabit these enclaves of ghettos and slums by default. And I think we have to be a bit more self-conscious about our social and urban planning to make sure that we don't end up trumping the very thing we want to see realized.

Orfield: I think that's right. Where we have housing projects, we do assign people where to live, because people who live there don't have any other choices, and they have to live there. And we usually assign them to live in a terrible neighborhood with terrible schools. I think we know how to run those things much better, if we wanted to. And it's a very important goal. Another way we do it—and I have to agree with Michael on this part—suburban communities that forbid poor people or working-class people, or anybody else that's not upper income, to live in their community at all, by not allowing any rental housing, and not allowing any kind of affordable housing of any sort, are assigning everybody who's not in a certain very high economic strata to live someplace else. Well, they're soaking up all the tax resources they can from everyplace else.

Tapp: I want to touch on one or two more things before we run out of time here. And one of them—and let me just paint the bleakest picture possible, because we've heard some depressing things in this conversation—we have a polarization about race, about class, over politics, black/white. We've got an integration that never really occurred, which we all say, when the pollster calls us, maybe we really believe in, but it might not be demonstrated by our behavior with regard to where we live, work, and send our children to school. I'm wondering how we begin to knit all that together. And I want to start actually with addressing a problem, before we go to that more positive way. So let me start with you, Arturo Vargas. There are tensions between African Americans and Latinos from all countries and all continents. And I'm wondering how one begins to address those tensions if, in fact, we're going to deal with the demographics, the change that we alluded to in the beginning.

Vargas: Well, we don't have to talk about all continents, and all countries. Let's talk about this continent, this country, about the, I think, real way for us to engage in a conversation between blacks and Latinos about power sharing. And there's a real challenge we have in our communities. And we don't want to talk about it. But there are many Latinos who are uncomfortable about being represented by African-American politicians—many African Americans who are uncomfortable about being represented by Latino politicians—because we have generated this whole mentality in our own communities that Latinos are the best representatives of Latino communities, and African American politicians of African American communities. But as these communities are changing, that is not going to be possible. And we have not engaged in that conversation yet. And we're going to be forced to do that very quickly, in a few years, as we talk about how we share power. I do have a lot of hope, because what I see emerging among some of the younger generation of elected officials is more of a willingness to talk about these issues.

Tapp: I want to ask you if you feel there's a problem with racism *in* the Latino community. And I know I'm making a wide generalization here. But is there a problem with regard to African Americans? And even think back to the example that Michael Eric Dyson used in the beginning, the view adopted by the Polish immigrant. Is that a problem?

Vargas: Of course. Latinos are racist, blacks are racist, whites are racist. There is racism in every community. People are uncomfortable with people who are different than them. But I do have some hope, because as we talk to people about these experiences, you always hear people saying things like, "Well, I don't know," or "I'm uncomfortable with all these immigrants, but I like the immigrants I know." And I think there is an element of hope there. I think because we're so segregated sometimes, we don't know each other.

Tapp: I know a lot of black people who have been hanging onto that element of hope for a long time, Michael Eric Dyson. You know, you've talked in your work about needing a black leadership that acknowledges the centrality of race, without asserting its exclusivity, that transforms race. Talk about that a little bit.

Dyson: What I mean by that is that we can be race specific without being race exclusive. That is, you never fail to pay attention to the particular manifestation of race, or racism, in a particular geographical region, or a particular issue of importance. At the same time, we can't be racially exclusive. That is, we have to pay attention to how issues of sexuality, issues of gender, issues of class intersect. And that's very important, because you don't want to establish this kind of artificial hierarchy that says, "Race stuff is more important than ethnicity." "No, ethnicity's more important than the class." "No class is less important"—and so on and so forth. And I think that's very crucial. I think what Arturo just said is true—I, too, remain hopeful. And I think hope is a different virtue than optimism, as has been pointed out. Hope against hope is a deeply rooted virtue that suggests good despite what we see going on presently—and some of that stuff is depressing, be-

cause I think that there is racism all along. All of us are subjected to media, and
the media is filling all of our minds, if I can speak broadly here, with these racist,
bigoted perceptions about "the other." So "the other" becomes the Mexican over
here who's taking my job, the Latino who's taking my job. And I think what we
have to do, then, is to acknowledge that we have much more in common than
when we're apart. Number two, we have to acknowledge the realms of difference,
and then deal with those. And thirdly, what we have to do is forge a coalitional
politics that pays specific attention to our issues while saying how we can come together as groups to mobilize our political agency.

Tapp: Garry Orfield, give me the last word.

Orfield: I think if you look at where we're going, and the kind of leadership we
have, you can't see how we can get to where we need to go from where we are
now. But that was certainly true in the 1950s. And it was certainly unimaginable,
what was accomplished in the 1960s in the South. We need to have some serious
leadership realize we have to spend some serious intellectual, political, and economic resources on these issues. But we still have some tremendous assets as a
country, I think. If you look at what black families and Latino families, and Asian
families, and white families want, it's the same. They want safe neighborhoods,
they want decent homes, they want education for their children. They believe
passionately in education. They believe in the values of this country. They want
it to work. And we have had a lot of people who have gone beneath that, and
stirred it up and divided us. We still have some very powerful common possibilities. And we have cultural resources that are of incredible importance for the
world, if we can figure out how to use them. And I just think we've got to give up
the dream that it'll all work out without our working on it, and realize that it's the
challenge of our generation.

2

THE GREATEST AMERICAN EVER
The Radical, and Human, Martin Luther King, Jr.

with Tavis Smiley and Taylor Branch

On the King holiday in 2000, I traveled to Washington, D.C., to appear on *BET Tonight*, hosted by media marvel Tavis Smiley. My conversation partner that night was Taylor Branch, the renowned King chronicler whose monumental trilogy of "America in the King Years" has set the standard for King scholarship. I had just written *I May Not Get There with You: The True Martin Luther King, Jr.*, a controversial volume that probed King's radical legacy while also grappling with his flaws, especially allegations of promiscuity and plagiarism. Smiley stood in for black America that night, vigorously questioning my motives and probing my arguments in an often friendly but spirited exchange. As both Branch and I contended that night, our work on King, warts and all, had only increased our appreciation for his singular genius. King must be engaged with our historical eyes wide open. That has not diminished my estimation of his unique stature nor my admiration for his brilliant thought and life, as the title of this chapter makes clear.

Tavis Smiley: Good evening. Welcome to *BET Tonight*. Tonight Americans across the country commemorate the life of Dr. Martin Luther King, Jr., a man who, indeed, had a powerful impact on all of our lives. Tonight we ask: who was the man behind the myth? In his new book, Michael Eric Dyson says, "King's image has suffered a sad fate. His strengths have been needlessly exaggerated, his weaknesses wildly overplayed. King's true legacy has been lost through cultural amnesia." I am pleased to be joined tonight by our guest, Michael Eric Dyson, author of a provocative new book, *I May Not Get There With You: The True Martin Luther King, Jr.* Also joining us tonight—you cannot have a critical conversation about King without having on the panel Taylor Branch, author of *Pillar of Fire: America in the King Years*, the second book in what is expected to be a trilogy about the years during the civil rights movement.

Michael, let me start with you. I had a chance to dig into this thing, man, and I don't know how close I want to sit next to you with some of the things you say in this book. And I say that with all due respect. This book, without question, is a radical reinterpretation of the life of King. But I can only imagine if some of our white brothers and sisters [are] watching right now, and reading that quote on the screen: "King had a mistrust of white America." You've got to explain that one. Because a lot of folks look at King—not just black folk—white folk look at King as the end-all, be-all. How dare you tell me that Dr. King himself distrusted white America, when he said he wanted his kids to live in a nation—you know the script. How can King mistrust white people?

Michael Eric Dyson: Well, I think that mistrust lived on the same block as his continuing faith in them, but he was chastened by his experiences later in life when he believed that you had to take a different approach to make white America do the right thing. Early on, King had deeply invested in his Christian faith the ability of white America to have its conscience appealed to and, therefore, to make change. But King, later in his life, said, "Look, I have to admit that most white Americans, and most Americans, are unconscious racists." Because the disease was so virulent, it was so nasty, and it was throughout the body politic, and in the institutions of American government and society. In fact, the last speech that King gave, the last Sunday morning sermon he gave, was at the National Cathedral, the Episcopal one, here in Washington, D.C.: "Remaining Awake Through a Great Revolution." And in that sermon King said that it's a sad thing to admit, but America's still a racist country, and white people have to come to grips with that. So that kind of mistrust was not a cynical disdain for white America; it was the embrace of a more aggressive strategy for social change. And that aggressive strategy was: Let's deal with the reality that white people don't want to change and, therefore, let's look for the ways we have to *force* them to change.

Smiley: Obviously we're talking tonight in retrospect, but how does one square away, juxtapose for me if you can, the reality of this image that we have of Dr. King—white America, I'm talking of now, Taylor—with the statement that you attribute to King that most white Americans, at the end of his life, he thought were unconscious racists. I don't know that you can square that in the minds of most people, given the image that we have of Dr. King.

Dyson: You're exactly right. And that image is one that I'm trying to defrost. We've frozen King in 1963 when he gave that prophetic speech at the sunlit summit of his oratorical career, "I Have a Dream." But the reality is, he said other stuff after "I Have a Dream." Even, he said, that "later that year I began to rethink that dream and I saw it turn into a nightmare on the streets of our cities." So how we square it is by saying, "Listen, you've got to change your image." King's roles are part of his evolving strategy, and what we have to do is come to grips with his ever-evolving philosophy. He became much more radical, he became much more progressive, he became much more reflective, and he became much more pessimistic about the possibility that white American could, *on its own*, change. It's not that he believed they couldn't change any longer. He said, I've got to adopt a different strategy. Because if you appeal to their conscience and they [change], that's one thing. But, when I've appealed to their conscience and it doesn't change, I've got to have some different strategies in my arsenal here. And King moved to a much more radical coercion of white America to hear his message.

Smiley: Taylor Branch, nice to see you.

Taylor Branch: Nice to see you.

Smiley: Thanks for coming on, man. There are some things I want to cover with you. I want to give you a chance to comment on the argument that Michael makes in his book that King, for lack of a better term, at the end of his life, was becoming more cynical about white America. And whether or not they can handle, or deal with, or make any progress, if you will, on this issue of racism.

Branch: In general, I think that's right. And I don't think you have to listen to his words very much. I think you can divine that from the tone of his voice before you even hear his words. His voice is a furnace in the tone. And what's burning in that furnace is the despair over the injustice that's going on, set against his belief in common humanity as the only salvation for all of the world menaces like hatred and war and nuclear weapons. That's where King comes together. This war, inside him, in his soul, over whether or not there's hope or despair. And certainly, towards the end of his life, the virulence of racism and staying power in the time of war, because the country got filled more with hate during the Vietnam War. It did make that furnace get a little hotter.

Smiley: Michael, one of the things that strikes me as interesting is a quote that you've used in the book, that we mentioned earlier. You argue that, in many respects, King's "strengths were exaggerated and his weaknesses were overplayed." I mentioned a moment ago we all know King, in many respects, was a flawed individual. Some would argue that showing the flaws of a man like King makes him more human, and convinces all of us that we can all make a difference in our own lives in a variety of ways. And even a man like King, who was flawed, made monumental differences. The flip side of that argument, I would think, is that people are going to have a lot of issues with you over digging up a lot of dirt about King. I want to talk for a moment about some of the flaws of this man. You talk in this book in detail about the promiscuity of Dr. King. You talk in this book in detail about plagiarism by Dr. King. Now, that knocked me back on my mind, I confess. I mean, King is, without question, in my mind at least, the greatest orator we have ever produced in this country. *And Michael Dyson's telling me that King stole some of his stuff!*

Dyson: It's a very good point. I think we have to make a distinction between what he did on the academic side, and what he did in terms of his oratorical capacity, in terms of his public presentations. Academically, I think there's no question that he engaged in falsification. He stole other people's words, he presented them as his own, and he represented them as his own original work. And that's a problem for anybody, like myself, who's a scholar in the academy and who wants to get toward a notion of doing your own work. Now, we can have big debates in this country about when notions of plagiarism began. You have to have a certain notion of capitalism and ownership of the word so it doesn't become rhetorically promiscuous. But that aside, the point is, the man jacked other people's words, [including] Jack Boozer, who had completed his dissertation three years before Dr. King, under the same person who led Dr. King in his own work, L. Harold De-Wolf. So there's no question about that.

But there's a difference in talking about Dr. King in the oratorical sphere. You know the old canard among black preachers: the first time you hear something you say, "As Tavis Smiley always says." Second time you hear it you say, "Like somebody said." The next time you say it you say, "Like I always said." [*Laughter*] We have no Harold Bloom "anxiety of influence"; we be rippin' stuff off as a matter of occasion. But it's because we see language as more or less a communal property, and that what we hear is what we can say. Because we learn to speak our own voices by speaking like somebody else until we grasp hold of what is our original register. King was equally influenced by William Holmes Borders, by Sandy Ray, [and] by Gardner Taylor, the acknowledged poet laureate of the American pulpit. But he developed his own unique style. But you do that by sampling.

And what I argue in this book is that King operated much like Puff Daddy does in terms of his rhetorical capacity. He borrowed somebody else's speeches, but when he finishes King-izing them things, you can believe it's a different thing. And here's an interesting thing. Some of the people from whom King borrowed some of his sermons kept inviting him back to their churches, as if to say, "Please steal some more of my stuff, 'cause it sounds so great from you, and when you charge it with a kind of moral efficacy of the civil rights movement, you give it a higher moral trajectory because of the impassioned way in which you speak it." Because in our community, it's not just what you say, it's how you say it. Some people mistake that for saying black people are obsessed with style over substance. No. Style becomes a vehicle for substance. When Michael Jordan puts that ball behind his back and around his head in 360 degrees, he's still scoring two points, still being the lead scorer. So the effective substance is there, but it's packaged in a different way.

Smiley: Taylor, with all respect to my friend, Mike Dyson, one could again, I think, make the argument that it doesn't take Mike Dyson writing a book this thick, and talking about all the dirt, alleged dirt, that King ever engaged in, and got on himself–it doesn't take doing all of that to make the point that King is "the greatest American we've ever produced." Why can't the book have been much shorter, or why couldn't Michael have written a book that talked about King in a critical sort of way without talking about the promiscuity? It reminds me–with all respect to Michael again–it reminds me of the book by Abernathy. You remember the book by Abernathy? That *one* line in the book–he was Dr. King's *boy*–he uses one line in the book about what King was allegedly doing the night before he died, and that's all that folk talked about in that book. And don't tell me Abernathy didn't know that was going to cause some controversy. Why does it take talking about the dirt this man was engaged in to tell me he was the greatest American we've been able to produce?

Branch: Well, with all due respect, I think Michael's book has a lot more in it than that. Because it's saying our whole image of King has been shaped in thirty-five years of backlash, when the whole country, black and white–and I will say this, black people contributed to the mythology around King just as enthusiastically as white people trying to de-fang him. But that's happened. And that is a huge subject. Our whole country has been brainwashing itself to be convinced that the '60s, and this whole era, was harmful in some respects. So there's a lot to do to recapture the authentic history. During King's life, those more up close and personal with Martin Luther King [knew that] major universities withdrew speaking engagements toward the end of his life. He was *never* a warm and cuddly figure here, even before the Vietnam War. So this is a tough subject. People were at war with themselves in their guts over what race means, over what America means, over what freedom means. And Michael is trying to get us back to that, because it is a healthy prospect.

Now as to Abernathy and the sex matter, Abernathy's controversy, it seems to me there are two things that need to be said about it. Number one, Abernathy had a jealousy of Dr. King that was an undercurrent of his entire life with him, that festered up in that book and was controversial for that reason, because all the people around Dr. King knew that but never spoke of it. Another factor, though, is you've got to understand [that] the minority psychology is a very powerful thing. If you are a minority of the country and you're trying to change all of its power relationships with no army, and no money, and no police force, and only a minority of the minorities involved in the movement, and they're at each other's throats, you don't want to be too forthcoming about your inner divisions, and therefore it's made it all the more sensitive when people have discussed the ordinary flaws of a human. My approach on this is that Dr. King is a human being, and those who don't share his faults, or claim not to, ought to be that much better.

Smiley: I'll buy that. Let me ask you right quick Michael before I get back to Taylor: I can only imagine, having read this book [*I May Not Get There With You*], that you are no longer—if you ever were—you are no longer in the good graces, shall we say, of the King family. I wonder what the reaction has been? Have they seen the book? Have they read the book, do you know?

Dyson: I think some of them have certainly seen the book. An excerpt appeared in *Emerge* magazine that they did not take too favorably. And I think there certainly have been some repercussions and some anxieties. And I sympathize with the King family to the degree that I can understand them wanting to protect the legacy of Martin Luther King, Jr. But I think, by grasping it so tightly, they have indeed choked it, as opposed to allowing it to flourish. Because King is brave enough, brilliant enough, courageous enough, and, I think, flawed in the right kind of ways to be able to withstand anything that I or anybody else can say about him.

Smiley: They would argue, though, Michael—I don't speak for the King family— they would argue that all they're really trying to do is to protect his intellectual property. They are the sons and daughters and wife of him. What's wrong with them trying to protect this man—as they see it?

Dyson: Well, nothing. But let's make a couple of distinctions. First of all, the intellectual property debate is one that they point to Dr. King having protected himself. He sued 20th Century Fox, and somebody else, right after the King speech, as Mr. Jones, who works with the King estate, points out. But he sued them with the point of giving the proceeds to the movement. And the FBI records prove that King wanted to sue them for the express purpose of recuperating those revenues to give to the civil rights movement. Now, if the King family wants to do the same thing, that's their decision. Number two, it would not be immoral for the King family to make money off of King's legacy. But it would be immoral for them to pretend King would like it. So on the one hand, they use the advantage of being his biological heirs to prove their connection to this legacy, but if we hold them to the same standards that King did, giving most of his $200,000 of income away to the movement, arguing with his own wife and best friend, Ralph Abernathy, about the dispensation of that $54,000 he won from the Nobel Prize, then we have to say, "Look, if you're going to be heirs and legatees of King, then be honest about how you have departed from that tradition, and allow us to scrutinize that." And furthermore, I think the attempt to control the intellectual representation of King by those papers not being available—and perhaps them going to the Library of Congress now bodes well for those of us who want to dig deep into the archives to understand what King did . . .

Smiley: They just cut a deal to sell the papers to the Library of Congress for $20 million?

Dyson: $20 million, if it's approved. But let me give you another, more splintering problem. The reality is, if King sampled some of this stuff, if he took from Prathia Hall the "I Have a Dream" phrase . . .

Smiley: Hold up, hold up. I think I just heard you say that the speech that Dr. King is most known for throughout the world—and God knows, in perpetuity—is the "I Have a Dream" speech. I mean, we all get bothered by the fact, as someone mentioned earlier, that too many of us act like King only gave one speech. That's in part because we hear that, and see it 24/7. You're now telling me that King jacked—he lifted the phrase—"I Have a Dream"?

Dyson: Improvised. Improvisation.

Smiley: Say it ain't so. Say it ain't so.

Dyson: It's the deal. Listen, he listened to a young woman, who is now one of the fifteen great black [female] preachers according to *Ebony* magazine, Prathia Hall, who was a student then in Albany, and she was praying one night about "I have a dream." And like any black preacher, King listens for the eloquent phrases that can be recontextualized so that they can have a broader meaning. So he heard her praying "I have a dream," and picked up on that image. Furthermore, Archibald Carey delivered to the 1952 Republican Convention a great speech that includes, "Let freedom ring." That whole section of, "Let freedom ring from the prodigious hilltops of New Hampshire"—you can hear that cadence, right? But part of that, a lot of that, is jacked, if you will—sampled, appropriated, stolen, ripped off, whatever you say—from Archibald Carey and given by Martin Luther King, Jr.

Smiley: Taylor, help me out here. Tell me how it is that we ever continue to view King—I mean, he obviously was not a perfect man. But there is something to revering what this man stood for that I think has to be maintained if we ever are going to aspire to having people want to be like Dr. King, and to love, and to be good neighbors, and to talk about dealing with racism. We gotta keep King on a pedestal of a certain sort, and I'm starting to get concerned that, as time goes on, we're going to so tarnish the image of Dr. King, trying to "keep it real" and trying to come correct, that we'll do ourselves harm long term.

Branch: All I can tell you, Tavis, is I started out on this project in 1982, not knowing a whole lot about this except that I admired the man. And my life is fundamentally affected by it. I've learned all these things and many, many more. I've
been at it eighteen years and I respect him more than I *ever* did.

Dyson: Yes.

Smiley: Tell me how that's possible. How is that possible, to learn [these] things
. . . I grew up in a Pentecostal church. I mean a conservative church. We couldn't
go to ball games, we couldn't play pool. I remember, as a kid, I used to win speech
tournaments all the time, doing my own oratorical interpretation of King's work.
And one day I saw that famous picture of King with a cigarette in his hand in a
pool hall. And I almost had a heart attack, as a thirteen-year-old, when I saw Dr.
King with a *pool stick* in his hand. And what I'm hearing now is so much beyond
a brother playing pool. I'm wondering how it is you can learn these things about
this man and then tell me that you respect him more now than you did eighteen
years ago.

Dyson: I do, as well.

Branch: Because he kept going with a greater faith against more—he realized all
of these limitations, and all these odds, in as sophisticated a way as you could ever
hope for, and went through that despair, and you still hear those speeches and
that voice. *And*, not only that, he kept his conviction, his belief, and he lifted the
whole country up into politics to try to, you know—his whole thing was, "I don't
want to be an Uncle Tom, but I'm never going to be afraid to be called one," because it's not just about finding principles and falling on your sword. That's not
gonna get you anywhere.

Smiley: You in fact argue in your book, *Pillar of Fire,* that King was not just . . . a
dreamer. You argue, at least, that he was one of the most brilliant political strate-
gists this country has ever known.

Branch: Absolutely. That's what Selma was about. There's still a debate going on
between Bob Moses—God love him—and all of the followers of SNCC [Student
Nonviolent Coordinating Committee] down in Mississippi about where the Voting Rights Act of 1965 came from that enfranchised five million new voters. And
whether it came from Selma or Mississippi. The fact of the matter is that King endured a lot of abuse at the time to try to make that march to Selma something that
would not only come off, and be true to principles, but would land in legislation.
And he endured abuse to do that. That puts him there, to me, with Lincoln, in
the sense of making principles count in history. And that's not easy to do.

Dyson: I think that's absolutely right. He made those documents live. He moved them from, if you will, parchment to pavement. And he marched there right with those words. He marched them into history. And he marched them into flesh. And I think the great thing about Dr. King is that you say, "How can we discover all this and appreciate him?" Because he had that much more to overcome. Saints make poor role models. Give me somebody with some flesh-and-blood flaws. And if we're going to really give new clothing to history, if we're going to re-tool it, then the bleached bones of history must have flaws. The flesh must have flaws. It has to have pimples. It has to have darted skin. But the reality is that King was able to rise above all of that and still do what he did. Here was a man who was depressed, clinically, for the last four years of his life.

Smiley: Whoa, whoa, whoa. Hold it. You're telling me now that Dr. King was a manic-depressive the last four years of his life?

Dyson: I'm telling you, Dr. King—how can you receive death threats every day of your life; how can you live under the pressure of death; how can you live, as he said, "with the surging murmur of life's restless siege," and not be able to acknowledge your depression? This man had a depression so profound he would go for days in a kind of internal chamber of, really, psychic torpor.

Smiley: You telling me King was depressed. King was lifting *us* up!

Dyson: But that's his genius. He preached himself out of that depression by giving to others. He embodied in his own life the very altruistic principles for which he died. And I'm saying, that's his genius. Here was a man beset by every imaginable injury to the psyche that one could endure, and yet, in spite of that, rose above that by bringing eloquence to bear upon his own situation and crisis, and then using that as a principle to defend the people whom he loved. That's an amazing thing. I think he's the greatest American we've ever produced. His death reaffirmed the fact that black people are often rejected *into* the American creed because race is the defining crisis of the American soul.

Smiley: Before I get back to this question of affirmative action, Taylor and Mike, one of the things that I know some watching—black folk and white folk, all kinds of Americans who revere and love and respect and quote Dr. King all the time—no doubt might be asking two questions as they sit here now. One, with all due respect to these thick polemics the two of you have authored, what gives you all the right to sit back and Monday-morning quarterback about King on a variety of different levels? And number two, isn't it true that much of what you all refer to, much of your research and much of what appears in these books, comes out of government files? How in the world am I supposed to believe, Mike, that I can trust what the FBI has to say anyway? You talk about the FBI files said this, and Taylor says the FBI file says that. Don't tell me about no FBI. I *know* what conspiracy theories are all about.

Dyson: Right. Well, I think first of all, about the Monday-morning quarterbacking, I think none of us presumes that we have any moral perfection or some kind of Archimedean objectivity, that we stand outside of the flow of human history. We are human beings as flawed as Dr. King, if not more so. But I think that our obligation as intellectuals, and as scholars and as journalists, is to take what we know and examine it with as much scrutiny as possible, and as much analytical rigor as possible, and as much fairness as possible, [and apply it] to the historical subject that we're studying. And try to see what's going on there. So I don't do it for moral perfection, because many of the flaws that Dr. King had can be exponentially increased in my own life, number one. And I'm a paid pest. That's what an intellectual is. [*Laughter*] And number two, in terms of the FBI records, it's no doubt that the FBI records reveal distorted perceptions of Dr. King. But they also unwittingly provide for us an interesting historical record of the greatness of Dr. King that they didn't intend. I mean, when you see Dr. King wrestling with his own conscience about how people are characterizing him in the press as hungry after material rewards when he's giving most of his money away. Or characterizing him as being hungry for media attention when, indeed, he's trying to really figure out how to focus the spotlight on the condition of black people, and poor people, themselves. Then the FBI really helps us understand the depth of his integrity, and the height of his altruism, and the breadth of his humanity. So I think that's clear.

But let me tell you what else. It's not simply the FBI records—although they are crucial. Georgia Davis, who's a former State Senator from Kentucky, wrote a book, *I Shared the Dream*. Need I tell you that what she shared was more than a mythical abstract conception of that dream?

Smiley: I can only imagine.

Dyson: She shared a flesh-and-blood embodiment of that dream. Here was a black woman involved in the movement who herself told the story. See, the problem with us as Americans is that we demand perfection from the people who are perfectly suited to the jobs that God, I believe, sent them to do. So I don't think Dr. King has to be perfect. And to deal with his flaws—listen, this is why I talk about hip-hop culture. You want to talk about Dr. King's flaws, and say he was a great man, but you want to look at Tupac Shakur and Biggie Smalls, and say, "Oh no, no, no, they're the refuse of the earth." The same people cutting slack for Dr. King, saying he's the greatest thing ever produced, are the same ones turning around to tell Tupac Shakur and Biggie Smalls, and a whole generation of young black people, that they are nothing. And I'm saying to you, if Dr. King died at twenty-six years old, he would have been known as a regionally important leader who stole other people's words and wives, and who had a great future potentially, the same [as when] Tupac and Biggie died. I'm saying to you that Dr. King overcame those flaws, was able to live out of the bag that he was put in and then make a great contribution. If that's the case, let's cut the same slack for our young people. I'm not saying they are Martin Luther King, Jr. I'm saying they have the potential to be useful human beings in our community.

Smiley: Taylor, no one is suggesting—I'm certainly not—that Dr. King needed to be or, in fact, was a perfect individual. He, like the rest of us, was not human and divine. The man was just human. I'm not looking for King to rise to the level of perfection. But—and I cast no aspersion on your work, and correct me and disabuse me of this notion if I'm wrong—while I don't want King to aspire to perfection, you are asking me (by *you* I mean you "paid pests," to use Michael's phrase) and those watching to at least entrust a certain modicum, a certain amount, of trust in a man like Hoover to believe much of what we read. You're asking me to believe [what] a man like Hoover, with his FBI, put in these files—and to believe much of what we read these days about Dr. King. How do we do that? Why should I do that?

Branch: First of all, I think you've got to be careful about disbelieving anything blankly. If the purpose is to find out what we share with Dr. King, where our beliefs are, then we can take the flaws and move them. If we don't have any beliefs, or we're not sure what they are, then everything is doctored . . . We have to remember, Dr. King's whole career was an appeal to the whole people of America to vindicate our fundamental premises *through* the federal government. I remember right-wingers saying, "He hated the federal government just like we do." Nothing could be further from the truth. The Supreme Court decision of '54 was the federal government vindicating those principles. The sit-ins were a plea to the federal government. The Freedom Rides, Birmingham [in '63], were a plea to outlaw segregation. Selma was a plea to the federal government to outlaw discrimination in voting. There was faith in the federal government that extended even to the FBI. If you're down in the South, in Mississippi, and the Klan is outside, you don't call the police, you call the FBI, because, relatively speaking, they're the better [choice].

Smiley: You raise an interesting question. Michael, how do we appropriately deal with the political right misappropriating, as it were, King's words to suggest, as Taylor just mentioned, that he was opposed to, was antigovernment, that he would have been opposed to affirmative action? You know the rationale. King said, as you repeated, in the "I Have a Dream" speech, that I want my kids to "live in a nation where they will not be judged by the color of their skin, but by the content of their character." The right takes that line to suggest that King would have been opposed to *anything* that was color based, that was race based. So consequently King would have been opposed to affirmative action. And as you detail in the book, there are a litany of political issues that we now deal with and grapple with every day, where the right now takes King's words to suggest that King would have been much more on *their* side on these political questions, than he would be on the "liberal" side.

Dyson: Yeah, well, thirty-four words, spoken when he was thirty-four years old, lifted out of context. And that golden phrase about the "content of our character," I think, has been so abused and misinterpreted. First of all, that was a different time in which King was living. When people like Ward Connerly appropriate those words, jack those words, rip those words out of their rhetorical context, rip them out of their moral context, rip them out of their political context and resituate them into the present, contemporary situation *without* any interpretation mediating the two, then what you end up with is just sheer interpretation. And I think Ward Connerly, et al, all of these conservative figures, need to really be rebuffed for their refusal to acknowledge those differences. And let me tell you this—Martin Luther King, Jr., was an advocate of something much stronger than affirmative action. He said, "Let's have a GI Bill for the disadvantaged. If the government, and the country, has done something *against* the Negro for so long," he said, "let's do something special *for* them now."

Furthermore, Dr. King understood that racial compensation was a systematic thing. It couldn't be a hit-and-miss kind of deal. The GI Bill for returning soldiers created the white middle class, essentially, in this country. Gave them the ability to go to college; it gave them the ability to have a home. So everybody wants a crib and a college degree. And they got that. Now, the same people who benefited from that affirmative action are now the ones who are turning against African American people, saying, "You should make it on your own," when, indeed, all of us were enabled by that process.

Smiley: I wonder whether or not, were King around today, you think he would think that integration is as worthy, in retrospect, as it was on the other side. I wonder whether or not, as we get further and further away from the time of Dr. King, that more and more folk are going to not think so highly of that ideal called integration.

Branch: I think probably they are. But my guess is, I may be on the other side on this issue, because I think that the idea of integration has been poisoned by these thirty-five years of backlash. On the black side, it's been taken to mean, "We have to be just like white people, and live up to their standards." If you listen to the end of the "I Have a Dream" speech even, he says, "And when that day comes, when freedom rings, we'll be able to look forward to that day when all God's children will be able to join hands and sing a black spiritual." He's inviting white people into that culture. That's what integration is. But we've poisoned that, in a way, to think, "Well, for integration to come about, black people have to be just like white people, and eat white bread and cut the crust off." Well, that ain't right.

Dyson: I think that's absolutely right. And I think King was never a romantic about the notion of integration. There's a difference in his mind between political integration—which meant that black people were going to be able to share the resources of the larger circle of American privilege—and moral integration, where he understood that we were part of the same polity, that we were part of the same quest for radical democracy. And psychic integration, where you had to give up being black—this is what Taylor's talking about now—give up the distinctiveness and the uniqueness of your blackness in order to be accepted. Martin Luther King, Jr., ten days before he died, spoke before the Rabbinical Assembly of America. Abraham Joshua Heschel, the great prophetic rabbi, introduced him as the moral leader of America. And King said there, ten days before his death, that black people must practice "temporary segregation, because if we're not careful, we're going to integrate ourselves out of power." But he said we have to have a temporary way station of segregation on the way to the larger goal of true integration into American society. So King always understood, and his notion of integration was always chastened by, the political realities that impinged in the meantime. But the ultimate goal was always toward a kind of holistic integration where people were truly equal. Without radical democracy, integration for King was political suicide.

Smiley: Let me ask you this question. I have less than a couple minutes left here, Michael. There are two major Baptist conventions. You've got the National Baptists, you've got Progressive Baptists, and all the Baptist preachers hit both conventions every year. And people don't know the story of how that convention got to be splintered. Tell that story in thirty seconds. It's a fascinating story.

Dyson: It's brilliantly told in Taylor Branch's book. But essentially, there was a fight in the convention between J. H. Jackson, the conservative leader, who got voted into office on his ability to reject the notion of tenure. But then, when he got there, like any other powerful figure, he loved it. He wanted to stay. So there was a big brouhaha in the convention. Gardner Taylor, the great prophetic figure, and pastor, of Concord Baptist Church [of Christ] in Brooklyn, New York, was voted on as president. There were warring factions. Both of them were elected. They rushed to the stage. A minister in Kansas City, I think, in '61, was unfortunately and tragically killed, pushed over the side. King then joined L. Venchael Booth and other figures later on to form the Progressive National Baptist Convention [because] J. H. Jackson and the National Baptists were refusing to acknowledge King's role as a civil rights leader. They said, "You're going to be a preacher, but don't involve us in these political shenanigans."

Smiley: And the convention split over King.

Dyson: Exactly.

Branch: One of the most moving days I ever had [was when] I told that story in [Gardner Taylor's pulpit], at Concord Baptist in Brooklyn, and he said that the only reason he was as good a preacher as he was is because he lost. And that that was the turning point in his life. It's an amazing story, amazing history.

Smiley: We're almost out of time. But I want to give Michael and Taylor just fifteen seconds each to tell me, in your own words, the most radical lesson we ought to learn about Dr. King's life, despite his flaws.

Branch: First of all, that he, himself, said the movement was much larger, and many times he was behind the students—and at times even small children—in Birmingham, [in] the movement. So it's not just about King. It's about all of us in reaching these values.

Smiley: Michael, last word.

Dyson: King is the central metaphor for the progressive movement and realization of democracy in our country. And the untold story: the invisible heroines are the black women whose integrity and whose diligence made it possible.

3

TOO LITTLE THOUGHT,
TOO LITTLE ACTION?
Black Leaders and Intellectuals

with Jesse Jackson; moderated by Tukufu Zuberi

In January of 2004, I had the privilege of engaging in conversation and debate with Rev. Jesse Jackson about Martin Luther King, Jr.'s legacy and the role and responsibilities of black leaders and intellectuals. I have known Jackson since 1990, when I served for more than a year as the official writer for his proposed autobiography. I had traveled with Jackson to London to meet with Nelson Mandela shortly after his release from prison, and accompanied Jackson across the nation as he worked tirelessly and creatively on behalf of dispossessed Americans of all colors and classes. Jackson is, without question, one of the most brilliant people I have ever met, and his quick, luminous intellect is generously displayed in our conversation. Our engagement became especially charged when we debated the tensions between black leaders who criticize the inaction of intellectuals, and intellectuals who decry the failure of some black leaders to sufficiently think through their actions and vocations. In the end, I gained even more respect for a man whose prodigious contributions to the civil and human rights movements continue to astonish.

Tukufu Zuberi: We begin with the question: what is the significance of Martin Luther King, Jr.'s legacy for social justice today, in the United States and in the world? What does this mean for how we ought to spend this day every year honoring his legacy? And, Rev. Jackson, I believe you spent the last birthday that Rev. Martin Luther King, Jr., had before he died, so you might be able to offer us some particularly unique insights in that way. Does it suggest how we ought to strive to make this a better world in celebration of his legacy? What does this struggle mean for people of African descent?

Jesse Jackson: Let me express my thanks to you and Michael for being part of this discussion tonight. On January 15, 1968, around eight o'clock that morning, he had breakfast with his family. He had convened a national staff meeting. Around ten o'clock we met in the basement of his church. He had on his windbreaker jacket and blue jeans. A few whites were there from Appalachia. And some from Caesar Chavez's group were there from southwest Texas. Some Jewish allies were there, [including] Al Lowenstein's group out of New York. There were also some Native Americans. Some blacks from Marks, Mississippi, from the Deep South, were there, and members of labor where there too—a kind of multiracial, rainbow coalition of sorts, focusing on a job or an income for every American, and health care and education. [We were] organizing a mass action march to Washington to engage in civil disobedience—to come by train, by car, by plane, and set up camp in front of the Lincoln Memorial, because the Emancipation Proclamation promise had been broken. A mass action in Washington. It had to be multicultural because [Dr. King] knew that there was not going to be a day when you had black full employment, and didn't have brown full employment, or white full employment. It had to be a multiracial base driven by a shared interest: a job and an income for every American. He knew full well that most poor people are not black. They're white, female, and young. He had to get beyond whites who tend to vote their fears rather than their interests. And [he had to rouse] the hopes of blacks with despair. So it was ten to about one o'clock on how to challenge government policy.

Around one o'clock, Xernona Clayton brought in a cake. We stopped and saluted his birthday. Then from two to five o'clock we spent on how to end the war in Vietnam. The monies were designed for the war on poverty, not the war in Vietnam. So he spent his own birthday A) at home with family, B) organizing the coalition for direct mass action, and C) how to end the war in Vietnam. Those who were there under him on that day [were] planning how to eliminate poverty, how to end wars, how to make the economy work for all of its people. That's how he spent his own last birthday.

Zuberi: So you think the significance is that's what we ought to do to celebrate his birthday.

Jackson: Well, because his legacy is mass action, unlike any leader before him. It's mass sacrifice—he was jailed twenty-three or twenty-six times; stabbed before he was killed. His impact was to change laws. No other leader changed *laws*: the '64 Public Accommodations Bill; the Voting Rights Act of '65; the Open Housing Act. Mass action, bodily sacrifice, and changing of laws puts him in a category all by himself.

Zuberi: In many ways, when we speak of the significance of the legacy of Rev. Martin Luther King, Jr., I take it that you're suggesting forms of social action.

What is the depth of active appreciation of this aspect of Rev. King? Like other holidays, has King's birthday also been stripped of its meaning, such that it becomes just another day off from work, and has he become just another empty icon that we look at? Do you think that, when we are talking about Martin Luther King, and we're talking about Martin Luther King's birthday, that we're talking about the problem of incorporation into the consumerism of modern society? Are we entering the time when we will go to K-Mart or Target for a Martin Luther King sale comparable to Labor Day sales or Presidents' Day sales?

Jackson: Well, *he* has not become empty. Many of the celebrations have become empty, and diversionary, and de facto conservative. I go to too many churches with a picture of Dr. King in the vestibule, and Malcolm X in the study, and a [Jerry] Falwell theology in the pulpit. Just downright retarded and backwards. [*Laughter*] For example, I would challenge every governor to have a commission in the tradition of the Kerner Commission. Every December they should issue a report, state by state. What is the state of racial inequality in Pennsylvania, for example, and the growing class gap? So you have some objective data, as opposed to anecdotal [stories], where folks are locked at the elbow but locked out by circumstance. For example, what is the infant mortality gap? It's measurable. The life expectancy gap? It's measurable. Access to public education gap: measurable. Access to college gap, grad school gap: measurable. Access to life insurance: measurable. Access to capital: measurable. Impact of predatory lending: measurable. Black people and brown people work harder for less money. Pay more for less: more for cars, more for insurance, more for houses, based upon race discrimination. We work harder for less, pay more for less, live under stress and don't live as long. That's our real profile.

So if the King Day celebrations [are effective], we say, "Now as of 2003, what is the plan to close the gap?" That's why we cannot throw away the Kerner Report. Because most poor people are not black, they're white. There are more poor whites in Appalachia than there are blacks in America. And they, too, are people. And we must whiten the face of poverty to make it real. John Kennedy held up a black baby in his arms in Harlem in 1960. It was dismissed as a campaign trick. They said, "He's a liberal guy from up North, and they talk funny, and he's got a black baby, and he's trying to please Adam Powell." It was just dismissed. Bobby Kennedy held a white in his arms from West Virginia. That baby's bloated belly— that baby's running nose and teary eyes—that picture triggered the war on poverty. White poverty is less tolerable than black poverty. To that extent Dr. King knew that a multiracial coalition was critical to changing public opinion. You will not get public policy to change because black people are hurting. Matter of fact, you might gain votes from whites by proving that blacks hurt. If I can hurt blacks, I can get votes on counterculture. That's why Bush could put the picture of Dr. King in the White House one day, and send [Ted] Olsen to argue against affirmative action the next day. Because he knew that our reaction would gain him votes on the other side. It's called countercultural politics. He could go and lay a wreath at Dr. King's gravesite one day, and the next day put people on the court [to hurt us]. He knew that our reaction would gain action on the white side. That's a calculated countercultural political act. So we must be able to think these things through. Again, Dr. King's legacy became not just mass analysis, but mass action for mass change.

Zuberi: Professor Dyson, do you have anything to add?

Michael Eric Dyson: Amen. [*Laughter*]

Zuberi: Tell me, to what extent do you think that we are achieving Rev. King's dream, both nationally and internationally?

Dyson: Well, I want to thank Professor Zuberi, and of course, the incredible and brilliant President Rodin. We're sad to see her leave. God bless her on her path. And to be here with Rev. Jesse Jackson is beyond words and description. I've shared so much time with him. We went to London to meet with Nelson Mandela in Oliver Tambo's house in London. And I saw him interact with other giants. And I've been with him to San Antonio when, without cameras, he argued for the rights of poor white workers who have been disenfranchised; and [the same for] library workers in South Carolina. He's a hero. I think that, in regard to the legacy of Martin Luther King, Jr., and in regard to whether or not we are celebrating his birthday in a specifically redemptive fashion, I think Rev. Jackson has spoken to that. I think that we are incapable in America of acknowledging the genuine threat of a militant figure who weds the vocabulary of American democracy to a revolutionary tradition generated out of the womb of an African American spiritual tradition. That was a profound marriage.

So when I think about Martin Luther King, Jr., and I think about his challenge and his legacy, and I think about what the state of that dream is—no, we're not celebrating the incredible dream of Martin Luther King, Jr. We have frozen Martin Luther King, Jr., into a narrow framework that says he was talking about a dream in 1963. We haven't even listened to that whole speech. "Five score years ago, a great American in whose symbolic shadow we stand today, signed the Emancipation Proclamation. This momentous decree came as a great beacon light of hope for millions of Negroes" who had been enslaved in the manacles [of chattel] slavery. Then he talked about, "We have come to the nation's capital to cash a check." In other words, nation better have my money! [*Laughter*] But it wasn't just money! He said, "I refuse to believe that the great vaults of democracy are empty." And, "the whirlwinds of revolt will continue to shake the foundation of the nation" until the Negro is granted his citizenship rights. And, he said, I want to make it pure and clear that "the Negro in the South can't vote, and the Negro in the

North believes he has nothing for which to vote." Then, Mahalia Jackson, after he was speaking about police brutality, shouted, "Tell them about the dream, Martin." Then he got into the rhetorical articulation of the hope and aspiration that black people had projected into the world, and made it credible and concrete, convincing white America to hear their dream. "Later that year," Dr. King said, "I saw my dream turn into a nightmare when those four girls got blown up at the 16th Street Baptist Church in Birmingham, Alabama."

So we have frozen Dr. King's legacy to a single moment: "I have a dream one day my four little children will live in a nation where they will not be judged by the color of their skin, but by the content of their character." We have turned him into a rhetorical ventriloquist. We're using him to speak words that he articulated without the meanings that he intended. So now, we have conservative brothers and sisters, and forces aligned against us—what Rev. Jackson brilliantly has talked about as countercultural politics—that have seized upon the rhetoric of Dr. King while emptying the meaning out of it. The ambition of progressive politics has now been turned against its best use because of that language. So I don't think that we've A) comprehended the complexity of that dream, B) challenged roping King into a narrow rhetorical moment, or C) talked about the third movement beyond that dream, which is economic and social justice.

And when we think about that dream, we think about Rev. Jesse Jackson. We think about figures on the front line who see that poor white people in Appalachia are just as dissed as the poor black person in Harlem. And yet, the manipulation of their bigotry, for poor white brothers and sisters, makes them vote against themselves, against their own best interests. When I think about that dream—that dream was brilliantly spoken about by Dr. King long before that speech. But it was also talked about after that speech. And what we have to do then is to excavate, dig deep, get underneath, the rhetoric and get down to the moral aspiration. What I mean by that—the hope that we will hear and embrace human beings who are dissed wherever they are, not only because of their race, but because of their class, because of their sexual orientation, because of their economic inequality, because of their inability to get access to education, because of the gap between the have-gots and the have-nots, especially within African American communities where we have the upward mobility of bourgeois Negroes in the White House who speak against the interests of those on the outside.

Jackson: I actually think we make a big mistake in referring to it as the dream speech. It was not the dream speech; it was the broken promise speech. He had a profound sense of history. He knew that we were on a timeline from 1619 to 1865, where blacks were legally enslaved. Along the way, 1776, July 4th, the United States was freed from Britain while not freeing the enslaved. Seventy-six years later, they said, "[Frederick] Douglass won't you celebrate [Independence]?" "I can't, I'm a fugitive from slavery," eleven years before the Emancipation Proclamation, and seventeen years before 1865. On that timeline, there is 1619; 1776; 1852, Douglass; 1857, Dred Scott; 1863, Abraham Lincoln; 1865, the Thirteenth, Fourteenth, and Fifteenth Amendments.

King said, "Here I stand today. Lincoln, you *promised* the Emancipation Proclamation. We got the Proclamation, not the Emancipation. Congress, you *promised* the Thirteenth, Fourteenth, and Fifteenth Amendments. You promised. We joined the Union to stop those engaged in secession, slavery, sedition, segregation. Now you honor those who betrayed the nation. You honor those who engaged in treason; they've got statues in the Great Hall of Congress, and we can't use the toilet. You broke the promise." My high-school senior class in South Carolina couldn't take a picture on the lawn of the state capitol. The dogs could. Our money was counterfeited. We couldn't buy a hamburger. We couldn't rest in a Holiday Inn. Black soldiers sat behind Nazi P.O.W.s [on trains]. King was saying, "So here we are today, a hundred years later—1863 to 1963—with a broken promise." The focus must be on the promise, not on the dream, because the dream doesn't have a budget attached to it. The promise was reparations. It was repair for damage done. The promise was the Freedmen's Bureau. The promise was education for the previously enslaved. The promise was some land, some capital. The dream really was about "I dream of a day when" and the media has taken the soothing rhetoric of it. King with his dream would have been unnecessary if the promise had been fulfilled. The march would have been unnecessary. The march was about a hundred years after the promise. We would do well as scholars to study, because a lot of the talk now about reparations is a search for something, we know it's kind of there, but it starts with the promise of it—repair for damage done. Even the Congress recognized you cannot have two hundred fifty-six years of slavery, and walk out and say you're free. Douglass said, "What, free to starve?" There must be some repair for damage done. I would hope we could begin to put our focus, not on Dr. King's dream, but on America's broken promise. The Congress promised; the White House promised, and those promises have not been honored. And therein lies our struggle: not King's dream, but the government's promise.

Zuberi: Last week I returned from Senegal, and while I was in Senegal, I was driving around town, and I looked up and I noticed I was on Martin Luther King, Jr. Boulevard. And I went into a bookstore, and I counted at least ten books translated on Dr. King. And it was interesting to me that there was a great amount of enthusiasm about Dr. King's work in Dakar, in Senegal, in West Africa. To what extent do you think Dr. King's dream is relevant—or the promise has not been fulfilled—for the rest of the world? And is there some comparable promise internationally that King's message is relevant to?

Jackson: See, here's the reason I keep challenging the "dream" rhetoric. Nkrumah went to Lincoln University, here in Pennsylvania, and many of the

African students went to Morehouse, and Howard, and other schools in the country. So they were aware of American, British, and Portuguese colonialism there, in Africa, and apartheid here. So as our struggle began to move, they were aware of it. Dr. King, 1955 in Montgomery, and Nkrumah in 1957 in Ghana—there was a profound sense of relationship. You with me so far? So that what happened was, the movement *here* [became internationally recognized] because America *is* the most powerful nation with the most capacity to project—our clothes styles become international; our music styles becomes international; our hair styles become international. And so does our struggle. So kids in Sharpsville, South Africa, were singing "We Shall Overcome." In Tiananmen Square, [protesters were] singing "We Shall Overcome." In Gdansk, Poland, [protesters sang] "We Shall Overcome." *We* see ourselves as grasshoppers; we're giants. *We* have the power to transform the whole world. The world gains strength from our struggle. Much of the third-world countries' struggles, the decolonization movements in Africa and third world countries, came from our struggle. As we marched in Alabama and North Carolina, we had no sense that they were listening to us on radio, watching us on TV and newsreel. That's why we here tonight must project that which is redemptive and not that which is degenerative, because we have the power to take the world up or down. We have that power.

Zuberi: In many ways the national election almost four years ago denied, avoided, and downplayed very crucial issues. Not enough was said about inner cities. Very little was said about levels of unemployment, underemployment, and misemployment, and almost nothing was said about the inequalities in wealth and income. And nothing was said about the fact that more men of African descent are in American jails than in American universities. What does this imply for social justice today? What did Martin Luther King, Jr., do or say that can provide us hope and optimism in the face of these realities?

Dyson: I'll be very brief because I know Rev. Jackson has plenty to say on that. I think that when you look at the social calculus—how you figure out, how you measure [our social realities]—I think what was important about what Rev. Jesse Jackson has said time and again is that this stuff is not nebulous; it's not vague. You can measure it, you can see it in the incarceration of disproportionately African men, and increasingly women, in America, to the tune of a million folk. More than two million are incarcerated altogether. We're the only industrialized nation in the world with this kind of incredible commitment A) to capital punishment and B) to the expansion of the prison-industrial complex on the backs of black and increasingly brown people. Poor white communities—about which Rev. Jackson spoke earlier—in Appalachia, in our Northern industrialized areas, and in the outlying areas across the heartland, now find their economic futures bolstered by the privatization of the prison industry. It becomes an enterprise, and it becomes commodified—turned into something to be bought and sold on the open market. What is that "it"? The future of black and brown America. Why is that? Because increased incarceration means that you can then subsidize the local economy through privatized enterprises that now deal with [imprisoning blacks and browns]. So that the funky reality is that black and brown people are being warehoused in these incarceration pens for the capitalist expansion of local communities that need economic support—but [it shouldn't be] at the expense of brothers and sisters who are black and brown!

We've also got to deal with the incredible concentration in America of the harshly reactionary, and draconian, consequences of incarceration. You know, half the people in prison have medical problems. What do you think happened when Ronald Reagan threw away all these people who were homeless, because they were mentally diseased? They're in prison now. So we end up criminalizing an essentially medical problem. Then there are those who have certain IQs who fall beneath the pale, so to speak, who never get addressed. So when you look at the incredible concentration of so-called social pathology around incarceration, it becomes very apparent that we are doing a terrible job. Let's not forget that Martin Luther King, Jr., himself was a prisoner. He spent time in jail. One of the first experiences he had when he got arrested [is that] when they were taking him to jail, he didn't know where they were going because they went way out of the [usual] way [to jail] in Montgomery, and it scared the crap out of him. Then he talks about going to Birmingham, where he wrote one of the most famous letters ever penned from his Birmingham cell. Martin Luther King, Jr., was a political prisoner. We have people now who are political prisoners as well, but we don't call them that.

In this country, we would rather put Lionel Tate in prison for a mistake he made at twelve or thirteen years old, dooming him to a life of perpetual suffering in an adult situation where we're not rehabilitating him, [but instead] inculcating in him the very values we want to avoid. We're teaching him, and others like him, how to become the very thing we say we want to reform. And at the same time, we allow other people in our society, who don't have darker skin, to plea bargain when they've stolen millions and millions of dollars out of the purses of ordinary people. And Martin Luther King, Jr., would talk about the economic inequality and fundamental social injustice that is both ethnically based and racially informed, but also class based, because poor white people themselves have been duped by politicians who don't have their best interests at heart. So he would talk to them about corporate capitalism and the enormous greed that has destroyed so many infrastructures of political possibility for poor people.

Let me end here saying this: [my analysis] doesn't mean that we're not [disturbed by] people who do the wrong thing. It means that [we must read] the Amnesty International report that said that black and brown kids are put in juvenile detention centers, which become warehouses for imprisonment as adults, for the same crimes that their white counterparts are slapped on the back of the hand for. And black and brown people have a stern view of crime and punishment—"if you did the crime you do the time"—failing to understand their children are being sold down the river for the same infractions that young white kids get little punishment for. Black kid gets put in jail for DWI; white kid becomes president of the United States. There's a hell of a gulf right there.

Zuberi: Rev. Jackson, what did Martin Luther King, Jr., do or say that can provide us hope and optimism when faced with these particular realities?

Jackson: Let me make this point first. Noelle Bush, Governor Bush's daughter, was charged with using crack three times. The law calls for a mandatory sentence; instead, she's getting rehabilitation, love, and monitoring—which is what she should get. But it should be fairly applied. Rush Limbaugh is admittedly drug sick. He may even be breaking government laws with cashing of checks. But no one went up into his house looking for more drugs as they did into Michael [Jackson's] place. So Michael gets a three million dollar bail without being charged, while Phil Spector gets a million dollar bail and is charged with murder. Rush Limbaugh gets no charge—and still has all of his stations and all of his commercials. So there are two sets of rules that drive all that.

Dr. King would say two things. Not only would he cry out against a jails-for-profit industry, he would also challenge those who go to jail for risky behavior. That's the other side of this question too. Dr. King did not go to jail for antisocial behavior. He meant to go to jail twenty-five times. He was on the offensive. He went to jail with moral authority. They wouldn't let me come to jail. They put me out of jail. [*Laughter*] Because I went there with an authority different than having been caught selling drugs in the name of "my thing." I was in [Chicago's] Cook County jail Christmas Day. Twelve thousand inmates, nine thousand beds. I said, "I want you to help me close this jail down this spring." I said, "How many of you finished high school?" Ten percent stood. As bad as schools are in Chicago, they're better than they ever were in Mississippi in the Deep South. They chose not to go to school. Last year in Chicago we lost $133 million for daily absenteeism. You get money for daily attendance, and lose money for daily absences. We have the power to end that. $133 million for not going to school? Willfully choosing entertainment over education? I said, "How many of you finished high school?" 10 percent stood. "How many of you have a child at home?" Almost all of them stood. Two children at home. Most of them stood up. Three children at home. I stopped; almost all of them stood again. I said, "Now how many of you are in on a nonviolent drug charge?" And 15 percent stood. Now I know that 85 percent of all rural arrests are white. 76 percent of all urban arrests are white. And 55 percent of all those in jail are black. So I know what the data is. I said, "Would you help me close the jail down?" They screamed, "Yeah. What can we do?" I said, "Don't come back no mo'." [*Laughter*]

My point is that we have the power to stop recidivism. It's no given you've got to go back to jail. There's no given that you have to have drugs. There's no given that you have to rob people in your own neighborhood. There's no given that you have to rape people. So he would challenge both sides. Yes, there is a jail-industrial complex. There's also some burden to make right choices, because every choice has a consequence. I got every "pathology"—as they are described—that a black man can have. Born out of wedlock; teenage mother; born in the Deep South. All of that stuff. I've seen the consequences of my choices. I can not avoid being responsible. I have the right to fight for the right. But I must sharpen my tools to win the fight.

Zuberi: Martin Luther King, Jr., as you well know, never ran for public office. Yet he was a great politician. But he did not do it inside of the electoral arena, as you very well know, Rev. Jackson. You were in the heat of battle and struggle with Dr. King in those very important moments during his life, and during our past. Today, African American voter turnout has increased, even though it trails behind non-Hispanic whites. In 2001 there were about 9,101 elected African American politicians, representing only less than 2 percent of all the elected officials, yet a tremendous increase over none. Are these political leaders the leaders of black America?

Jackson: Yeah, but you've got to deal with [the fact that] politicians are elected to get re-elected. And they tend to do a lot of good work in their zone. And that's become a big problem for us in recent years. There was a time, if dogs bit us in Birmingham, we bled everywhere, [and we cried] "Let's go to Birmingham." Emmett Till got killed in Mississippi: "Let's go to Mississippi." Now you get a killing in Philadelphia, it's not Wilmington's problem. It's not Camden's problem. There's a radical sense of turfism. Almost a capacity to not care that there's a problem in Chicago. We've lost a sense of national vision and put forth a series of turfs that makes unity impossible, so today we're not so much divided philosophically as we are disconnected. More phones and more e-mails and more stuff and miscommunication about things that matter. Most politicians that are elected may focus on getting reelected, which is significant, but it's not the stuff of which change is made. It's the stuff of which maintenance is made. Most change does not come from politics in the first place. Abolitionists were not elected officials. Those who were elected *reacted* to the abolitionists. Those who ended segregation were not elected; they didn't have the right to vote. So there's a role to play outside of electoral politics. Those who are not elected can set the climate [of change]. So in many ways John Kennedy could say to Dr. King, "Your nonviolent demonstrations enabled me to do what I do better." If there was a case of [Police Commissioner] Bull Connor beating black people in Birmingham, and black people doing nothing but sitting passive, John Kennedy couldn't say, "I went to Birmingham one day and I saw blacks couldn't use the hotels and motels, and let's have a change." They'd think he was crazy. He had a *choice* between King and Bull Connor; he chose King. So we must always provide the creative activist alternative.

Second, I don't find any consolation in our voting patterns lately, even though I know in Florida we won the election, and Bush won by the margin of the "stop counting" votes from Florida A&M, Bethune-Cookman College, and the Haitian folk who had problems with the lack of language support so they could vote. So I know he stole this election. Ordinarily the president selects the Supreme Court. This time the Supreme Court selected the president. Having said that, tonight, tonight, tonight there are nine hundred fifty thousand blacks in New York unregistered. Four hundred and fifty thousand New Jersey blacks unregistered. Four hundred thousand in Pennsylvania unregistered. About four hundred thousand in Virginia unregistered. Six hundred thousand blacks in Georgia are unregistered, and we lost the Senate seat by thirty thousand votes. Four hundred thousand unregistered blacks in South Carolina, and we lost the governor's race by forty thousand. Six hundred thousand unregistered in Florida. So really we cannot make a case about "the Man"—if we don't use our vote.

And that's where Dr. King would not spend so much time on analysis. Analysis is easy but registration—that's work. Dr. King said, "Selma was exciting. You know, the dogs were there, and the police were there, and the cameras were there. So now, let's leave the dramatic part for the drudgery of day-to-day work—door knocking, church by church [canvassing]." How can a black high-school principal with one hundred fifty seniors not register every high-school senior to vote? How can you be a pastor with unregistered folks in his church and preach past that empowerment? So in some sense we have *betrayed* Dr. King's effort by our inaction. You cannot compensate for action with analysis. We about to overdose on analysis, and about to trip out on action. Because action makes analysis make sense. Analysis describes action, but action is the base of it all. When we act, people analyze what we do. If we don't act, ain't nothing to analyze. [*Laughter*]

Dyson: Absolutely right. But the critical thing is, King got a Ph.D. at Boston University, to make it available [to his people]. That's your point—brilliantly taken—but analysis is critical. I know you're not dismissing it, but I want to underscore the necessity for it. Because I've seen a whole bunch of people acting without any analysis, and it becomes empty. Action wedded to analysis becomes redemptive movement. And I think that's what you did. I think that's what Dr. King did. I think that's what C. T. Vivian did. I think that's what Jo Ann Robinson did. I think that's what Fannie Lou Hamer did. I think that's what a whole bunch of people who had critical intelligence brought to bear upon social problems. Because one of the pathologies you spoke about in young people is this anti-intellectual attitude, where they think, "I ain't got to hit the books, I ain't got to dig deep, I don't have to be critical. I can write a rap song but I can't learn a mathematical formula." And I'm not dissing rap, because I respect both [rap and math]. But my point is that critical analysis is important to understanding what we're doing in terms of the social justice movement. Because what Dr. King did brilliantly in the "I Have a Dream" speech, which is "broken promises," was make an *analysis*. The analysis allowed space for action to come after that, and it was the product of that action. You're absolutely right. But I think it's a reciprocal, dialectal process.

The point about the politicians, I think, is brilliant as well. John F. Kennedy didn't want Martin Luther King, Jr., to do the March on Washington, as you know, Rev. Jackson. Kennedy said, "Don't do it, you're going to mess things up. I've got to have things prepared for Congress. You're going to create this backlash." Martin Luther King, Jr., et al—A. Philip Randolph, John Lewis, and a whole host of people who were there, especially Bayard Rustin—understood that a moral commitment outside of parliamentary politics would create the heat on the politicians. Because I think what we have to understand, as Rev. Jackson said, is that extra-parliamentary procedures—that is, people outside the political process—make politicians accountable. If you and I, who are part of the citizenry, don't make them accountable—they are to represent our interests. Black politicians very much have to be responsible to the social justice issue. Many of them get up there and get a pass because they are black—because they have black skin don't mean they represent black interests. And black interests are not narrowly defined.

Let me say this: the reason I went to Princeton to get a Ph.D. was not to be high-falutin' and to be soundin' high and mighty. It was to *join* the Reverend Jesse Jackson, it was to join the legacy of Martin Luther King, Jr. But it's also to make the life of the mind sexy to young people [so they can] understand that this critical intelligence can be brought to bear to create the *urge* to action. Because as we know, only 10 percent of black people got involved in the movement in the first place. The rest of the people were on the sidelines, watching it on TV, looking at it in the restaurant, complaining about it, grumbling about what Negroes were doing, and they weren't doing nothing. And then, when the goodies came, they got involved, and ain't none of them turned it down. The reason I write books, the reason I write articles, the reason I'm on the front line trying to write in the *New York Times* about Rev. Jesse Jackson and about social justice, is because the pen is mighty, the insight is critical, the analysis important—because it's an adjunct to, not just separate from, the action. So I just want to say it's both of those together.

Jackson: I guess, my point is, Michael, as we talk about Dr. King's legacy—here's where philosophy and King came together. Those who are analysts are not, by and large, leading action. They just analyzed it—and are well endowed to do so. Dr. King, with his Ph.D., could have been the preacher at Riverside Church. He was a profoundly intellectual, analytical black preacher. He went down to Alabama, where applying his intellect would mean something. And so today, the issue is, where are the Ph.D.s who can talk the common language [and use] critical analysis, using their ability to lead people somewhere? Show me another Ph.D. that's using that brilliance to trigger enough hope to have a following. That's what made him different. He was a man of analysis *and* action. He said we don't want to get the paralysis of analysis.

This last point again—this idea of a timeline. I hear people say, "back in the civil rights days." [*Laughter*] I say, "Has time been warped?" If our mission statement is, "defend, protect, and gain civil rights, and even the playing field" [we're not through]. We're out of slavery. We're out of legal segregation. We have the right to vote. But is there a plan for access to health care? [Enhancing] life expectancy? Access to colleges, universities, capital? To that extent, there's no reason to sink back in because it is not over. The question is, can we just intellectualize ourselves to the goal line—or must we run the ball? You can't wish up a touchdown; you got to run the touchdown. And you got to run the risk of getting tackled. And when you just analyze what other black people do, there's no risk involved. And part of what Dr. King's legacy was, was an at-risk ministry. He took the risk of getting stabbed; the risk of going to jail on his own terms twenty-five times. You don't have to be in his tradition. There are a lot of other traditions. But in *that* tradition—there is analysis, action, risk, sacrifice, and countercultural activity. Activity—that's what made him different. He had lots of friends in class with Ph.D.s. He was with that. But what made him different was the at-risk factor; the sacrifice factor; the going-to-jail factor; the countercultural factor; the inspiring-common-people factor. Those things made him different.

Dyson: I agree with you, Reverend. I agree with all that. Where are we having this conversation? The University of Pennsylvania. King came here. President Rodin talked about it. In a schoolroom, in a class lecture, he heard the great Mordecai Johnson—himself not a possessor of a Ph.D., the president of Howard University, but brilliant as all get out. He didn't need a Ph.D. because his intellectual acuity was of such a nature that he was able to command the leadership of men and women. But he had gone—*action*—to India, and came back—*action*—and spoke about it—*analysis*. So to me, it's not a contradistinction between an either/or, it's a both/and. So when Mordecai Johnson stood in 1948 in the University of Pennsylvania, and Martin Luther King, Jr., heard him, and having heard the ideas presented about Mahatma Gandhi, he went to read the books about this "little brown saint"—Fisher's book on Gandhi—because he wanted to be better acquainted with this man who was deeply in tune with Jesus' ministry and yet had a global application of it. I'm saying to you, there is necessary sweat work that *you* have done, obviously—without question one of the smartest human beings I've ever met in my life. You! And I'm saying, I don't want to downplay or to negate that, or to make it appear that there's action over here, and analysis over there. Well, of course we prefer the action. But the action has to be informed.

And I'm saying this finally as well. For those who make a serious attempt to do serious analysis—[conceding] your point about the paralysis of analysis as Martin Luther King, Jr., said—well, Martin Luther King, Jr., was quoting folk in all of his speeches. "Five score years ago"—reference to what? The Gettysburg Address. Archibald Carey—"let freedom ring." What was it—'52 Republican Convention? He pieced that together. "I have a dream" itself was taken from Prathia Hall. So

I'm saying that when we look at Martin Luther King, Jr., the rhetorical landscape upon which he cast his eye was derived from intellectually credible human beings who paid the price, the sweat [of study and analysis]. He said himself, "Stay up late at night to study." Martin Luther King, Jr., was able to have brilliant action because he read books written by people who informed his analysis, so that he could move towards serious action. I'm not trying to privilege the analysis over the action. Obviously, people do stuff, and people write about what they do. I'm saying, however, that the critical intelligence necessary to do the analysis is, itself, a form of activity. Not getting bogged down in [it], not doing it for the sake of [doing it]–I mean socially redemptive, theoretically sophisticated forms of thinking that can inform those people who are activists so they have something to pull on.

If Martin Luther King, Jr., didn't get trained at Morehouse, fifteen to nineteen [years old], go to Crozer Theological Seminary from nineteen through twenty-one [years old], and then go to Boston University and become educated–not simply schooled, but educated–in the complex analysis of the culture, then, I think, he would have been a different kind of figure. He wouldn't have had that kind of powerful, insightful movement towards social justice. So I just don't want to downplay the necessity for analysis and study. Because we know there's a whole bunch of leaders out here who "talkin' loud and sayin' nothin'" and what they're doing is leading and misleading. So if we want to talk about the paralysis of analysis, let's [also] talk about the leaden leadership that we've seen manifested in an American society where Negroes have pimped other ignorant people without being accountable themselves. I want to join those two together.

Jackson: My point is, some of those misleaders would not be misleading if those who were educated were active. The nature of politics has gone backwards. In many small towns, the NAACP leader may be an auto mechanic; it may be some leader who works for the union. And across town, in the universities, there are very well-informed black intellectuals, who analyze what other black people do, and get paid for it. [*Laughter*] I was at James Madison University the other night, in Virginia, and some community people came from the NAACP and some other social organizations. But none of the professors on campus were involved in any of the action. They were working on their tenure and stuff; they were not involved. I'm challenging that.

You know what impressed me so much about Mandela? When Mandela first came out of jail–and I had known his family for some time because I had been to South Africa, sometime in 1979, I guess it was–and somebody said, "Man, Jesse, if you can just get to Mandela, tell him, 'You've been in jail twenty-seven years, so if you'd just spend your time writing a book, or doing a movie. You've paid your dues, Mandela.'" The first thing Mandela did when he came out was rejoin the ANC. It took an organization to bring about change. He tried to build a vehicle [for social change]. It was going to rain. God didn't tell Noah to teach swimming lessons. He said to build an infrastructure. [*Laughter*] So, the ANC's leaders [taught] the Ph.D.s [ANC leader] Mbeki and those guys went away to college and came back and joined the *struggle* struggle. They were not analyzing the struggle; they were the leaders of it.

Dyson: They weren't only analyzing it.

Jackson: Well, they were analyzing and acting. They added the analyst-activist sacrificial dimension. They could have stayed in Europe, where it was much more comfortable, because they were all bright. They could have stayed in America. Instead, they said, "We going back home." So if those who got the learning go back to Mississippi, as it were, or maybe Philadelphia; go back to South Carolina. Those who know are burdened with going to those who don't know. Those who know the most have the most obligation. So I'm saying that sometimes we go forth in the streets talking ignorant talk 'cause the informed people are not acting and talking.

I tell you today that we have enough black intellectuals in our country to take the country over. But except for a handful of y'all, most cannot be found. When they were doing chokeholds, and killing blacks in LA–I mean chokeholds–and Maxine Waters and I were leading a demonstration against *killing our people*, they wouldn't leave the campus and join us. I was in Goose Creek, South Carolina, last week, and the police came in, and conspired with the school officials, came in with guns, glocks, without safety locks on them. Hemming our children behind a hallway and handcuffing them. They had dogs sniffing between little girls' legs, looking for drugs, and did not find them. Those who are possessed with great knowledge wouldn't come to the rally, wouldn't come to the march. I'm not indicting those who are doing it, but in Dr. King's tradition, he would not have just analyzed Goose Creek, he would have gone there. That's what makes a difference.

Dyson: Absolutely. I'm down with you on everything and take a lot of heat for it. Don't get me wrong–I'm not saying this from a position of security. Especially in an academy A) that looks down on and is skeptical about being able to speak to a broader audience without using jargon or obscure language and B) that is suspicious of the intent to want to speak to a broad audience. So you're not talking to somebody who doesn't understand that. And I've been with you in marches plenty of times. But this is what I'm saying: when I worked at the car wash, I worked the windows. Homeboy say, "You hit them windows?" I say, "Yep, I got 'em." Now I can't also do the front lights, because homeboy in the front got them, and homeboy in the back got the tail pipe; and somebody's got the side doors. Division of labor is critical. That's like me asking a factory laborer, "How come you ain't at the university teaching?" He'd say, "Cause my job is to be an arc-welder." And I've been an arc-welder, 'cause I did that before I went to college at twenty-one. So I'm saying that division of labor is critical.

The reason why white conservatives are ahead of us: they ain't playa-hatin' on men and women who all day long, all they do is write books and make analysis. And you know what those white conservatives do? They take that analysis and turn it into public policy, because the leisure of critical, conservative, white intellectuals is transformed into serious public policy. They understand the division of labor. We should do the same. All I'm arguing for—I think we're on the same page—is that we [can] have concerned, committed intellectuals who make the choice to make their gifts available [to a broader public]. But [we must remember] this cat here can't do this, but this person over here can do this. "I can write, I can think, I can make sociological analysis. My name is William Julius Wilson. I can write a book that can inform public policy for the next fifteen years. I don't have to march because my books become the fodder for the cannons being fired on the front lines of those who march."

And let me say this. If we're gon' get real about it, many of the leaders I know—you were right to challenge us; let me challenge the leaders. Half the leaders I know are insecure. A Negro come up here with some intelligence, they go, "Oh, hell, who is he? [*Laughter*] I'm not going to get the glory anymore because now this person is there." Insecure, incapable of accepting intelligent, articulate people who just want to help. So it goes both ways. More analysts would be involved in action if the Negroes leading the action weren't insecure about the analysis.

Jackson: I don't think that applies to [NAACP president] Kweisi Mfume. I don't think that applies to [National Urban League president Marc] Morial. I guess all I'm saying is white professors can afford to just analyze and let other white reactionaries use it. But we can't be like white people. You are an intellectual activist, which makes you rare. You ain't like the folk you try to defend. And to defend those analysts who don't act is trying to put a square peg in a round hole. It will not fit. You are defending that which you ain't. I'm not trying to defend leaders who don't make sense, because a lot of them just don't. But I guess I'm concerned that often those who *do* lead are leading in vacuums, without calling anybody's names. For example, Mike, say black people get killed in Philadelphia. Who will go to Mary Mason's show and talk about how terrible it is, and what this means? Who will have a press conference here and say, "They killed our people. This is not right." Well, if the ministers don't have a press conference, the intellectuals don't have it, and the politicians who say, "they're not in my district" don't have it, there's a vacuum. And up comes Mojo talking about whatever. Well, he stepped in a vacuum. All I'm saying is, those who know have the burden to express when it matters. I don't think we have the option to be detached from that action. That's my point.

Dyson: You know, Reverend, I'm down with that. Because I agree with everything you just said. And I don't want to necessarily make the template of my behavior the norm for everybody to follow. I *do* believe the reason I got this degree wasn't to impress nobody. It was to help somebody, because I was disenfranchised my dadgum self, and seen as a pathological, nihilistic "nigga" who couldn't do it. So when I came up off of welfare, as a teen father—got some of them "pathologies" myself—I understood what that meant. But I understand this as well. Your point is brilliant in the sense that the creation of the [leadership] gap itself is a judgment against those of us who have the critical intelligence and analysis, and need to do it. I agree with that.

I'm just saying, though, if that's not this person's *skill,* they may not be able to get up at no press conference and talk to nobody. But dammit they can write a book. And the book that they write—the activist who ain't got time to do all that research, can look at that book. Dr. King borrowed liberally from a whole bunch of people's books, and made his analysis, and made some points that were powerful. So I agree with you. I'm just saying, division of labor means this: some people don't have the gift to stand up before a press conference, or go on a television program, or to write an article that's lucid in a certain way. Some people got some skills that are narrowly defined. And I'm saying, I agree with the challenge to us; I just don't want to disenfranchise those people who want to participate as citizens and scholars. That's all I'm saying.

Jackson: I give. [*Laughter*]

Zuberi: You know, as time passes and the FBI and CIA files get released, and books get written, the image of Dr. King becomes more imperfect. Recent discussions of King, including this one, have attempted to demythologize him by acknowledging his humanness. Most of us have heard of Dr. King's extramarital affairs, and maybe less so his possibly plagiarizing his dissertation. We face this issue with other leaders as well, including Thomas Jefferson and, more recently, President Bush. How can we balance Dr. King's moral accountability with his moral complexity, without totally absolving him, on the one hand, or totally condemning him, on the other hand? And what lessons are in that for current leaders today?

Dyson: Well, I'll take this first. I wrote a book on Dr. King, *I May Not Get There with You: The True Martin Luther King, Jr.* A lot of black folk got mad at me. (I'm talking about Rev. Jackson). [*Laughter*] They called me up on radio programs. And I remember I was in Chicago, and I got the spirit of Jesse Jackson in me. And I said, "Have you read my book?" "Naw." I said, "Hold it. If my book you do not read / do not attempt to make me bleed." And here's my point: they didn't read my book, comprised of thirteen chapters, [only] a couple of them dealing [with King's flaws]. We complain about white folk who take our history and mess it up, guided by their narrow ideological concerns, so they don't want to deal with what they find, they deal with what they want to find. So they dismiss it. First of all, these FBI wiretaps on King are going to be unsealed in 2027. That ain't that far away, number one. Number two, Martin Luther King, Jr., is great enough to withstand anything that any *analyst* could ever say about him, think about him, or understand about his life.

Number three, it's critical for those of us who want to hold high the mantle of scholarship to talk about the good, the bad, and the ugly, not pretending that the ideological and political contexts don't make a difference. I knew that some white folk would read that book and say, "See? We told you he was a pervert. We told you he was a plagiarist." And so on. But my book addressed that. It addressed that because it was honest about the failures of this man, and yet the conclusion of my book, in my opinion, was that Martin Luther King, Jr,. was the greatest American produced on American soil. So, my point is, we don't have to deny accusations of plagiarism. This is why this analysis thing [that Rev. Jackson and I have been disputing] is so critical to me. Because obviously, Martin Luther King, Jr., saw it fit enough to be able to present himself as an intellectually credible person in a white supremacist society that denied Negroes being seen as intelligent. If Martin Luther King, Jr., hungered after that credibility at that level, we can't dismiss analysis.

But what is more important is—and I think it was Rev. Jesse Jackson who said, "I'm not looking for his footnotes; I'm looking for his footprints in the sand of time"—it's very important to put Martin Luther King, Jr., in a broader context. Did he engage in extramarital affairs? Absolutely. Did he engage in plagiarist activity? Absolutely. And the point is what? The point is, he did those things. The point is not to try to pretend he didn't. But the point is also to put [his flaws] in the context of his entire life. Here's a man who died at thirty-nine years old. He was on the road for twenty-eight days of most months out of the year. That's not a justification, that's an explanation. Somebody threatening you that morning—a credible threat, not a fake threat—and you down in, say, Saint Augustine, Florida. And that night, in the respite from the horror of the moment, I could imagine that a woman offering Dr. King consolation—I'm just trying to keep it real. My life is being threatened, and this might be my last night on earth? [*Laughter*] Bro, I don't know about you. Holla! [*Laughter*]

So he's not a *god*. He's a *man* in the context of a movement where white folk are trying to kill him; black people are scared of him because of what he represents; the authorities have put a bug under his bed. Can *you* stand that? If somebody put a bug under my bed, have mercy, Jesus! You been gettin' your freak on and somebody got a tape of it? [*Laughter*] "Girl, you better come in here tonight 'cause I'm a lay it on you *right now*!" [*Laughter*] Nobody can stand that. It's deep enough to stay married without the government on you. This man is trying to stay married in the midst of a holocaust, and the government is trying to undo the man. I'm saying that in the context of the life he lived, in the times in which he emerged, Martin Luther King, Jr., in my estimation, is a great, powerful, and ingenious American leader.

And let me say this, because I know it's implicit. Let me make it explicit, although I know Rev. Jackson can speak for himself. I wrote an op-ed piece in the *New York Times* about Rev. Jesse Jackson. And I said, about Dr. King and Rev. Jackson, that you don't have to be perfect to be useful. You judge a person's life by the entire sweep of his life. When we look at these figures—Martin Luther King, Jr., with all that education, put it on the front line. Rev. Jesse Jackson could have been a billionaire in corporate enterprises, but he gave that up to speak for those who are powerless. And I have been an activist on the front line with him, without the cameras there, without them celebrating him. I wrote that out of conviction, because I have seen this man's life. I wasn't willing to allow people to besmirch his character, since you cannot reduce the complexity and genius of the creative inspiration that God has breathed through his body and mind, to a mistake that human beings make. That's why I celebrate and acknowledge and stand up for the man.

Finally, if we are serious scholars, credible intellectuals, we must not turn a blind eye or a deaf ear—to use those troubling metaphors—to what we find out. We are not made less by the more we know about Dr. King. We are ennobled. And this is why I join in the hip-hop culture. You mean if Martin Luther King, Jr., did this and yet still achieved, [you can't do the same for] those little black boys that you don't want to give a chance to, and those little black girls that you're dismissing? This is especially my challenge to the civil rights generation. You can look at Dr. King—and I'm not saying Dr. King is Tupac or Biggie. Don't be ridiculous. What I *am* saying is that if Dr. King had died at twenty-five like Tupac, he would be seen much differently than having died at thirty-nine. So my point is, give young people a chance to mature and develop. You don't know what potential's in them. So let's not castigate them and dismiss them. That's why I wrote my book on King. And that's why, with Dr. King, I think it's important for us to deal with [his flaws] and not lie about them. Because we don't have to pretend Dr. King was perfect. Like singer Grace Jones said, "I ain't perfect, but I'm perfect for you." Martin Luther King, Jr., was not perfect, but he was perfect for the times to which he spoke in the nation that received him.

Jackson: You know, I worked with him directly for four years, [and it's] like when you eat food: the part that gives you vitality, you use, and the rest goes in the toilet. I have to use of Dr. King what's nutritional to me. The rest of that is not important to me. And so those who want to go that route, it's alright with me, but when I see him, I see the most militant guy of his era, who engaged in the most mass action, to change laws under which all of us live. The very idea of focusing on his private sexual appetite is used so viciously to undercut our struggle. That's why I wouldn't give it much time—for that reason. They accept Jesus as perfect, because we worship Jesus. If we didn't, we'd raise questions about him and Mary Magdalene. Because we worship him, he's just untouchable. We believe about

Jesus: the Holy Ghost is the Daddy, and not Joseph. So we worship him. Non-Christians don't believe that. To Christians it doesn't matter, though. And so I'll accept from Dr. King what he gave to us. It *matters* to me. That's why I stop right there. One thing is clear: those who pounce on him, they jump on *him*, but they're really jumping on *us*. They're saying we're not worthy to have public accommodations. We're not worthy to have the right to vote. And look at this guy leading y'all; something wrong with him means there's something wrong with y'all. So that is why, to me, it's the politics of the scholarship.

To put it another way, I argue there are four stages in our struggle. If I was writing a Freedom Symphony, I'd have four movements. James Brown fans think it's two, but there are four movements. [*Laughter*] The first movement was to end slavery. The second movement was to end legal segregation. The third movement was the right to vote. The fourth movement is access to capital. You can be out of slavery, out of segregation, have the right to vote—and starve to death. So now we are in another stage of our struggle. We spent too little time on the fourth stage, still arguing about stages two and three. So what does it mean, for example, tonight? There are $7 *trillion* in mutual funds. One of every three Americans invest in them. Ten companies control $3 *trillion*. We collectively control 5.5 billion—billion with a *B*, trillion with a *T*. As we follow Dr. King to his logical conclusion, we're fighting for our share of capital. There's a trillion dollars, a trillion, in 401Ks. We manage none of it. GM has $120 billion in pension funds; Boeing has 54 billion, with a $17 billion government contract pending because of the scandal. Our control of pension funds: zero. Harvard, 20 billion; Yale, 15 billion; blacks and browns manage none of it.

When you look at $54 *trillion* in institutional assets, we seek to manage 5 percent. Just as we took pensions out [of corporations doing business with South Africa] to end apartheid there, we can [end up] investing in apartheid here. And so the struggle before us is not for public accommodations or the right to vote. In front of us is the last mountain to be scaled, the mountain of capital. We are substantial investors in Wall Street. And every now and then, somebody says, "Jesse, you're on Wall Street, what does Wall Street mean?" There's a graveyard there; the whole Federal Plaza is the graveyard of our people. Wall Street was built on the shipping industry and commodities exchange. We were the ship; we were the cargo and the commodity exchange. At that time blacks were more valuable than land was, because land was basically uncultivated. So we were moving stock. Wall Street was built on us. We are the base of it. Yale has twelve colleges, ten named after owners of our people. Yale was a bastion of slavery, in fact. The first state against slavery was Vermont.

I come at it this way because I'm trying to keep us focused on: where are we going? We're going to finally get an even playing field. We cannot run from our share of capital. Some of our folk said, "Slavery doesn't matter. After all, when we die, it will be all over." That was a cop-out from fighting with abolitionists. Some of our folk said, "Segregation doesn't matter; they don't want to be bothered with us, we don't want to be bothered with them." That was a cop-out from fighting. Some of our folk said, "The right to vote? That doesn't matter because it's dangerous; politics is dirty." We were afraid to fight the fight. Some of our folk say, "Capital is for them." No, capital is for us. It's *our* money. We have a right to our share of capital. We must now be intellectually prepared to fight for our share of capital in this country, and peace in the world.

If there's one other legacy of Dr. King, it's that he internationalized our thought process. The fact that we could fight for peace in Vietnam, suggests we can fight for peace in Iraq too. Because before Dr. King we didn't quite feel we had the authority [to be internationally minded]. When Dr. King spoke out against the war in Vietnam, other civil rights leaders attacked him. They said, "After all, you're out of our zone." He said, "No, no, no. Vietnam is our zone." Today, Iraq is our zone. Afghanistan is our zone. Putting Bush out in November is in our zone too, and we're going to do it.

4

MYTHS, DISTORTIONS, AND HISTORY
Affirmative Action

with Ward Connerly, moderated by Yvonne Scruggs-Leftwich

In August 1998, before a massive gathering of thousands at the national meeting of Blacks in Government (BIG) in Washington, D.C., I debated Ward Connerly, then University of California Regent, who spearheaded the movement to bring affirmative action to an end most recently in Michigan, and before that in California through the ballot initiative Prop 209. Our nearly two-and-a-half-hour debate was carried live on C-SPAN, and then rebroadcast on the network several times. Mr. Connerly and I had a warm-up of sorts when we were paired on opposite ends of a panel debating affirmative action a year earlier at the University of Wisconsin, Milwaukee, where Connerly was joined by Charles Murray and Linda Chavez, and I was joined by Christopher Edley and Judith Lichtman. At our BIG debate, the proceedings were always civil, often lively, and occasionally humorous. And yet the two sides couldn't have been more clearly stated or actively contested as Connerly and I defended our radically different visions of racial justice and affirmative action. I have often been stopped by folk over the years who told me that this was one of the most important and enlightening debates about affirmative action that they've witnessed. I was glad to defend a policy whose existence has preserved the right of millions of deserving minority citizens to get a quality education and gain satisfying employment.

Ward Connerly: Let me just say, first of all, that it's a delight to be here. I also want to state to you that I am delighted to see the recognition that you gave Dr. [Oscar] Eason, although I will indicate that, had you proceeded to stand as I was introduced, I'd be worried, thinking you might be walking out. [*Laughter*]

This is a serious issue we are discussing. My grandmother always used to say there are always two sides to the smallest pancake. And I hope that tonight you can suspend any predispositions you might have about the subject or my position, and in the fullness of the evening, perhaps, we might find there is more agreement than there is disagreement. The [debate] resolution poses the question of whether affirmative action, which I support in most of its forms, has essentially brought women, minorities into the American mainstream. Indeed it has. That question, however, requires a little bit more explanation than how the question is presented, and I will try to explore that.

It seems to me that the question really ought to include the subquestion of whether affirmative action, as a system of preferences, will best serve the nation and all of its people in the years ahead. Not just the past, but in the years ahead. And I would respond accordingly. First of all, I think that affirmative action, as a system of treating people differently on the basis of race, sex, color, ethnicity, national origin, color, sexual orientation, or whatever, by the government, by any franchise of government, is morally wrong. That was the position that this nation embraced back in 1964, '63, and that's the position I believe we should embrace today and forevermore. I believe any system of government that says, "Because of your skin color, we're going to hold you to a different standard," is just morally wrong. So, number one, I think that affirmative action as a system of different treatment, different standards for people, is wrong morally.

Secondly, I think that affirmative action as it has evolved, in most venues, has become a system that marginalizes people. Government agencies by the score will hire people because of skin color, thinking they have celebrated diversity, only once people get in that door, [they] close the door and [the government does] not allow people to move up into certain jobs because they don't fit the profile. There is an awful lot, from my experience, of government agencies that won't consider especially people like me—and I don't mean black and bald necessarily—to move into certain positions. Finance positions, CEO positions. Those positions frequently are not considered for black people because of the very paradigm in which people are hired. Government agencies are discriminating against people on the basis of skin color, so that it becomes a double-edged sword because of the marginalization that I believe all too often happens with affirmative action preferences.

More importantly, affirmative action has become a political decision in which black people are getting sandwiched in between two dynamics. The first is the rapidly growing Hispanic population. Because of immigration—some illegal, [some] because of a high birth rate—the fastest growing segment of our population happens to be Hispanic. And in many agencies, the powers-that-be feel a certain pressure to reach parity. In the county of Los Angeles, a lot of people are being held back because they happen to be black, because the Hispanic population is growing as rapidly as it is, and there is a population parity ordinance in the county of Los Angeles. And as a result of this ordinance you have, on the one hand, the pressure of keeping the black number at a certain level, because of that pressure of the growth in the Hispanic population. This is not said to pit anyone against another, but it is said to suggest to you that the rapid growing rate of the Hispanic population, if we're going to hire people by the numbers, by the de facto numbers, is going to work against the interest of black people.

The second thing is the Asian population. In the state of California, and I suspect throughout the nation, there are people who come to our nation, and we welcome them, who want nothing more than a chance to succeed. They will open up businesses—nail salon businesses. They will open up donut shops. They take a great interest in education. It is not coincidental that, in the University of California in 1968, the percentage of students who happened to be Asian was 11 percent. Today, thirty years later, that percent is 40 percent, solely because of an interest, a respect, for education, higher education. Now, no affirmative action was involved in that, none at all; simply a respect for education and preparation, preparation, preparation for higher education. Sandwiched between these two—a rapidly growing Hispanic population that is saying it's now our turn and wants to use affirmative action as a device for moving into that middle class of America, and the Asian population that is saying, "All we want to do is compete"—we have black people that, in too many cases, are saying, "We're not preparing ourselves and we want affirmative action." Those are the two dynamics that I see in the state of California.

And there's a growing awareness—you've heard it from Colin Powell recently, you've heard it from Jesse Jackson, you've heard it from Hugh Price—that the time has come for black people to say, "We're not going to overly rely on affirmative action; we're going to prepare ourselves to compete, get our kids ready for the competition." That is my perspective, that the forces that are affecting us are no longer the forces that existed in a black/white paradigm twenty, thirty years ago. We're living in an environment which is very competitive. And the only way that we're going to compete with this rapidly growing Hispanic population that wants to use affirmative action to accelerate their progress into the mainstream (and I can understand their perspective) and the Asian population that is competing, competing, competing is for us to get off this treadmill of affirmative action preferences and compete ourselves, and not to rely on anybody else to foster our progress.

My position is that for the last thirty-five years this has been a struggle for legal equality. For the next thirty-five years it is a struggle for respect. And if we get that respect, [and use] the legal equality that has been provided, and use the opportunities that are available, then the rest will take care of itself. This is not to suggest that discrimination has been erased from the face of this land. It has not. But I think the time has come to forget about dealing with this through the device of affirmative action preferences and to get our kids prepared for the competition that exists.

Yvonne Scruggs-Leftwich: Speaking in support of the resolution that affirmative action has been one of the most effective vehicles for transporting African Americans, Hispanics, other people of color, and women into the American mainstream is Dr. Michael Eric Dyson, who will also have ten minutes. Dr. Dyson.

Michael Eric Dyson: Thank you very kindly, Dr. Scruggs-Leftwich, and to Mr. Eason, and to my co-dialogist, Mr. Connerly.

Nearly thirty years ago, to the date, Martin Luther King, Jr., standing at the sunlit summit of racial expectation, in an optimism that was directly contradictory to the pervasive white supremacy that he confronted on the streets of Birmingham and in his home state of Georgia, declared that he had a dream. Thirty-four words [have been] extracted from his speech: "I have a dream my four little children will one day live in a nation where they will not be judged by the color of their skin but by the content of their character." Thirty-four words, uttered when he was thirty-four years old, have been used as the rhetorical and ideological backdrop against which people assault affirmative action, and to suggest that Dr. King believed in a color-blind society, the predicate for so much of the resistance to white supremacy that he and his colleagues waged in the 1960s.

But the reality is that Dr. King, in the latter part of his life, grew much more weary about the potential of solving our racial conundrums, our racial paradoxes, our racial problems, by believing in the inherent goodness of our white brothers and sisters, or the inevitable progress that would be made once our preparation, once our intelligence, once our spiritual values, were proved to be comparable to those of our white brothers and sisters. And so the reality is that we need some government intervention. First of all, because the government has worked against us, the government must now work for us.

It is clear that one of the most powerful battles African Americans and, subsequently, other racial minority groups have waged is the battle against legal proscriptions—and legal prohibitions against black people living in the same neighborhood as their white brothers and sisters, going to the same schools, sitting at the front of the bus, transportation, hotel accommodations, and so on. But there was also an economic factor that we have not yet grappled with. I agree with Mr. Connerly that it's not simply about a black/white paradigm; it is about an economic one. If racism is destroyed tomorrow, many poor people who are black will continue to be poor.

But it is a logical fallacy to assert, on the one hand, precisely because classism operates in American culture, that race doesn't also continue to be a force in our lives. Race and class continue to gang up on African people in America to deprive them systematically, and to exclude them in very powerful ways. To marginalize them, yes—but not by bringing them into American society, or into the larger circle of American privilege, but by continuing to deny them the legal and moral access that their talents certainly merit.

So for me, as a background, affirmative action has been quite successful, first, because it recognizes the government has worked against African American people and other minorities, especially Latinos, Native Americans, and, of course, to a certain degree, Asian American brothers and sisters. So the first predicate of my argument is that the government has been a factor that has hindered the realization of African American and other minority interests and, therefore, it should now become an intervening factor.

Second, the reality is that affirmative action is not about retaliating against white Americans. It is about recognizing the legal and moral consequences of practicing subjugation for well over three hundred years. I wish this was a kind of sitcom, perhaps *Bewitched*, where we could wrinkle our noses and erase memories of racial and ethnic bigotry and brutality. But the reality is that we live in the aftermath, with the consequences, of the systematic exclusion of African Americans and other minorities from the larger circle of American privilege. This is not about the politics of *ressentiment*; it is about the politics of justice and equal opportunity. And equal opportunity means we not only have to pay attention to the past, we must pay attention to the present. After all, it's in the present that Texaco and Denny's operate in our own lives.

Number three, what we're really arguing for is not preferences. One of the ingenuities (and I must hand it to them) of the conservative brothers and sisters in our own political community is that they have seized the rhetorical upper hand. They have taken the dead carcasses of the words that civil rights figures used to use—level playing field, equal opportunity, and opportunity not in terms of result, but opportunity in terms of being able to get a job and hold a job by virtue of talent—and have ingeniously seized the rhetorical upper hand by using the words they had forced us to stop using and now abuse them in a more powerful way. But I think that's a kind of rhetorical legerdemain—it's a sleight of hand.

The bottom line is that in our society it is not about preferences of African Americans and Latinos and Native Americans and others that have gone first. First of all, white women have been the overwhelming beneficiaries of affirmative action in America. Number two, look at the American sugar production which, in one sense, violates environmental codes in Florida but is protected by a governmental tariff. Look at tobacco, which is protected knowing that it causes harm to our bodies, and yet it has a tariff. Look at the export tariffs that are waged against tomatoes grown in Mexico in deference to tomatoes grown in America. That's affirmative action!

Look at the systematic exclusion of every person who is not a white male property owner for three hundred and some odd years in terms of educational access, in terms of corporate access, in terms of business access, and in terms of shaping American doctrines and interpretations of fundamental notions of democracy, justice, and freedom—and we see that these realities continue to spread influence in our lives even as we speak. I am for affirmative action for those who most deserve it, not for fat cat elites within American corporate structures who don't deserve the tariff and have it given to them.

And then, let me say two other things before I close. First of all, merit has never been the exclusive predicate upon which we have based the distribution of goods in American society. You know, when I was at Princeton a lot of people wanted to go to Princeton. A lot of folk couldn't get into Princeton. A lot of folk want to go to Harvard. Talladega. Morehouse. But guess what? You all can't get in. And a lot of these folk are not only willing to be prepared; they *are* prepared! But the competition is deep and stiff. So the reality is if you've got ten or twenty thousand people trying to get into a school, and they're all equally qualified, what is the basis for distributing resources and goods so as not to be unequally disposed towards the person who is excluded? You've got to have some reason besides merit. Maybe somebody plays the violin from South Carolina–"We need them up at Harvard this year." Maybe somebody who is interested in mathematics, and who is a skilled rhetorician on the other hand, and joins those talents together, gets into Princeton this year. Merit has never been the exclusive basis for distributing resources in American society. Merit is a contingent good. It depends upon what environment it operates in to determine its efficacy and its relevance.

And, finally, I want to say this. Affirmative action often accounts for the legal and the moral, but it does not often extend itself to dealing with the cultural and, shall we call it, the aesthetic. You can never measure the disdain that some people have for a person of color when you look into their eyes and know right away that you will not get that job. You can't prove it. Ain't no statistics to verify your feeling; no empirical verification for your sentiment. But you and they know, because of a history of aesthetic revulsion to black skin; a history of not liking slanted eyes; a way of disdaining women who wear skirts–and yet whose intelligence and power is not only comparable, but overmatching the man who stands there to judge them–it's [these] factors that we don't often account for. And affirmative action needs to be in place in order [to] continue to exercise and leverage the moral authority of democracy for which black folk and other minorities have given their lives. Thank you very much.

Scruggs-Leftwich: We have five minutes' rebuttal by Mr. Connerly.

Connerly: Well, that was a great speech. And once he comes out of his shell, he's going to be all right. [*Laughter and jeers*] Michael doesn't take that in a bad way.

This isn't about Texaco. This is not about Denny's. This is about our government, and whether our government should be allowed to treat us differently. And when you strip through that very powerful, very eloquent statement, Dr. Dyson is saying yes. He's saying it's okay for our government to treat some of us differently. He's saying there are aesthetic reasons and all kinds of reasons that may be compelling to you, but they're not to me. It is not compelling for my government–I'm not talking about Texaco, I'm not talking about Denny's–it is not compelling for my government to say it is going to treat me differently than it treats somebody else. What that is essentially saying is that we're going to give our government the power to discriminate. I thought we said we didn't want to do that. When is it appropriate for the government to engage in that? You can use all kinds of words that you want to say that, "Well, we're not talking about discrimination, we're talking about diversity. We're talking about compensating for the past." I don't care how you describe it. You're essentially saying it's okay for the government to treat people differently on the basis of certain characteristics.

Now, I don't subscribe to a total meritocracy at all. And the system that we put in place in California, and at the University of California, is not a total meritocracy. In fact, it allows the administrators to take into account students' ability to overcome obstacles; to take into account their income, their social circumstances, and to weigh that along with academic measurements. It is not a total meritocracy. And Dr. Dyson knows that. And he will tell you that. As a result of the system that we've put in place, this year the number of students who are what we called "historically underrepresented" went up. Yes, last year it took a precipitous drop. One black student was admitted last year at Boalt Hall. This year there are nine. [*Boos and jeers*] If you would let me continue. If you would let me continue. I know that you have a bias, but if you would let me continue to give you my point of view. What I'm suggesting to you is that, by adapting the system to new realities, we have reversed the trend. And those numbers will go up. But to say we're going to reject merit, my friends, and allow the government to decide who's going to get in on the basis of skin color or whatever characteristics—I submit to you, in the long run, it's wrong. It's wrong for the nation, it's wrong for all of its people. Merit, however you define that, is something we can rely upon. It doesn't mean that merit has to be solely academic measurement. They can take other things into account. But whatever we define merit to be, it ought to be applied across the board evenly, fairly to everybody. And not one standard applied to black people, another standard applied to whites or Asians or whatever. You can disagree with that. But that is my position. That is a position I will carry with me. It's a position that the courts have basically set.

A lot of the affirmative action programs that many of you think ought to be on the books and ought to be applied, I would remind you, the courts have thrown them out. The courts have very narrowly defined when you can use rights. It is an inherently suspect classification, according to the courts, and there are very limited circumstances in which it can be used. What I'm trying to do is to appeal to you to say that, in the long term, it is wrong, it is not in our best interest to allow government agencies to use race for seemingly benign purposes. I think that those purposes—and history has proven me right—can end up being very, very harmful. Thank you.

Scruggs-Leftwich: Dr. Dyson, you have five minutes for rebuttal.

Dyson: Well, as Mr. Connerly knows, and we both agree, it is not that I believe in pure meritocracy. We have to dismantle, deconstruct, demythologize—get real about—merit. Because we know it ain't equal, and it's not equally applied. So we agree on that. But philosophically speaking, if race has functioned as a demerit for such a long time, it seems to me only just and fair that it function as a merit during a certain period. Not forever. But long enough for us to balance the im-balance introduced as a result of the governmental exclusion of opportunity for African Americans, Latinos, Native Americans, and others.

I don't have the kind of faith and optimism in governmental agencies that Mr. Connerly seems to entertain and enjoy. Because the reason we're celebrating the March on Washington is because the government wasn't about doing its job, and social strategic action had to mobilize passion and sentiment so that it could reach up to the halls of Congress and shake the Supreme Court to make sure that they understood that these Africans in America, and other people, [who] had given their lives in defense of democracy on foreign soils wanted a piece of that pie right in America. It was not because the government was good or willing; it's because it was forced to do the right thing.

Now, Mr. Connerly says that, to a certain degree, I believe in unequal applica-tion of merit. That is not the case. I believe in affirmative action, again, for those who merit affirmative action. I am not asking the government, in that sense, to unequally apply law. I am asking the government to do what it intended to do with affirmative action when LBJ signed that executive order; when Mr. Nixon, ironically wanting to bust unions, forced affirmative action into the place of unions and the American political consciousness. I want [affirmative action] to do what it was intended to do: A) reverse the historic patterns of discrimination that have dominated and excluded African Americans and, subsequently, other peo-ple's lives; B) make sure that the wide opportunity available to everyone else with white skin in American culture would be extended to African Americans; and C) continue to acknowledge the historic manifestation of patterns of discrimination, and historic forms of exclusion, and redress those with dispatch by the govern-ment and by private business.

So, for me, it is not asking the government to, in one sense, condescend to me, because—Ward will recognize this—the government, when we were meritorious and prepared, did not acknowledge our equality before the law. So if merit was the big deal, and it was all about being fair, [explain why] Joe Louis couldn't get in through the front door and he made a whole lot of money. Martin Luther King, Jr., had a Ph.D. from Boston University and couldn't get into the door. They were prepared. Merit alone will never become the decisive factor for mak-ing sure that opportunity is equally applied. It is about strategic social action and political consciousness together, when they are wed in the blissful union of mind and mood and determination.

Scruggs-Leftwich: The moderators have two-minute questions. My question is for Mr. Connerly. You have four minutes to respond. I'd like to go back to your sta-tistics on Boalt Hall. They're a little different from the ones that I know. The sta-tistics that I know about [for Boalt Hall], the law school in California, is that the last number of blacks admitted before Proposition 209 was eighteen. Eight were accepted last year. Only one enrolled. If you've accepted nine this year, I don't know how many are going to enroll, but the statistics underscore the interest of African American students not to be insulted and not to be offended, and they are not applying. The University of Texas, following the *Hopwood* decision, the same dynamic occurred: zero students enrolled at the University of Texas last year.

I don't know what the admissions statistic is this year, but we picked up the paper yesterday on a report on this study, "Miles to Go: A Report on Black Students in Post-Secondary Education in the South," and it says: "On many college campuses in the South, the percent of black students enrolling is in decline after years of gain, and their likelihood of graduating is no better than it was when the region first desegregated universities decades ago." It goes on to say that, "Researchers suggest that recent court rulings and voter decisions to limit or abolish affirmative action at public universities in California and Texas have made college officials elsewhere reluctant to create or expand outreach programs to minority students. There's a kind of paralysis setting in on this issue."

And finally, we know that in an area where our life resources are addressed with regard to medical school, that African American students are not applying to medical schools at the rate that they applied before the anti-affirmative action effort. All that is said to raise the question with you: how, then, do you reconcile your philosophy about the existing level playing field, and the need to abandon these old tools, with the performance we're seeing increasingly of African American students being, in an accelerated way, eliminated from, not only the playing field, but the game altogether?

Connerly: Well, in the first year after SP-1 went into effect—not 209, but the Regents' action—the number of black students and Latino [students] who applied to Berkeley and UCLA was down dramatically. We can speculate all we want about the reasons for that. We really don't know. Not only were the number of applicants down; the number who were admitted was down and the number who enrolled was down. At Boalt Hall, there was one student who attended Boalt Hall—that's the law school—last year, a black student, and he wasn't even admitted during 1997. He was admitted in the prior year and he was rolled over to 1997. This year, the number that is actually enrolling is nine. We admitted far more than that, but after some very aggressive outreach, the number who actually accepted our offer to attend went up from one to nine. And that is a significant—we're not totally satisfied with that—but that is a significant increase, from one to nine who will actually be attending.

Now, one of the things that's happened to, I think, reverse this, and to start our moving those numbers back up, is the fact that this year we put far more money into targeted outreach. Up until the last year, the amount of money that the University of California was spending on outreach—which is preparation and advertising and all of that—was about $60 million. And [in] the budget that was signed three days ago by the governor, that was negotiated with the legislature, that number is up to $138.5 million. So we've more than doubled the money we're spending on outreach, which is trying to achieve the admissions without the use of preferences. And we're talking about preferences, applying different standards on the basis of race.

We hope that we can increase that outreach by another $60 million next year. But the reality is that we're trying to do everything that we can to make sure that the students are prepared for the competition. And we're trying to do it the right way, through the outreach. The K through 12 system in California is terrible. Everyone knows that. And we've known about it for I don't know how many years, because we had the shortcut that we could use called affirmative action. Now we're trying to achieve this the right way, and outreach is one way of doing it. We're going into the lowest performing high schools, going into the lowest performing junior high schools, and trying to bring about a better performance on the part of the K through 12 system.

Scruggs-Leftwich: Mr. Connerly, there's a redirect option here and I want to exercise it, because I want to remind you that, before the anti-affirmative action policy, eighteen students enrolled in Boalt Hall. And the other thing I want to remind you of is that outreach is apparently another word for affirmative action.

Connerly: No, it's not.

Scruggs-Leftwich: How is it not?

Connerly: You're using the terms to say that I'm anti-affirmative action and I have said, I don't know how many times, I am not.

Scruggs-Leftwich: No. What I'm saying is that you appear to be finding another nomenclature for what many of us call affirmative action. And I would like to understand how outreach differs from what we're saying has been an effective tool for assuring—not that kids who weren't going to succeed or weren't interested in college got into college—that the kids who are motivated, and have been supported by their families, do get accepted into college.

Connerly: Well, I guess the difference is that the outreach in which we're engaged right now is not on the basis of race. It's on the basis of those who come from single-parent households, who come from low-income families . . .

Scruggs-Leftwich: Who are black.

Connerly: Who are not necessarily . . .

Scruggs-Leftwich: You have just a minute to answer.

Connerly: I think it's a fallacy to presume that the term *black* equals low income. Or that the term *black* equals low socio-economic conditions. When I say that we're designing our outreach program to try to benefit those on the basis of need, that is not saying that we're trying to benefit black or Latino, anybody, on the basis of race. The programs and the policies that we had in place previously were solely designed to benefit historically underrepresented minorities. That's the way the terminology was framed and those were the programs that we had. Now we're simply saying we're going to benefit those who have needs on the basis of factors other than race, sex, color, ethnicity, national origin. I don't know why that amuses anyone. We're using different factors to try to benefit people.

Scruggs-Leftwich: Dr. Dyson.

Dyson: I think that Mr. Connerly's argument about the possibility of finding factors other than race to distribute goods—like education, access to jobs, and so on—is a compelling one that has been made by a variety of people who have sought responses to the erosion of the moral authority for affirmative action. I think that Dr. Scruggs-Leftwich here has posed a challenge to Mr. Connerly that I think he hasn't quite eased himself out of. If you say that outreach becomes a euphemism for strategically intervening upon a free market reality—that is, students out there—there's no other reason to get them except they score well, which is what merit is about. But he's already conceded that merit is not the only predicate for distributing these goods.

Well, then, if there's something other than merit—but he's also arguing that merit is important—well, which one is it? If merit is the primary means, outreach only [means you] send letters to those whose test scores are so startling, and so stunningly brilliant, that they will either choose to come to your school or won't, because several schools will be reaching out to them. So the outreach will be about their merit. We can concede that point. But he's already subverted that possibility by saying that the outreach is predicated upon—aha—class.

Well, I know that *black* don't equal po' [*laughter*]—in my house it did, but I understand that. Black is a multivariegated, deeply complex reality. But the deal is, one-third of black folk [are] below the level of poverty in America. That means, therefore, that we don't equate blackness and low socio-economic condition. We assume, predicated upon our empirical reading of the numbers, that a proportion of African American people struggle not only with race, but with class issues. So why is it legitimate to distribute goods based on class and not race [when] the reality [is] that racism continues to be the major hindrance to the realization of goods for African American people? The very argument that Mr. Connerly has put forth shows the resistance to race while it embraces class. If most poor people in America, proportionately speaking, are African American and Latino and other minorities, then the reality is that's affirmative action by the back door. I don't want to be Sneaky Pete about it; I want to be up front about it. Let's be honest about what has gone on.

And then let me say this: I'm glad when my conservative brothers and sisters become Marxists, because now they're concerned about the class issue and economic inequality. I've been there all along. I'm all down for the class issue. But don't say class *or* race; say class *and* race. Let's yoke them together and then begin to do a deep thing. Because if we get poor white folk who have been excluded from American society to join with African Americans and Latinos and Native Americans—*we can turn this mother out!*

Oscar Eason: Dr. Dyson, how do you respond to the basic proposition of the opposition to affirmative action when they declare that affirmative action is racist in and of itself? That each time you give a group of people a preference over another group, that is discrimination in itself. How do you answer the question, what has my great-great-great-great grandfather enslaving your great-great-great-great grandfather—what does that have to do with my son giving your son preferences on a job? How do you respond to the question that each time a preference is given to a person in the workplace that it is at the expense of another group of people? How do you respond to the question that what has busing my kids all the way across town to a school when there is a perfectly good school next to him to do with your kid's inability to compete with my kid? Those are basic questions dealing with the whole position, the whole concept, of affirmative action that need to be answered. Could you give us a response on that?

Dyson: Yes. I think, first of all, we've got to take such complaints, such carps, such legitimate criticisms, quite seriously. Because in American society, where we're concerned about the moral efficacy of our political practices, we ought to be concerned about what affirmative action means to the people both whom it defends and the people, obviously, whom it offends.

How I answer that, however, is by first of all arguing that we've got to revoke our citizenship in the United States of Amnesia. We cannot—and we must completely refuse to—pretend that the past doesn't affect the present. But it's not a one-to-one relationship. The past has a variety of impacts upon the present. First of all, some people ask, "what does my great-grandfather being a bigoted racist have to do with you and I now as we compete for a slot in, say, a schoolroom?" Well, the reality is, those same people don't deny that they subscribe to the Bill of Rights, none of whose words were written during their lifetime. The Constitution or the Declaration of Independence, none of whose words were written during their lifetime. But they appeal to those precious words and those incredibly able documents which codify basic humane propositions about the nature of political organization. They continue to go to the Supreme Court to appeal to those words to justify their own political practices, and to adjudicate—that is, decide between—competing claims about what's good and what's right and what's just. If those documents, crafted in the past, can continue to exercise powerful impacts upon our contemporary lives then, likewise, issues of social disorganization and chaos around race continue to exert a lethal impact upon our contemporary situation.

But even more important, let me get down to brass tacks and knuckles here. The distribution of land and resources was occurring in a powerful way in American society: first, with the gift of suffrage, if you will, to a white, male, propertied working class. And as Werner Sombart says in his 1906 work, *Why Is There No Socialism in the United States?*, the reason we have no class consciousness in America is because white men who came here were given property, and didn't have to strategically argue for their gifts, or their benefits, or their citizenship. Number two, as a result of that, anybody who was not a white male was on the outside looking in. And that has a powerful impact now, because the accumulation of wealth, of property, of access, of skills that were predicated upon those with that access, and the accumulation of money that allows people to leverage their own powerful authority for their children and their children's children, means that African Americans and others were systematically excluded, and continue to be disadvantaged, as a result of something that happened some three-hundred-odd years ago.

Even more important is the reality that when it comes to talking about the distribution of goods, like education or access to employment, black people and other minorities are not asking for a handout—are not asking, from lack of preparation, for access. We have been *over* prepared. We used to teach our children that you got to be twice as good, smart, and able as the next person. We ain't never been lacking in terms of our own preparation and education. But the reality is that exclusion was not predicated upon merit; it was predicated upon our race and our class and, to some degree, our gender and ethnicity.

So what I'm arguing now is that that history has shaped and molded not only legal practice; it has molded those intangibles that we can't put our hands on, but that have an impact upon how we are treated. If you read William Julius Wilson's book, *When Work Disappears*, look at statistic after statistic that documents how employers refused to hire black men because they thought they were untoward, that they needed behavior modification, presuming only on skin color and upon geographical region how they would be successful or not. So my point is, as I end here, that I am not arguing against the distribution of goods predicated upon a philosophical commitment to equality. I'm talking about the real world, where we know equality ain't never been something given out. It has to be argued for, and it has to be constantly ratified by our political practices.

Connerly: That still doesn't explain why a low-income white child should get different treatment than a child who happens to be black from an upper-income family. It still doesn't answer it. It doesn't answer why we would hold a Latino to a different standard because he or she is a historically underrepresented minority than we would hold an Asian. Doesn't answer it. And the only answer I have for all of that is that, as Lincoln said, "I must keep some standard of principal fixed within myself." As a nation, I think that we have to have a certain standard. And that standard ought to be that we will treat each other the same. We will not look at three hundred years ago. You may disagree, but you invited me here to share my point of view with you, and I'm going to do it. I think that we have to treat each other the same. We cannot go back three hundred years. We cannot go back fifty years. Public policy—and you're in government, you know this—public policy is based on some standard of behavior that we're trying to set for those that you're governing. And it just seems to me, as clear as day, that we cannot say we're going to treat one group differently on the basis of their skin color, and treat another group differently on the basis of their skin color, and another group differently on the basis of their skin color. This isn't just black versus white. It is all shades of the rainbow. And we're treating immigrants from Russia, who are classified as white, differently than we're treating immigrants from Mexico, because they're classified "historically underrepresented minority." That, it seems to me, makes no sense. And you cannot rationalize that within the context of this black/white oppression that Dr. Dyson is talking about. You can't do it.

And so I would argue that, in the long term—and he can say that this is a temporary solution—I'd like to know at what point do we stop it, if it's just temporary? Is it five years? Is it ten, is it twenty? Whatever. I believe that at some point we as a nation have to say this is going to be the policy: we're going to treat everybody the same. If there is discrimination then, doggone it, deal with it. But I don't think we're going to fudge it by saying, "Yeah, it's okay to do it in this case. It's okay to discriminate here." And it's discrimination. When you treat one person different from another you can call it all you want—it's discrimination. I don't want it done against me, and if I don't want it done against me then I shouldn't be willing to have it done against somebody else.

Dyson: Just very briefly—Ward raises the conundrum of affirmative action.

Eason: Dr. Dyson, you have one minute.

Dyson: The bottom line is that when you talk about treating a poor white person differently than an African American, I can see that there are enormous inequities in the present forms of distributing goods based upon color. But the reality is that affirmative action is an attempt to address a specific set, a finite set, of conditions that existed in this country that have to be reversed. To reach out to poor white people is not the burden of affirmative action; it's the burden of a government that you don't want discriminating against them. Because affirmative action didn't create their inequality. That's number one.

Number two, I think it's *not* a black/white issue and divide. Of course it's not. It's much more complex than mere blacks against whites. It's Latinos, Native Americans, Jews for that matter, and other racially excluded ethnic groups in this country. But to say that it's beyond black and white—the reality is that the black/white divide [is central to our history]. And thirdly, as I end here, let's be fair. Ward wants fairness, by doggit, he wants honesty and equality. I'll tell you what. Let's only have affirmative action as long as we had slavery. And then we can call it a day. [*Laughter*]

Eason: Mr. Connerly, you have one minute.

Connerly: Well, I'm writing down some of his quickies. You know there's some good ones there. [*Laughter*] I come back to the point that this is a moral question for me. And at some point, I have to say to my fellow Americans, "You done me wrong but I don't want you to do it again." And try to put in place all the tools that we can to deal with discrimination. If the tools are inadequate, let's keep trying to hone them to the point that we get them to be adequate. But I don't think we can go on with policies that say we're going to hold someone accountable for something over which they say, "I didn't do that. I'm not responsible for that." When we give a preference to somebody from Vietnam in the area of employment because some government agency wants to make sure there is parity in that agency, I as a black man say, "I didn't do anything to the Vietnamese. I'm not responsible for any oppression that you might have. I'm not responsible for any adversity you may have encountered. So therefore, you should not receive any preference over me." To me, that's simple. There has to be some standard that we apply. And for me, that standard is: our government treats all of us the same. The same.

Dyson: Can I have a minute? Because I think Ward has raised a very powerful point here. You see, two things. He says he wants to be concerned about morality, and it's a moral issue. If it's a moral issue it's not about a one-to-one relationship between whites who wronged African American people and blacks who were wronged, neither of which are here. But we are their children and their grandchildren and their great-grandchildren, and we are here. We are the product of a past that is invisible, that we can't see. Our genetic structure testifies to the ability of the past to leverage its impact upon our present. Number two, when Ward says, "Well, I didn't do anything against the Vietnamese"—I've been up for jobs where women have gotten the job because they wanted in that case a white woman or black woman. And I didn't say, "Oh my God, I'm equally qualified, and I want to be able to have that job, too." I realize that I'm a male supremacist, inevitably, because I'm born in a patriarchal culture, and as a man, I willingly say, "I want to forego an opportunity not necessarily by birth mine, anyway, to make sure that women's voices and presences are represented within the context of American society." My legality would rule against that, but my moral vision says that's got to be the truth and the case.

And if we're concerned about morality, let's be concerned about the fact that we have to be responsible, not only for ourselves, but for our brothers and sisters. The predicate of American democracy is about opening an opportunity for those who have been closed out. When my son wrecks a car, I've got to pay for it. I didn't wreck the car, but I'm the one who got the cash. That's all I'm saying, America. Martin Luther King, Jr., said, "Be true to what you said on paper." So I would amend what Ward said. I want to say, too, "Hey, you done me wrong. I want you to do me right. But just in case you don't, let's have the rules in line to make sure you do."

Scruggs-Leftwich: This is the last rebuttal.

Connerly: I don't want to be held accountable for the omissions or the sins of somebody else. I don't want my son to be held accountable for something that I do that he had nothing to do with. That is a standard rule in our society. Yes, if my son wrecks the car, because he is living in my household, if he were, I'd be responsible for that. But it's a standard rule of our society that we don't hold people responsible for the conduct of their sons and their grandfathers. That's a standard rule, Michael.

Scruggs-Leftwich: Ladies and gentlemen, we're going to take a brief intermission so you can array yourselves at the microphone.

Question: The question is to Mr. Connerly. "Why should my tax dollars support educational institutions to which African Americans are not admitted?"

Connerly: Well, if there were some policy that black people were not being admitted, your tax dollars shouldn't be used for that purpose. But to say that there will be no preference to anybody, and everybody's going to be treated the same, is not saying that your tax dollars are being used at a place where black people are not admitted. We're simply saying that everybody should be treated equally. Everybody should be treated the same, without regard to their race, their sex, their color, their ethnicity, in my view their sexual orientation, their religion, whatever. And if you apply those rules fairly then I, as a taxpayer, don't have any complaint if, at the end of the day, the outcome is favorable or unfavorable to me.

Dyson: Very briefly. But the question, I think, Mr. Connerly, is about subsidizing ones' own inequality. And the question goes to the fact that that opponents of affirmative action often argue that they will not subsidize inequality because it is a fundamentally reverse racist system. As a result of that, we must divest from it. That is, the government must refuse to pour more money into those programs: set asides, contracts, timetables, goals, and so on. So I think the question he's really asking is that the most powerful forum that African Americans have that decides political representation with the government is through their own tax system. And if they are subsidizing a system or an institution that is depriving them of equal access, how does your particular understanding of affirmative action redress that? How does it acknowledge A) that such an inequality exists and B) how can they, in one sense, dis-invest or divest in a system that continues to be unfair to them? I think that's a very powerful question.

Connerly: I don't think it's investing in inequality when you have a policy that says the state shall not discriminate against or grant preferential treatment to any individual or group on the basis of race, sex, color, ethnicity or national origin. That's not inequality. That's the ultimate expression of equality. And to say that at the end of the competition there aren't enough of this or that or whatever in any venue is, to me, a word game to say that equality really remains inequality. I don't see that.

Question: This question is directed to Mr. Connerly. "If it is a fact that you have advanced due to affirmative action, how is it that you can now say that it is not fair? Was it fair when it was done in your favor?"

Connerly: First of all, I went to a community college in 1957. Although I had about a 3.8, the [folk from my] neighborhood [never] attended UC. I didn't have transportation. So I went to a community college, and I don't think I got into a community college because of affirmative action. I went to a state college—Cal State Sacramento—in 1959 through '62. There was no affirmative action there. The one time that I can see where I benefited from affirmative action was when I was appointed to a twelve-year term—unpaid, I might add, almost a sentence—on the Board of Regents of the University of California. And if there is any preference involved in that other than, candidly, political cronyism, because I knew the governor, then that's wrong. But I think that any time our government makes a decision about any of us on the basis of skin color, I think it's wrong. And I have spoken out against that for all of my adult life, and I do now. And I will probably continue to do so.

Dyson: What I think the question is getting at is that, inevitably, without regard to choice, most of us who are African American in a culture that has been deeply racist have benefited from the incredible and strategic social action of those people who marched in the civil rights movement, who made sure you could go to community colleges, that we could go to institutions of higher education. So I think that is number one. Number two, when we think about the issue of who benefits and who doesn't, the reality is that affirmative action is not about assigning worth to people who don't deserve it. It is about acknowledging the preexisting condition of worth that was *not* recognized. And so for me, affirmative action is not about, again, trying to shake white America down, or trying to force the

government to do something it is not morally obligated to do. The moral obligation of the government is to redress not only past discrimination but continuing
patterns of discrimination.

So I wonder why, Mr. Connerly, [you are] only against affirmative action in regard to race or sex, but what about alumni [advantages]—and I know you stand
against them, but if you stand against them why not have, not the civil rights initiative, but the alumni children's initiative, to go throughout this country making
sure any child who gets into any institution of higher education as a result of his
or her mother or father going there, or having given a great sum of money,
should somehow be socially stigmatized and castigated? Why not have a movement in that regard?

Connerly: Well, again, I'm pleased that you acknowledged what my position is,
because I have fought very vigorously against alumni and legacy preferences at
the University of California. But as far as my going out and having some movement on it, that doesn't strike me as odious as the notion of my government treating me differently because of my skin color. [*Murmurs*]. I'll wait until you finish
with your response. I just have a problem with that. And you can disagree with
it. But I don't want my government treating me differently, or anybody else, on
the basis of race, sex, color, ethnicity, or national origin.

Question: This question is directed at Mr. Connerly. "It has long been felt by
many that affirmative action is just as much about power as it is about equal opportunity. As we live in a society where power, be it political, social, or economic,
rests primarily in the hands of the white majority society, how can we logically
justify equality until we can logically justify the power structure within our society, especially when Frederick Douglass has taught us that 'power concedes nothing without a fight.'"

Connerly: I think affirmative action *has* become a debate about power. And it is
precisely for that reason that I think we should not embrace policies which are
aimed at power. When you look at the state of California, and probably Texas,
and probably Florida, the percentage of black people in the overall pie of the population is going down. Right now, in the state of California, black people represent about 7 percent of the overall population. The most rapidly growing segment
of the population happens to be Latino. It is no coincidence, as I have said before,
that the last two speakers of the California assembly following Willie Brown are
Latino. And the reason is that the Latino legislative caucus votes as a bloc. And
you look at districts throughout the state of California that might have been black
ten years ago, that are now going Latino. If you want to look at power and the exercise of power, if you want to look at how the Democratic Party and the Republican Party are so concerned about the Latino vote—and that's their business if
they want to do that—if you want to bring up power, and the exercise of power,

then I would submit to you that you're not really looking far ahead when you start looking at the dramatic rise in the Latino population of the nation and the static numbers of black people. If you're talking about power, and how that power's going to be exercised, you're playing a very, very dangerous game.

Dyson: First of all, that's assuming that power is not already the object of the political game. Number one, what world are we living in? The world in which we live, *realpolitik*, dictates to us that power is precisely the game that American society has been about. And our not acknowledging that is certainly to our own demise, and certainly we will be somehow excluded. But look at this: Latinos, Native Americans, Asian Americans, and African Americans constitute about 25 percent of the population together. They have about 6 percent of our nation's operating businesses. These businesses account for about 1 percent of the nation's gross business receipts. Now, it don't look like to me, there, affirmative action done made a helluva lot of dent in the operation of economic benefits toward most white Americans.

Number two, I teach at a university. You know, all of this brouhaha about affirmative action changing the landscape, and identity politics subverting this objective condition of meritocracy prevailing—I ain't seen a whole lot of Negroes, or African Americans, and women and gays and Leftists and guerilla Marxists taking over the institutions of higher education. We still can't hardly get a job. If we got one, we're overworked and we're underpaid and we're trying to make a wage. If I look at my students, these students are hardworking, intelligent, articulate young people who want to do the best job they're able [to do]. Who are the people—this kind of colossal, collective straw person—that they put forth as the object of derision for the anti-affirmative action forces when, in the real world of numbers and empirical statistics, the bottom line is we still at the back of the line: Latinos and African Americans, Native Americans, only to a certain degree Asian Americans, and collectively, we still don't make a dent in the large edifice of American democracy, equality, or money. And until we're willing to concede that fact, we'll be arguing about apples and oranges and not getting down to the real fact. It *is* about power; it *is* about the distribution of resources predicated upon power. Let me say this one final thing. As somebody was pointing out, only 20 percent of jobs are advertised in the paper. The rest of the 80 percent—you know how they get got? "Hey, Bill, my son just graduated from Harvard." "Cool, tell him to call me on Tuesday." That's how he gets work. How to get a job in America. That's how it be going, all right? And that's about power.

Connerly: Well, again, one of the dangers when we look at this on a national basis is that we don't look at specific situations. In the state of California, Latinos represent about 30 percent of the population. And by the year 2015 they are expected to be the majority. Now, that's a lot more than the 20 percent that Michael is saying. All I'm saying to you is that if you're trying to play a game of people-of-color politics, it is fraught with danger. It is fraught with grave danger. Because as a black man, I think we lose that game down the road. I think we lose it, just on the basis of numbers. And I can show you city and county in the state of California where those demographics that are changing are forcing changes based on ethnicity that will bear out what I'm telling you. Get a clipping service and look at the city of Lynwood. Look at the county of Los Angeles. Look at the state of California. And I'll tell you, my friends, this game of identity politics, if you're trying to say, "Well, we can forge a people-of-color coalition," it is fraught with long-term danger. And I think the one that loses in that game are black people.

Scruggs-Leftwich: Let me comment by pointing out that current polls—the *National Council of Christian and Jews*, the *New York Times* poll, the poll by the *Joint Center for Political and Economic Study*, and the *Gallup Poll*—these polls all indicate there is stratification *within* the communities of color which is destructive in the extreme. And what we know about politics, looking at California, looking at Chicago, looking at New York, is that the majority white male population has developed a strategy for exploiting those differences within groups. And building tension between the racial groups so that the national polls show that in a rank order hierarchy of any kind, about any negative issue, including who would you hire last, and who would you fire first, and who would you like to work with, asking Hispanics, Koreans, white Americans, and blacks, blacks are at the bottom of every hierarchy. And so the issue of power becomes a critical issue. It may be insurmountable in the final analysis. But it may also be the only alternative to annihilation as we get to 2050, when white Americans are going to be less than 50 percent. And if you think there is fear and backlash now, just wait.

Question: This is directed to Dr. Dyson. "Many times it has been said that history repeats itself. The mood in white America today toward affirmative action is the same as in the period following the Civil War, the period of Reconstruction. We know that after Reconstruction, programs were eliminated, Jim Crow laws were enacted. Given the mood in the country today, do you think it's possible we could return to Jim Crow laws?" [*Nervous laughter*]

Dyson: Jim Crow the Third. [*Laughter*] That's a very perceptive question and comment. And I think all I want to do is add a layer to that and then, of course, respond. I think there's no question that not only does history repeat itself; it recycles itself in very predictable patterns. And our obligation as citizens of a commonwealth predicated upon democratic institutions is that we gotta be the ones who understand that we're behind the curve, as people of color. And the brilliance of what Dr. Scruggs-Leftwich just said is that the very people who are fomenting the internal dissension, and exploiting that stratification, are the very people that Mr. Connerly calls us—I think, if he doesn't mind me saying, because he's a distinguished gentleman—rather naïvely to trust, without asking any measures or mechanisms of balance and check be instituted. I think that's politically not only destructive–it's self-destructive.

The patterns of history are very real. Not only are we living through a kind of second post-Reconstruction, but the reality is that even at the height of populist politics in the early part of the twentieth century, white populism was, itself, a deeply racist project. So that even the populism about which we speak in high tones and with great regard has to itself be filtered through the prism of understanding the racial politics that somehow undergird it. Number two, what we are forgetting is that the enormous program of affirmative action that the government gave to the GIs returning from the Second World War transformed the American middle class and remade economic opportunity, and thrust upward mobility as the real possibility of returning white soldiers. When you've got a loan to buy your crib and to get into school, and to have a few points on a test so you can get in, that's the deepest, most prolific, most profound, most structural form of affirmative action that has ever been delivered in the history of the twentieth century on behalf of the enfranchised white male.

And let's be honest here. Let's concede the point that affirmative action by and large and in the main certainly targets those of us who are prepared to take advantage of it. But that's only half the argument. The other half is that affirmative action *creates* a middle class that either becomes powerfully preoccupied with its own narcissistic upward mobility, or those who realize, "We got in the do', we got to leave it open to make sure somebody else gets in." And we know it ain't about merit, it ain't about, simply, qualification. It's about creating structures of opportunity that leave the door open.

Yes, we can get back to a kind of Jim Crow situation *only* if those of us who are privileged, those of us who have resources–M.B.A.s, Ph.D.s and so on, law degrees and doctors–only if we refuse A) to recognize our moral responsibility and culpability to the least of these within our community, and B) to make sure that we're not only concerned about race, but that we're concerned about class. Because "them niggers" and "them spics" and them so-calleds is us! Right? And we are them. That's why we've got to constantly fight against not only racism from the outside, but classism and economic inequality from within. Otherwise, we will revisit Southern apartheid.

Connerly: I think it is absolutely ludicrous to think that we're going to go back to the era of Jim Crow. We're not helpless. The people in this room, you occupy prominent positions in government. We're decision makers. [*Murmurs*]. I'll wait until you finish.

Eason: Please let us remain silent while our guest is speaking.

Connerly: I think it is absolutely ludicrous for us to sit here thinking that we're going to allow our nation to go back to the 1950s and '60s. I mean, that idea, to me, is the most mind-boggling idea that I've ever heard. No we're not going to let that happen. That isn't even in the realm of possibility. [*Murmurs*]. So my answer to you, whether you agree or not—I really don't care, I really don't give a damn—my belief is no. No. It's not going to happen. No.

Dyson: May I just very briefly respond—and let's certainly extend to Mr. Connerly the kind of consideration we would want to have extended to us. But I must say that your reception here, Mr. Connerly, is what most black people face on a daily basis in hostile white institutions that you're asking us now to . . . [*Laughter*] And Ward understands that. I'm not saying that to be nasty. I'm saying that to be real.

Your point is we're not going to allow that to happen. That's the point: we've got to work together to make sure that doesn't happen. It's not going to happen if we work against it. But we [can't] leave it to the inevitable forces of governmental intervention, [where] the economic benefit of racism has been so powerful and overwhelming, which is why so many people are invested in it still. So my point is that, like our Jewish brothers and sisters—and we ought to rip off a page out of their playbook—they say "Never again," because they were saying the same thing in Hitlerian Germany. "Hey, we running the joint, we very much established, we upper-middle-class people. That ain't gonna happen to us." Next thing you know . . . I'm not arguing, as you say, the literal possibility that ovens will be cranked up in America. But I want to say to you a lesser-known word from one of Dr. King's sermons when he said, in 1968, that if we're not careful, the genocidal impulse that is at the root of American democracy, so to speak, will in one sense have a powerful backlash on African people in America. And he says, "I don't know about you, but I've been on the reservation too long. I don't want to go back to being interned like our Japanese brothers and sisters during the Second World War." Now, we may say that's ludicrous and that's ridiculous. But the reality is that our own, if you will, experience with the forces of white supremacy prove ain't too much that's—as Barney Fife said—"beyond the ken of mortal man" for what goes on in American society. Unless we are vigilant, there is no guarantee that these things will not happen.

And finally, I'll end here. The point is not simply whether or not we trust our white brothers and sisters. We love them. If anybody doesn't have to prove that they love white folk, it's black folk. [*Laughter*] Right? It ain't about love. It's about justice. And justice says that "Even if I love you, don't use my love for you to exploit me." Let it be about justice. It's not about dissing our white brothers and sisters, it's about acknowledging that labor was lost over slavery, and that post-Reconstruction denial of benefits has had a devastating effect, and a lethal impact, upon African American life. And I don't know what world we're living in, but the real world I live in says that despite our economic advantage, and despite our intelligence, and despite how cute we think we are, and how colored we are, that if we get caught on the wrong street at the wrong time, our name could be Ennis Cosby and we can go down. That's the world in which we live.

Question: Mr. Connerly, "Who is making the merit scale to determine the merit?"

Connerly: Well, I think it's each agency. I know within the university system, we allow each campus, the administration, to devise within a certain framework the standards for admission that they have. And we say that each campus can admit a minimum of 50 percent and a maximum of 75 percent on the basis of academic measurements alone. The remainder can be admitted on the basis of a combination of academic measurements and supplemental factors, which include leadership, which include socio-economic status, which include overcoming obstacles. And it might be interesting for you to know that we do have a zero-sum game in most of our campuses. At UCLA, where one of my constituents is seated right now, we have 31,000 applicants who apply for something like 3200, 3500 seats. And of those 31,000, 12,000 have 4.0s or greater.

And so, as we look at merit, someone with a 3.8 and 1200 on an SAT score is not necessarily more meritorious than someone who has a 3.78 and 1180 on an SAT score. They're all basically within the same range. Now, at that point I think you can begin to take into account: Did this person come from a low-income background? And did this other person, who may have the 3.8, which is a shade higher, did that person have to work after school? Merit—if somebody had to work after school or they had to overcome obstacles, that's part of their merit. And so we allow them to take those factors into account. It's not just who scored the highest on a test, but it's also other factors that influence somebody's merit. And we let the individual agency make that determination.

Dyson: But that's all we're asking for in regard to race. We're not that far apart, Ward. The reality is that the other factor that determines whether or not a person can acquire a certain set of skills is precisely conditioned by socio-economic background, by racial origin or ethnic origin, and other factors. So it's not that we're arguing for this arbitrary litmus test to be evoked to distribute these goods, and to adjudicate between competing claims between who can get in and who can't. All we're saying is that race has manifested itself as a criteria-influencing factor. And if race has manifested itself as a criteria-influencing factor, then why not let it account *for* the person as against him? That's not inequality; that's bringing restitution, rehabilitation, and balance to a system that is out of whack.

And then, finally, let me say this. Look, let's be honest. When we talk about getting into schools, first of all tests only predict what people will do, *maybe*, the first year. Let's go back and do interviews of Alan Bakke, where he is now in the famous [*Bakke*] affirmative action case in California, and the brother who got sued and kept out [of school]. And if we do an analysis, as somebody recently did, Alan Bakke is not faring as well as that other brother. That's because tests alone don't determine character or intelligence, or the ability to perform in the real world. You can be a test pilot and get real good on a video game, but when your butt got to "fly the friendly skies of United," that's a different story.

And finally, let me say this. That for me, understanding the place of merit in American culture—let's apply it equally, then. Let's apply affirmative action to the football field, and the basketball field. Tell me them brothers making 12 to 1500 on the SAT and 18-whatever on the ACT! That's big-time granted affirmative action, and white men will go to their death in Southern institutions, where big-necked black boys play ball on the gridiron, to defend their right to get in, 'cause merit ain't about SATs; it's about can you run a 440 in record time to boost the economic wherewithal of my university.

Connerly: You're right. We're not far apart on the basic issue. And it really does reduce itself to the fundamental question of whether you believe it's appropriate, or I believe it's appropriate, to use race as a means of determining whether I get admitted to school, whether I get a contract, whether I get hired. I believe it's not right, that the government should not do that. And we can argue 'til the cows come home with a different point of view. The one philosophy is, race matters, and the only way we can get beyond race is to use race. And the other philosophy, to which I subscribe, was enunciated by John F. Kennedy on June 11, 1963, when he said, "Race has no place in American life or law." We're not there. I know we're not there. We're not a color-blind society. But I think that the only way that we get to that point—and race is still that one big mountain that we have to climb—the only way we get there is to say we want to get there, and we work at it. We practice, practice, practice. To say that we're going to use race temporarily, in my view, means that we never get there. We never try to pursue that dream of a society in which none of us are having our futures, or our lives, determined by skin color. We may think it's all right, right now, for government to do that for benign purposes. But how do you know? How do you know when the government might change its mind and treat someone differently on the basis of skin color? I just want to have a policy that I can wake up in the morning and know what it says. And what it says—my government won't use my skin color against me. I feel comfortable with that.

Dyson: Well, here's my point. John Kennedy, when he made that statement, had to be forced [by the civil rights movement] to make that statement, number one. African American people are [rightfully] appreciative of him placing a well-timed call to Martin Luther King, Jr., in a prison cell that allowed the black voters to get behind him.

Number two, when John Kennedy made that statement, he lived in a world in which race ruled and was so dominant against the interests of African American color, that to articulate a conception of color-blindness was to speak in *behalf* of African American people. That's the fundamental paradox of universal notions of race objectivity—that when you talk about color-blindness in the '60s, you're talking about defending the interest of people who are excluded from an already universal document. Wait a minute, now. We got competing universalisms! First of all, if the documents—the Bill of Rights, the Declaration of Independence, the Constitution—were already universal, why would you have to argue for black folk to get included? Because universality itself don't make a diddly-squat difference—it's the application of that ideal. And so in the ideal world, yes, I agree with you. I don't want race to rule. I don't want race to matter. But in the real world race matters. Race rules. Race makes a difference. And until we get to that nirvana of racial objectivity, we got to live with what we got right now. And that is, making sure that we are not so naïve or ignorant as to believe the goodness of our brothers and sisters to do the right thing. We don't even believe our husbands and wives do that—that's why we have a contract to marry them, and if we get a divorce, we go to court. [*Laughter*]

Question: A short comment and then a question. In America, Jews have received reparation. The Japanese have received reparation. The Native Americans have received some form of reparation. And the Vietnamese have received reparation. Do you think—this is to both panelists—do you think African Americans should receive reparations? If so, what and how?

Connerly: No.

Dyson: Hell, yes! [*Laughter*] If you don't want yours, give it to me—I'll take it. [*Laughter*]

Scruggs-Leftwich: Would either of you care to elaborate on those cryptic answers?

Connerly: No, I think that goes back to the question of whether Joe Sixpack is responsible for the sins of his great-great-grandfather. And I just happen to believe no.

Dyson: Let me read from Martin Luther King, Jr., the architect of the color-blind dream, according to many of our brothers and sisters. This is from his book, *Why We Can't Wait*. Listen to this. "No amount of gold could provide an adequate compensation for the exploitation and humiliation of the Negro in America down through the centuries. Not all the wealth of this affluent society could meet the bill. Yet a price can be placed on unpaid wages. The ancient common law has always provided a remedy for the appropriation of the labor of one human being by another. This law should be made to apply for American Negroes. The payment should be in the form of a massive program by the government of special compensatory measures which could be regarded as a settlement in accordance with the accepted practice of common law. Such measures would certainly be less expensive than any computation based on two centuries of unpaid wages and accumulated interest. I am proposing, therefore, that, just as we granted a GI Bill of Rights to war veterans, America launch a broad-based and gigantic Bill of Rights for the Disadvantaged, our veterans of the long siege of denial."

That is an argument for reparations. That is an argument for reconstituting American political life to make sure that democracy prevails. And if it's so ludicrous to assume that black people can be paid wages when our Jewish brothers and sisters, our Vietnamese brothers and sisters, our Japanese brothers and sisters have been restituted—why not African people in America? Hell, yes, we should be able to have that right. I'm not asking for forty acres and a mule. Maybe an acre on Wall Street. If you can't find me a mule give me a Jaguar! That'll settle the case. [*Laughter*]

Question: The final question of the evening. "Dr. Dyson, could there be another way to level the playing field other than affirmative action? And if yes, please comment on the alternatives."

Dyson: Listen. Martin Luther King, Jr., didn't die for affirmative action. Get real. Affirmative action is the basement. But because the shift to the right has been so radical and thorough, and completely divisive, we now believe it's the ceiling. Affirmative action is the mere beginning toward a larger, gigantic, more ennobling, edifying goal. And that is the goal of human equality, not only before the law, but in the custom and traditions, and in the folkways and mores, of American society. Affirmative action is a vehicle to get to that end. It is not an end in itself. But if our white brothers and sisters, and other dissenters of our race, cannot even acknowledge the necessity for reaching that goal through that vehicle, then we are in a pitiful estate.

Of course there are other means and measures by which we can strategically argue for racial equality. And, by the way, for economic equality. But affirmative action is a crucial pillar in the larger edifice of making sure that democracy prevails. Are there other ways? Of course there are. But I am suspicious of a government and people who, in the face of the obvious justice of the moral claim for affirmative action, can't even do *that*. Can they really be up to the test to do the more radical thing, which is to redistribute wealth, which is to make sure that the poorest belly in this country is fed, and the most ignorant mind is filled with knowledge? I cannot believe that in the face of denials against affirmative action, we can do that. So affirmative action is not the be-all and end-all, the panacea; but it is the strategic, crucial means by which we can achieve that greater, grander destiny of American equality. That's what I believe.

Connerly: Absolutely. I think that there are other ways of getting to where we want to be. I think most of us agree with the goal. We want a nation in which all of us have the freedom and the opportunity to participate without regard to our race, our skin color, our gender, our national origin, our ethnicity, our sexual orientation, our religion. I think most people of goodwill want that. The question to me is whether using those factors is the most expeditious, the most fair, the least painful way of doing it. I believe it is not the least painful. But we have found at the University of California—I hate to keep coming back to that, but that's my frame of reference—that there are other ways of getting there. You may think that the term outreach is a euphemism for affirmative action—okay. Fine. I won't quibble with you over terms. But it is non race-based. Race is a raw nerve in America. We know that. And so if there are other ways of getting there, why can't we try them?

I don't say stop all affirmative action—at all. And I certainly don't say stop all affirmative action cold turkey. Every state has to look at this in its own way. But I think we want to get to the point where skin color, which is fundamentally what we're talking about when we talk about race, is not going to be used by our government for or against us. And the only way, it seems to me, that we get to that point, is that we start putting in place policies that help to bring people into the mainstream, that help people without using that forbidden characteristic that we call race. So, yes, there are other ways of getting there, in my opinion.

Dyson: Let me just say one final thing. But if there are other ways of getting there, and we know affirmative action is *one* way of getting there, how come we can't come up with the ingenious idea of, "Let's try *all* the ways at the same time"? G. K. Chesterton said it's not that Christianity has been tried and failed. Christianity, he claimed, had really not been tried. Affirmative action has not been tried and failed. From its very birth it's been attacked. People have tried to abort it. Let's give it a chance to breathe. How long? I don't know how long. But at least for the next twenty to thirty years, to make sure we can preserve the very principles this government claims to live by. Malcolm X says, "You can't stick a knife in my back 9 inches, pull it out 6 inches, and call that progress." "You can't cut my legs off," Malcolm said, "and then accuse me of being handicapped." We've got to deal with the structural reality of how this government has handicapped us, and now must rehabilitate us to make us walk powerfully into the future. That's all I'm asking for.

Eason: Thank you debaters. You now have two minutes to summarize.

Connerly: Although it's clear that my position does not comport with a large number of you, I respect the audience that you've given me. I respect the fact that, for the most part, you have been respectful in listening to my point of view. With every fiber of my being I say to you, I want to get to the same point that I believe you do. We do not have a monolithic point of view on this subject. And if we are people of goodwill, people of reason, we can sit down and figure out what is in the best long-term interest of our nation and ourselves. I believe that policies which treat the American people differently on the basis of skin color, race, sex, and all of the other characteristics that I've mentioned are fundamentally wrong. They're poisonous. They build resentment. We know that we cannot sustain those policies forever. We know that.

Michael, who is a good man, has said, "Yeah, they're only temporary." Well I say, let's start the process now of unraveling a system that I believe is going to cause great, great harm the longer we go. Whether it's five years or ten years—if I were king and I could negotiate that, I'd be willing to do that. I'd go along with ten years, perhaps. But I think that at some point we have to come to terms with the fact that we're holding on to a dying engine. It's dying. So the thing, it seems to me, we should do is say, "How do we put in place policies that ensure that our kids and our grandkids have an equal chance to compete?" And then we have to prepare them to take advantage of the opportunities that are available. But never, never should we agree with policies that say we're going to treat somebody differently on the basis of their skin color, their race, their national origin, or their ethnicity. I happen to believe that is wrong, and that is not in our long-term best interest. Thank you.

Dyson: In an ideal world, I suppose I absolutely agree with Mr. Connerly, himself a good man, that race should not make the huge difference that it makes in our own lives. And yet I come from a people—who have taught me, who have prepared me, who have loved me—who proved time and again that they are more than capable and competent to embrace the full repertoire of gifts that America is willing to give to those whom it cherishes and whom it favors. And yet, for too long, systematic exclusion from the larger circle of American privilege has been our lot in life. This is not about victimizing or victim-mongering. It is about the real analysis of how America operates.

When Martin Luther King, Jr., and other figures in the 1960s argued for a color-blind society, it was within the context of a struggle—a bitter, colossal struggle—for freedom, equality, and justice. And black people have given their very birthright to this country. They have mixed their blood with the soil of American society to defend rights that they could not themselves enjoy at home. And if African American people, and Latino people, and Native American people, and Asian people, and the Vietnamese and Asian Pacific Islanders and whosoever—these "huddled masses"—have come here seeking opportunity, and have had that opportunity, to a certain degree, extended to them, then we must embrace the American dream as an extension of the democratic project. But to the degree that we continue to face barriers that hinder us from living out the true meaning of the American creed, we must fight tooth and nail on behalf of people who, unlike Mr.

Connerly and I, will never make it on television or get degrees from institutions of higher education. Those black people who through no fault of their own, those Latino brothers and sisters who through no fault of their own, those Native American people whose genocide is the predicate for the expansion of American democracy who through no fault of their own have been closed out of opportunities that they deserve.

In the ideal world we should not take race into account. In the world in which *we* live, as James Brown would say, "howsonever," we got to take race into account to get to the point, as Supreme Court Justice Harry A. Blackmun said, where race will no longer make a difference. Until that time, we have to take race into account. And affirmative action is *a* means by which we can reach that racial Promised Land. Until that time, we got to fight, and fight hard, and make sure that we never forget where we came from. As we get our degrees and our education, don't think you-all that [we've made it]—because it could be snatched away tomorrow. Fight on behalf of those you know deserve that opportunity.

PART II

ETHNICITY

5

RAINBOW COLLISION?
Black, White, and Brown

with Angelo Falcon; moderated by Mara Tapp

This conversation and debate between me and Puerto Rican activist and intellectual Angelo Falcon was the second panel I participated in at Wingspread in 1998. Our dialogue explored the similarities and differences between black and Latino communities, and how elements of class play out in each group. Falcon is sharp-witted and humorously, and strategically, self-deprecating, and offered a stimulating debate partner for our hour together.

Mara Tapp: Angelo Falcon, I want to start with you. And let's start really wide angle, wide open, and try to define what we mean by class with regard to Latinos.

Angelo Falcon: Usually, when I'm at meetings, even with some issue with the Latino community, we talk about the issue for a while. And at some point someone stands up and makes a statement, and says, "All this stuff is really about class." And it's like an epiphany in the room. Everybody says, "That person's right." And then we proceed with the discussion and just ignore what they said. But there is this recognition that we're in a very profoundly class-divided society. But that issues of ethnicity and race are really–[in] my understanding–are really so intertwined with the class question that you just can't separate the two. And you can't say one is more real than the other. And I think that's what makes things very difficult sometimes to deal with in terms of organizing, in terms of defining issues–that [with] the mixing of the two in a very profound way, you can't extricate one from the other at certain points. It makes it hard to conceptualize it, because we're used to talking about one or the other, and I think that's one of the difficulties in talking about these issues today.

Tapp: I asked you a very unfair question. I said, tell me about class for Latinos, which, of course, is preposterous on its face. Break it down a little bit in this sense.

Do we think what you just said, that intertwining, applies to Puerto Ricans, Cubans, Nicaraguans, Mexicans?

Falcon: It does, in many ways. One of the issues it raises as well is that you can't also talk about these various communities as themselves being monolithic, and that there are kinds of class divisions within all of these communities. But at the same time, while you acknowledge that, race permeates all of that up and down—that class hierarchy—and that's what makes it difficult. Let's say, within the Latino experience, Cubans are more middle class and have no problems, and Puerto Ricans are very poor and we're not even on the class structure—we're underclass. History is an interesting kind of thing, where you may have had a certain selectivity in the early part of the Cuban migration, but then in 1980 you have a lot of poor, black Cubans coming in and raising those other issues. So while a lot of Cubans at one point, in an early part, may have felt superior in many ways, now they're dealing with many of the same issues that, say, Puerto Ricans are dealing with, in terms of welfare, in terms of school dropouts. So it's kind of a very fluid thing, that is very American in that sense, which makes it difficult to develop class-based kinds of social movements as well. Because of that certain level of fluidity that you have, and a certain feeling of openness in terms of the class structure. Again, it makes it very difficult to talk about these questions in a very definitive way.

Tapp: This won't stop us here today, of course. We'll keep coming back at it. And I do want to come back at it. But I also want to bring Michael Eric Dyson into this conversation, and I want to ask you the same question that I started with. Talk to me a little bit about race, about blackness, and about class.

Michael Eric Dyson: Well, race has been "de-classed" and class has been "e-raced." When people think about race they don't often think about the divisions within African American communities. Within African American culture, class is not exclusively about economic status; it's also about a sort of cultural style and aesthetic that marks one's own class orientation. That's been the complexity of thinking about class within African American communities. But that being said, there's a tremendous lack of attention paid to the internal divisions within African American culture—until recently, when it became in vogue to think about the so-called underclass. Williams Julius Wilson, who helped spearhead that sociological orientation toward class matters, began to prefer the term "the ghetto poor." But the reality is that there's this persistently poor group of people within African American culture whose lives were paid insignificant, or insufficient, attention to until they began to be pathologically visibilized. By which I mean, only when their pathologies were being paraded was there discourse around who they were, why they were where they were, and what we needed to do about them. And that was a very difficult thing to do, because as many commentators have said about

American society, it's probably even more difficult to speak about class than it is to deal with the difficult subject of race.

The way class has been "e-raced," if you will, is that all of this brouhaha recently over identity politics has permeated the labor movement, for instance, in this country. And you see all of these conferences quite recently about the labor movement: "Where is the labor movement headed?" And part of it is predicated upon this nostalgic recuperation of a time when the labor movement was about economic inequality, and it was about class warfare, which meant white working people. Now, they're ignoring the fact that Latinos, and Native Americans, and Asian Americans, to a certain degree, and certainly African American people who are laborers, have been concerned about issues of economic inequality all along. But their bodies don't count. Their particular niche on the socio-economic ladder makes no difference. It doesn't constitute, or count as, a legitimate labor issue and, therefore, a class issue. So for me, the class/race intervention and the class/race intersection is quite crucial to understanding why people are where they are. And I'll end by saying this—if racism is destroyed tomorrow, as vicious as it is, many poor people who are black will continue to be poor. Many poor people who are Latino will continue to be poor. How, then, do we deal with these underlying issues in regard to the race/class dialectic, is what we need to attend to.

Falcon: That's what I meant to say. [*Laughter*]

Tapp: Stuck in there was something that went by a little too quickly, and I want to pull it back out. I think I heard you say it is more difficult to talk about class than race. Is that what you said?

Dyson: Yeah. I said in many instances that's absolutely right. But the difficulty of class is that it's this invisible variable that has been quite difficult to "out." You know, we're still in the closet about class. We're out about race. We're wearing our identities on our sleeves for a variety of reasons and with a variety of consequences. But the class issue is so much more muted, because we're not able to find an analytical vocabulary that allows us A) to know what's going on and B) to be able to grasp hold of it, because it's so messy. As Angelo was saying, it's so fluid as to be rendered ambiguous at certain points.

Tapp: Let me throw out another theory. Angelo Falcon, maybe the reason that we have trouble talking about class is that we still like to believe that we are a classless society. That is the whole North American construct, isn't it?

Falcon: That's the basis of much of liberalism, and I think the idea, also, that we're a middle-class society. I'm amazed at the optimism about the society's ability to grow and just incorporate all sorts of people, at least theoretically. You start thinking about some of the stuff that comes out in terms of social policy and how people are looking at this increasing pie, even though they're cutting back left and right. But somehow the optimism about this society being able to absorb all sorts of groups of people, turning this into a middle-class society, at the same time that we know that this is basically a class society, in the sense that you can't have everybody being middle class. Otherwise the system won't work. You need inequality for the system to work. And so you have that contradiction in the way we look at things. Ideologically, this optimism, it permeates the way we talk, the way we think about American society. But then the reality, when you sit down with the numbers and you start saying, well, how does capitalism work? How does it move forward? Well, through exploitation of people, through this inequality. If you don't have that, the system doesn't work. But yet, we have this denial about that reality, about how capitalism works.

Tapp: I'm wondering if we can pursue that for a moment and go back to this notion of trying to talk a little bit more realistically about Latinos. If we think about that structure that you've just described, this false belief that we're classless, how familiar or unfamiliar is that to groups of immigrants? Again, you're going to generalize—I understand that. But if we talk about, say, for Puerto Ricans. Is that a shock? Mexicans. People from various parts of South America. People from Spain. People from Portugal.

Falcon: No, it's part of it. I think the motivation for coming to this country, and if you're here already, of trying to make the best of it here, is the idea that somehow you can make it in society. We did a survey back in 1990 of Latinos, called the Latino National Political Survey. And we caught all sorts of hell, because we found things like: Latinos were very loyal to this country. Gee, Latinos really thought this was a great country. A lot of our academic colleagues were saying, you know, this is racist, terrible—you must have done something wrong with the survey. And the reality is, I think there is, again, a tremendous amount of good feeling, ironically, about coming to this country and making it in this country. The reality kicks in once you're here, and you don't make it, and so many of your people are poor. So you have these kinds of myths that are out there—and that immigrant myth about streets being paved with gold—that are alive and well. Now, does it mean that people really think that society works that way? Or that they will be the exceptions and be able to reap some of the bounty or create a little niche for themselves and make it that way? I mean, one of the interesting things is this idea that somehow Latinos are these subversive people that are coming, that are anti-American, which you couldn't tell from really talking to real Latinos as opposed to maybe a couple of crazy academics. But what happens in this society is that Latino consciousness, and the idea of being "other," or being a minority, is very much an American phenomenon. It's not something we bring with us. The term *Hispanic, Latino*—that's not something we use in Latin America and the Caribbean, that's something we create here in reaction to American society and how it treats us.

Tapp: I want to actually stay with that and pick up again on something you just said, for a moment. And I want to hear from both of you on this. Why didn't it work? This immigrant dream of coming here and working hard and being patriotic and doing all the right things and succeeding—why isn't it working? What's happening?

Falcon: There are economic realities. Latinos come into the society and they find very quickly that there are certain places for them to fit in, in terms of the economy. That while there may be certain groups that are small, that may find a niche here and there, once our population gets large enough, the society starts looking at us in a very different way. Puerto Ricans, for example, came in large numbers in the '40s and '50s, up until the '60s, had very high labor force participation rates—Puerto Rican women being in the forefront of all women in this country by having very high levels of labor force participation rates in the '50s and the '60s. Then in the '60s you have this profound economic restructuring. You have, in the Northeast where we were concentrated, in New York, a lot of plant closings, moving to other places. Our community never recovered from that, those economic forces. Our community also, as a newcomer—and also not part of this black/white kind of dialectic that you have in this country—also were not able to hang on to certain policies, like affirmative action, or public sector employment. So we wound up being very much a welfare population, going from a very productive service industry, blue-collar community, to becoming, in a matter of a few decades, basically a welfare community. So today, for example, in New York City, 59 percent of the people on welfare are Latino, overwhelmingly Puerto Rican. So I think it has to do with these structural forces in this society, not some sort of immigrant ethos. And I think that is a reaction, not to some sort of ethics on our part—we didn't all of a sudden become lazy people that didn't want to work and wanted to go on welfare. It was a reaction to real structural forces around real people. And that's really what did it.

Tapp: Michael Eric Dyson, I want to bring you into this conversation as well, partly to react a little bit to what you've heard from Angelo Falcon, but also to put in here a point I think we need to make. There's a difference between coming to this country as an immigrant, which is to say, voluntarily, and coming or being a descendent of a group of people who didn't come voluntarily. And I'm wondering how much color—pun intended—colors this whole experience here.

Dyson: Well, first of all, to respond to Angelo, there's no question that those same forces, what we now term, in high-falutin' social theory, postindustrial urban collapse, disproportionately affected heavy immigrant populations as well as indigenous African American populations. The restructuring, for instance, of the automobile industry in Detroit, or the steel industry in Pittsburgh, and so on, has had a profound effect on the ability of African American people and other immigrants to participate in the labor force, and a precipitously negative effect on every other arena of their lives. For instance, their ability to own a home, their ability to send their kids to the best schools that were possible, their ability to maintain a level of subsistence that was above the poverty line. The dream of Henry Ford—Fordist capitalism—provided the possibility for individual workers to exercise their economic agency by accumulating enough capital to have the American dream. So despite the fact that you didn't have access to higher echelons of elite education, you were able, by dint of your own sweat and your brawn, to have access to high-waged, low-skilled jobs that gave you the possibility of supporting your family.

In relationship to African American communities, there's no question that I think the color issue does, indeed, pigment [this debate]. We live in what scholars have called a pigmentocracy. And that's the rule, reign, and tyranny of issues of skin color. And color is much more than about the tone of one's skin. It's about the political identity that's ascribed to people of color. And I think that recently arriving immigrant groups, or well-established immigrant groups, have a very difficult time assimilating into the larger circle of American privilege. But that's even more especially exacerbated for African American people who—though an indigenous pool of labor that has, in one sense, supported the global expansion of American capitalism—have never been able to reap its gross benefits. And the ongoing tragedy is the persistence of issues of bias and bigotry toward African Americans individually and as a group.

For instance, William Julius Wilson, in his book, *When Work Disappears,* goes to extraordinary pains to point out that there are employers within Chicago who treat African American people differently—especially in this case, the target pool of African American men, having assumptions about who they are, what their work habits will be, what kinds of criminalization they've been exposed to. And as a result of that, going in the door, they are prevented from having access to this larger circle of American employment. So the issue of pigment, the issue of color, exacerbates an underlying structural reality, which has had a devastating impact upon both recently arrived immigrants, as well as older immigrant groups, as well as African Americans. I think that's something we have to pay attention to.

Falcon: Also, I think it's important to challenge the notion of voluntary immigration or migration. In the Puerto Rican case we're technically migrants, and not immigrants. I think if you look at the history, for example, of Puerto Rico, it's interesting the way the government on the island, the colonial government, has been able to basically export excess labor in very strategic ways. I mean, we have one of the first migrations of Puerto Ricans being laborers sent out to Hawaii in 1901, a lot of them getting lost along the way. So you wind up having these pockets of Puerto Ricans, for example, in San Francisco, having some of the oldest Puerto Rican organizations because of that labor migration. And the horror stories that got back to the island in terms of the way people were lied to and treated. That whole history of how people get here, also that notion that they're here voluntarily, is I think also a big myth. So I think color isn't how we basically deal with the society. It's not simply people who just decide one day to pick up and come here.

Tapp: Do you think it's a myth, Michael Eric Dyson?

Dyson: One of the things we have to contend with, however, once here, is the differential treatment assigned to African American people because of the kind of skin perception, and the attempt to exploit indigenous labor, over migrant or immigrant labor, where the relative value of the capital is assigned precisely because of their ability to assimilate or mix in. This is the great carrot seductively held in front of many immigrant or migrant groups: "You're more like us, the white majority, than you are like them, the African American minority." So when we think about it—not only in relation to Puerto Ricans, but Chicanos and Mexicans and Cubans, and African Americans too—poor whites, the untold labor base for much of the so-called working class and underclass, has never seen its fate tied up with that of African Americans and other minority workers. Poor white workers neglected to forge solidarity and coalition with African Americans and other minority workers precisely because they derived a psychological benefit from their white skin. They engaged in what I call a comparative racial taxonomy: "Because we're not the niggers, because we're not the Puerto Ricans, not the wetbacks and so on, we are therefore able to enjoy a level of privilege over against these people"—not realizing their economic benefits, or their economic devastation, was tied very closely to the real structural realities of minority communities.

Tapp: There are some, though, who would argue that that even happened within various Latino communities, that the whole ideal of whiteness is still very much a problem. We've talked a little about this before, but let's just pursue it again for a moment. And let me just throw another ugly little thing in here as well—the struggle between colonialism in parts of South America, and in the Caribbean, and where speakers of Spanish fit, and where people of color fit into that, black people of color, people who may have come from Africa through the slave trade—I mean, this gets really complicated if we add all that in.

Falcon: The way we look at race in Latin America and the Caribbean is different than in this country. Here you have that one drop rule. In Latin America they've found ways to have a whole gradation where you can basically *buy* into whiteness, or marry into whiteness. And so it's more complex, but no less pernicious. It's not the kind of thing where you're saying, "Well, there is no racism in Puerto Rico." Well, how come none of the major government officials or the heads of corporation are dark skinned? That issue is not being addressed. But you have a very segregated society.

Tapp: You can see there are so many examples, and we could take up the rest of our time here by giving them, but let me just give one. I was astounded to be in Barcelona in the middle of Catalon Independence, and watch TV, and everybody was blond. Now, to be sure, there are lots of blondes in Spain. But that doesn't mean that everybody on television should be blond. And everybody was blond.

Dyson: Well, in one sense, the ingenuity of American popular culture has been the export of an ideal of American identity that punishes people throughout the world—punishes them for their difference, and their deviation from the so-called norm. And one of the perverse ingenuities of American pop culture has been the marketing and the retailing globally of this notion that whiteness is the ideal identity. For me, issues of whiteness are extraordinarily important when we talk about issues of class, because even within immigrant populations, as well as within African American populations, there is this uncritical celebration, sometimes unconsciously, of a white ideal. Even the degree to which we measure ourselves as human beings so often pulls from the sort of psychological and the cultural capital of whiteness. And that I think we have to pay attention to.

Tapp: Since you mentioned the export of this American notion—idealized whiteness—let's talk a little about another notion we may be exporting. And I think it will factor into the issue of race and the way that it intersects with class. I know in your work in the past, Michael Eric Dyson, you've said we don't live in a democracy, we live in a juvenocracy. I guess I want to pull the youth culture out here and talk a little bit about it, and ask you to begin by defining a juvenocracy.

Dyson: Well, what I meant by that rather flippant term: I'm talking about the way in which young people under the ages of (and the older I get, the older youth is defined in my work) let's say twenty-five years old, in postindustrial urban centers—Detroit, Philadelphia, Chicago, New York, and so on—have found disproportionate forms of influence within their culture by virtue of informal economies related to drugs, related to the fencing of stolen goods and so on, especially in the late '80s, where the retail of crack cocaine to black and Latino youth provided an enormous influx of cash into these devastated urban centers. Already there had been the hemorrhaging of resources in the postindustrial urban centers, so that they had gone out to the suburbs. The transportation network had gone out to the suburbs; the informal network of employment had gone out to the suburbs. So we had all forms of capital flight as well. The exposure of the vulnerable postindustrial urban center, which was largely black and brown, left this gaping hole. I agree with William Julius Wilson when he says that out-migration—that is, the flight of black and brown people from these so-called ghettos and barrios—left people devastated in many ways. But one [of those forms of devastation] was not, as some have argued, the lack of moral turpitude among those people. There was a tremendous moral center still left there, but it was not as visible as before, because it didn't have the—again, this is a deeply classed issue—it didn't have the visibility of professors and lawyers and doctors who heretofore had lived in at least close proximity to these centers, or within their boundaries. So for me, a juvenocracy is about the tyranny of a youth-led experience that is largely illegal.

Now, it's often linked to the rise of hip-hop culture which, of course, has been driven by black and Latino youth—initially in New York, but throughout American culture now. And the hip-hop revolution has, I think, exposed enormous class divisions within Latino and African American cultures specifically, as well as many other [cultures], because the generational divide is, in reality, and at root, a class divide. African American youth and Latino youth are speaking about issues of economic inequality, are speaking about issues of persistent racism, are speaking about the kind of bourgeois-ification of Latino and black communities, in ways that we used to hear from prophets in our pulpits or in our synagogues, certainly in our churches and temples. And now the expression of that rhetoric of prophetic criticism of persistent forms of social oppression has been left to these urban griots who often wield their rhetorical authority with violent metaphors. So they fuse their powerfully emergent rhetorical culture with forms of deep violence that are quite problematic to bourgeois black and Latino people who think, "This is not the correct way to act. This is not the correct way to be. The aesthetic of your revolution is deeply problematic, because it's linked to, and driven by, the engine of a violent preoccupation with economic immiseration." So what we have to do, then, is to acknowledge the class basis of much of the criticism of these young people—which is also the basis of their expression of dissatisfaction with their own people in their race, as well as the larger white society.

Tapp: Let me turn that on it's head a minute, and let me press it, and let me pull Angelo Falcon in here as well. Part of being young is rebelling against things. That's part of growing up. Testing things, finding out where you really stand on issues. And one of the reasons that growing up is called growing up is because you do go through phases. You find your tastes change. You try things out and you reject them. That works fine in a society that has age integration. However, in a society that is dominated either through the stuff that we see on television, the books that were sold, what we read in our newspapers or in our communities, by youth, we don't have the opportunities to go through those phases. Now, let me ask you, Angelo Falcon, does *that* factor in here?

Falcon: There are certain things we take for granted in terms of American history and the way American society develops that just aren't working today. For example, when you talk about neighborhoods, and when you talk about the process of class formation, something profoundly different is going on. And people like Wilson and others have documented it. The whole idea that somehow you have a poor working-class neighborhood that begins to turn into, and develop, a middle-class component to it, and then that middle-class develops businesses, and then there's a succession, and a new group comes in, and then your kids go off to college. That stuff is not happening. And so the process by which people, especially people of color, get integrated into society, how they deal with these types of questions, is profoundly different. The way our youth is developing is profoundly different in terms of the kind of resources they have around them, and in terms of the people that they have as not only role models, but the people that they have to deal with, and the profound impact it's had on family structure. So there's some real differences there going on that I think have had this kind of impact, where you have a disconnect in many ways, and you don't have the kind of more organic development of communities that you may have had at another point.

Tapp: Stay with this for another moment, and take us through it. I'll use the example of *There Are No Children Here* by Alex Kotlowitz, where we saw sketched out, in I think a fairly fair way, which is to say a nonjudgmental way, a society in which there was a great presence of—and we know the statistics are here on this—single-mother families with lots and lots of kids. Is that what you're talking about? Is that going on in Puerto Rican communities, too? Is that the welfare situation in urban areas among the urban poor of color?

Falcon: We did an atlas of Latino neighborhoods in New York City, and we weren't able to find a solidly middle-class Latino neighborhood. What we had were neighborhoods where the poverty rate, while for the community as a whole may have been 40 percent, going up as high as 65 percent. Communities that really didn't have certain basic institutions that you would think would be part of any kind of neighborhood. What you had was people moving out, professionals moving out, even the process of suburbanization being turned on its head. Where before, I thought you were supposed to go to suburbs when you did okay, and you could buy a house and stuff. Well, now you've got poor people moving to the suburbs. And you have pockets of poverty. It's like all the processes we took for granted that would help in terms of social mobility have been turned on their head. So what we have now are populations that are basically trying to deal with this question.

I think the other issue is the one that makes it very difficult. Because we can't talk about blacks, Puerto Ricans, Latinos, West Indian blacks at the same level, either. That's one thing that's been very difficult to get across to people, that there's even a notion of a hierarchy of powerlessness. For example, I did an analysis once looking at black/Latino coalition building in New York City and compared the resources that African Americans bring into the political process, compared to Latinos. And it was interesting. Because many of the institutions that came out of this slavery turned into political resources. So, for example, in the black community, where you have a black church that provides tremendous leadership and, in many cases, much economic development, you don't have a counterpart in the Latino community. What you have is a very colonial church, a Catholic Church that basically still plays that kind of outsider role. Historically, black colleges have also been a tremendous resource. We don't have a counterpart to that. Public sector employment—you could make the argument that, in fact, one of the outcomes of the Great Society programs has been to allow the black community to develop the basis of a middle class based on public sector employment. People don't understand that issue, that hierarchy, also. And I think our cities are becoming majority black/Latino/Asian. We need to understand that dynamic, and how class and the different history these groups have kind of also play the part in how they work together.

Tapp: Michael Eric Dyson, I know you want to jump in.

Dyson: Yeah. I think talking about a notion of hierarchy is very rich here, indeed. Because what ends up happening is that there's a politics of resentment that is projected onto the next or competing group. What's interesting about that is that each group then thinks the other has the power now. When he talks about churches, the public sector, and when he talks about colleges, there's no question that the institutional assistance of certain forms of organized life within African American culture have led to an inversion of oppression into a source of power. So that slave religion became a central organizing principle for social revolution, and prophetic resistance to forms of oppression, as well as black colleges became the sites of resistance—as well as, by the way, tremendous conservatism on both sides. But at the same time, I think what's interesting is that within these communities as well—that is, within Latino communities and within African American communities—the competition for scarce resources has indeed allowed us to, in one sense, bicker and talk about each other's powerlessness, or relative victimization, within a hierarchy of power, and within a hierarchy of visibility. But we've also got to acknowledge the seductive principle and practice of whiteness within the Latino communities, where the distribution of agony has largely followed a color axis. And that's where the difficulty of bringing in the issue of class comes about.

Tapp: I want to stay with this a moment, I wanted to talk a little bit about this black/brown connection. We all sit here and we say, "It's gotta happen," and then nobody wants to talk about it. So talk about it. What's the problem? And please, if you wouldn't mind, Angelo Falcon, throw class in there as well. Why can't this connection happen?

Falcon: To me, it's not something you talk about, it's something you do in terms of coalition building. It's something we find ourselves always involved with. And it's almost within a family. You know, you have your squabbles, and you try to deal with these issues. But one of my conclusions in trying to work in terms of coalitions is the notion that somehow you can talk about it in terms of an educational experience—we should know more about each other, we should understand each other better. But unfortunately, it comes down to a question of power. And that is of respect of each other's communities. Because right now, one of the biggest claims, or biggest problems, that Latinos face in working, say, with the African American community, and other communities, is the idea of being junior partners. The African American community is very powerful. See, the thing is, you talk to African Americans about this stuff and they go, "Are you crazy? What are you talking about, that we're powerful?" We have Latinos feeling that African Americans are gatekeepers, have much better networks. It's kind of sometimes pathetic. You see a lot of reports coming out of these Latino groups in Washington, and they're constantly saying, "The Latino problem—an American problem." While, ironically, from a legacy of slavery, you have more of an American consciousness of black history, of the black dilemma. Latinos still feel that we're these foreigners that no one understands, and that there's no American connection to what we're doing. And so one of the biggest problems we have is that question of being seen as people who are foreigners, who really have no claims and no stakes in this society.

Tapp: And let me throw some other hurts in here—that there are perceptions, again, that on the part of African Americans, that Latinos in South America oppress them. And on the part of Latinos, that African Americans are those lazy—and we're going with stereotypes. We're dealing with racism here. No one wants to say those things. But they're there. Aren't they, Michael Eric Dyson?

Dyson: No doubt. Supposedly, minority people consume as much, if not even more, popular culture, especially television, than any other group. There's no doubt, then, that we're receiving the same televised stereotypes that filter through the minds of our white colleagues. So the reality is that each group does wield a certain amount of stereotypical thinking or bias and bigotry. And what we have to do then is to break down, to de-mythologize, some of the mythologies that aggregate around the notion that blacks wield more power and that Latinos are junior partners, if you will, to borrow that corporate metaphor. So what's interesting, then, is to talk about the ways in which relative powerlessness operates both between blacks and Latinos, and the larger white society—and between blacks and Latinos within the group. So I think there's no denying it, on both sides, there would be tremendous hurts that have been expressed historically about what blacks feel about Latinos, what Latinos feel about blacks.

If we're talking about coalitional politics, we must acknowledge the way in which, as has been argued, the black/white divide is being challenged, and the black/white paradigm of racial relations is being challenged by Latino experience. Let's be honest about it. First of all, the black/white divide needs to be challenged. But the black/white divide has been the major artery through which the blood of bigotry has flowed throughout the body politic for most of the history of America. So what we have to be careful about, and cautious about, is the opportunistic exploitation of that relationship by others outside of African American cultures. And that includes some Latino groups who, on the one hand, acknowledge their solidarity with African Americans as oppressed people through affirmative action, but on the other hand disclaim their relationship to African Americans in terms of a racial distinction, as opposed to an ethnic distinction.

Let me say this about African Americans, and especially Latinos and youth. One of the things that's interesting to me is that for young people who "grow up in public," issues of violence and issues of public space are very important for both black and Latino youth. And one of the ways we can organize political coalitions around issues of identity is to understand the way in which black and Latino youth both face issues of declining public housing, declining education, and the inability to claim their public spaces. When you have rappers like Biggie Smalls say, "Back in the days our parents used to take care of us / look at them now, they're even f–ing scared of us / calling the state for help because they can't maintain, Damn, things done changed / If I wasn't in the rap game, I'd probably have a key knee deep in the crack game / 'Cause the streets is a short stop/ Either you're slinging crack rock or you got a wicked jump shot / . . . Damn, it's hard being young from the slums, eating five-cent gums, not knowing where your meal's coming from / What happened to the summertime cookouts? Every time I turn around a nigga's being took out." Now, that may not satisfy your Max Weber quotient of sociological analysis, but it does qualify as a kind of homeboy ethnography of trying to figure out what the hell is going on with the collapse of public spaces, especially under Reaganomics.

And finally, the introduction of drugs, for instance, on the West Coast—that was a large argument, like other so-called conspiracy theories, that gets written off against black peoples' and brown peoples' hypersensitivity about their relative economic inequality. When the real deal is, that in a culture that has systematically prevented the flourishing of black and brown people, conspiracy theories become the escape valve for the real political and material analysis of the forces that continue to make our lives hell. That's the necessity we have to deal with, instead of merely the bickering back and forth.

Falcon: I would disagree. I think that the story I began with about the guy who gets up at a meeting and says, "It's really class," I think that's exactly what you just laid out. And I think the big difficulty and the big challenge now is, in fact, to deal with that bickering and to deal with how we conceptualize each community's role in society vis-à-vis the racial dynamic here. And I think that's something that hasn't really been dealt with. And I said that one of the interesting things that is forcing that discussion is the fact that, when you're talking about Chicago, or New York, you're talking about cities where blacks and Latinos are becoming majorities of the population. And not one group has dominated. And that's going to force a discussion that we haven't had. And those kinds of issues, like, "Hey, this

is a lot of baloney, it's gossipy kind of stuff"—I think those are going to become
much more important. And we have to deal with those issues. In the Latino case,
all the discussions in this country are between black and white. Where do we fit
in? Is there a third way? There are some people saying, well, we're really more
white. There's this whole discussion about how Hispanic we are, and how connected we are to Spain. And by the way, a lot of these kinds of situations are not
simply the influence of American culture. I mean, you talk about European Spanish culture. So we have a lot of devils that we have to deal with within our own
cultures. And the way we also just deal not with just our African roots, but as well
as our indigenous roots, and how we deal. And so I—

Dyson: When I say bickering, I'm talking about getting rid of the inessential elements and dealing with the profound structural ones that are precisely of the character you're speaking about. For instance, we have to do some hard-headed thinking here when we say, "Hey, there's a black [way] and there's a white [way] but
there's a third way, Latino." I'm going, "Well, help me out here." Because Latinos
themselves are suffering from tremendous forms of oppression within Latino
communities, where Dominicans are given short shrift, and [dark-skinned]
Cubans are given short shrift—light-skinned Cubans who are deeply Republican
and reactionary, conservative are talked about as Latinos who provide a third
way. That ain't nothing but the white way with a Latino face! Similar to previous
immigrant groups like Jews and Poles. And if that's the case, then, let's put our
cards on the table, and don't just talk about "people of color." Let's talk about
people of color who are arguing about their self-definition in relationship to political economies of color that have had negative consequences for black people
even within Latino cultures. That, to me, is not bickering. That's structural realities that have to be contended with.

Falcon: Right at the center is that debate in the Latino community today. And
until we, within our community, really come to some clarity in that issue, it becomes very difficult to have a coherent discussion about where we're going to go.
And that's the thing that worries me. What is a third way? I don't know what the
hell that means.

Dyson: That's what I'm saying. To merely evoke the Latino way as a third way
is essentialist, it's reductive, and it's not very helpful in terms of on-the-ground
kinds of analyses of the real contestation for scarce resources that blacks and
browns engage in. So what I want to do, then, is see a much more expanded dialogue that acknowledges the colorocracy among Latinos themselves, so we see
that there's an enormous internal division about the relative value of color, and as
a result of that, the consequent assigning of privilege or lack of privilege thereof.
And that's what needs to be contended with as well.

Tapp: Privilege, and/or class status. I think there are some other questions we need to get back to. Let me pick up on something Michael just said. Let me frame this question in the most general way. Does moving up the ladder of success mean assimilation? Does it mean if you're Irish or Jewish, becoming white, or does it mean redefining that? And actually, Angelo Falcon, let me ask you that one. Because that is a struggle that I think we've seen in a lot of Spanish-speaking communities.

Falcon: First of all, we have to be clear that everyone here goes through assimilation. I think that's one of the reasons why we can all kind of talk and eat the same food. I didn't bring any plantains with me so I could digest the food here. So that's a level of assimilation, I guess. We have to be careful about these kinds of pure ways we sometimes talk about these things. But I think one of the things that, to me, has been fascinating is, I remember when I was starting my organization, I would have these Latino and Puerto Rican professionals come up to me and say, "Hey, you still doing that community stuff, man? I'm getting a job with this corporation; later for that community stuff." And five years later, there's this brown ceiling—can I say that?—and they would come back and they all of a sudden became radicalized. And I think we're seeing that kind of process going on where, yeah, there's a certain level of assimilation, upward mobility. We had a little game people used to play. Puerto Ricans used to call themselves Hispanics. Guys calling themselves Hispanic, they're Puerto Ricans. Well, turned out Hispanics seemed a little bit more sanitized, because Puerto Ricans are on welfare. Remember the decade of the Hispanic that had the nuclear family with the nice house, and that was a Hispanic? Then you have Puerto Ricans. So we have those kinds of games going on all the time within our own community, in terms of people trying to project themselves out there.

But then the reality is setting in. In New York City there is a tremendous diversity of Latinos. You have not only Puerto Ricans, Dominicans, you have Colombians, the Argentineans. And one of the things that strikes me is how when they hit the society full head on—and it's not theoretical anymore, it's not some sort of little enclave of like three middle-class Colombian professionals, but the communities start growing—then you see things like police brutality affecting them. You see the issue of employment discrimination. You look at the Spanish language newspapers—horror stories every day: immigration abuses, police brutality. That's what starts basically fueling a Latino identity. And it's not, again, something we bring with us, because people come here very optimistic. But it's something this society kind of imparts on us. And that's part of that racial dynamic in this country. And I think one of the things Latinos need to understand is that continuity.

Tapp: Let me turn it on its head, and then, Michael Eric Dyson, let me throw it back to you. What is so wrong with assimilating? It's a bad word, suddenly. What is wrong with adapting? What is wrong with learning to live with other people? And what is so wrong—and I know you're all patriots here—with saying, "I like the concepts, not always perhaps the realities, but the concepts that underlie this democracy. I like the notion of personal responsibility. I like individual rights. I like being in a majority rule situation." What is so wrong with all of that? Why have we gotten to a point where we have to say this might be an evil thing?

Dyson: Well, it's not that we've got to that point. It's that America has had amnesia about the fact that it systematically denied that opportunity to a group of people—and in this case, we take African Americans who weren't treated as individuals in slavery, because they were enslaved regardless of their education, their IQ, their geographical distribution along the African coast. So the reality is that America's quite hypocritical about saying that to those people who have paid the price, and borne the burden, for allowing Americans to be individuals. Slave owners were allowed to be individuals because they made a collectivity, and an oppressive one, out of African slaves. That's something we can't forget, as the background to what I'm about to say. There's nothing wrong at all. And that's, by the way, one of the tensions between black and brown people. Because recently arriving immigrants of whatever hue who are grateful to be here have not yet gathered the revolutionary fire until they meet the brown or yellow or lighter-brown ceiling, and then they come back and rediscover their pigment.

What's interesting about African American people, then, I think, is that nobody has been more individual than us. The claims of the civil rights movement were never primarily about black versus white; they were about right versus wrong. The moral energy of the civil rights movement, for instance, was always about the revolutionary transformation of American society predicated upon the very dream that America articulated through Thomas Jefferson's inscription of the Declaration of Independence; through the Bill of Rights. Martin Luther King kept saying, "Somewhere I read of the freedom of speech." Somewhere he read was the very foundations of American democracy as codified in those documents that eloquently articulated America's desire to remove every form of tyranny. Now, all of a sudden, black folk get re-read as not wanting to be individuals, not wanting to be patriotic? What more patriotism can we express than in the face of our own severe denigration within the borders of American society to support America as she went to war against fascism? Here were black men and, to a certain degree, women, going to foreign borders and fighting for what they didn't enjoy here. Excuse me, what kind of revisionist historiography are we subscribing to that denies the integrity of that narrative?

So there's nothing wrong with assimilating—*if* assimilation means we are integrating into an economy of identity. What I mean by that is a way of distributing identity that doesn't say one thing is better than the other. If we had an American society where whiteness was not the conscious and unconscious, the express and the implicit ideal, then we could have a society where we say, "Well, whatever you are, you are." But the reality is, we still, as people of color, have in our minds the boogeyman of the white person inside us. That's why Malcolm X said, what's most important is not the white slave owner standing outside of you; it is that internal assent to self-abnegation that white supremacy evokes in the black and, we can add, brown unconscious. So for me, when we say assimilation is not wrong, I go, "Great, if the assimilative ideal is for all of us to enjoy this large amorphous American identity." But so often, the universal gets translated as white. People ask me all the time, "Are you black first, or are you an American?" Like I can make that kind of decision, where I can get up in the morning and put my pants on— "Well, I'm going to be black today, but also be an American, as opposed to West Indian, or I'm going to be a human being as opposed to an orangutan." The simultaneity of my identity is what I get up with every day. I'm already an American, as an *African* American. I've helped define the central operation of American democracy. So I'm saying this—that within American society, the assimilative ideal has always been a coded representation of a white norm that never gets outed as itself being specific, and contingent, and particular. And until we come to the point of demythologizing whiteness as the universal norm, we will never get to the ideal of assimilation being for anybody.

Ralph Ellison said, "Listen, I don't want to know how white black people are; I want to know how black white people are." Because when we think about American society, people want to be black or brown when it's convenient. We market multiculturalism in ways that help us capitalize our businesses. But when it comes to bearing the burden of blackness or brownness, or being Asian American, that's not something you want to do. Until we get to the point in this country when assimilation means white people can stop being white, we ain't going to really arrive at a point of real assimilation in American society.

Falcon: Con yo! That's a Cuban term.

Tapp: Meaning, agreed. What more could one add to that? I mean, there is this problem. It goes back to the whole notion of "separate but equal," except actually separate but unequal. Is that the problem, Angelo Falcon? It's just not working?

Falcon: Well, I think part of the problem is also filtering. First of all, people always tell me I don't look Puerto Rican. Sometimes it's supposed to be a compliment. The thing is, there's a filtering also of what it is we're talking about in terms of representing the values in our own communities. So when I say I'm with the Puerto Rican Defense Fund—I'm on a television show or something—the assumption is, I'm for big government, I'm against personal responsibility, I want everybody to be on welfare. And no matter what I say, people don't listen to what I'm saying, or don't believe what I'm saying. That, in fact, our reality is much more complex. That in our community the notion of self-help, the notion of pulling yourself up by the bootstraps—all that stuff is well and good. There are movements and leaders that do that. But that doesn't come through, because right now I feel like a cartoon character in American society. I feel like this two-dimensional thing that basically people just point to us as an example. So the left is saying, "Well, you guys are to blame for the destruction of the left." And I'm saying, "Gee, thanks for all the power." Then, on the other hand, you have the right wing saying, "You know, you people control everything through bilingual education." Gee, thanks for the props. Then I go home. I got no power. What are these people talking about? I have absolutely no control over how I project my community's agenda and our issues.

Tapp: We have to talk a little bit about violence. Because we can relate that, I think, to power and to race and to class, and kind of tie everything up as we close here. And let me just recall the rap that we heard earlier, that Michael Eric Dyson did. And let me say that one of the things that interested me about it was it was a bit of a stereotype breaker, in the sense that we heard a rapper, someone of that youth culture, that juvenocracy, bemoaning the loss of let's call it family and class structure, shall we? And bemoaning the very things that the right wing calls for, the left wing sometimes calls for, and everybody says they really, really want. Now let me wrap all that together, and let me ask you how violence fits in. Because I think one of the things that I've heard you talk a little bit about, Michael Eric Dyson, is that if we talk juvenocracy, and we realize that we're all a little bit more aggressive when those hormones are flying wildly around our bodies, maybe somehow there's a link to the violence that we're seeing in some communities. I don't know. Is there a link there?

Dyson: Well, there's a link to this degree: American culture is itself violent. I mean, when H. Rap Brown said that violence was as American as cherry pie, people went off on him. But the reality is violence is an American birthright. It's the ritual that we deploy to become Americans. But what's interesting to me is who gets a chance to be violent in American culture is deeply racialized and deeply classed. When Arnold Schwarzenegger is doing his thing, it's all right, because he's a right wing Republican. When Bruce Willis is doing his thing, he's a right wing Republican. And guess what? We never think that Bruce Willis is going to go home and deflate body parts of Demi Moore—or, in the past, he could have had that possibility—or Arnold Schwarzenegger with Maria Shriver. We never think they're going to go home and lacerate their children and cut their heads off and bury them under their beds, never to be seen for the next fifteen years. And yet, when Snoop Doggy Dog promotes violence, or when Biggie Smalls or Tupac Shakur promotes violence, it's a deeply racialized [effort]. Now I'm not denying at all the lethal intensity, and the moral ferocity, attached to certain forms of a culture within hip-hop expression, because I think it's very problematic and deeply troubling.

But I am arguing that, when we think about violence—*Thelma and Louise*, when that movie came out, people went off the deep end. "My Lord, here are these women talking about killing men." That's because men for the first time saw themselves as the victims of violence, and not the perpetrators. There was more violence in the first three minutes of *Lethal Weapon* than in the entire movie of *Thelma and Louise*. But because women were now deploying the violence, they were threatening to do something to men, it was problematic. So the reality to me, then, is who is doing violence? Francis Ford Coppola makes *The Godfather*. When you hear Marlon Brando, as he looks at James Caan's decimated body, go, "Look at how they massacred my boy," it is one of the epiphanic moments of American cinema in the latter part of the twentieth century, because the Mafioso has become the sublimated metaphor for the convergence of violence and family and honor and respect and machismo in American society. But what about when Snoop Doggy Dog says, "Woke up, jumped out of my bed / I'm in a two-man cell with my homey Lil' Half Dead / Murder was the case that they gave me / Dear God, I wonder can you save me?" They don't hear Tupac Shakur when he says, "Somebody help me, tell me where to go from here / Because even thugs cry, but do the Lord care?" They don't understand when these young people are articulating their concerns about violence. Now, I'm saying all that to say these two things. First of all—

Tapp: Wait a second, wait a second. We're talking about a movie or a rap. We *know* what the statistics are. They're bad. Black against black violence, it's out of control, right?

Dyson: No doubt. But, see, what I'm saying to you is American violence, in general, is out of control. I'm not trying to valorize racialized conceptions of violence and defend them because they happen to be black or Latino. What I'm arguing here is one thing: that violence is problematic, but it becomes *more* problematic when it's seen to be in the hands of certain people, when the guns are in the hands of certain people. Number two, real violence in American culture *does* make those people in ghettos or barrios who deploy violent lyrics to defend themselves or to define themselves—it certainly makes them more vulnerable because they don't have these so-called social buffers that will absorb the kind of excess of their imagination and teach them, "Hey, that's not how you do it." But let me say this. Because it relates back to the statement you made about single parents. See, what I'm concerned about is the kind of rhetorical pathology of the people who bear the brunt of American culture's vices. So that single black mothers or Latino mothers are made to be the bearers of everything that's wrong with American society. When we begin to break these stereotypes down, we see the business of a very complex group of people who have fought against the odds to make sure their children will be provided for—the real miracle, to me, is not that so many so-called poor people of color are violent. The real miracle is that not more of them are violent in an ethos which is fundamentally inimical to them. So violence is terrible, but I'm arguing that unless we take into account the gendered and the racialized character of this violence, we will scarcely be able to move this discussion forward.

Tapp: I want to end by going back to Angelo Falcon, and I want you to drag class back into this. And let's talk about data for a minute. There has been much work by the now defunct Latino Institute in Chicago about class, and particularly with regard to the multigenerational Mexican population in Chicago—Mexican and Mexican American. Middle class, solidly, loves those family values, connected to the church, connected to the community. And yet, when that research is presented there is always someone saying, "Oh, this is biased research. That can't be real." Now, in nice middle-class communities, we don't have a big tolerance for violence. I'm wondering if you can connect that. It's complex, but I think there are connections.

Falcon: It's a little out of my experience. Also, I'm not a violent person. Again, trying to project those images of middle classness and those kinds of values has been very difficult. We've been able to document it, and there's a rejection—again, you feel like you're being used in this polarized discussion, where none of those things makes any difference. And so that drives it more to issues of how, within the Latino community, we organize and, in fact, begin to develop agendas that begin to address those issues. And we're a long way from that, because we do have all sorts of class divisions within the Latino community. There are issues of race within our community, issues of coalition building. You know, we're talking about coalitions between blacks and Latinos—well, there's a lot of heavy issues of coalition building within the Latino community. And here you start with the question of class, from the point of view of the stratification within the Latino community; questions also where, as we start getting larger and larger, we've begun to be seen as markets. So you have the corporate sector beginning to appropriate us, beginning to bring us in, in very, very exploitative ways, and many of our old middle class, upper middle class buying into that, and distorting our own agenda into more and more of a corporate agenda. So we have these battles.

And I think one of the problems we have with this type of discussion about race and ethnicity in this society is, I think we're in a point of transition now. I don't think sometimes we even have the words—although I think you make up a lot of that stuff, those terms. I'm going to get a dictionary—

Dyson: I'll break it off to you later. [*Laughter*]

Falcon: But what he's trying to do, I think, is the kind of thing we're all trying to do, and that is trying to create a language for this stuff where it may not be there.

So we're in this transition, where I think we have more questions than answers. And I think that's what's frustrating. And something's got to give and, again, one of the things that will be driving this a lot are the demographic changes we're seeing. But that's not going to be the answer. I think we need our intellectuals to begin to really address these issues in new ways. I think we need our leadership to be much more aggressive and much more open to these questions, and to see that we are at a major turning point in this country. And that the way we define these issues now is going to determine the future of this country. These are not really little questions about this little minority group here or this little group here. We're talking about the shape of American society in the future. And I think we're at that point. And the frustration a lot of us feel is that we're right in the middle of this kind of turning, this kind of transition, and we don't know sometimes what to make of it. So I don't walk away feeling pessimistic. The fact that there are people asking these questions, to me, at this point, is good enough, and gives me something to start working on.

Tapp: I think it's always good to end on a note of optimism. Thank you.

6

MEMBERSHIP HAS ITS PRIVILEGES
Coloring White Identities

with David Roediger, Peggy McIntosh, Anna Meigs;
moderated by Ray Suarez

In July 1998, I participated in a wonderful conversation about the field of whiteness studies on NPR's *Talk of the Nation*, hosted by distinguished journalist Ray Suarez, now a correspondent with *The NewsHour with Jim Lehrer*. My partners in dialogue that day included David Roediger, a gifted intellectual who has helped to establish the scholarly legitimacy of the field, and Peggy McIntosh, a pioneering thinker in exploring the often unconscious privileges of whiteness. Since our discussion, many colleges and universities have explored the varied and conflicted meanings of whiteness in courses, conferences, and curricula.

Ray Suarez: Whiteness is a funny thing in the lives of white people, certainly in this country. People have gotten into a habit in the twentieth century of making being white the normal state of affairs, the condition of a regular person. Race, then, is used as a marker to describe people who are set apart from that normality. We use race as a label of non-whiteness. But whiteness itself? It's transparent. White life in America is just life in America. White history is history. Even for those who complain about race designation as social constructs, that is, something we impose as an organizing tool on society in the absence of any real biological difference, whiteness is transparent. People hostile to racial designations see those labels as something that white people lay on blacks and others, and white people are left out of the equation, sort of by elimination. Is there a construction of identity around whiteness that is not the kind found at white Aryan resistance meetings? Is there a history of whiteness in America, the ideas around it, its uses, its definition that is a worthwhile field for academic study?

The scholars who are taking those first pioneering steps into this lightly charted territory answer: yes, you bet. But what is there to study? What is there to write about that doesn't end up treading well-worn territory? What is there to say that isn't a prisoner of the repetitious and sometimes kind of boring arguments we've gotten so good at having in America? Peggy McIntosh, is whiteness studies a fully fleshed-out area of academic inquiry yet?

Peggy McIntosh: Not yet fully fleshed out, but well worth working on. It's the complement to the development of black studies and ethnic studies in the last couple of decades.

Suarez: Do you have a sort of definition-of-terms problem up at the top, where you have to tell people what it is and what it ain't?

McIntosh: Well for me, it was best to start autobiographically, in realizing that though I had been taught I didn't have race, other people did, I came to realize that having skin of the color I have opened many doors for me and gave me conditions of existence which I had been taught never to see. These conditions of unearned advantage that I saw that I had were transparent to me, and to the people of my race, place, and class that I grew up with.

Suarez: Does it undermine the attempt to build this as an academic field, that so much of what we say about race either starts with autobiography or personal narrative?

McIntosh: Well, of course, by the academic standards I was taught in three degrees from Harvard, for example, yes, any personal testimony undercuts the objectivity of scholarship. I now believe that, for me anyway, it was best to start testimonially. And in fact, the power of my analysis rests in the fact I don't claim it applies to all white people. I claimed only to mine my own experience, for what turned out to be a list of forty-six ways in which I daily experience, and know that I experience, unearned advantage based on my skin color, relative to just one tiny sample, which is, African American women in my building in my line of work.

Suarez: Well Michael Eric Dyson, you're right now a professor of African American studies, do you go along with Peggy McIntosh's assertion that white studies is implied by the existence of black studies?

Michael Eric Dyson: No question. I think that the development of white studies is itself in response to—similar to whiteness—the existence of blackness, of black studies, of African American studies throughout the Diaspora. So that in one sense, blackness and whiteness are called into existence mutually by one another, not always in equal fashion or form, and not, certainly, on an equal playing field. But nonetheless, they exist in a symbiotic relationship to one another. So when we think about whiteness studies in the academy, as Professor McIntosh has indicated, not only does it have to do with one's own autobiography–"Who I am as a white person and thinking about the psychology that structures my consciousness; unearned advantage; the ways in which those advantages work for me that don't work for other people"–but also about coming into an awareness of how, in relationship to African Americans or Native Americans or Latinos and so on, that whiteness is reinforced in very powerful ways. It stigmatizes the things that fall outside of its circumference.

So what we have to do is to begin to break down the transparency and the invisibility of whiteness–the way in which it is silenced–and name it for what it is, to allow it to speak in its very powerful vocabularies. Because as Professor McIntosh has indicated, whiteness is a very huge, multivariegated thing. It's a very differentiated thing; it has a lot of different components. We talk about so-called white trash on the one hand; we talk about elite whites on the other hand; we talk about the white working class, about which Professor David Roediger has written brilliantly. So, I think when we think about whiteness studies vis-à-vis African-American studies or other so-called ethnic or area studies, it is good, because it forces white Americans, and those of us who write about race and ethnicity in this country, to understand that not only do whites possess a race, but the invisibility of thinking about that race has really led us down some very treacherous paths that we need to really make up for.

Suarez: But, it's easy to see, I think, where the lines of inquiry are, if you're writing about oh, black freedmen in Charleston or Norfolk in the nineteenth century. It's easy to see what it is you're talking about because you're talking about the survival of a minority within the bounds created by a majority. But if you go to do studies at a county in Indiana where 97 percent of the population is white, what you're writing about is the state of circumstances of life. Where does whiteness come into it?

Dyson: Well, that's a very good question. And I think that even taking that example of Indiana–for instance, Indiana is not unfamiliar with, say, the rise of the Ku Klux Klan. So when we think about Indiana, that specific example, we think about one of the birthplaces of a very virulent strain of whiteness that has existed, and to a certain degree, has been allowed to survive, precisely because it has remained untheorized. That is, people don't ask questions about how whiteness exists, what it exists against. Implicit in your question is the presumption that because it's normal, or because it becomes normalized, it doesn't have anything against which it pitches itself–that is, the background against which we understand whiteness. Whiteness looks like the universal, therefore it never gets talked about in any particular fashion.

So I think in that example alone, the difficulty–but also the reward of thinking about and interrogating whiteness–is that you begin to say, "Hey, how did something that's very specific and particular, growing up in Indiana as a white person where 90 percent, or 95 percent, of the population is white" [which] only begs the question, how can we get beneath the surface, as it were, to find out what makes us white? Why do we think about ourselves as not having a race? Why, when we think about race, do we think about those folk across the river, say a few miles down the road in Chicago or over in St. Louis?

Why don't we think about ourselves as possessing a race? And what difference does that make? And how has that made it painful for other people to exist? And also, how has it really deprived us of some intellectual resources to think about our own lives? So, I think in that sense, even though it is more invisible, it well re-pays the effort of thinking about it, because white people then, and people who think about whiteness, have to come to grips with the complexity, and the variety of whiteness, and that's often masked by assuming that all white folk are the same.

Suarez: Well David Roediger, a lot of the twentieth century has been spent by left-of-center academics trying to explode the use of race, and using class analysis and the styles of economic relationships between groups, between people, be-tween professional groups, between people who live in different countries. Using that way of unlocking; unbundling what it is that human beings bring to life. What's tough about bringing race into the equation, especially with whites?

David Roediger: Well, my work actually grows out, very much, of that tradition, and my interest is in whites for whom whiteness doesn't pay off. And I think it's kind of easy to understand why, for example, a plantation owner would identify with white supremacy. My interest is in trying to figure out why white working people—whose wages, whose benefits, whose privilege don't really measure to a lot—also identify with whiteness. I'm a labor historian. It's really out of those kinds of class questions that I felt the need to bring in white racial identity, and to begin to ask the question: why do people call themselves white workers, and within that, why do they accent the white more often than they accent the workers?

Suarez: And is this kind of inquiry going on basically in the research, in the pub-lication, or does it exist as a practical matter, in the course catalog, for university students? If I want to take white studies at your own University of Minnesota, what would I sign up for? What would greet me on the first day of class?

Roediger: Well, I don't think there are any such courses at Minnesota. I know that I teach classes on race in the United States, and race and class in the United States. And although I identify with what Peggy said at the start, sometimes I think that the way to study whiteness is in a constellation of racial relationships, and I'd be a little bit hesitant to teach a course that's just on whiteness studies, and I certainly wouldn't envision departments, programs, et cetera, of white studies. In that sense, I think it's not symmetrical to black studies.

Suarez: Peggy McIntosh, do you agree?

McIntosh: Well, picking up on what David said, a very good course on whiteness studies taught by Arlene Avakian at University of Massachusetts in Amherst differentiates between many kinds of white people's experience. And I think it, therefore, does both recognize and avoid that pitfall David is talking about—the pitfall of assuming that white skin privilege works equally for all whites in all circumstances. However, to go back to both the Indiana question and the working-class whites question, here, I'm gonna read three things from my list which, indeed, I would say working-class people do benefit [from], and white Indianans do benefit [from], in ways they may not know about.

I wrote in one of my forty-six points: "I can turn on the TV or open to the front page of the paper and see people of my race widely and positively represented." I should add, that's in cases where the front page has anything positive on it at all. Next: "When I'm told about our national heritage or about so-called civilization, I'm shown that people of my skin color made it what it is, or gave it its best qualities." And a third: "I can be sure that our children will be given curricular materials that testify to the existence of our race, in every single course at every single grade level and every single subject area." Now, whether or not you're a laborer or a white Indianan, those things are working for you to put some sort of floor under your sense of identity.

Suarez: And if you're living in Indianapolis and heading for the phone, I mean, I just picked Indiana out of the basket folks. [*Laughter*] There's no prep that went into singling out Indiana. Petaluma, California, is our first stop this hour. Hi ya, Rick.

Caller: Hi, I'm really excited to be on the air here today. And I wonder, with each of your panelists, if there is any consistency in how many races each believes there are. And I wonder if they could each go around and comment on that, and delineate them for us?

Suarez: Notice how they're all jumping in here, Rick. [*Laughter*] It's not a question for which there is an easy answer, I'm sure.

Caller: I think that astrologers might actually have more coherence in their comments about their schemes of categorizing people, than people who think long and hard about race.

Suarez: But Rick, isn't self-identification almost as important as sort of hard-and-fast rules that we might set up about racial categorization?

Caller: I think that internal definitions really *are* important and that's how we *should* judge people and think about people, in their own terms, and not apply our classifications upon them, but I–

Dyson: Well–

Caller: –would like to do this experiment and have them each say how many and what they are.

Suarez: Michael Eric Dyson.

Dyson: Yeah, I think, in response to that–and I won't dodge the bullet, I'll answer finally. I was just having lunch with my wife at a restaurant here in New York, and I was among the only black patrons with my wife in the restaurant, and noticed that I was getting short shrift in regard to the waitress. And the burden of race, it seems to me, is that one is forever fixed by external categories that people impose *on* you. So that I have to think: "Is she treating me this way because A) I'm black or B) she doesn't like the Chicago Bulls shirt I have on, because she voted for the New York Knicks, or is it that she's having a terrible day? But she's speaking so kindly and so fluidly to the other white patrons." So that the atmosphere that is poisoned by the presumption I have about who she is, and perhaps about who she thinks I am, is something that's beyond my control.

So, when I think about race, and I think about racial identity, it's not something that people control, or they can merely categorize. I can answer by saying I think that there are as many races as people need there to be. You know, if we talk about Tiger Woods, who as a youth called himself Cablinasian, trying to fix on the map of identity the coordinates that constituted who he was. Well, all of us have that problem in the final analysis, but I'll tell you what: I can go out here in New York and tell the person that I want to pick me up in a cab, "Hey, listen, race is a metaphor; it doesn't exist; it's a social convention. We're all just part of the *human* race, and so let's not categorize each other." But you know what? That cab driver constantly refuses to stop for me at certain times in New York. So, it's not about a simplistic way of me saying, "Hey, I want to get beyond race and racial categories." The real question is how does race function, in a very serious way, to deny me social benefit, to make me uncomfortable, to reinforce my disadvantage, and to remind me of my place in the hierarchy of American priorities. So, to me–

Suarez: But, I think Rick was also trying to get at the arbitrariness of it all, which is, I think, an important thing to remember too.

Dyson: There's no doubt that it's exactly arbitrary, except it's arbitrary in consistent patterns, right? That sounds like a contradiction. It's arbitrary all right, because it can show up at any point. It can blow up in your face at any point. It can name you or deny you at any point. But there's a consistency. The cab metaphor I used, for instance: there are a lot of black men, and black people in New York, who can't get a cab. And so it's arbitrary on the one hand because I never know when it's gonna happen and when it's not gonna happen. But there are some consistent patterns of treatment, and that's just one of them. And I'm sure David and Peggy would have many more to add to that, but I'm indicating that the arbitrariness of race has to do with the inability to name and predict when it's gonna show up in our faces and hurt us and harm us, or give us advantage. But what's not arbitrary is the kind of hierarchy where race is assigned a certain privilege–whiteness and blackness exist, Latino identity and Native American identity exist, in very specific ways, that I think are not quite as arbitrary as we'd like to make them to be.

Suarez: Peggy McIntosh.

McIntosh: Both biologists and anthropologists agree that there is very little basis for clear distinctions between races, but what Michael Eric Dyson says is absolutely true in my experience, that race functions as social categorization, politically constructed categorization. And I have stood on the curb in New York City in order to hail a cab for an African American man who could not get one to stop for him. So, we have different kinds of melanin, and they do play out in what gets projected on to us in the way [we are considered] trustworthy citizens, or rich citizens, or people able to pay a cab fare, or safe citizens. And that's the part of this whole matter that makes me not want to simply abolish a term like race. And it's a little bit like male and female in that there are tremendously verifiable differences between male and female. On the other hand, there's lots that men and women share in common. Yes, because of projections on to us, we were raised to think of ourselves, at least in my subculture, as opposite sexes. So we were made to seem more different than we actually are. If you do cognitive studies on men and women, our thought processes are much more similar than they are different. We are not opposite in the ways we think. But, the language has the social and political force of making us seem very different, and therefore justifying quite different treatment of the two sexes.

Suarez: David Roediger.

Roediger: I think it's clear that there's one human race biologically. Beyond that, though, we speak of the social construction of races, and Michael and Peggy both emphasized that this has consequences. And one of the things that I like to tell my students is that, when we talk about socially constructed races, the buildings that we work in, live in, are also social constructions. They're the product of groups of people getting together and making them over time. Now realizing that, we can't jump through the walls of the buildings. We can't ignore the realities of those constructions. I spent a great deal of time in South Africa in 1990 during the liberation period, and one of the favorite sayings of freedom fighters in South Africa was, "The way to nonracialism"—which was the goal of the freedom movement—"is through race." And I think that that's still a reality here in the United States—that we need to think about racial privilege if we're going to get to this ideal of nonracialism.

Suarez: South Bend, Indiana, is next. Hi ya, Lisa.

Caller: Thank you for taking my call. I'd like to make a point about the idea of whiteness as property, or whiteness as a social wage, and what that can add to President [Bill Clinton's] "dialogue on race." The idea of whiteness as a social wage comes from W. E. B. Dubois, and what he meant was that whiteness is a form of symbolic compensation for those of us who don't control Wall Street or Washington that are white. And the idea is that even if we're not in charge, at least we've got something to keep us off the bottom, which is that black folks are down there looking up at us. I think that the conservative whites showed us that people can be mobilized politically by their property in whiteness, and that the message of the right has been: pay attention, you're losing that property in whiteness.

My point is that I don't think the president's dialogue on race is going to get very far if it continues to be a conversation about how to achieve equality for black people and brown people, because where white people are invested in whiteness as property, equality is very difficult to achieve. And politically, what we need to recognize is that white privilege is something that we need to resist and transform politically, by dismantling the laws that support it. So, for example, we could start by changing the practice of funding schools through property taxes, 'cause that just encourages white flight to the suburbs where you can tax yourself to pay for good public schools and leave the urban schools to crumble. I'd like to ask the panel, as scholars who study whiteness, what would they recommend to the president to dismantle the privileges of whiteness that you've been talking about?

McIntosh: That's a great question. I'll answer briefly and give it to the other two. But I think until those dialogues themselves address the fact that white unearned advantage does exist, then they can't get anywhere at all on all of this.

Suarez: But, I'm sure you realize that that is a very, very hard nut. I mean, a lot of people just will not stand for that argument. Their first—

McIntosh: No, I think it's—

Suarez: —answer is, "What are you talking about white skin privilege?"

McIntosh: Well, I know. I was taught to see racism only in individual acts of meanness, and not in invisible systems that confer dominance on my group. Therefore it's a matter, I think, of conceptualizing differently the consequences of having lighter skin for people. You say they will be resistant, but I say, Ray, that this idea isn't yet even in the public world. It's in the universities, without question.

Dyson: I think that whiteness functions—and that was a great question from Indiana—in a variety of ways. It functions as an identity; it functions as an institutional expression of supremacy, or deference to that supremacy; and it functions as an ideology of superiority in a culture where, as David Roediger has indicated, and Peggy McIntosh [as well], this constellation of relations makes sure that brown and black are rendered inferior to white and so on. Ray, you're absolutely right, it's very difficult to ask the president himself to unmask some of the ways in which whiteness has been deployed by his own administration to protect him. And I'll give you a couple of quick examples and be quiet. First of all, when he was running for president the first time, he played the race card, if we can use that metaphor, in a very violent, and I think vicious, way that appealed to whiteness. That is, when he indicated that he would be running for suburban issues and not the cities, that was a real play toward whiteness, and I think that that's crucial. And then also with the Sister Souljah incident, where he refused to acknowledge that he was playing the race card.

Suarez: Today, we're talking about the emerging academic field often called whiteness studies. Joining us now is Anna Meigs. Welcome to the program.

Anna Meigs: I'm happy to be here.

Suarez: So, what do you study about, and what do your students write about?

Meigs: Well, this is a course, basically, in what I like to consider a "racial literacy," where the students learn to see race and to talk race. And given that the vast majority of the students in my classes are white, we spend a considerable amount of time in the class on these issues that your panelists have been discussing—you know, whiteness and race privilege—that people of color in the class, and whites, can see whiteness, name it, talk about it. And talk about it not just in general and in theoretical terms, but in terms of their own life. What happened today, what they saw today on the TV, or heard on the radio, or talked about at lunch.

Suarez: A lot of the places this conversation has been going so far, frankly, concentrate on the negative content of that vessel we'll call whiteness for the purposes of this conversation. Is there a disinterested critique in the functioning of whiteness, or does it inevitably get to the bad things white people do or have done, or the malign systems that they've put up for other people to negotiate? I mean, does this all end up, somehow, being an attack on the actions of white people through history?

Meigs: From my perspective, whiteness is about domination, and that's inescapable. It is about nothing else but that. But the good news is that in facing that, and dealing with that as a white person, you can come to stand in a place which is more positive, more helpful, more productive. I can't think of good things to say about whiteness. So I suppose from that perspective, there is a downer aspect to it, yes.

Suarez: And can you give me an example of some of the term projects or papers that some of your students have written? The kind of places they've been going to look for fresh questions to ask?

Meigs: The project that they do that I think they like the best is a thing called "race discourse analyses," where about ten times in the semester, they're required to turn in a paragraph or two which describes a racial incident. Well, the assumption of the course is that all incidents in the United States are racial, and that what they're looking for is to try to unpack, discover, what is racial about the interaction they had at lunch; the course that they are taking which isn't apparently about race; what someone said. The ideas we have about race are ideas that our culture gave us. We didn't generate them ourselves. We don't have the burden of that particular responsibility, but we do have the burden of carrying the ideas that the culture has given us. And now we try to discover where we are using them and where other people are using them. And let's look at them; let's look at what's going on here racially. So that's the literacy aspect that I'm looking to teach them so they can decode the events of their environment, the things they see on TV, from a racial perspective. And of course, whiteness is an important part of that. If they're only thinking it's racial if they see a person of color, well, they're missing an awful lot.

Suarez: And are these heavily signed up, these courses?

Meigs: Yeah, this course of mine is—well, I haven't been teaching it for very long, but it was one of the first to close. It enrolled very rapidly this past semester. And students are very enthusiastic about it. White students are eager to understand what it means to be white so that they can take responsibility for it. That's something that students here, at least at Macalester, are seeking—not all of them, but certainly the students in my course and beyond as well.

Suarez: Professor Meigs, thanks for being with us this hour.

Meigs: You're welcome.

Suarez: Did anything that Anna Meigs just say give anybody pause?

McIntosh: I think white privilege has positive aspects which are conditions of life that I would want to have available to everybody. So, though I respect her work and I'm delighted to hear that the students do too, with regard to the list I wrote, this kind of thing I'd like to be true for everybody, not just for whites. It's not negative; it's positive. "The day I move into new housing that I have chosen, I can be pretty sure that my new neighbors will be either neutral to me or pleasant to me." Or, "I can go shopping in the department stores of my area without being tailed by the store detective on grounds that I might be shoplifting or soliciting men." Or, "Whether I use checks or credit cards or cash, I can count on my skin color not working against the appearance that I'm financially reliable." Now these are things that make my life easy and I would like such ease to be there for all people. So to answer Anna Meigs on the fact that she can't find much positive to say about whiteness, I just want to say that the freedom from anger that these privileges allow me is a freedom I would want for everybody.

Suarez: But denying any positive value to the content of an entire culture, for want of a better term, I think starts from a proposition that we do not extend to any other field of ethnic studies.

McIntosh: Yeah, well that's interesting and I am sure the other two panelists have something to say about this. I've been trying to study what it is that the habit of being a colonial ruler developed in people of my skin color that is, in the lineup of human attributes, useful. I mean, I think among other things that this business of organizing everybody, though it was too concentrated in just a few—but that's a highly useful habit. Or categorizing; or making encyclopedias. They may have stemmed from an urge to get control of *everything*, on behalf of *everybody*. On the other hand, they did develop skills in some of white male culture, or colonial culture, that, I think, are part of the array of what the human brain is capable of. So, I wouldn't want to write it off.

Dyson: I'm torn in this regard because I think that I'm highly sympathetic to, and deeply, deeply committed to, the project of understanding whiteness, and how whiteness functions—and have learned, especially from David Roediger and from

Peggy McIntosh, in the abolition of whiteness movement, about really abolishing those very fundamentally scurrilous expressions of whiteness that have undermined the very civility that all of us want to enjoy. And that Peggy McIntosh has written about and talked about here, and certainly David Roediger. But I'm suspicious also—or skeptical may be the more correct term—about labeling whiteness itself as impervious to any redemptive or uplifting or edifying term. Now, if we understand whiteness to be the same as dysfunction or colonizing, or if we understand it as undermining and subverting, then of course whiteness has got to go. But if we understand whiteness as a much more complex phenomenon, that is both good and bad, if you will, both edifying and degrading, then we've got to figure out ways in which whiteness has functioned in our culture.

I'm reminded of Martin Luther King, Jr., who argued with those foes of his within African American communities about whiteness—and these were some of the most brilliant interpreters, if you will, of whiteness—when he said, "Listen, whiteness is not just one thing; it's a whole bunch of things at the same time." And the simultaneity of whiteness means that we've got to learn to differentiate it. We have to have a kind of grassroots ethnography where we begin to interrogate the forms and function of whiteness on the ground as it were—and where it has cohabited with blackness, with Latinoness, with redness, with yellowness. Where it's been made, and remade, in conjunction with, and in cooperation with, blackness. I mean, there are tremendous degrees of complexity within whiteness. At the same time I am skeptical, [I am also] embracing of the abolition of whiteness movement because I think that it's a very powerful movement to at least force white Americans, and the rest of us, to see that whiteness is not given. It's not natural. It's not something that we have to be stuck with our entire lives. But we've got to figure out ways in which we can allow white people to exist, while destroying the very meanings that they have created around whiteness itself. So, I'm quite frankly torn about that.

Roediger: I think that clearly there are antiracists who are white—I'm involved in part of an effort to re-celebrate John Brown Day for example—and I think that that kind of highlighting of variety of white perspectives is useful. But I wonder if there is a white culture outside of domination. On that point I agree with Anna. And Peggy moves the discussion to: what do colonial officials do? And that's still around the issue of domination. I once asked a class at the University of Missouri what they'd put in a white cultural center—there was a debate about a black cultural center. Some conservative white kids said, "We need a white cultural center if we have a black cultural center." And I said, "Well, what then would go in a white cultural center?" And there was the longest silence that I have ever experienced in a classroom after that. And the silence was broken by a hand going up, and a shout: "Elvis!" And then laughter, that Elvis would somehow be considered unambiguously white. [*Laughter*]

Suarez: Let's go to Burbank, California. Tom is with us now. Hi, Tom.

Caller: Hi. I would bring the point that I'm an Irish-American, and I am a Catholic. And some of us, when we filled out our 1990 census, put "other" and put "Irish," because to me, white in this country means White Anglo-Saxon Protestant. And not only is there no Anglo-Saxon Protestant bone in my body, my sense of American history is the Know Nothing Party against the Catholic immigrants from different countries, the Molly Maguires, the IWW and the organizing of working people. When my grandmother Annie Gleason came into New Orleans, the French side of my family called us "Shanty Irish," and it took me a few years to understand that that was not a compliment. So, I think that there is a white European ethnic Catholicism which is not part of any colonialism. The Irish didn't colonize anybody; we were colonized. We were subjected to the last bigotry besides racism, which is anti-Catholicism.

Dyson: I'm sure all of our panelists are thinking about Noel Ignatiev's book, *How the Irish Became White,* and I'll defer to my colleagues here to explain the complexities of that text in the next five minutes. But I think that Irishness itself is a very specific ethnic grouping. And you're absolutely right—there have been contests over Irish identity in this culture. And as a result, we think about schools that were prejudiced against the Irish in the early part of this century, and I went to school with Irish people. So, there's no question that there's a whole range of differences between, say, white Anglo-Saxon Protestants and the Irish, about notions of who is white and who is not. But the perverse ingenuity of whiteness is that it absorbs people by virtue of skin color. So that many people who are unable to tell the difference between Irish or Scottish or British, or white Anglo-Saxon Protestant for that matter, are the same people who understand that whiteness functions beyond ethnic groups to unite different ethnicities within white European countries, for example, around the issue that, when they come to America, they're made the same. [Whiteness] has a kind of pulverizing homogeneity; it makes people of similar skin the same despite those internal differences. And I'll add this one further point: the restaurant I was speaking about, in which I had the enormous problem in regard to the waitress, indeed was an Irish restaurant.

Suarez: Well Tom, if you're gonna drop out and no longer be white, I guess you're gonna have a lot of company if you're gonna use that fairly restrictive definition of whiteness. Was Michael Dukakis white?

Caller: No, I considered him an ethnic American.

Suarez: Okay. And—Telly Savalas?

Caller: Well, I consider white to be an anomaly that should actually be extricated. I'm much more in favor of hyphenated Americanism, because I think it shows a pride in one's own culture, one's own addition to the melting pot. I mean, I came to understand, to the extent I can understand, the black experience in America when I spend time as I do every year in the ghettos of Northern Ireland. And I was explained to by my Irish brothers and sisters in the North that they followed and modeled their civil rights movement, before Bloody Sunday in Derry, on Martin Luther King. And they understood immediately what happens when there is tumult and there are problems in the urban centers of this country. And I visualize Belfast and Derry and Armagh and the rest, and that is where I started to get some sort of wisdom about being a subjected people.

Suarez: Sorry. Before we close for the hour, thanks for your call, Peter in Saint Paul. We have a couple of interesting letters. Herbert Lewis, who is a professor of anthropology in the Wisconsin University system, writes: "Whiteness does not refer to any group of people that shares a history, a music, a culture despite the obfuscations of the advocates of this view. Most of what we're hearing about whiteness consists either of resentment against whites, or of simple-minded stereotypes of so-called 'white people.' This is no way to understand the complexity of our lives. It can only result in confusion at best, in unpleasantness and division at worst. We will not understand ourselves, our culture or history better. We will only be more angry at each other."

And Amy writes from Seattle, Washington: "Chatting about this in the classroom is OK, but doesn't mean much until it enters the everyday. And since that's where racism destroys and degrades actual lives, I think most of us want to see how this work is going to help change society for the average Juan y Juana. Cheers to your panel for addressing practical applications."

That's all the time we have for this hour. Thanks to everyone who called. And thanks especially to my guests.

7

THE MEXICANS ARE COMING
Immigration and the Borders of Fear

*with Maria Hinojosa, Henry Cisneros, Macarena Hernandez,
D. A. King, Archbishop Jose H. Gomez, Richard Langlois,
Lee Teran*

The immigration debate heated up again in the spring of 2006, when rallies around the country were held by Latino immigrants and their allies to highlight and protest the injustices, inequities, and grievances they experienced. More than four hundred thousand Latinos gathered in both Chicago and Los Angeles, and some seventy-five thousand rallied in Denver. In May 2006, a town hall meeting was convened in San Antonio, Texas, to discuss and debate the issues surrounding immigration policy and the recent flurry of protests. Hosted by journalist Maria Hinojosa, the roundtable featured, among others, former HUD Secretary Henry Cisneros, talented journalist Macarena Hernandez [whose work *New York Times* journalist Jayson Blair plagiarized], and D. A. King, a noted critic of immigration policy. I was invited to join the group and to draw parallels between black freedom struggles and the Latino immigration struggle, no mean feat in light of the severe black critique of Latino immigration and protests. I believe this is one of the most important debates I have engaged in, for no other reasons than to show solidarity with Latino immigrants and to further combat the stereotypes of blackness that many of them transport and inherit. Since Latinos and blacks are the largest minority groups in the nation, it behooves us to explore common ground in creating a potential alliance that can have substantive impact in the political and social arena.

Maria Hinojosa: Good evening. It's been an unprecedented time in our country. On that, I think, all Americans can agree. Talk to any Latino, recent immigrant, or long-term resident about the rallies, and their eyes will light up and they'll tell you how energized they are by this exercise of democracy and visibility. But others see something else entirely—a presumptuous gathering of people who are here illegally in the first place. What right do they have even to demonstrate? But one thing is clear. The estimated eleven million undocumented people threaded into the fabric of our lives are not likely to be going anywhere anytime soon. So, how do we move ahead? We're going to just dive into our conversation with our panelists.

But first, I want to throw a question out to the audience. It may be a little uncomfortable, but I want to ask you, how many of you know an undocumented person? Show of hands. And our panel? So that's just about everyone. Okay. Not to put you on the spot, but a question to you. How many of you think—think, maybe without knowing—but think you may have at one time employed an undocumented immigrant? Okay, just a few of you are willing to raise your hand. But that's okay. So what's changed here is not really their presence, but rather their visibility. Right, Henry Cisneros, former mayor of San Antonio, former secretary of Housing Urban Development? Tell me what you name what's going on in this country.

Henry Cisneros: Oh, I think you name it change. And I think you name it a time of an important national dialogue. But I don't think you name it chaos or panic, or a time of societal meltdown, or cultural Armageddon. I don't think it's any of those things that some people are panicking about. I think it's a time when our country is going through some fundamental demographic changes and economic changes that I think, in the long run, are going to work to the benefit of our country. This is going to revitalize our nation with new, young energetic workers in the midst of an American society that is aging. I think that's what's happening.

Hinojosa: Same thing, Macerana? Energized, or not?

Macarena Hernandez: You know, Latinos have never been good at organizing, so when I saw half a million people in Dallas, I thought, "This is great; it's wonderful" because not all the people that were marching are here illegally. Some of them are people like me who are children of immigrants. So I think it's great that we're mobilizing. And maybe we can use this energy to address other parts of our community that need to be addressed.

Hinojosa: You're a journalist with the *Dallas Morning News*, a columnist and editorial writer. Are they seeing the same thing that you're seeing, your bosses?

Hernandez: People in Dallas who write to me—I have hate mail in my in box. No, they're not seeing the same thing, and I wonder why is it that they're not seeing the same thing. And I think some of the message is getting lost in the translation. Because if you're out there, and you see these kids in strollers, these grandfathers in walkers, these people wanting to say, "We just want to come out, be out of the shadows, contribute to your society, because we already are America." And I think that's still energizing and encouraging.

Hinojosa: Okay. D. A. King. You are from Atlanta—Marietta—and you're an activist. You call yourself an anti-illegal alien activist.

D. A. King: I'm against illegal immigration, yes.

Hinojosa: So just tell me how you respond when you're hearing Cisneros and Macerana Hernandez saying what they're saying. What do you see?

King: I see it a little bit differently. The way I look at it, what we're going through now is a decision on whether or not the United States of America will be permitted to have borders and enforce its own laws. I see it as a very large sovereignty issue. And I agree that the rallies were very, very impressive. Again, I look at it a little bit differently. I think the rallies that we all saw on TV the last couple of weeks have done more to open up the average American's eyes on how large an issue, if not a problem, this really is. So I am urging people to have more rallies like that.

Hinojosa: Archbishop Gomez—Archbishop of San Antonio—an issue or a problem? What do you see?

Jose H. Gomez: Oh, I see an issue. And I think we see a global reality. That people are moving. The means of communication are better now, and people are going from one place to the other. You see it in Europe, you see it in Latin America, you see it in the United States. I think it's the reality that we have to be aware, and what we are looking for is the best possible solution for this issue. I think, as Secretary Cisneros said, and also the bishops of the United States have said, it's a blessing for the United States, the presence of so many Hispanics in our country.

Hinojosa: Michael Eric Dyson, University of Pennsylvania. You're a writer, you are also a radio show host. From your perspective, what you're hearing in the African American community—a lot of people kind of thought, "Oh, everybody's going to be rallying here together." Not necessarily. A lot of Latinos are saying this is the new civil rights movement. Is it the new civil rights movement, and what do African Americans have to say about that?

Michael Eric Dyson: Well, I think there's undoubtedly an element of civil rights struggle here: self-definition; the reorganization of the logic of what it means to be an American; American citizenship. Most of the people sitting here are immigrants to America—just at what point did you come? This is the fourth great wave of immigration. Think about the first wave—the Western Europeans who founded the nation. The second wave [was] in the middle of the nineteenth century, when you had Eastern European people coming in an influx. Most Jews and Poles and

Italians arrived in the mid-1800s, late 1800s, or early 1900s. And of course, the nation was undergoing profound industrialization then. The third stage [included] the first two decades of the twentieth century. When you think of Ellis Island—a million immigrants a year came to this country, largely from Europe. [The fourth stage] since the 1980s—twenty million people, mostly from Asia and Central America, are coming to this nation. So there's an extraordinary expansion of what it means to be an American. *E Pluribus Unum*—"out of many, one."

From African American people, I've heard some distressing and discouraging moments of resistance, an appropriation of American white supremacy, xenophobia—that is, resistance to the other. The reproduction of this, I think, pathological notion of pure American identity. If we're a dog, if we're a canine, we're mongrels to begin with. This ain't no pure nation. So, for me, I see African American people who are afraid because they figure the Mexicans are coming over to take our jobs. And if the Mexicans take our jobs, and if they work for less than half the minimum wage, they're going to displace us. And so I say to them, "Stop that. It is the people from above—corporate interests—who manipulate African Americans and Latinos against each other." And we don't get at the real problem. The real problem is the inability of America to acknowledge that our borders are already permeable, they're already flexible. Let's stop with the xenophobia. Let's open up to honest dialogue and discussion, but the resistance, as if this is a racial or ethnic Armageddon, is way overblown.

And it *is* a civil rights struggle. When black people say, "Well, they're going to take our word and term." Let me see, when Martin Luther King, Jr., visited with Jawaharlal Nehru in India, I wonder if the Indians said, "Well, African American people are now trying to appropriate Gandhi and nonviolence for their purposes." It's a universal thing. It's a universal struggle. And I say to Latino brothers and sisters, "Amen, and welcome to the struggle. And let's continue to expose the realities of American ethnic bigotry."

Hinojosa: Okay. Lee Teran, you are an immigration rights lawyer—have been for many, many years. Your students at St. Mary's University, your own children, are they calling this a new civil rights movement, or not?

Lee Teran: They are. My students are, yes. And I agree with them. I think it is a new civil rights movement. And for me, as an immigration lawyer, it is watching the effects of many ill-defined immigration laws, immigration statutes that have passed over the last ten years and really affected negatively this community. And I think finally the community is reacting, and saying, "Enough! Enough punishing us. Enough punitive measures against immigrants." This is a struggle of migrants coming, and jobs being available for them. And to turn to the immigrant community and say, "This is your fault," and punish them both in civil and criminal ways—I think the community has had enough, and they're finally getting together.

Hinojosa: Thank you. Now Richard Langlois, you are the president of the local Republican Party of Bear County here in Texas.

Richard Langlois: Chairman.

Hinojosa: Chairman. So what's happening within the Republican Party? And you should know that we did ask several elected Republican officials to come. None of them said yes. And we wondered a little bit why. Is there a crisis in the Republican Party about this particular issue, and what are you telling them?

Langlois: I don't think there's a crisis. I think, like in any organization, there's a division of views. First off, I think we have to look at the fact that I don't think the word "immigrant" should be used. Because these people that are here illegally, they're not immigrants. They're people that broke the law by coming into our country and did not use the means to come in through Ellis Island, like we did back in the past, and things like this. And that's where the problem has been created. I don't think they all ought to be put in prison or anything like this. But I think that's where we have to get some legislation going in so that we can handle this situation, so that they can achieve their identity. It's not a civil rights movement, because they don't *have* any rights. They don't have the rights that the blacks had, because the blacks were brought over here. These people came over themselves, illegally. And that's where the crisis has developed, is their illegal status.

Hinojosa: This is what I find fascinating, where you can say they don't have any rights at all. And you've heard this a lot after the May 1st National Boycott Day—almost a sense of, "These uppity immigrants. Who do they think they are?" But would we want them to stay indoors, then? Is that what we want? Do we want these undocumented immigrants who are here to stay behind closed doors, to not come out, to not take to the streets?

Cisneros: There are a series of factors, they're called push and pull factors, that brought something like twelve million people to this country. Push, because there weren't enough jobs in their home countries so they are pushed out. But pull, equally powerful, by economic forces here, that pull people to jobs that need to be filled. Whole industries—agriculture, stoop labor in the fields, food processing, labor in construction, and many others that are crying for people to work. So that's why twelve million people are here now. That's the core of it. That there are twelve million human beings, with rights—they have, at minimum, human rights, and certainly ought not be exposed to the kinds of abuses that they are today. They're living in the shadows without protections, children living in bad circumstances, the way people should not have to live. So what we have to do as a country—I think the legislation that's being now discussed has to have three elements.

Yes, border enforcement, because a country has to have sovereign control of its borders. But also, some kind of guest worker program that allows people to be recognized as workers, to be able to come and go with procedure, see their families, and so forth. And thirdly, a path to legalization, which is the heart of the problem in the present legislation: that many are opposed to that legalization. But without it, then we leave people in the shadows. So some kind of path to legalization, and that's where it gets real technical. Because some people say, "Well, yes, but they have to go home first." That's not a practical answer.

Hernandez: And when people say it's not a civil rights movement, they forget that [for] a lot of these families, while our government turned a blind eye, didn't enforce its laws. They came across, they bought homes, they have the two kids who were born in America, the cat, the two-car garage. They have full lives here. Maybe if some people believe that they don't have rights, their children, as American citizens, do have rights. And that's why I feel like it's a civil rights movement. As for me, as a Latina whose parents were immigrants, this is like the first time I see any kind of movement, any kind of saying, "You know what? We're done being invisible." And what's so bad with being visible? It's kind of the sense of, like, "Que igualdos. Como se atreven." ("How dare they equate themselves to us.") And it's, like, you know what? No one wants to create a second-class citizenship, an underground world within a country, because that only will affect all of us.

Hinojosa: So what do you think about that, Michael? I mean, this notion of staying behind closed doors. What Richard is saying, "They don't have the right to be on the streets." If we say that, what does that say about us as a democracy?

Dyson: Well, we've got to come out of the democratic closet. I think that it's akin to being gay—hiding your sexuality, hiding your ethnicity, hiding your nationality. I think it's ridiculous. First of all, I find it interesting, and altogether amusing, that people who stood tooth and nail against African American people—even arguably today—would then appropriate our experience and say, "Well, they're not like the black people." Well, they don't have to be like us to draw from similar situations and circumstances. But I think in many ways, they are. First of all, we broke the law too. It was against the law of America for a black person to be free. So obviously, I don't genuflect before the altar of the law. If I gave ultimate precedence to the law—Martin Luther King, Jr., broke the law. Rosa Parks broke the law. So breaking of the law means that they adhere to a higher moral law.

Secondly, when you talk about "They have no rights"—they have a right because they breathe! They have a right because blood flows through their veins. We are part of a global community. America's imperialist and, I think, very narrow conception of what it means to be a world citizen is the problem here. So I think this isolationist impulse needs to give way to the best of American tradition.

What is the best of American tradition? "Come to our borders." What does it say on the Statue of Liberty? Now, some people would say, "Well, it says legally." What did "wop" mean? Without papers. (Guap, of course, was a derogatory term that meant pimp or ruffian). You say it like, "We, the Italians?" There were people here who were sneaking in under the border. You have the difference between the "wet foot" and "dry foot" policy among, say, white Cubans versus black Dominicans or Haitians. So we know that there's incredible internecine squabbling going on *even* among Latino communities.

But my point is: America needs to own up to the fact that it shouldn't have submerged populations who are in the shadows. Come out and be free. We've exploited these people. They have been our gardeners. They have been our nannies, despite what people have said—that they haven't hired them. They have done everything for us. How can we have a lazy Mexican stereotype when they got about fifteen jobs? And if you think they're going to take over in America, the reality is that they have been here, they have contributed. What we need to do is to acknowledge their presence and then, as Brother Cisneros says, get a pathway towards legalization that acknowledges their humanity. But to say they have no rights—we are not God. You cannot dismiss off the face of the earth human beings who have come here and made a contribution, and now we bellyache and bemoan them, because it's not to our advantage to acknowledge their presence or, at least, to give them rights.

Hinojosa: Okay. D. A. I know you've just been—

King: The question has to be asked: "Is it a human rights violation for the United States to secure its own borders? Is it somehow un-American for us to enforce the law equally?" I am a child of the '60s. I heard the words "xenophobe" and "bigot" a minute ago. I have been called considerably worse than that for simply saying that we should apply the law equally as we were taught in the '60s. I firmly believe that if we do not secure our borders, we don't have borders. And it's my observation that if we don't have borders, we don't have a country. I hear a lot about the globalization of the world, or the global economy. There are a great many Americans who are not willing to give up the United States of America in the name of globalization. For me, and I think for most Americans, this is not about ethnicity or color. But neither do I recognize it as a civil right to come into my country, illegally, take a job for less than an American of any color, and then demand that you be allowed to stay. And I think later on we'll probably get into the last time that we tried the path to legalization. In 1986 we were told, as a nation, "We're going to legalize about a million people." (It turned out to be nearly three million people.) "And after we do this, folks, then we're going to secure our borders. Then we're going to sanction these criminal employers and the bankers who are, in fact, the magnet that draws these people here." Does any of that sound familiar?

Dyson: What about the people who come in from Germany, Sweden—for the information superhighway? You're talking about push and pull economic factors— the expansion of the opportunity along the information superhighway has brought a great degree of immigrants who are highly educated, because you've got a severely segregated market. Either they're well educated and highly fluent in the languages of American commerce, or they're at the bottom of the economic pool. There have been a lot of people coming over to this country from non- Latino based countries, and we haven't cried, we haven't kvetched, we haven't bellyached or bemoaned their presence. And I think at that level, Brother D. A., I would at least say that race is a signifier. Ethnicity is a signifier for a kind of re- sistance to the opening of American borders. It is a civil rights struggle for me, be- cause we have exploited their labor, we have allowed them, as Macerana says, to come in and to have jobs and families and so on. We even say, legally, possession is nine-tenths of the law. Where they're here in America, they've had children who are now citizens. Would we, for the sake of trying to enforce the border, tear up families? What happened to American family values? I thought we were the people who were concerned about mothers and fathers and everybody living to- gether. Why would we then separate families in deference to a political ideology which is not a conservative notion to begin with?

Hinojosa: Archbishop Gomez, there are some people who say, in fact, that there are some laws which are meant to be broken. There are some laws that may not have the moral base. And I know that there's a lot of contradictions around what people are saying. But what do you think?

Gomez: Well, I think this dialogue, it's exactly what people are talking about: how to put together the reality of the undocumented people that are in the United States, and the dignity of the human person, and our laws. Because I think what is clear is that something is wrong, because somehow we allowed twelve million people to come in without papers. So I think that something must be wrong.

Hinojosa: In fact, some people say we're placing the blame on them. But some- how, we allow them to come into the country, because we weren't policing our borders and, my gosh, they got jobs too. So is it all their fault?

Gomez: First of all, no one wants to be undocumented, or illegal. And I think we all agree that we need to protect our borders. But we need to be realistic and solve the problem. Like you said, first of all, even before naming someone illegal, he or she is a human person. And every single person has the dignity of being a child of God, for us, at least in the Catholic Church. So that makes a big difference. I think the important thing for all of us is to find the solution to the problem. So our prayers are that we are able, as a consequence of this dialogue, to really find a solution for our reality. That's going to be a blessing to all of us.

Cisneros: Maria, in the interest of just trying to get a solution, at least in this little group: if we were to concede, D. A., that the border needs to be protected, so that needs to happen. We need to put more money into border protection of all kinds—all kinds of electronic devices, and human resources, etcetera. So this country has a right and a duty to protect its borders. Now, we all should do something about the workers, because the country needs the workers. And so some kind of guest worker program, which the left and labor have traditionally opposed, they are now willing to concede. But it has to be linked to some method of humane treatment and legalization of the twelve million people who are here. What's your answer to that?

King: My answer, Mr. Cisneros, and first of all—

Cisneros: I mean, in the spirit of kind of finding a middle ground, if there is such a possibility.

King: I'm told that the definition of insanity, or something that Einstein said, was "Insanity is doing the same thing over and over again, and expecting different results." I think we have already tried the middle ground, in 1986, and it's a recurring theme in my discussions—most Americans are not even aware of the fact that we had an amnesty for three million illegal aliens in 1986. So the middle ground, sir, must be, first of all, to punish the employers, if not the government that didn't punish them. We, as the American people, did not allow these people in here. Our government has failed us.

Cisneros: But all of that has *happened.* Those are realities. Twelve million human beings—

King: There's the reality word again.

Cisneros: So what is your answer to twelve million living, breathing human beings?

Gomez: I also think technology has improved a lot. I mean, now every single person that comes to the United States that is a foreign national, they get fingerprinted and a picture is taken. That didn't happen in 1986. So I think we can protect our borders better just using the technology that we have here.

Hinojosa: Here's what I want to know, D. A—and you and I have gone back and forth on this several times. What is supposed to happen? I need you to explain to me, to all of us, what happens with twelve million people? Do we ask them to leave, and hope that they will? Do we go door to door? What does that mean? In your dream-o-vision of the solution of the problem of getting rid of the illegal aliens in the United States, how does it happen?

King: I want to dispute the twelve million figure. I believe it to be in excess of twenty. But the answer is that this problem did not develop overnight. This took twenty-five, thirty, maybe forty years to happen to us as a nation. Neither will it be solved overnight. Nobody I know, no reasonable person that I know, expects people to be rounded up and taken out of the country by sundown tomorrow. People are giving—the people who don't study this—two choices: we either legalize the millions of people who are here illegally, or we round them up. But as you said, there is a third option that should be discussed more. It's called attrition by enforcement. Nobody breaks into Disneyland if they can't ride the rides. If we begin to punish the employers and the bankers, the people who are profiting from this, the magnets, if we actually enforce existing law, then I believe people will begin to go home and improve their own countries. Now, it is true that we're going to have to deport some people. And nobody likes that thought. But Mexico deports more people every year than does the United States. So it has to be part of the answer. Attrition by enforcement, to answer your question, Maria, a gradual decrease of the population, I think, is a very reasonable answer to that.

Hinojosa: Richard Langlois—and the Republican Party is going to step up and say—

Langlois: It's got to be a two-way street.

Hinojosa: But tell me about the Republican Party, the Republican Party now in power, [what will they do about] D. A. King and his position?

Langlois: Well, I think President Bush has proposed legislation pretty much to what Mr. Cisneros has said. But he also mentioned we need more money in border security. We do. But they've also kicked up border security tremendously. You can't come from the border without going through Checkpoint Charlies. These people still get through.

Hinojosa: In fact, it's the most money *ever*, in *history*, that has been spent on securing the borders now.

Langlois: Yeah. Many more customs agents, ice agents, whatever you want to call them. And they stop people every day. It's an ongoing cycle. But the real situation is this: we do have twelve, twenty million people here, many of them in Texas, who have a driver's license, that shouldn't be registered to vote, because they're not a citizen. And that's what I meant is, they don't have *that* type of right. So the question is this: we do have to enact legislation to provide some census of who they are. They have to come forward and say, "Yes, I'm not documented; I'm such-and-such." And then we have to have a mechanism to identify and determine whether or not they can qualify to become legalized in some respects. Do they get some kind of a residence card, or something like this? But they have to take the initiative too. Yes, it has been a push and pull. Yes, a lot of people want to employ them and things like this. But on the other hand, we've got to put a stop to the illegals from coming in somehow. We have to have an accounting device for who's here. Get them certified for whatever way we're going to legalize them, or whatever. I don't believe we should send them over. I don't think putting people in jail or prison who are here illegally right now—if we did that, I told a congressman this within the last month—if we put anybody in prison who is here illegally right now, we'd have a million grandmothers, who have probably been living here for twenty or thirty years, in prison. We don't want that. The Republican Party doesn't want that. I think a lot of people in the Republican Party are very level-headed about this. I mean, there are some groups that want to hang everybody. But that's not the way it should be.

Hinojosa: Lee Teran, are you seeing levelheadedness within the Republican Party on this—

Teran: No.

Hinojosa: —or are you seeing lots of contradictions? And, in fact, in terms of the politics and the legality of this, are Democrats putting forth anything? Or are you more concerned about the legal issues here?

Teran: Well, I don't think any of the proposals are going to solve the problem, frankly. I think that yes, there should be border security, but you're not going to get border security by building walls or by increasing border patrol. We've been doubling border patrol since IRCA [Immigration Reform and Control Act] in 1986. Every time there's a legislation, we double border patrol. We've put an enormous amount of money into prisons. There are prisons all over south Texas filled with undocumented workers. It's not going to stop the flow if the employers are still here bringing in the workers, and the workers are still coming in from those countries needing a place to work. There has to be some way—other than immigration law, I think—to deal with the migration of people and the employers bringing them in from another country.

Dyson: And I think, on top of that, speaking of what Brother D. A. talked about vis-à-vis reinforcing the legality of existing laws—maybe we've come to a point where we see the laws are not working. Maybe the actual existence, God forbid, of the free market—I've been a critic of that, but I thought my conservative and Republican brothers and sisters were down with the free market—if the free market has dictated that people be drawn here as a result of the economic conditions of the construction business, of retail, of food industries, where black and Latinos compete over ever scarcer resources—but in an expanding job market for opportunity—well, maybe the laws are out of tune and out of touch with the actual practice of American democracy. Maybe what's bursting at the seam is a rethinking of what it means to be an American. And maybe this new development has suggested that we have to change the law to reflect the new America in which we live.

King: Before we give up on the law, Michael, I would ask a twenty-year period of time where we actually try to enforce it. We have had a series of administrations who have refused to punish these employers for bringing these people in.

Hinojosa: But, D. A., the question is, it's not as if they don't see what's happening. So they're making a choice?

Cisneros: Let me just say, for me, what I don't understand is, fundamentally, the American economy is almost as strong as it's ever been. And it's the strongest force on the globe. And immigration has contributed to that, including illegal immigration, whether you want to acknowledge it or not. I mean, pricing and production and just almost every aspect of our lives—construction boom, home ownership boom, retail sales. I mean, we've got glitches like gas prices and such, but fundamentally we're very, very strong. And so, this has been part of the success. What really bothers people, I think, and what causes this anger, is that these new immigrants look different. People are afraid of cultural change in America because they see different faces, and different last names, and different languages, and so forth. But I would say, "America, you need to get over it," because this is going to be the salvation of the country. Japan, Germany, Italy, France—losing populations, aging rapidly—we're not going to have that problem, because we're a good country, and these people come here. I live in a neighborhood where I see these people on my street. These are human beings who come here to work hard, raise their children, have a better life, go to church, pay their taxes. They're paying their way. What is the problem?

Dyson: Samuel Huntington, who wrote that famous book, *Clash of Civilizations*, of course [has written] about the Hispanic threat. And the very thing that Brother Cisneros is talking about is real here. And this is why I think that [we need] much more progressive voices, even with Latino communities, who've absorbed the discourse and rhetoric of, "We're *grateful* to be here in America," to begin to challenge some of the negative fallout from American ideology, which is an "us versus them." It's very sharply drawn. And so now, it *is* the fact that we've got to speak a different language: "Are they talking about me in my face? Are they speaking about me in ways that are untoward? I don't know what they're saying. I can't control the language, and if I can't control the language they're contaminating the nation."

And I think that, unless we confront the fundamental racial issue–and Brother D. A., I'm not speaking about you personally, because I don't even know you that well, right?–I'm talking about a broader orientation where I've seen the fear in white people. This is white panic. This is really a kind of white panic about the redefinition of borders, recruiting, ironically enough, African American people who, because they're crapped on by the existing "powers that be," now forge alliances with the very people who disdain them, to argue against the Latino brother and sister. And I'm saying, "No. Let's do the best of what we do in America." Martin Luther King, Jr., joined Cesar Chavez to talk about a march to Washington against poverty. Let's talk about Archbishop [Oscar] Romero, who said, "When I feed the poor, they call me a saint. When I ask why they are poor, they call me a communist." So my point is to figure out how we can join together. If blacks and Latinos would come together and forge coalitions and alliances, we could challenge some of the economic inequality in this country. And I'll tell you what else [makes folk] fearful: if we actually have reform of immigration law, that's better for everybody. That rising tide lifts every boat. Because now the people who have been crapped upon–who are black, or Asian–who have been subjected to unfair labor law, now are advantaged and, as a result of it, are benefited by the reform in the law. So I think there's nothing but good that can come out of opening these borders and making a new America that acknowledges who we are.

King: Now we've gotten to it. Would you like to see America without borders, Michael?

Dyson: No, not at all. The border's in place.

King: Well, I think that's the path we're on.

Dyson: But it's what borders we're talking about.

King: Well, the existing borders and the existing law. Earlier you said the law's not working. I maintain that we haven't really tried to enforce them. I'm not going to get drawn in a black/Latino thing. For me–and I know you don't know me, but please take my word–that is not my issue. And neither is it the issue of most people who are upset about this crisis. If we do not secure our borders–and I hope we can all agree that the very, very first thing that can be done, before we do anything else, whatever else this discussion goes to, I hope we can all agree that American borders have to be secured, period. Is there anybody here who does not agree with that?

Hernandez: I think that when we talk about borders, we just point to the Rio Grande, and it's not like any of the hijackers [on 9/11] crossed the Rio Grande to hop on their planes. So when we talk about securing the borders we really need to get serious about securing *all* the borders. Because then, it seems like the discussion is geared towards Latinos. And that I think is the most dangerous thread out of this whole argument.

King: Nobody said secure the borders against Latinos. We're saying, "Secure the borders."

Hernandez: We keep pointing to the Rio Grande.

Dyson: The reality is that the massive amounts of people who are from Latino border states, and border countries, who come here are the water carriers, if you will, for the burden of this new wave of Americanism. Let me say why I think "borders" is a questionable proposition here. Because as a person who was *brought* across those borders—as you've acknowledged and other people have acknowledged—historically speaking, I'm a bit skeptical and suspicious of people who now want to reinforce borders, when it wasn't border patrol when you're bringing Africans as marketplace enhancers a couple of centuries ago. Now you say, "Well, that's a long time ago." Well, the reality is, we continue to be advantaged and benefited by the process of opening up what it means to be American. When I hear "borders" that's a code word. The code word is: "They're not us. They're not white people, they're not Anglos, they're not people from Western or Eastern Europe." Because we didn't have a problem when *they* were coming over. We didn't have a problem with the masses of people who were flooding this country who are people who can become white. And part of the problem with some Latinos, as well, is the virtue of white skin privilege. So they get in here, hibernate, think they're white, and then what this debate makes them understand, "Naw, you down here with the brothers and sisters. You have been re-Mexicanized. You have been re-Latinized. And so now you've got to forge a coalition and connection with those who [have borne] the brunt of anti-American fervor from the beginning."

Langlois: I don't consider this to be a racial issue, like Brother Dyson's trying to make it. It's not a racial issue.

Dyson: It's ethnicity.

Langlois: One thing is: who has ever asked an immigrant what they want? What do they really want? That's a real issue about where we're going: Do they want to come in the country, work, and then keep their family in Mexico and not become citizens? Or have a certain amount of them been here so long that they have assimilated into the system, but yet they don't have their citizenship, and they've been undercover, so to speak, and now they want to throw the covers off and come out.

Hinojosa: But what do you think, Macarena? What do you think they want? Do they want to come here? And not only come here, but do they want to come here and change America? There are many people who've said they want to come here, they never want to speak English, they don't want to assimilate.

Hernandez: That assimilation argument is so old. By the third generation, most Latinos speak only English. Half of them will marry outside their ethnic box.

Hinojosa: In fact, within Latinos, aren't people worrying, "Oh my God, my children aren't going to speak Spanish anymore.

Hernandez: Oh yeah.

Hinojosa: "They're not going to marry a Latino. Oh, my God."

Langlois: But many of them that I'm familiar with—and as a criminal defense attorney, I've represented many of them—they will come in here, and part of them want to stay here and assimilate, like you say. A lot of them want to keep their identity back in Mexico.

Cisneros: What happens is that life intervenes. A young man comes here to work. And he works two or three years, and he misses his family back home. But then he meets someone, and they get married, and they have children. And this young man continues to work two, three jobs. This is the hardest working group in America.

Hinojosa: But they don't learn English fast enough, Henry Cisneros.

Cisneros: And they have children, and now going home is really not an option because life has intervened and taken over. These are human *beings*, right? And if America would only understand that the motivation behind most of these folks is to live a better life. And they will sacrifice to make that better life in this country. And make the country better.

Hernandez: It all has to do with how long they've been in the country. When my parents came here in the late '70s, [they] had been crossing the border since they were eight years old, working in the King Ranch, picking cotton. So it was back then when the traffic reaching both countries was a lot more open. And my parents always said, "When you guys turn eighteen we're going to go back to Mexico, and we'll see you." But you know what? Life intervened. They had kids who had no desire to go back to a little ranch in Mexico, where there's no A/C, and no running water. So that became, like, "This is your life now. You have kids here. You can't go back." And my mother still says, "When I die, you're going to have to bury me over there." A couple of months ago she's like, "I'm rethinking that, because who's going to go and give me flowers? You guys don't even want to come back here."

Dyson: This is home.

Hernandez: Exactly.

Hinojosa: But let me ask you this—because there are a lot of issues around the question of assimilation. And many, many non-Latinos who call themselves liberal or progressives say, "On this particular issue I'm a little bit concerned. My gosh, you know, they don't speak English, they don't want to learn it, they don't want to assimilate." There's all this talk. Where, in fact, in a study that came out of State University of New York, they said that a number of people from the left and the right are underplaying the modern signs of assimilation. They're viewing American society as much more fractured along ethnic and cultural lines than appears to be the case. That actually, the Latinos are not that different, Archbishop Gomez, than other immigrant groups. But at this moment it doesn't seem like that's what's playing out with many Americans.

Gomez: That's correct. Well, I kind of prefer integration instead of assimilation. Because I think we have learned the value of every single culture—the Italians, the Irish, the African American.

Hinojosa: But some people might say, in this particular case with Latinos, that's what makes it different: there's too many of them. And they're always going to be here. And they're always going to continue to come.

Gomez: Right. But that doesn't mean that they're not going to participate in the life of the country. I mean, every single ESL [English as a Second Language] school has a long waiting list, because people want to learn English. They know that if they don't learn English, they'll never make progress in our society.

Cisneros: But that concern has confidence in the American system and way of life. It is so strong, and so powerful that these folks want to be Americans in short order here.

Hinojosa: But the perception, Henry Cisneros …

Cisneros: I know what the perception is.

Hinojosa: So how do you—

Dyson: It amazes me—when you think about Poles, and Jews, and Italians, and Lithuanians—this debate about assimilation is not a Latino-specific debate. This debate has been going on from the very beginning of time. Again, we're talking about Eastern European versus Western European: Are you going to assimilate, are you going to speak, are you going to stay in Italian communities, are you going to be in the ethnic barrio, are you going to stay in the ghetto? No. The reality is, there's always a give and take, and a push and pull, between being part of the larger fabric of American society and maintaining distinct ethnic and racial identities. I think that the fear, again, is not about assimilation. But the Archbishop made a critical point: the difference between assimilation and integration—what's the difference? Assimilation assumes that the white norm is the only value that should be emulated. If you go back to Samuel Huntington's book about the Hispanic threat, he said [paraphrasing]: "Look, when those white Europeans came over, it was beautiful. We have an Anglo-American country whose values we respect. Now that the Latinos are trying to come over, they're subverting the very unanimity and solidarity of our community." And I'm saying that's hogwash. The reality is that assimilation means I have to be like you in order to be accepted as an American. Integration says we bring the beauty and the diversity and the multidisciplinary realities of our identities together to form—whether you want to call it—a quilt, a stew, a melting pot, whatever analogy works for you. The point is, I don't have to give up being me in order to be part of white America. I help define what this nation is. I don't want to bleach my black skin in an ocean of whiteness. I don't think you have to bleach brownness in an ocean of whiteness.

Hinojosa: Macerana, I want to ask you about the question around living in two worlds. When you and I first spoke you said, "My God, I've always felt like I've lived in two worlds, but never as much as now." And I think it's a question that Latino activists, and immigrant rights activists, have to answer. And even Samuel Huntington said, "Will a bilingual society be a disaster? Not necessarily. But it will be a different a country." So, is it a problem to be in a different country? Do we have this notion that this country can't change, so we legislate a halt to change?

Hernandez: You know, I think this question of assimilation and fear is probably—like I started saying earlier—is probably the most dangerous threat of the whole immigration debate. Because it puts people like me—I go to Mexico. They don't think I'm a Mexican. At all. I'm a *gringa*. And I'm here in the United States—they don't think I'm an American. I am a Mexican. So I'm a "Pocha," okay? [Pocha/ pocho used to be a derogatory term that Mexicans called Mexican Americans, who can't speak Spanish and aren't really Mexican.] And I embrace the word, because that's the only space that I tend to fit in, especially in these days. And I think that kind of talk, that fear, just fuels this kind of marginalized sense, where people like me are going to feel like they're not either one. And this whole question about what an American is—it's, like, Americans come in all flavors. There are all different kinds of Americans. And people look at me, and they've always asked me, "Where are you from?" and I say, "From south Texas." "No, no, no, really, where are you from?" "Oh, La Jolla, you won't even know where it is on the map." "Is it on the other side?" I'm like, "Oh, are you asking me what my ethnic background is?" And I think that as long as people look at me and don't see an American, we're going to keep fostering this divide.

Cisneros: Maria, I think it's important to, out of this dialogue that our country's going through right now, refocus on what it means to be an American. And what it is, is a set of values. Values like due process—

Hinojosa: But many people, that's exactly what they're afraid of, having to redefine what an American is.

Cisneros: —freedom of speech, freedom of religion, a sense of enterprise, a recognition of private property. And those values, people of all ethnic groups can respect. In fact, people from other countries come here because they know this is a superior system. They come here because their system didn't work, and they're coming to sign on to this dream. And they're going to have the passion of the convert for this system. And I don't think Americans need to be afraid of that.

Dyson: But there's some insularity going on there as well, because we're the only nation that is proud of our monolinguisticality. We speak one language—A-muhr-rican. We don't even speak English; we speak A-muhr-rican. 'Cause you ain't speaking what T. S. Eliot spoke; you're not speaking as Tennyson spoke: "Though much is taken, much abides / And though we're not now that strength which in old days moved earth and heaven." You're not speaking their variety of English; we're speaking A-muhr-rican. And the problem is, we've got cabdrivers that we think are our servants, who speak four languages and three distinct dialects, and we think we're superior. They're so much more educated; they're so much more world citizens. We rely upon an isolationist impulse. And I think the reality is, we could agree or disagree with Secretary Cisneros about what constitutes an American, because we could quibble about that. But the bottom line is, those fundamental values need to constantly be rethought. That's the beauty of the American way of life, to rethink. The Declaration of Independence and the Constitution, the Bill of Rights, didn't include black people and women. We fought hard to redefine that to include and expand what our notion of America is. There's nothing wrong with constantly rethinking and opening the borders of American identity so that we can include everybody who's here.

Hinojosa: Is there something wrong with that, though, D. A.?

King: First of all, every time Michael has spoken he's brought up either color, race, or ethnicity. Every time. I hope that we're not here talking about that. I came here to talk about illegal immigration. And it is my respectful observation that no matter what color you are, or no matter from where you come, in this country the rule of law is what we were founded upon. The language thing: press one to speak Celtic in Japan. We are not the only monolingual—and we're no longer, by the way, a monolingual nation.

Hinojosa: You have a problem with that, don't you, D. A.? You have said, yes, your focus is against the illegality of the immigrant. But you have said that one of your concerns is that Georgia is going to become "Georgia-fornia."

King: It's a term that I coined to try to get people's attention. Nobody that I know is afraid of America evolving and changing. But it's like someone coming into my house, and I cook them dinner. It is my decision. If they come into my house and take my dinner it is an entirely different situation. If America is going to be changed because people are allowed to come here simply because, in violation of our laws, the laws that most of us are held up to—if America's going to be changed because our government is not enforcing our laws, because it is profitable for the people who put them in office, I reject that change.

Hinojosa: And what do you do with that, though, D. A.? I have seen you, because you walked along the streets of Atlanta, and you stopped undocumented immigrants and you asked them to present their papers. That was something that you once did. I'm not sure if you're doing it now. But what do you do with the issues that you have? Are you protesting in front of the Department of Homeland Security? And saying, "Come on, go police the border?" Are you in front of President Bush, in the White House?

King: Actually, last April I had about seven hundred people doing exactly that at the White House. I protest in front of banks who are making mortgage loans to people they know to be in this country illegally. It's a federal felony—

Hinojosa: But they're doing it. And somehow it's allowed.

King: Because someone is doing it doesn't mean it can't be stopped. This is not a weather event. We can. And we should stop pretending that it's impossible for us to stop people coming into this country illegally. We should stop pretending that it's somehow un-American to equally apply our laws. The language thing that Macerana—I agree that if you were to stop illegal immigration now, you could slow the flow enough so that everybody would eventually at least have the option of speaking English. But the theory that the third generation has assimilated, or integrated, or whatever word we're presently using, and then is speaking English, does not take into account that we are as much as being told that it's somehow un-American to stop the next wave who comes in. The track that we're on now, you will always have, if we don't enforce our laws, you're always going to have another group. We've proven it. '86, we had *x* amount of people here; we made them legal. It's a miserable failure. Amnesty is not the answer. I cannot allow myself to be accused of being somehow unworthy of being an American simply for insisting that the law be equally applied.

Dyson: What amazes me, again, is that in a culture that puts the burden upon those of us who feel the heat of both the ethnicity, [and] the racial—we can expand gender and sexual orientation, but right now we're talking about race and ethnicity because it is [about race and ethnicity]. D. A., I respectfully disagree with you. When I bring it up, all of a sudden now, we want to live in a naïve society where we believe that the argument over immigration—for Germans and Italians and Swedes and so on versus those who are Latino, or from Asia or the Pacific Rim—is not racially or ethnically coded. We can see the difference even between allowing Cubans to come in, in Miami, versus Haitians who are kept back. I would submit to you that, across the board, those people who want to live like an ostrich with its head in the sand, to refuse to see the racial and ethnic fallout from this debate, don't have history on their side. That's why I, as an African American—

King: No argument Michael—

Dyson: —understand that debate.

King: —but it's not the main issue here—

Dyson: I'm saying it's a huge part of it.

King: —and neither should it be. And for a large part of America it is whether or not the law is going to be effective. And I don't believe, by the way, that "borders" is any kind of a code word. I believe borders, in Mexico, for example—Mexico enforces its borders quite well and has an interior enforcement act whereby they remove people who are in the country illegally. I don't think "borders" is a code word in Mexico. Neither do I think it's a code word in—

Dyson: It becomes a code word here when we only want to discipline and police the influx of those people who happen to be from Latin America and—

Hinojosa: I really want the two of you guys—let's go out to have a beer after this. But I do want to bring you in, Richard Langlois. When you hear this kind of a conversation back and forth, and it's really at these opposing points, and the Republican Party in power with not necessarily a clear leadership here. Except for the president saying he believes in a guest worker program, or perhaps that these twelve million undocumented immigrants won't be going anywhere. What goes on for you when you see this kind of debate?

Langlois: The question is, the people are here, what are *they* going to do? And what do *they* want? And how can we recognize who they are? We don't know who they are because they're here illegally. Mr. Dyson's talking about all these people who have come in, but they've all come in through immigration. Your parents came in here, but they became citizens, I'm sure.

Hernandez: Thirty years later, and thanks to Pete Wilson.

Langlois: Yeah, okay.

Hinojosa: Proposition 187 in California.

Langlois: The Party's open. The Republican Party, for Mr. Dyson's knowledge is—the Republican Party in Texas was actually started by blacks. Did you know that?

Dyson: It was a different Republican Party, brother, to be sure.

[*Laughter*]

Hinojosa: Okay, let me do this now, because we're about to wrap up. And I do want to ask all of you to think about one thing specifically. Because this is about individuals, right? It's about everybody's personal life being somehow affected or impacted by this, from all of us here. So when we leave here today, what are each of you going to do specifically around this issue? What can you do? Fifteen seconds. We'll start with you, Richard.

Langlois: Well, I represent people. And I interact with a lot of Hispanic people that are here both legally, illegally. I think the issue is not what I'm going to do, it's what are illegals going to do? Are we going to forgive and forget? We have to start somewhere. It's got to start with legislation.

Hinojosa: Macerana.

Hernandez: I think the marches have been great because they raised the visibility of the community, and there are issues beyond immigration that we need to start talking about. And those are issues I tackle in my weekly columns. But I hope to also keep pounding away that, at the very core of this, we're talking about families.

Hinojosa: Michael Eric Dyson.

Dyson: Elevate the discussion; try to expand the boundaries of our perceptions about what's at stake; and fight for truth, justice, and democracy, as I always have on this issue and all issues. And I think when we do that, we'll protect our borders.

Hinojosa: Do you feel you have more of a challenge when you're dealing right now with the African American community?

Dyson: Oh, absolutely. I think that, again, many African American people are reacting out of fear and a refusal to acknowledge the tremendous problems in this debate, and negative responses [black people have had] prove we need to expand our understanding of what is truly at stake.

Hinojosa: Henry Cisneros.

Cisneros: I think we're very close to the potential of a national compromise that has those three elements: border enforcement, guest worker, and path to legalization. You can't have one without the others and hold the whole thing together. It will work. People like D. A. have to understand the path to legalization piece is as important as the border enforcement. We all have to work to get that compromise done.

Hinojosa: And you, Lee.

Teran: I think we have to change the focus back to making immigration law what it is supposed to be, and that is to keep families together, and turn our attention maybe to do a Marshall Plan to help Latin America or Mexico rebuild its infrastructure so that maybe the workers wouldn't have to come here.

Hinojosa: D. A. King.

King: I am going to encourage our government to go ahead and secure our borders. If the compromise that Mr. Cisneros brought up is the answer, then how about this time we secure the borders first, stop illegal immigration, and punish the employers, and then leave the third part of that for another year? I don't think that's an unreasonable request.

Hinojosa: Archbishop Gomez, final word.

Gomez: I'm going to pray that we all in our country can have a principled dialogue on this issue, respecting the dignity of the human person, and for elected officials to find a reasonable solution.

Hinojosa: I want to thank you all for joining us. It's been a fascinating conversation. And as for me, as a mother, as an immigrant, as a journalist, as a Latina, and as an American, I think I'll be spending a lot of time in the next few years exploring these issues, which I think really are at the very heart of our democracy.

PART III

CONFLICTING LOVES

8

I SAY YO, YOU SAY OY
Blacks, Jews, and Love

with Elliot A. Ratzman

Blacks and Jews have had an occasionally tremendous, often tense, and sometimes tortured relationship. Common struggles against oppression have opened doors of mutual interest, while competing stories of racial and ethnic identity have deepened collective wounds. In the summer of 2006, I sat for an interview with Elliot Ratzman, then a Princeton doctoral student and a member of the editorial collective of *HEEB* magazine, an irreverent take on Jewish identity, arts, culture, and politics by sophisticated young Jewish intellectuals and artists. Because I was interviewed for *HEEB's* "love" issue, Elliot engaged me in a conversation, and occasional debate, about Jewish love for blacks, and black love for Jews, and how the two groups express love in their own worlds. I loved doing this interview.

Elliot Ratzman: I remember seeing you at the Tikkun Conference in '94, in New York. You said it was the first time you preached in a synagogue. Have you preached in a synagogue since?

Michael Eric Dyson: Yeah, I've preached in two or three synagogues, man. I had a memorable experience in Maryland doing so. A couple other places as well. It was a wonderful opportunity to share my thoughts about a common Jewish and Christian heritage, and to think about the vocabulary I had inherited all my life, having read Martin Buber and Abraham Heschel, two of my favorite thinkers. I've obviously been trained in a religious discourse that owes its metaphors and its language to Jewish prophetic articulations. So it was a beautiful thing.

Ratzman: The Jewish crowd loved you.

Dyson: I had a good time. Look, when I think about my own intellectual development, about books, and the self-understandings that I've been able to garner reading as a child, and as a young person, and being reared in a black Baptist church where both Hebrew Scriptures and that Jewish cat named Jesus were vital to us—I definitely have a rapport at that level. Both in terms of intellectual tutelage but also the kind of common discourse about changing the world and believing that words—and actions wedded to words—make a difference in people's lives.

Ratzman: You know what I think is interesting is, Jewish folks can only deal with the Jesus language when black people are speaking it. But you think about the way in which faith is used in politics, it's only when the black church is articulating it that Jews don't roll their eyes.

Dyson: That's an interesting point. I think partly that has to do, first of all, with our common suffering as a people. So the experiences of black people and Jewish people have in common a concrete reference to the North Star of oppression and suffering, and the struggle against oppression and suffering, by means of words, by means of thought, by means of aesthetic expression, and by means of trying to figure out your place in the world by locating yourself in relationship to God. It's a big deal, *even* if you're a secular Jew—

Ratzman: And who isn't?

Dyson: —or a black person outside of the *official* black church, but still within the moral and political arc of black religion. On both sides, you can be outside of the official perimeters of those religious communities, but you're still going to be deeply and profoundly influenced by the stories, the narratives, the myths, etcetera, that have been put forth. So I think between blacks and Jews there's a common understanding that black people have suffered, and I think it may be easier to take from black people—that is, thought and discourse about Jesus, despite the inherent anti-Semitism of certain moments of Christian tradition—because it's at least moderated by the common expression of oppression. And the whole point of that religious language is not to prove, "Aha! Once again, the Jews killed Jesus." It's not a Mel Gibson-like intent to subvert the authority of Jews as the originators of prophetic thought or to claim some kind of moral propriety.

Ratzman: In some ways the religious experience of Christians, of Jews, is always in some ways abstract. Like what Marx said: The everyday Jew is a different story. So in the last sixty years, there's been this love/hate relationship in major urban centers—because Jews are mostly living in the cities, and African Americans mostly living in cities. But there's still that strange dynamic. People talk about this a lot. In some ways—and you see it in the *Tikkun* sanctuary—where Jewish people love black people on *some* level, at *some* time. And you see this through the civil rights movement in a sort of maudlin, maybe even strangely reverent relationship that liberal Jews have towards blacks. You see it in hip-hop. What do you make of that? I haven't seen that you've written that much about that.

Dyson: Yeah. Well, that's a very important question. I think part of that love—you said love/hate and we'll get to the love/hate part later—but part of the love, the pure love, is about the politics of identification. I mean by that, the way that liberal Jews admired African American people for a staunch commitment to freedom, for a kind of express intent to, at all costs, find the natural level of liberation in our own community. That is to say, you ain't got to be a civil rights leader on the front line. You just want to find some possibilities for joy in your own neighborhood. And that kind of *joie de vivre* cannot be translated simply into the politics of affirming your identity as a black person at a broad national level with political language. I'm talking about the individual, at the crib, in the neighborhood, in the projects—a determination to live as freely as possible from the constraints of the dominant white supremacist culture. There's a real identification, I think, with Jews and blacks at that level.

But there's a sense of reverie and nostalgia, too. I think many liberal Jews look at black people playing out the scripts and narratives of what Jewish people had to confront at the latter part of the nineteenth century, but especially the beginning of the twentieth century. Because don't forget, blacks and Jews shared a lot of physical space that really is not often spoken about. I mean, in these ghettos. Of course I'm not talking about in the European world, the *shtetl*. We're talking about in the new world, in the industrial economy. Blacks and Jews were grist for that mill. So they spent time together in physical spaces that were dominated by anti-Semitism and white supremacy and, as a result, forged serious bonds.

As Jews experienced upward mobility over the early part of the twentieth century, they left those ghettos behind—and they left behind black people whose culture was still being shaped by those experiences. So at one level, there's a sense of identification with the black experience by many Jews, who may conclude: "This is what our people struggled with."

And by the way, it's not difficult to understand why even the everyday Jew could understand that the everyday black person still appeals to these stories and myths and narratives in the Hebrew Bible to talk about their experiences. "By the rivers of Babylon, there we sat down, yea, we wept, when we remembered Zion. We hanged our harps upon the willows in the midst thereof. For there they that carried us away captive required of us a song; and they that wasted us required of us mirth, saying, Sing us one of the songs of Zion." I mean, that's the blues; that's black gospel music, that sense of longing and nostalgia and trying to do something in foreign territory. So I think that there's a kind of liberal Jewish identification with the stories and myths that black people kept alive in their experience, as a means of survival, which obviously owed a debt to Jewish ideas, even if they weren't explicitly articulated. Smart liberal Jews understood the outlines of the influence implicitly; they didn't have to be told, and black people didn't have to announce it. It was there. They understood it. And that was partly forged in a culture where we could understand blacks and Jews being knit together in the womb of common resistance against oppression.

But as Jews began to experience upward mobility, black people got left behind, and there's a growing class chasm. You're talking about these urban spaces where Jewish brothers and sisters have departed as neighbors, but returned as business owners and the like. You begin to find a tremendous level of racial hostility and animosity; there's scapegoating by blacks and Jews. Of course, there are legitimate gripes and complaints as well. Martin Luther King, Jr., for instance, said that one of the tragedies that was revealed in some of the riots [in the '60s] is that some Jewish brothers and sisters who had been depended upon as stalwarts in the civil rights movement had now turned slumlords to further the internal oppression of black people in these communities. So with Jewish success came black resentment, some scapegoating, and some legitimate critique—and, quite frankly, the development of Jewish criticisms of black lifestyles, behaviors, and poverty. Thus began the fracturing and fragmentation of that implicit relationship between blacks and Jews.

But beyond that, the cultural moment—whether it's preaching or music—still holds great promise for blacks and Jews coming together to express love for, and appreciation of, each other. There are Jews who admire the tenacity and the power of the spoken word in black culture. And there are blacks who admire Jews not only for a culture where literacy is critical but the ability to forge solidarity and tell the white man, "Kiss our butts. If we can't force you by law to treat us right, we're going to force you by business and commerce and ethnic solidarity to deal with us." Now, that stuff was exaggerated by many blacks—'cause we've got to ask, "Well, what Jews are you talking about who come together?" Not all Jews see things the same way. There are Jews who read and admire *Tikkun*, and those who read and admire *Commentary*. That's the mythos in many black communities: that all Jews come together. But there's enough truth to the functional solidarity among Jewish communities that black people, to this day, continue to admire, and continue to point to as an example of what we can do. "Why can't we do like Jewish brothers and sisters? They're 2.5, 3 percent of the population, and are significant and influential in so many arenas. That's what we've got to do." So currently, you've got that back and forth between blacks and Jews.

Ratzman: Let's get some specific examples: This year's strangest hybrid, Matisyahu. The thing was, the commentary was not the fact that he was white, or that he was Jewish, but that he was Orthodox.

Dyson: Yeah, you know? And I was thinking that, brother. I saw him on TV, and I said, "How much sense does this make?" And it's not just black and Jew, right? It's not just white and black. It's an *Orthodox* Jew and reggae. So that a particular form of Jewish identity, and a particular form of African identity in the Diaspora, are forged here. On the one hand, what does it show? It shows that there's a kind of inherent politics that unites Jews and blacks in common cause against oppression through music. On the other hand, what it suggests is that, in strange and interesting fashion, the rhythms of blacks and Jews, despite taking a battering from the politics of the last twenty-five years, can lift our groups when those rhythms express hope and love. And look, as an Orthodox Jew, his fellow believers at some level might find what he's doing offensive, irreverent, interesting, and provocative. So he's taking a risk even within the boundaries of his religious identity. Forging a connection with blackness is an implicit judgment of certain moments of Orthodox Judaism. But it's also calling into question the politics of purity, identity, and authenticity within black communities.

Ratzman: There's this strange hybrid of the construction of Zion in West Indian culture, right? And it's as if to say, "Okay. We're talking about Zion here." We're talking about kingship and David and all sorts of Hasidic stuff that regular Jews don't know anything about. He's using the reggae medium to push it. I'm not sure I'm not convinced—I don't know if you said anything about this—that his project is not a sort of uplift of everybody at issue. It's a promotion of Orthodox Judaism in some way.

Dyson: That's a great point. It's an interesting politics of reappropriation, and a politics of reversal. Usually it's black folks saying, "Well, white folks, we're going to take our culture back." Here's an Orthodox Jew saying to blacks, "Check this out: Zion, in your religious discourse, is an appropriation of Jewish language, thought, and metaphysics. How about this: I'm jacking that back. I'm taking that back for purposes of Orthodox Judaism." But it's not an uncomplicated reappropriation. Because in one sense, it's acknowledging that the "stranger" and the "enemy" has been more brilliantly capable of speaking about Zion than those within the religious circle. It's a judgment at one level. At the same time, I think about the Falasha Jews of Ethiopia in relationship to the issue of skin color, pigment, and melanin within the larger circle of Judaism. In a sense, Matisyahu's reappropriation of Zion raises the question of whether, intentionally or not, this is an incorporation of the black Jew within Orthodox Judaism by Matisyahu touching the hem of Bob Marley's garment, so to speak. He's speaking about Zionism, but he's also reappropriating a reggae conception of Zion, and Rastafarianism, back into the fold of Orthodox Judaism. Matisyahu represents an interesting moment of reappropriation that speaks volumes about the politics of black and Jewish identity right now.

Ratzman: Alright, stand-up comedy. I don't know if you've written anything about it. I know about the Cosby book, but I haven't read it, so I'm not sure you talk about comedy per se. Because as I said, Jews only put up with Jesus language from black people. How much criticism can Jews put up with from anybody, I'm not sure. But I think that I have seen many liberal Jews take a lot of criticism from black people, from black intellectuals, or black speakers, and sort of uncritically say, "Yes, yes, that's right." I'm not sure if the reverse is true, either. But I want to probe the dimension of loving criticism: that you have a love for a group, or you stand in solidarity with a group, but you can also offer a few criticisms. I want to explore how that dynamic works. I wanted to point out a few people: Ali G and Sarah Silverman, who I think are two of the most interesting performers who experiment with race.

Dyson: Oh, yeah. I've been on *Real Time with Bill Maher* with Sarah.

Ratzman: I don't know if you've seen her movie, *Jesus Is Magic.*

Dyson: No, no, but I've heard it's an amazing—

Ratzman: Listen to this. This is the opening song, sung very upbeat. "I love you more than bears love honey / I love you more than Jews love money / I love you more than Asians are good at math / I love you more than Puerto Ricans need a bath / I love you more"—et cetera et cetera. "Black people don't tip." And "Jews driving German cars is the opposite of FUBU [For Us By Us, a black clothing line]."

Dyson: Sarah Silverman is a mouthful, a pocketful, and a handful. Having been on Bill Maher with her, I saw how she skirted dangerously close to the edge for some people. I know there were some black people who were thinking, "Oh my God, is she a racist?" I was cracking up. The ability to be self-critical in relationship to the group you love is an extremely interesting phenomenon. Most of us are incapable of having that broadly defined love. Because the thing is with blacks and Jews, we feel we're under such attack anyway, and some members of our groups ask: "Why add to it?" But that's to forget that the purpose of art is not simply to embrace and coddle, or to affirm and to edify. Artists are also supposed to be irreverent, and to poke fun at pieties, and to force people to think more critically about themselves, right? There's a way in which Jewish comedy, in terms of its vast ranges of signification, has now become American comedy. The genius of Jewish comedy is to be able to translate Yiddish idiosyncrasy—and an engagement with their particular marginal slice of the world—into what America is about. It's similar to what happens with certain fields of intellectual and academic pursuit—say with sociology. Jewish alienation at a certain level gets translated into conceptual apparatuses that began to articulate universal ideas about difference, anomie, and strangeness, which is genius.

The same thing goes on in comedy. American comedy has such a huge debt to pay to Jewish sensibilities. Now, people usually take that up in the negative: "Well, you know how Jews run Hollywood. You know how they've done X, Y, and Z." I'm not talking about a conspiratorial, anti-Semitic argument. I'm speaking about the positive imprint of that Jewish adage among artists: "Think Yiddish and write goyish." That's the mantra of Jewish comedians of a certain generation. Not to speak of what's going on even now, with Adam Sandler and the like. Think about earlier. Shecky Green. Think about the whole tradition and generation—

Ratzman: There was an erasure of Jewish identity.

Dyson: Right, there was an erasure at one level. But there was an appropriation of Jewish idiosyncrasies at another level: Shlemiel. Shlemazel. Yiddish language was transmuted into terms of American identity that accompanied, and in small ways, offset, the erasure of explicit Jewish identity. And this dual process happened on all levels, by the way, and not just with comedy. Think about Kirk Douglas. "Kirk Douglas? Damn. We missed that. He's Jewish too? Oh, my Lord." It comes out when he starts writing his novels. In the same way Anthony Quinn was Latino, although it wasn't widely known until the end of his life.

Ratzman: My parents gave my brother and me middle names that sound very Anglo-Saxon in case we wanted to be performers. And we could cut off our last names.

Dyson: There it is. You know, Firestein to Firestone. It happens in business too. So the easy erasure of Jewish identity for purposes of survival was also accompanied by a resistant, and rebellious, moment of Jewish identity where it gets translated into: "If we can't beat them, we'll make them join us." Oh, that's a brilliant strategy on a certain level. In other words, the terms of the debate will be shaped by our particular preoccupations translated as universal. So when you see that going on in comedy, the Borscht Belt becomes—

Ratzman: But now it becomes reversed. Now the Jewish identity becomes the center of something. And here's the weird thing with Ali G and Sarah Silverman. Sarah Silverman, her persona is, "I'm the naïve Long Island upper-class Jewish girl full of racist stereotypes." So when she sings, "I love you more than X," she's saying, "These are the exaggerations of daily life." Ali G, who's into drag in some way—remember the first few episodes, you didn't know what ethnicity he was, whether he was Pakistani or something else. And at some point he spoils it by saying, "Is it 'cause me black?" But the racial ambiguity, I thought, was the root [of his appeal]. He did his master's degree at Oxford on black and Jewish relations in the South. But here's the thing—he's playing with race in order to show that the stereotypes still linger, and the racism is still embedded. And I think Sarah Silverman does the same thing, but nobody gets it that she is also in drag.

Dyson: And the reason they don't get that she's in drag, I think, is because of how Sarah Silverman's irreverence cuts both ways. So it's one thing to say, "I'm going to appropriate, at an intellectual and discursive level, all of these stereotypes to turn them on their head." That's the kind of straight form. But to say that as an upper-middle-class Jewish female comedian, "I'm going to signify on how these stereotypes hold sway and, as a woman, challenge them"—you can't underestimate the gender of Ali G, versus Sarah Silverman, as to who has authority to do that. Think about it in the same way that *Lethal Weapon* had more violence in the first four minutes than *Thelma and Louise*. But when *Thelma and Louise* came out, folk, especially men, went crazy. "Oh my God, it's so violent. Why do women do this? This is unacceptable; it's intolerable." Well, it's intolerable because now women are appropriating—

Ratzman: You're dating yourself!

Dyson: Exactly. We'll just say, "I hope you all saw that movie that made Brad Pitt a star long before *Brangelina!*" But here's the reality: it's problematic when women appropriate a male domain, especially one where men have been permitted to go far afield and have free reign over what they think is good or true or viable—or over what they think is irreverent. Women for the most part have been cut off. Sarah Silverman has been cut off in a certain way. We don't understand her signification. We don't understand the modes through which she expresses her sense of irreverence or irony or parody because we're not used to women at a certain level doing that. When we discuss Sarah Silverman's art and craft, we can talk about Jewish comedians, about female comedians, and even about Jewish female comedians in particular. But the reality is that women don't get the chance to be that ironic or parodic in a way that signifies on stereotypes like Ali G can. I think it's partly gender. But also, her comedy moves in two directions because she's trying to force Jews to think critically about their own stereotyping and about how they're being stereotyped. And that give and take, that kind of postmodern Jewish irreverence, may not go over well.

Ratzman: But you know, it hasn't broken out to the point where the Jewish community realizes it's being made fun of. It won't be until there's a moment in which there's Israel criticism. I do stand-up, too. When I do Israel jokes, it's like: "Well enough about Jews." But your penchant for iconoclasm has gotten you, I think, in a bit of trouble. What's your account of how you are critiquing lovingly black heroes, and also fellow black intellectuals? Your list [in your essay on black intellectuals] at the end of your *Michael Eric Dyson Reader* is pretty intense.

Dyson: I want to say, "I understand you, Sarah Silverman." My loving critique in part reflects the class divisions and the class chasms in black America. In one sense, in my essay on black intellectuals, I'm bringing to the academic front, and to the intellectual fore, the signifying, gently dozens-playing traditions that shaped me on the streets of Detroit. And it's not that you didn't have rules there. They were probably more implicit than explicit. They were improvisational. And they were flexible. But still they were observable. And you had to acknowledge them. Because even if you made them up, you had to agree to them and you had to abide by them. So I think that kind of raucous, irreverent discourse finds its way into my particular arsenal, so to speak.

But that's not the only thing I learned in the streets. One of the most important things I learned was just the willingness to speak out on behalf of those who have been marginalized because they're poor and black. And the willingness to be lovingly critical—but more often, harshly judgmental—of black people is a habit that is usually only practiced towards poor black people. There ain't no such thing as being lovingly critical to well-off blacks, at least not in their minds. As long as you can practice a kind of politics of *noblesse oblige*, or condescension, or moral myopia, about poor blacks, it's fine. The moment you begin to talk about heroes, or "respectable" folk, it's like, "Wait a minute, now. What are you doing? What are you saying? You're a race traitor. You are disloyal to the race." But my response is, "Wait a minute. It's the same impulse. If you're asking for us to be lovingly and affirmingly self-critical, and to be caringly critical of our heroes—not to dismiss them, but to, in my estimation at least, forge a connection between those on a pedestal and the black people who are left behind, which is one of my points in my book on Martin Luther King, Jr.—then the same should apply for the poor. If we create compassionate narratives and stories and explanations and justifications for Martin Luther King, Jr.'s flaws, then we at least ought to be willing to do that for our children and young folk so they can grow out of their flaws to become strong men and women. There's a deep class bias in black America that I've run up against, quite frankly, not only in the King book but especially in the Cosby book.

Ratzman: There's a lot of talk about loving one's people. What does that mean to you?

Dyson: Well, for me, loving one's people means that you are deeply invested in their survival; that you inherit the intellectual vocabulary they used to make their way in history; that you appreciate and can document the struggles that have been waged in the past to make your present position or vocation possible. To love your people means that you only add to their survival by being willing to be critical about the bad things. You've got to talk about the vices. Celebrate the virtues. And say how complex things are. That's why I can never give in to a positive versus negative in black life. I think it's about complex versus simple. That's the biggest division that exists.

Ratzman: Does that make it agapic or erotic?

Dyson: Well, probably *agaperotic!* Agapic praxis is about a kind of love that, no matter what this person may say or do to you, you will hold fast to it. It celebrates this kind of Kantian tradition of, "I'm going to love you regardless." Or, as some of the brothers would say, "irregardless." It involves a sort of Archimedean point—not of objectivity but of stability—that says, "No matter what happens, as Jesus says, 'pray for those who despitefully use you.'" That's an agapic practice. But that rests upon claims of disinterest. The erotic level is about a more intimate and personal investment in the knowledge of your people. It's an epistemology of intimacy. And at that level, I think it's got to be both agapic and erotic. I think it's got to be an erotic engagement with the intimate details of struggle to understand that people's lives are at stake. That even as you do everything you do, that people are making decisions, and public policy, about poor black people. Or about the people you love. And at that level, you have an ethical responsibility to use whatever is at hand to defend these people that you love. And even if they think what you're doing is unloving, even if what they believe at any given moment is fundamentally and squarely set against the perpetuation and the survival of the people, you've got to hold to that if you really love them. That's part of the irony and the conflict between agape and eros.

Ratzman: So Hannah Arendt comes out with her Eichmann book, and she gets taken to task. Gershom Scholem says, "You don't show 'Ahavat Yisrael,' love of Israel. You don't have that sort of love in your heart. You don't have this love of Israel coming through." And she replies to him, "I don't love abstractions. I love my friends, I love my family, but I can't love a people. I've never denied that I'm part of that people, but . . . "

Dyson: That's tough. I'm a huge Hannah Arendt fan. I went to see, in New York, the Kate Fodor play, *Hannah and Martin*, that dramatizes the relationship between Arendt and her mentor, and later her lover, Martin Heidegger. There are so many moments where her brilliance is blistering. In that Eichmann book she talks about "the banality of evil," how evil has been made routine, even acceptable. And that has been an incredibly important concept for me in trying to explain how the groundless grotesque, and the transcendent tragic, can get reduced to routine, to the quotidian, to everyday stuff that comes out as pathology. So first up, her work has been very important to me.

I think I understand the intellectual point she's trying to make there, especially as a critic and intellectual. Because what you're wrestling with is a love of nation, love of people, love of tribe, and solidarity with group—the kind of telos of love for that particular group that can pull you forward and lift you up. But it can also weigh you down. Maybe what Hannah Arendt is trying to get at is that roots should nurture, not strangle.

But loving an abstraction—that would be tough for me to say, though I understand one of the parallels in black communities: certain kinds of nationalist narratives that say unless you are an Afrocentrist within black studies or unless you display a certain kind of aesthetic attraction to Africa by the way you dress (by the way, a lot of that stuff is made in Korea), then you're not African. I say "no." There are many different ways to love your people. Now I hear Hannah Arendt's criticism, and I join her in that.

Where I would demure, where I would say, "Wait a minute, I want to put an asterisk on that thought," is when it comes to standing with one's people, especially when they have been collectively demonized and deliberately misunderstood. Even so, you've still got to make morally illuminating critiques of your people. But there is something to be said—Condoleezza Rice and Clarence Thomas—for strategically standing beside your despised and degraded folk.

Ratzman: All right, let me put on my critical hat here and disagree with you. A lot of times, in your work and your talk, there are moments when we have a particular instance, whether it's Rice, or whether it's black on black crime, where your analysis flies up to a sociological level. Not to a sort of middle, let's say Foucaultian physics of power, but it flies up to the contextualization. And I was thinking, what would it look like if I did that to, let's say, Israel, right at this very moment? I consider myself a Zionist but totally critical of Israel's policies toward Palestine. So if I were to do the same analysis that you were doing, I would start to say, "Well, what's going on in Lebanon is bad, but you've got to understand the larger geopolitical history of Islam being very violent, of colonizing religion." I'd have to say things like, "Well, these particular Palestinians, I feel sorry for them, but in the larger context their leadership didn't make the right decisions back in '48." So in some ways that discourse, which I don't accept—that line of thinking in the Jewish context, which says, "You know what, let's tie this into a larger narrative in order to understand"—sometimes I feel that you veer too close to that.

Dyson: That might be true. That's the risk you run in trying to bring the *Sitz im Leben*, or the "situation in life" as Biblical scholars call it, to bear, and to figure out what we're dealing with, especially when it involves the micropolitics of managing existential realities that are in conflict, both with each other and with stories and narratives that try to explain them. So sociologically what I'm trying to do is to situate those truths and bring context to bear. Now, I'm not against a kind of Foucaultian understanding versus a Weberian conception—Max Weber located power in hierarchy, rationalization, and authority, whereas Foucault said, "Yeah, but power breaks out everywhere." Foucault recognized that there are ways in which people who are powerless compete with one another over scarce resources of legitimacy, or over self-definition on a limited political terrain. I'm down with both of those. I'm Weberian *and* Foucaultian at that level. But I don't think that an empirically abstract Foucaultian conception of power would yield much in benefit to those who are trying to figure out the next move in the Palestinian-Israeli dialogue and struggle for liberation—

Ratzman: Well, you end up with postmodern resistance. And here's where maybe some of my personal questioning about the liberatory power of art, whether rap or movies, is raised: art is a moment, but the real life is in power, in politics, in organizing, in resources, in lobbying, in the material dimension of life.

Dyson: That's a great point, and that's what I'm coming to. At the end of the day, the question of politics has to be put to both Weber and Foucault. And, by extension, to those of us who follow sociological and contextual arguments, schemes of justification, and rationality (and that's Weberian analysis) versus a kind of Foucaultian argument that power is decentered and destabilized. And that we should map how it has metastasized across the ideological body and social landscape.

Cool. That's all important. That's true. But after that, we've got to ask of each of them, and us, what the next step is. And we've got to give answers. And how we give answers determines what kind of permission in the culture is granted to spaces where such pursuits can even be engaged. In a repressive Fascist regime, a Foucaultian question of power can never even be put, whereas a Weberian conception that locates power in a hierarchy and a political order may be the most critically analytical tool to get at the forces that undermine the freedom that allowed Foucault to even pursue his way of thinking. If that's the case, then I'm not for the postmodern abstracted from a kind of racial and cultural *realpolitik,* not in a George Kennan foreign policy sense, but in terms of actual on-the-ground resources at stake and what we're going to do about them.

And so, for me, that's why talk about context is not a way to dismiss questions of culpability. To talk about the environment within which certain things develop is not to avoid the issue of responsibility. It is simply to give a scheme of explanation a coherent expression among people who may have competing moral ideals. Because when you talk about Palestinians and Jews, for instance, you're talking about Thomas Kuhn's conception of incommensurable vocabularies. Are we really speaking about different ways of viewing the world? These might be different cosmologies at stake—it's not just different languages and different understandings, but these are different peoples constituted by different histories who have almost incoherent moral vocabularies—at least to each other—to express what they're doing. Intifada meets Prophetic Tradition. I think context is critical to both explanation and justification, and to trying to settle the ground where people enjoy even the possibility of exploring their divergent conceptions of what is good and true.

Ratzman: Let me switch the scene a bit. First, I keep this image in my head of reggae bands playing at frat parties, calling for unity! Now, let me juxtapose that to Mumia Abu-Jamal support rallies in Philadelphia, which I was somewhat involved with years and years ago. Here we have *Rage Against the Machine* playing a concert. We had rallies, we had young people out. What came of it? And I've gotten to be very critical about Mumia, not because of the merits of the case, but I was saying, "What's going to come of it? No voter registration going on. No concrete politics." People say, "Well, this is the beginning of interracial coalitions." And I said, "Where are they? What are they? What's going to happen?" So in some ways the Mumia rallies, which people might mistake for *realpolitik*, became an echo that led to nothing.

Dyson: That's a legitimate critique of what is seen as a moment in time that people have tried to stretch into a movement. I happen to be deeply and profoundly empathetic to Mumia and his plight for a variety of reasons. Part of it can be explained because, like John Edgar Wideman, I've got a brother in prison who's convicted of second-degree murder. Then, in Mumia's case, there's the manipulation of truth and story by both corporate media and white supremacy, and when they dovetail with police power and state forces, they have negative consequences on a black man getting a fair shake in the legal system. So I'm very empathetic to Mumia at that level.

But at the same time, I can be critical of the political consequences—not of Mumia, but of what is made of Mumia. Because what you're being critical of is not Mumia. You're being critical of the uses to which his own story have been put, and the political consequences and fallouts that may ultimately contradict his own complex and concrete obligation to render service to vulnerable people. Your point is, where's the beef, where's the pudding? So you're executing a Mumia-like examination of the use of Mumia's image for politics that have really been eviscerated, emptied out of their importance. Or, as you suggested, politics made needlessly ephemeral.

Ratzman: It's a politics of the spectacle.

Dyson: Absolutely.

Ratzman: When do we get to the point in which we actually do touch the reality of politics throughout our critiques? Now, I'll give you another example: Chomsky. Nobody's going to blame him for not having a thorough-going, deep critique of all sorts of structural and historical facts, economic dimensions, etcetera, etcetera. But where's the politics? What is one to do when one is so trapped? And here's where I think the agency talk, harnessed to actual projects, would make a difference: Here is what your life would look like if you were actually doing politics. That needs to be sketched out.

Dyson: That's true. But check this out. I'm a huge Chomsky fan too, and what's interesting is that the times have caught up with Chomsky's critique. In other words, the critique you made of Chomsky is a critique that might have been made ten years ago. "You've really got to talk about the concrete resources that are at stake if you want us to behave politically in the most progressive fashion. You've got to talk about how solidarity is gained. You've got to tell us what movements you're part of—or ones to join that resemble the appropriate performance of conscience as you recommend. Did you participate in the march against Iraq?" And I'm sure there are graduate students, a dime a dozen, who think they're smarter than Chomsky, who think he should have stuck to arguments over transformational grammar, and stuck to debating Foucault about the ethics and epistemological criteria of linguistic habits, but in terms of politics, well, he's simply out of date.

Well, the times have caught up to Chomsky. How? We're living in a time of enormous repression in terms of access to information and the squandering of civil liberties. I mean, even David Remnick—let's just specify the broad range of Jewish critique of the state—in the *New Yorker,* is drawing parallels between what Bush is doing with an imperial presidency, and what Nixon and Cheney and Rumsfeld and Agnew—remember his "nattering nabobs of negativism"—were doing under that regime in '69, '70, '71. So I'm saying, what's interesting is that the Bush imperial presidency, that rides upon nostalgia for an epoch in which the chief political figure was a monarch—well at least part of an oligarchy—has now made Chomsky's language especially useful and resonant. His very language creates possibilities of imagination that have been seen as nearly criminal under Bush. So, at that level, it's not an abstraction, or a Foucaultian projection of collective delirium, to suggest that Chomsky's words are creating very concrete pathways for people to follow. Because even to think the way Chomsky does now is a challenge to what Bush is doing in trying to tap us, survey us, and contain us. So even though you're right in terms of the political consequences that flow from Chomsky in discourse, the existence of a Chomsky now is a hopeful sign.

Ratzman: Yeah, Chomsky and his tradition of Jewish complaint—that's kind of like our blues. A lecture complaint—that's like the Jewish blues. Like, "Oh, the world's so horrible. Look how trapped we are. Look how horrible these people are."

Dyson: Well, you see that in former New York Knicks and Philadelphia 76ers basketball coach Larry Brown, too. In other words, the moral beauty and social usefulness of that culture of complaint—and they say Larry Brown is only satisfied when it's dark outside because when it's light, baby, he doesn't trust it and starts to kvetch—is to distrust even what you see as empirical evidence because you know that there's some potential flaw that has to be revealed. You'd rather anticipate the existence of the flaw and forestall it by the warning that's communicated through the complaint. So I just want to show some love for the efficacy of a certain kind of complaint within Judaism, whether secular or religious. It could either be like black blues, or a kind of Irish melancholia that registers as a principled resistance to the sunnier streams of optimism that have nothing to do with the real politics of their world.

Ratzman: Jeff Stout described me once as a counselor for a Jewish social justice camp. So let me give you a little optimism—well not optimism, because we know the facts don't bear optimism. You have the Bush imperial presidency, but we have everybody complaining about it, and everybody pushing on it, and everybody ridiculing it. So you couldn't have that happen in a real authoritarian society. There is the attempt—there's Bush saying, "Well, let's see if we can get away with this." It's like he's rounding third base there.

Dyson: But the thing I'm afraid of is that even as they are manipulating symbols and images on that level—and people are fighting against them—that the real subversive practices are going on substrata, or if we take the body politic literally, subcutaneously. That's what I'm afraid of. It's not just the stuff we can see and oppose. What about the stuff we don't even know about, that we should object to, that we could be in opposition to? That's the tragedy. And the intent of Bush is to politically obscure, and masquerade, and keep at bay, so that we don't even have access to the truth—this is partly David Remnick's complaint about what's going on in the Bush administration. They're manipulating the media in such a fashion—à la Andrew Card—because they understand that this is the fourth estate trying to challenge the authoritarianism of the state, or at least this administration, as they seek to bring a check and balance outside of the judicial, and the executive, and the legislative branches. That's what the media is supposed to do. And what the media and the rest of the world catches the Bush administration doing— think about it, that's just the stuff we know about. I'm afraid about the stuff we don't know. But it's like with Katrina: if this is what the Bush administration will do—or, as it were, *won't* do—when the cameras are rolling, when the world is watching, what the hell do you think they're doing when nobody is checking them out? That's the thing I fear about this Bush presidency, more than any other presidency since Nixon.

Ratzman: On lighter topics, but no less rigorous or important. Loving women. Tell me how you're kicking all these books out. Tell me about the repercussions of you writing the book *Why I Love Black Women*.

Dyson: When I wrote that book, I thought, "Oh, it's a no-brainer." Well, it's political, because black love is political, especially in an era where black people embracing and loving themselves—getting back to how it's not an abstraction in an Arendtian sense, but actual fleshly beings—is a political project that is opposed to the implicit, though no less monstrous, norms of white supremacy. In part, that deals with the question: What's beautiful? In the book, I'm celebrating broad noses, and kinky hair, and black women of darker hue and skin. Now, those things can be episodically exoticized and eroticized to the delight of a dominant culture. But when black people themselves are admiring other black people for their beauty—elevating black styles and forms of beauty as desirable, even taking them for granted as normatively attractive—that is problematic to certain quarters of the culture. See, it's alright to admire Julia Roberts, with her thick lips, but don't you dare say Cicely Tyson is beautiful. So I looked around and saw that the everyday black sister was getting dissed, and not simply by hip-hop culture. I wanted to say, "Yeah, but it's going on in other places of the culture too." And I wanted to give black women a love note from a black man of a certain prominence who was able publicly to affirm black women in all of their resplendent beauty, their poignant brilliance, their soulfulness, and their spiritual genius. I wanted to combat the lack of recognition by black men, even, of how important and wonderful black women are. So that book was an attempt to do so.

But I went on *The View,* before Star Jones was summarily dismissed, and I got beat down, brother, because I have a chapter entitled, "Another Saturday Night, or Have All the Brothers Gone to White Women?" And my point wasn't—it couldn't have been, trust me—that black men shouldn't be with white women. My point was, in a culture where many prominent black men were visibly defecting from any sense of erotic, metaphysical, spiritual, physical, and emotional allegiance to black women, that such a reality, at a certain level, was reinforced by a culture that already said these women were very little to look at, or to grapple with intellectually, to begin with. So, for me, the disdain for black women by visible black men, and others, replayed some of the vicious mythologies of black women that come straight out of the Massa's house on the plantation. Of course, such objections to black women never kept him from raping or abusing black women.

So when I went on *The View* I tried to explain that one of the arguments I was making in that chapter is that there's often a sociological exchange value between white women and black men when they marry each other. White women offer the allure of access to the dominant culture, especially access to the ideal norm of beauty that white women represent. And black men often offer, in exchange for that, elevation to a higher economic status. I didn't have to get into a neo-Marxist analysis. And I wasn't making a normative claim; I was making a descriptive claim. I wasn't saying this is how things ought to be; I was saying this is how they are! I argued back and forth with some of the women on *The View.* But I finally came to the conclusion, in the form of a Carly Simon philosophical edict: "You're so vain, you probably think this book is about you. It's not about you. It's about black women." It's about this inability of many white women to understand how black women's bodies have been abused, and symbolically dismantled and reassembled for white titillation or sport, or black male desire and ambition. Black women are rarely allowed to exist in their own intelligence and beauty *for* themselves.

Ratzman: But now you get into the tension between, let's say, a democratic egalitarianism which said, "love everybody," and the understandable endogamous direction—wanting to marry and have children within your own group. It's true of so many cultures: Polish, Russian, Greek—you saw *My Big Fat Greek Wedding* was all about that—and certainly Jewish. But the call for a certain kind of endogamy within the black community—

Dyson: Or a kind of cessation of interracial relationships. But that's not what I was arguing. My point was simply to draw attention to the demonization of black women. I would love to see a black man who happened to have chosen a white woman say, "I still love sisters. I appreciate and love them. I made a choice based upon individual, reciprocal, mutual intimacy and relationship. I met and fell in love with this woman." But it's one thing to have met somebody. It's another thing to pursue them as the object of your desire because they are a trophy in the racial showcase. That's different. And I think some of the pathology of black/white relations at the erotic level cannot be exempt from such considerations. But I'm certainly for erotic egalitarianism—love who you will!

Ratzman: In the Jewish community, we have a little Web site devoted to endogamous relationships. And *occasionally* a sister finds her way on—very interesting, wanting to go with a Jewish guy. What's interesting, I think, is the semiotics of it, because here you have the Jewish guy, who's always been, for the last three hundred years or longer, especially in the history of Christianity, feminized—he bleeds from the penis like a woman through circumcision. He's bookish and nerdy and Woody Allenish. So he's the most effeminate male you get, but he's also very wealthy or successful on some level. And he's pining after blonde non-Jews from West Virginia, like in *Portnoy's Complaint.* You have what Seinfeld called the "shiksa appeal"—the appeal of non-Jews to Jewish men. But there's also this pressure [for Jews to marry Jews]—like my cousin, Mark Ecko, Mark Milecofsky is his real name, who married an Ecuadorian, but she converted. But I think that Jewish men pine after in some ways the ideal blonde.

Dyson: Of course. A lot of men do.

Ratzman: And there's the demonization of Jewish women—you can see the parallel—of being a little zaftig, of dark hair. I mean, I love brunettes. I don't understand what all the upset is all about.

Dyson: What's telling is that when it comes to affections across racial and ethnic lines, seekers of exogamous relations have appreciated the very thing for which Jewish women have been demonized: the dark, swarthy look, the zaftig, voluptuous figure, the intellectual energy and engagement, the dynamism. Sounds just like a sister to me. They both seem to have that same sort of independence—the ability to articulate a self-defining persona that is not contingent upon, or derivative of, somebody telling them what to do. That kind of attitude is a rebellion against patriarchy at every level. So that the demonization of Jewish women within certain circles leads to a call for endogamy, leads to a call for preserving the race. You have the convergence of a host of conflicting agendas there. On the very conservative side is, "Well, look, the Jewish race has gone to hell in a handbasket in terms of the shrinking number of Jewish babies." And on the other hand, it could be recognition of the politics of self-love and self-regard. And I think that's a legitimate point. In other words, demonization of Jewish women, and the erotic deference shown to blonde, blue-eyed white women seen as the ideal women—not to disrespect or dismiss white women, since there's no necessity to be either/or. But looking at the history of Jewish women, of black women, against the relative pedestal-boosting and valorization accorded white women—not only at the erotic end but also at the moral level of white women—Jewish and black women, by comparison, have been so extraordinary in their ability to thrive. That's why I think this demonization has to be analyzed and attacked.

Ratzman: Look at the parallels: loudness, money-grubbing, gold-digging, wanting to get married after the second date. I was reading that chapter, I was like, "This sounds just like the demonization of Jewish women."

Dyson: It really is. And you know what? I'm empathetic to the forces that fight that off. I'm empathetic to any group of people feeling that the women who actually *produced* you, that physically gave birth to you—collectively—are now not good enough to bear in their wombs the perpetuation of your legacy. Man, that's genocidal. And not only on a metaphysical level; that's genocidal at a physical level. Because what ends up happening is that you're slapping your mother, retroactively. You're trying to commit retroactive abortion, by reseeding yourself in the womb of a dominant white culture that wants to produce you as their child.

Ratzman: Wow. Now how would we apply that to Jewish culture? I guess getting the Christmas tree. I actually broke up with a girl over a Christmas tree.

Dyson: That reminds me of the famous "Christmas Tree" episode on Larry David's HBO comedy series, *Curb Your Enthusiasm*. When I talk about not measuring up to the ideal standards of beauty and desirability, I mean this for Jewish women, black women, any group that falls outside of the panoramic view of white beauty. And here's the interesting thing: the possibility of white skin identification, of being literally grafted into the pigment of the dominant culture, exists for most Jews. But of course, there was the shaving off of last names to conform to Anglo-Saxon nomenclature; there have been the changes in physical appearance through cosmetic surgery. However, there has been a persistent, distinct beauty among Jewish women that often managed to bleed through such transformations. Still, the changes in name and body for women were often driven by what was considered beautiful in the culture at large: the blonde-haired, blue-eyed mythology.

Ratzman: A lot of the interracial relationships that began in the '60s, during the civil rights movement, their children are now roughly my age, late twenties, early thirties. I know a lot of Jewish friends of mine for whom the most desirable Jewish woman is a Jewish woman of color. Paleness implies the pale settlements, which are very Europeanized. But to find half-Asian Jewish women is the pinnacle for many people. You have now the children of the first generation of serious interracial relationships. So what is a white Jewish guy to do?

Dyson: You can celebrate the union of ostensibly opposing cultures, dynamically resolved in the genetic structure of the woman you see before you. That's a beautiful possibility that many seek to realize. Obviously there is the concern of always embracing and loving one's own. But in this case, "one's own" gets broadened. But for African American people, the mulatto—that was the negative term—the fusion of races in one body, at once resisted and reproduced the pathology of white supremacy. The resistance came in with the very act of loving across the color line and producing offspring who testified to such transgression. But the reproduction of white supremacy jumped in because there was favor given to those who were lighter, brighter, and whiter—those who were closer to the white norm of beauty, as opposed to those who were deep dark chocolate, the more clearly African American person. So the politics of demonization are associated with such fusions, because those children were automatically considered to be beautiful and desirable in some circles. Of course, they came in for cultural and racial drubbing themselves, often from both sides of the color divide. They often faced hostility from whites and questions from blacks. If you tapped into these children's psyches and listened to their stories—being torn between two cultures, being demonized by both, hearing that "You're not black enough" from some blacks, or "You're not Jewish enough" from some Jews, or "You're not Puerto Rican enough" from some Puerto Ricans, or getting the blues from whatever two or more groups with which they were mixed. So within African American and other dark minority cultures, it worked out a bit differently.

Ratzman: I don't think I know another writer who loves black culture as much as you and weaves it into his work. What does it mean? We already talked about a certain creative tension between violence and the troubles of the city. You've written about the troubles in your family, and your love for your brother in prison, who converted to the Moorish Science branch of Islam. There's also the tension you're having with the general opinion makers in the black community. How do you negotiate that and still remain so effective?

Dyson: Because you take your work seriously, but you never take yourself too seriously. And I think that if you have a real love for your people, the way I hope I do, then you're not afraid of them. That love allows you to tell the truth as clearly as you can and to defend your people in a principled fashion from both internal danger and external destruction. And I try to call on the resources of hope and love that have sustained black folk throughout our perilous but fruitful journey in the wilderness of America.

9

CAN WE ALL GET ALONG?
Racial Friction and the Beloved Community

with Marianne Williamson

Marianne Williamson is one of the most profound and gifted spiritual writers and leaders in America. When she was pastor of Renaissance Unity Interfaith Spiritual Fellowship, in Warren, Michigan, right outside Detroit, she invited me to speak at her church. After I spoke at Renaissance Unity in April 2002, in a special afternoon lecture titled "Race, Spirituality, and Politics," Marianne and I had a spirited conversation and debate about race, black identity, O. J. Simpson, Zionism, and the beloved community. I appreciate Marianne's openness and honesty, and her willingness to join spiritual matters to political ideas to help change the world. During our conversation, there were some tense moments. It is a tribute to her desire to confront difficult truths in dialogue and debate that our encounter was so authentic.

Marianne Williamson: Michael and I thought we would just talk a little bit with ourselves and with you, and just sort of take it [from there]. So I do have something that is up for me based on something that you said, and actually based on the reaction of some of the audience members that I want to take up with you. You were talking about the little fifteen-year-old boy who was lynched. And of course, we are all with you in consciousness that murder is murder. And I cannot imagine anything that would make me think [that that was okay]. And Martin Luther King said black supremacy is no better than white supremacy. And you said we must challenge any impediment to that.

But I feel Nicole [Simpson] was a woman and I'm a woman. She's a white woman as I am. But I think that just as there are some horrible racists who would say about certain black people, "Well, he killed him, but it was only a black person," I think there are some people in this society, as you said, who do think, "O. J. Simpson killed [Nicole], but look who it was. I mean, he shouldn't have been doing it to her to begin with." And the fact that she was a beautiful white woman somehow makes her life less valuable. And I feel it was an issue of a man's violence towards a woman. And I really feel a lot of discomfort with that conversation at some points, when I hear certain reactions, and want to challenge the view that somehow—it's one thing if somebody really doesn't think he killed her. But I'm talking about the view that some people have who would admit they think he killed her—and would admit that they think that he killed Ron Goldman. But that somehow *that* murder doesn't really matter as much. And isn't that the problem that we have here? So I have to share that, and bring that up in conversation, because I heard some of that here in this room, and I felt that pain that I feel whenever I—

Michael Eric Dyson: You felt that I was saying—

Williamson: No, no, no. I did not feel that you felt that. But when you said something about, "We don't think he's innocent, we just don't think he's guilty," and you spoke to that, there was some reaction from some people in the audience which, just as there are certain things that black people know in America what's really being said when certain things are being said—

Dyson: Yeah. Right.

Williamson: —I know what things are being said when that's being said. [*Laughter*] "He shouldn't have been doing it to her to begin with." Well, excuse me. And murder is murder.

Dyson: Thank you for clarifying that. First of all, absolutely, I think I was pretty clear about—

Williamson: Oh, you were.

Dyson: —whether O.J. was guilty. And when I said that it's not that we didn't believe he was innocent, [it's just that] we didn't think he was guilty—the response of black people was, "Yeah, we see what you're saying." And that's this: that the justice system has been disproportionately targeting, and disadvantaging, black people who for years have been saying, "But wait a minute, this person is not guilty." And [the response has been], "According to the law, that person is guilty." And we go, "But no." So the implicit statement behind what I explicitly said was the belief of many African American people that the justice system has never recognized the full worth of [black] humans to the degree that it has placed that worth on white Americans. Furthermore, the justice system has targeted and taxed black people in such unjust fashion that it is a horrendous affair to even speak about the possibility of getting justice. But I think you're absolutely right.

Let me take up the other side you're talking about there, in terms of Nicole being a white woman—absolutely right. Even when I said, "Well, I know he kills white people, but does he kill black people," I'm trying to acknowledge the backdrop of black people saying, "Well, O. J.–I believe he killed these people, and I believe that's punishable by the law. I also believe that the attempt to frame a guilty man was something that was implicit in the conduct of the police department."

Williamson: I agree.

Dyson: But let me say this one final thing. If we're going to push to be honest: There was a huge divorce and divide in American society over Nicole Simpson–specifically the relationship with O. J. Simpson. And it wasn't the fact that a white woman–blue-eyed, blonde-haired woman–should be any less valuable than anybody else. It was that she had been *overvalued* because she was a white woman, when a week before her murder, a woman in Brooklyn had been thrown off of the top of a fifteen-story building by a man, and then had her two children murdered, and there was no outcry. Now, we have to acknowledge, of course, that it wasn't done by a "famous person," so that O. J.'s celebrity added a sheen of perverse–and, some would say, worthy–recognition to that case. But there's resentment among black American people because they feel–as I talked to them in writing my essay on O. J.–that Nicole Simpson got so much love, and so much coverage, because she was a white woman. That Latino, African American, and even poor white women–every day–are murdered, are taken under, are treated in despicable ways, [are subject to] domestic violence–by black men, by white men, by Latino men–but will never receive commensurate consideration.

So I think you're absolutely right in challenging the presumption that because she's a white woman that she doesn't deserve, especially among African American people, equal coverage in thinking about the issue of race. But I think the subtext there, of course again, is that the privileging of a white female body over against a black or brown woman's body is something that was equally divisive to black people. Which is why, for instance, [it was interesting to see] Gloria Steinem versus Toni Morrison about this issue: Whose body counts? Why is it that the murder of a white woman would make more difference than the murder of a black woman or brown woman? And how can we come to a point in our society where we can acknowledge that domestic violence is just as real among African American people who refuse to acknowledge its centrality because the black men who are being victimized by white supremacy are, themselves, victimizing women through their discourse of male supremacy and domestic violence? But at the same time, those same black women supported O. J. disproportionately because they felt that the focus on white women had re-victimized them. So that's a very complex knot.

Williamson: That doesn't excuse it.

Dyson: Not at all.

Williamson: That's my point. Because everything that you were saying about justice towards black people in America—I couldn't agree with you more. I know it *was* true, and I know that it *is* true. But somehow, Nicole dying the kind of death that she died doesn't make it all right for black women in America. You know what I'm saying?

Dyson: Not at all. Not at all.

Williamson: That doesn't pay any ransom.

Dyson: But I'm agreeing with you.

Williamson: I know you agree. But hold on a moment. I know you do, Michael, and I heard you speak. Please don't get me wrong. What I'm trying to name here, first of all, when they explain the whole social-political context, you know I couldn't agree with you more.

Dyson: Absolutely.

Williamson: Okay. And when you're explaining the psychological impulse be-hind certain people claiming, you know, what we're talking about here. And you're explaining it to me, I understand that. But I still think it's something to be called, to be spoken to from a perspective other than, "Well, I understand." Do you understand what I'm saying?

Dyson: No.

Williamson: I understand that white women have been given greater—all that stuff that you said. It's just like when certain very subtle racist comments are made, or certain subtle anti-Semitic comments are made, and there is kind of a so-cial pressure not to call it, "Just don't go there." And those are usually the places where we need to go.

Dyson: Absolutely.

Williamson: And I think what is essentially a less than full-blown righteous stand on the subject of murder in the case of Nicole Simpson and Ron Goldman is something that should be called. And it's almost like sometimes you don't want to call something because you're afraid that you might appear blah, blah, blah, blah, blah. And so that's why I just wanted to say that. It was nothing in what you said. But there was reaction of some people in the audience, which we've all come to understand and know, which is somehow the self-righteous [position], "It's okay in his case." Well, I'm sorry. I have encountered that, whether that was in this audience or not. I have spoken to enough people who will admit—and I'm saying it's not necessarily even just black people—that they think he killed her, but that somehow he should still be free because, after all—

Dyson: Oh no, no—

Williamson: When you say "no," then you're saying your "no," and I appreciate that. But my experience is many people for whom they could not honestly say "no."

Dyson: Let me tell you what I respond to that. My point is: I do believe he killed her. But I believe the verdict was just.

Williamson: Why?

Dyson: Let me say what I mean. When I say "just," I don't mean that O. J. didn't kill her. I'm saying that, in the history of jurisprudence in American society—in the justice system—in dealing with black people, the question has never been the moral integrity of a system. It's been about what you can prove in the court.

Williamson: And they did. The police tried to frame him.

Dyson: Let me give an example. It is, for instance, the case of Medgar Evers. Now, did anybody really doubt that Byron De La Beckwith killed Medgar Evers? I don't think many people did. It took a long time. Let's talk about Nicole Simpson, let's talk about Medgar Evers. Medgar Evers: his case was finally resolved, recently, when there was enough legal evidence to substantiate the moral claim that we knew that this man was walking around and saying, "I hate the niggers," and still living. And still we had moral outrage against that, but guess what? Moral outrage doesn't translate into a legally sustainable justice to juries. Now I'm not saying that Byron De La Beckwith should have been walking around all those years, but I'm saying there was not a legal case to be made. And if a legal case could not be made, then Byron De La Beckwith could not—as much as I hated what he did—go to jail. But once they amassed enough evidence to prove that Byron De La Beckwith indeed was the murderer, then he had to go to jail.

So I'm saying to you, I believe O. J. killed Nicole Simpson. I also believe that white racist cop [was] involved with a very questionable assault on justice—it just happened to be O. J. was involved at the same time. So I'm saying that the consideration of Nicole as a white woman does not, in my mind, at all mitigate against her being treated fairly. I'm suggesting that the justice system, in its faultiness, unfairly punished Nicole Simpson and Ron Goldman by delivering a verdict that ended up being in the favor of O. J., but that we know was morally reprehensible. At least I believe that—I believe it was morally reprehensible. So that's what I mean when I say the verdict was just. I think it was just in the sense that the case against O. J. would not stand up, given the other impediments that were there.

Williamson: Absolutely. But even then, I think it becomes a case about violence against women, in many ways. Not just black and white. Because when you said something a few minutes ago about how she was treated so well, she had been treated horribly. She had called the police so many times, saying that her husband was beating her. And because he was a big star—and I don't think it was right— because he was a big star, a big white star in their minds for all the reasons you said, they let him go away. There's no way we can claim that Nicole Simpson was treated well by the system in terms of her violence.

Dyson: See, what I'm saying is that there are so many other women whose lives don't count.

Williamson: I agree, I agree, I agree.

Dyson: So I think part of the response, this is part of the anger that some [have toward] Tammy Bruce out in L.A., who was then the director of NOW, who got dismissed by the national office because they thought she was going overboard. Because what the black women who had themselves been abused had been say- ing is that, "Listen, we know about domestic violence, because you all ain't com- ing around here unless it's Nicole. You're not concerned about us." I'm not saying that, therefore, justifies Nicole. I'm saying, understand that when people respond to Nicole, they're not responding to Nicole, they're responding to Nicole as a symbol of a system that's refused to [be fair].

Williamson: But that is my point. That is my point. And also, even just a little bit—then we can get off it—you said they came around here because it was her. They came around, but then they basically did nothing.

Dyson: Because of celebrity.

Audience voice: She kept going back.

Williamson: So she deserved to die? Okay, we'll have a whole thing about women and violence.

Dyson: Absolutely, because it's equally about that.

Williamson: Then let's talk about whatever. We don't have to keep talking about that at all.

Dyson: No, but I'm glad you raised that question. Okay. Yes, ma'am?

Question: I'm from Detroit. I have a profound question for Professor Dyson that I have had on my mind for some time. Out of the Muslim and the Arabic world a concept has come, and that concept is: Zionism is racism. It was brought to the table in South Africa, and the United States refused to send a delegation because of that and [because of disputes about] reparations. Zionism is racism for the Arabic-Muslim world. What is the profoundness of this? What is your idea that these Arabic-Muslim people have come to this concept and brought it to the table and wanted it to be approved of?

Dyson: That's a wide open question. I'm going to try to take a stab at it, and I know Marianne–

Williamson: "I know a Jewish woman is standing right next to me while I do it."

Dyson: My home girl whom I love. [*Laughter*] Let me tell you this. First of all, many people who bandy around the term Zionism, and talk about Israel and anti-Semitism and Arab ideology and Muslim people, are rather sloppy in their thinking. Because first of all, you've got to distinguish between the author of Zionism, Theodore Hertzl, and what he meant by a Zionist conception–and how that was predicated upon the possession of land that was granted to Jewish people who had been destabilized as a result of the thousands-of-years-old tradition of anti-Semitism. So Zionism is a historically specific moment in the development of competing ideologies within Judaism, both sacred and secular. So when I hear the word bandied about, about Zionism, I think Zionism has had an intellectual component, an ideological thrust, and a political use. And so I think we have to be very careful in making those kinds of distinctions.

In regard to the Arab world, when you say "the Arab world," that's just like talking about "the Jewish world," "the black world." Now, what Jews are you talking about, what Arabs are you talking about, what black people are you talking about? Are you talking about progressives? Are you talking about moderates? Are you talking about people who are reformed? Are you talking about–within Islam–people who believe in jihad as the religious articulation of their belief about God and the sanctification of a certain kind of violence? Or what they perceive to be Oriental resistance to Westernism? So I'm very cautious about that. Having said all that, I want to take the question head on. [*Laughter*]

But history is crucial. I mean, the context is crucial to me. I think the World Conference on Racism was crucial. I think that the attempt to get at the underlying issues of racial domination and hegemony in the world is crucial. And it was multipronged and multistreamed. Now, there was a brouhaha occasioned around the United States' participation and Israel's participation. I think it was unfortunate that both Israel and the United States did not participate for the following reasons: as a person of color and, in this case, black American, I ain't never had the leisure of saying, "Hey, I disagree with you so I ain't gonna talk to you." I can't get down like that. I gotta go, like, "Hey, if I ain't there, my point may not be represented. And somebody claiming to speak for me might be messing it up, right?" Now, if Marianne was there I'd be all right. But she ain't always there. So that means that somebody else might be doing the okey-doke in my name. So I got to step up to the plate, 'cause I "got to be there." I don't have the leisure of saying, "I'm gonna take my ball and go 'cause you ain't gonna play with me." I'm gonna argue my point.

I think the United States, especially, even more than Israel although I hold Israel accountable too, should have been there, because Colin Powell was interested in going because the issue of reparations was on board, the issue of talking about white supremacy was on board, and the issue of speaking about the Palestinian-Israeli conflict was on board. This is why I think Israel should have been there. You don't turn around if you believe that people are going to say things that are insulting or, in some senses, subversive of your own culture. After all, that's what it means to be a participant in the modern West for people of color for the last— what—three hundred, four hundred years?

I think Israel had a legitimate beef about how they were being characterized and painted with one brush. This is why I think Michael Lerner gave one of the most powerful responses to that by saying, "Look, I am a progressive Jew who is a rabbi, who believes in forging connections with Palestinian brothers and sisters, but I'm not trying to surrender the integrity of my identification with Israel and what that means in terms of its politics, culture, and especially, its religion." So I think Israel had a legitimate beef about how it thought it was being mischaracterized, but the best way [to proceed], as Marianne has talked about, is conversation. Not *less* conversation, but *more* conversation. If on the table was a proposal about the nature of Zionism, debate that. Tell people, "You don't even know what Zionism is. You don't even understand the historical question of what Zionism is about and its misrepresentation by anti-Semitic people who deploy it." I'm not talking about just Arabs and Muslims, I mean people all over the world. There are some anti-Semitic Jews who, within the context of trying to defend their own understanding of their Jewish identity, end up hurting, harming, and subverting the potential affiliation they enjoy with their Jewish brothers and sisters. So my point is: more conversation, not less.

But I think Zionism has a complex history. It has had some negative connotations, as Black Nationalism has, and it has some edifying ones, as Black Nationalism has. Any nationalism is suspect to me, as well as Americanism. Right? That's why, after 9/11, I made a distinction between patriotism and nationalism. Patriotism is the critical affirmation of one's country in light of its best values. Nationalism is the uncritical support of one's nation, right or wrong. I can't go with that. No "ism" deserves our uncritical support—black, brown, red, yellow, Jewish,

Muslim, or whatever. The problem is fundamentalism. Fundamentalisms go in any religion, masquerade as any politics, masquerade in any ideology.

I think we need to be critical of Israel and not be called anti-Semitic. And we should be critical of Palestine and not be called anti-Arab. Like we can be critical of African American people, and disagree with them, and not be called racist. We have to have an open conversation where the dialogue is aboveboard.

Williamson: Ma'am, I want to ask you a question. When you were asking Michael about this whole idea that that conference called Zionism a racist phenomenon, do you agree with that? Is your thought that Zionism is a racist phenomenon?

Questioner: I really don't know. When you have the whole tenet of people bringing this forth, it comes embodied in something. We know that in 1948, when Israel was created, that the people were poverty stricken. In Israel, the people, the Jews, brought in a whole modern way of living, and the relationship is almost like black to white over there. The Arab people, most of them work for the Jewish people. They're modern. The women are [of a] different status. You know, the Arab women are more second class, the Jewish women in Israel are very modern in everything they do.

Williamson: Well, Zionism, the concept, is a separate issue from what you're talking about here, which is something that deserves tremendous attention and is getting it. But the whole concept of Zionism is the idea of a Jewish state. So the idea that Zionism is essentially a racist concept, I don't see how the concept that the Jews have a state, which was established by the United Nations, should be called inherently a racist concept. It's been very difficult for me, as a Jewish woman, over the last few weeks. I consider myself a very progressive Jew in my thinking. I certainly have the capacity to criticize Israeli policy, just as I have the capacity to criticize American policy. But I've felt in the last few weeks such a major anti-Israel impulse in this country that is, as you would say, Michael, so lacking in historical context, that I found myself having to defend in my mind the idea of just the existence of Israel—which is not to in any way defend this current policy of the Israeli government at all. So that's why I was curious what you thought Zionism meant. Because I had heard so many people talking about Zionism like it's inherently a racist concept. And I don't see that. Do you, Michael?

Dyson: No, I don't. Look, the existence of Israel is an idea, as Victor Hugo said, whose time had already come long before it was even established. So I am in no way critical of the establishment of a homeland for Jews. I think the distinction you made, however, is very crucial. The point you were making is not identical with Zionism.

Williamson: *Right*. It's a whole different issue. And that's why I'm asking the woman what—

Dyson: Right. But the practices of people who are unjust—we should be critical of them whether they are Jewish or Arab or Muslim or anybody else, which is what I hear Marianne saying.

Williamson: But that's not Zionism.

Questioner: The average layperson does not know all these deep things like you do.

Williamson: Okay, but one of the reasons I like Michael Dyson so much, and one of the themes that I heard Michael repeating over and over today, which is so important [is]: the American people have gone to sleep. You know, Martin Luther King said, "We need to have tough minds and tender hearts." Americans tend to be divided into two categories: people with tough minds *or* tender hearts. There are many people, clearly, in this country who have tough minds but do not have enough love in their hearts. But there are too many people with love in their hearts who need to read a book or two. Right? Too many people! The spiritual community in America is the lazy group of people that can afford to ignore the facts and read the books and learn what we're talking about. Right? And that's why I think Michael is so important. And you put it so beautifully, Marcia [Michael's wife], when you were talking earlier about how when you met Michael, you knew things but you didn't have [the words to name them like he did]. And so, if you're not careful, you become a sloppy thinker. And you can end up arguing the argument you'd be against if you'd read the book. Right? Isn't that true? And that's why we're so interested in bringing people like Michael here. We should be making the most eloquent intellectual arguments. And every woman knows that.

It's kind of like when Michael was talking before of the woman who is a pilot of a 757: we know she's at least as good as a man. And when Ann Richards talked about Ginger Rogers did everything that Fred Astaire did—but backwards and in high heels! So I say that women of America, if we know that we have to have our facts down in order to be taken seriously, then I say we'd better get our facts down. And so, when you said the normal person—I'm the normal person, you're the normal person, we're all [normal people]—you know what I'm saying? And we need to watch a little less television and read a few more books. Right?

Question: Thank you very much. What I have to say probably won't go over too popular here. But I want to congratulate you, Mr. Dyson. You're an eloquent spokesman for our cause. You didn't say any falsities. No lies. What you said is true. Racism is a root cause of overwhelming problems that we have in our country. I want to say that maybe a couple of weeks ago, one of our local leaders here in Detroit had comments that were printed in the *Detroit Free Press* complaining about racism in Novi [Michigan], which maybe has seventy-five black families. Racism right here in Warren, Michigan. Racism in East Flint, and the same day on the front page of the *Free Press*, there was a story of the three-year-old black girl who was killed watching television in her room by a drive-by shooting. And then a couple days ago the third black girl, pre-teen, was killed. And I think what you are doing is good, really good. But I think we need like a two-prong attack. We have deviant behavior in our black community that should be addressed. You know, absentee fathers. The woman [living on Linwood and Davidson, in Detroit's ghetto], she's not, I don't think, that concerned about white racism. [*Laughter*] She's worried about somebody breaking into her house, you know? I wish more leaders would address things that we could do in our own black community.

Dyson: Yes, sir. Well, you know what? The thing that Marianne just said is crucial and apropos here, too. There have been all kinds of books, all kinds of statements—Jesse Jackson's been talking about this for about thirty-four years. So this ain't nothing new, talking about black-on-black crime. Dick Gregory's been talking about it for that long, and more. But Dick Gregory said—and he said it tongue in cheek, so I say that before I say what I'm about to say—he said, "If you want to have integrated killing, you have to have integrated communities." Now, his point was this: that people kill where they live. So you're talking about black-on-black crime—most of the crime committed against white Americans is committed by other white Americans. But you don't hear it phrased as white-on-white crime. That's despite what was called the "super predator" about ten years ago by a then Princeton/University of Pennsylvania scholar, who then, when the statistics were deconstructed, ends up finding out that people kill in a vicinity. And kill people they know, by and large. So I don't deny at all the necessity of dealing with the problem. You can read the recent book put out by Alvin Poussaint that deals with this, a twenty-year anniversary edition of a book that dealt with [black-on-black crime]. I think it's Amos Wilson who deals with the relationship between black pathologies, so-called, and the kind of murder rate within African American communities. So sociologists have been working overtime on figuring what the heck is going on. And I don't think there's been any lack of serious, credible intellectual and moral outcry.

Lambasting black-on-black crime has been one of the rites of passage for many leaders in African American culture. Martin Luther King, Jr., if you go back and read some of the records, was being critical of some of the pathologies, if we call them that, that were in African American society. The question is, though, how do we place that within the context of understanding that, as Gandhi said, and others talked about, when you have people that you systematically oppress, if you then blame them for the pathologies that the oppression produces, without interrogating the pathologies of the oppression itself, then what you're doing is calling into question the victim without talking about the victimizer. That's no excuse at all of trying to get away from [personal responsibility]. But I think preachers on any given Sunday morning preach sermons about how we've got to clean up our act. I think local politicians have talked about it time and time again, and it's something that we have to be open and honest about in terms of our communities.

One of the things I think King was rigorous in was his own moral insistence that we deal with problems. That even though we think, "Well, white folk, if they hear us dealing with them, they'll just take advantage of us and then say, ah ha, we told you." So we have to be more morally mature than that. At the same time, understand we have to hold both the system and the so-called person who is a victim, and victimizer, [responsible] within that situation. Because let me tell you one of the brave things [about Marianne] is that, first of all, we couldn't have had this conversation in most places because they wouldn't be that honest. See what I'm saying? We'd simply be polite [and conclude]: "We ain't going to say what we know is the case." So we got black folk over here thinking one thing, white folk thinking another thing. I'm picking up on what the black folks are saying, you're picking up on what the white folks are saying, but we ain't going to say it. So we just pretend this stuff is all right.

And then we say the uncomfortable truth. And the uncomfortable truth is: Hey, we see this in different ways. And we see it predicated upon our experiences and our understanding. And so we don't want to deal with domestic violence and brutality. Well, that's what I meant [when I said] be racially specific but not racially exclusive. So the issue of black-on-black violence, or domestic violence within the context of our children, is another issue that we have to come to grips with. So I think you're absolutely right, but as Marianne Williamson said, there are a whole lot of books you might want to pick up that I can tell you about that can deal with that issue, as well as local political discourse.

Williamson: Or even good media. And I just want to say, before we take the next person, once again, what Michael not only exemplifies but points out the need for: If we are interested in forging a spiritually infused politics, we must be very mature thinkers. We must be politically informed as well as spiritually informed. This is really the time. I think you were saying something on the pulpit today—or maybe here—about reading when you're on the bus, that we must show up maturely on every single level in order to have the conversations that can contain the levels of nuance that are necessary for us to hold all the juxtaposed forces, painful as well as enlightened, that inform our human experience today.

Dyson: Absolutely. Yes, ma'am?

Question: What I'd like to pose to you is the conversation of the beloved community and the idea of the beloved community. We raise ourself to a level of consciousness of saying, "We want this to exist." Do we first cure the elements of society in order for the community to exist, or do we try to get the community to exist in hopes that the ailments of society don't come up to that level? I'll give you an example. In the African American community several years ago there was a church, and the church was set up such [that] they had the paper bag test. And for those of you that don't know what the paper bag test is, you held up a paper bag, and if you were a certain shade you were not allowed in that church. So what I'm saying is, in the beloved community, not just being color conscious, because this works conversely, too, in my situation. But there is homophobia, there's racism, there's ageism, there's even prejudice towards people with disabilities. When do we stop doing that? Do we cure the ailments of the community and then try to develop the beloved community, or do we develop the beloved community? Do we say, "Okay, these elements exist, but we love, and then develop the community and trust and pray that these elements will not follow?"

Williamson: First of all, you can't heal it. You don't have the option of healing the ailments first and then being a beloved community. Without love you can't heal them. But I think one of the things also that Michael brought up today is: love is not this namby-pamby passive thing. Love is present when real communication is present. So sometimes, when people are not yet reconciled, it's like when Michael was talking a few minutes ago, that *we* can have the conversation [here]. I was in a relationship with a man once, and something happened and I brought up something, and I didn't think it was a fight; I thought it was a passive debate. And he couldn't be with that. He just slapped that down. And I knew that day there was no way we were going to have a relationship, because you can't have real love if you can't fight good. [*Laughter*] Right? This is somebody not ready for a relationship—you know what I'm saying? Because part of being beloved is much like you were talking about what's going on here. I mean, we've got beloved talk, beloved get down, beloved, "Say that hurt me when you said that." And I'm going to stay in the conversation, though, because this is a great work, our love matters. So beloved community is not a static thing; it's a process. And when a community is not yet beloved, it's not going to get beloved by fear. And you're not going to heal all those wounds except through love. And that's why I think we do what we do here. And that's why I think we do the peace circles. And that's why any of us who have mature relationships know that. There are times in intimacy, there are times being beloved, where it's not going to be easy. Being beloved doesn't mean you agree; it means you're going to stay there for the conversation.

Dyson: That's perfectly stated. And all I want to add is that the beloved community is a regulative ideal and a governing norm. There's no doubt about it. If you read King—if you read Ira Zepp and Kenneth Smith's book on beloved community, about King—the very thing that Marianne is speaking about was so powerfully fleshed out, not just in the theology of King, but in the theologies he engaged in school and in the streets from so-called "ignorant people" who were morally literate. And as she said, that love is not only the ideal, but it's also the vehicle by which you get to the ideal. Love is both the body and the lens that helps it see better. Love is an incredible force. It's also a passion. It's noun, verb, adjective, and everything.

And finally, in terms of the paper bag test—which meant that there were hierarchies of color within black America—that's true. And it's still true today. And when you said a church [involved with] the color thing—there was the knowing look that maybe white people might not have understood when black people say, "Oh yeah, paper bag." And the ruler test: If your hair was straight as this ruler you're all right, and if it was contourtuplicated, better known as kinky, you wasn't gettin' in—not only the church, but sororities, fraternities, and a whole lot of other places.

But when Marianne said be literate, here's the point: one of the most vicious consequences of white supremacy is its internalization in the people's brains who are themselves the victims. Just like the greatest enemy of some women is other women—they be "cock-blocking" and "playa-hating" on another woman, as the hip-hoppers say. So what you gotta understand is that Malcolm X said that what we're worried about is not simply the overseer outside, but the overseer in our brain. So that the homophobia, the disinclination to understand and embrace gay and lesbian, transsexual, transgender, bisexual brothers and sisters; the reality of class and economic differences; or the differences between the so-called hip-hop and the civil rights generation, which is another huge, gaping event that we haven't addressed—all that is absolutely real. But I wouldn't equate that with the kind of force of white supremacy that seduces people into cooperating with it. We are all victims [of white supremacy], but we're not equally victimized as African American people. So we have to understand that as much as our brother over here, or our sister over here, is valorizing the idea of, "You're light, bright, almost white; if you're dark as a bark stay in the park"—divorcing us—that has to be dealt with as a symptom of the disease we're dealing with.

Williamson: I want to talk for a moment about the metaphysics, also, that you touched on here of the beloved community, when you talked about it being a verb. And of course King often spoke from the Gandhian principle that the end is inherent in the means. So if we want a beloved community—we were talking about this on the pulpit today—we have to claim in the present what we want in the future. I shared with some of you, I think, on the pulpit, when Coretta Scott King invited me to be one of the speakers at the Martin Luther King commemorative service this year. I did not know until I got there that Laura Bush was the keynote speaker. And I had to do some quick editing on my talk. [*Laughter*] And I had to do it very fast. But I thought that this was such a perfect principle, so perfect here on Martin Luther King's pulpit with Laura Bush in back of me. Literally, I'm speaking on Dr. King's pulpit with Laura Bush standing in back of me. Because what I want to say, basically, is that her husband is doing everything that's keeping the beloved community at bay. But if I'm not sensitive to the fact that this is the man this woman sleeps with, right? If I'm not sensitive to her as a woman, and if this is her husband, then I am not being of the beloved community myself. So it was such a challenge to me to be like Martin Luther King himself, to show her honor as a person.

Dyson: Right, right. And still tell the truth, as you did.

Williamson: Absolutely. Thank you. [*Laughter*] But that is a very important issue, to not talk about the beloved community as something other people need to establish. Because if I couldn't speak my truth and still honor this woman, then I'm not of the beloved community either. I'm just talking.

Question: I'm from Jamaica. I'm the product of my mother going to take five, six buses. And that's why I'm here today. I'm an engineer and I'm in corporate America. One observation: I hope we can continue to open a dialogue like this, because it's crucial, especially in the metro-Detroit area. My brother is one of three firefighters for the city of Warren, and I don't see them hiring anyone else. But my question to you is, since I'm in corporate America, I've noticed that there's virtually no dialogue between white and black males. I see white and black females starting to get the picture of coming together, especially in this church, and especially out in the community. But when it comes to corporate America, white and black men virtually don't talk about any issues. They don't talk about the substance dialogue that we should start talking about. My question is, how can we start that dialogue, because the "Big Three" [the automobile manufacturers] are not talking at all. Period. I mean, that is a deep subject. I've been trying to get the answer to that question, and I can't get it and I don't know how to start it.

Williamson: Well, there's a reason, subconsciously, why that conversation isn't happening. Because if you were to challenge that separation, you'd have to challenge the fundamental underlying principles that govern corporate America to begin with. The conversation about corporate America is probably the most morally challenging and critical conversation in the world. You know, people are fine. And the people who work within corporations are fine. Some of the corporations we might have the most criticism of are filled with wonderful human beings. The problem is, the human being has a conscience. The human being has the capacity to reflect. The human being has the capacity to appreciate nuance. So placing our faith, including our economic faith, in the hands of human beings who are regulated to a certain extent—that society deems necessary—I don't have a problem with. What has happened in the United States today, which Thomas Jefferson warned us about, which Abraham Lincoln warned us about, is that you get these gargantuan powers which are not human. They are not human. They are not entities who reflect. They are not entities with conscience. They are not entities who are appreciating nuance.

So whereas an individual, if I talked to a rich man or woman, and I say, "Well I understand that you'd make half a million there, but I'd like you to look at the oil spill. I'd like you to look at what the oil spill is actually doing, and then can we talk about whether it's worth the financial gain you're getting by not protecting us against the oil spill." I don't have any problem. The problem is, if I'm talking to a corporation, that means I'm probably not even getting to the individual who's making the economic accounting decision, and they're never going to see the oil spill. So that's a conversation that is the real issue of corporate America. Not how its members relate to each other. If the members start getting real with each other, pretty soon you're going to have a conversation among them about, "What the hell are we doing here?" Right? And that's why the system, on a certain level, re-sists a certain level of authentic, genuine human communication. Because it's al-most like a slippery slope there: once we start getting real, we're going to start ask-ing all kinds of questions.

Dyson: Right. Once you start getting real, you've got to keep it real.

Williamson: That's right. So there's a lot of subconscious aversion that I think goes way beyond race. It goes to the issues of power and control, period.

Question: There should be no dialogue?

Dyson: No, no, I don't think that's what she said at all. She's talking about the culture–

Williamson: –Subconscious resistance to it, within a corporate system.

Dyson: Right. And she's talking about corporate culture, especially among busi-ness elites. And it's not even about business elites. It's about the degree to which the regulating ideas of corporate culture discourage the very conversation you're speaking about, because then it wouldn't be the corporate culture. Because think about Reinhold Niebuhr's book, *Moral Man, Immoral Society*. This is what Mari-anne's talking about, right? Corporations don't think. At least, not in the way we're talking about individuals do. So that when you're speaking about corporate culture, you're speaking about the very rigorous attention to the very forces that allow it to exist without conscience at a certain level. That's what it means: cor-porate–without the individual response to the oil spill, or the money hemorrhag-ing. So that now you've got the mayor of Chicago trying to deal with the Ander-son employees because they got shafted–which is a metaphor for what happens when big business in general lights on these communities, especially in cyber-space, with the postindustrial forms of economy that are now developing.

But your question about black men and white men in particular is rather interesting, because in a patriarchal culture—that has conscious or unconscious beliefs that men's lives should supply the norms that dominate life—well, black men and white men might have some agreement about that. So they might both be patriarchal in that sense. But what's the greatest threat to you as a patriarch? A potential supplanter. Another patriarch. So even within the political economy of patriarchy, the greatest threat is another man—and this is why you see all these internal conversations between black men and black women. Brother say, "We can't get no job." Sister say, "Well, we can get hired *sometimes*." And then brothers—wrongly, wrongly—end up saying to sisters, "Oh, the white man is favoring you, and you gettin' over." No, no, no. What's happening is that the greatest threat in a patriarchal system is another patriarch. So black men often beat up, rhetorically speaking, on women by saying, "Hey, you should then be protesting." No.

We should undermine the system of patriarchy so that the distribution of goods like jobs is not predicated upon me identifying with you as a man, but how we can identify with just practices, so that we can disabuse ourselves of [such injustice]. Because if the only thing black men want to ask white men is how to get over, as opposed to how to make it more just, then we're not undermining the system. But black men represent a particular kind of threat in that patriarchal culture. Don't be mistaken about that.

Williamson: Can I say something really quick? I heard someone say this recently—one of my colleagues. I can't remember who it was, but boy, do I agree. And they were saying that we should really be careful about all this business of corporate make-nice. This idea that if we have enough feel-good seminars inside corporations, it gives it this nice face, which will make it actually easier to obfuscate some of the issues we need to look at more deeply, in terms of work behavior.

Dyson: That's the point you were making earlier. We've got to challenge it.

Williamson: That's not a criticism of people who work in corporations.

Question: Brother Dyson, may I make my observation? First of all, you sound so much like Fred Sampson. [*Applause*]

Dyson: That's my pastor. Thanks.

Question: As one who benefited from going to Tabernacle [Missionary Baptist Church] and hearing him in other places, it's such a compliment that someone came out of his church like you.

Dyson: That's an honor to me, brother.

Question: The other thing is: you know, we have a revolutionary sister who's a leader here. She got heart. Sister's got heart. She will confront no matter what. And we all love and appreciate how she feels and the heart she has. The question I have is: I'm a radical black Republican, okay?

Dyson: Wow. Wow.

Question: And I ain't afraid of nobody in this room, okay? You understand what I'm saying? I ain't scared of nobody in here. But I'm just suggesting to you that the conversation we had is a beautiful conversation. I'm a supporter of Jesse Jackson, and one of the things Jesse always talks about is [that] we [should] take this conversation into the level of public policy. Where do we go from this beautiful discussion that we had? I mean, even Marianne's comments about the comment that was made by the black people when you said what you said about the Nicole thing was a beautiful thing. Even though she may have misinterpreted what the black folks meant with their comment. That's alright. We understand that she got the right to misinterpret that, too. [*Laughter*] 'Cause, you know, as beautiful as she is, and as much as she understands us, she may not understand all of us because she ain't been with us, where we are. But the point is, how do we take this discussion we've had, and all the things we've talked about—and this translates into what Jesse talks about—[into] public policy? Where do we go from there to make this public policy? You know, I represent Pookie. I'm a criminal lawyer. I'm dealing with murder tomorrow. Okay? And I'm just telling you, I deal with Pookie on a daily basis. How do we translate this into public policy so we create fewer Pookies?

Dyson: Well, look, I think that public policy is crucial, and Jesse Jackson is right when he insists that it's not just about feel good sentimentality; it's about the translation of [ideas into] public policy. Because, after all, the law has to be changed for the policies to be enacted. And the change of the law was fundamental, right, which is how he made a distinction, for instance, between the Million Man March, with its organization of passions directed against the state at some level, versus the 1963 March on Washington, which led to the Civil Rights Bill and the Voting Rights Act.

How I intend to [translate public policy]—first of all, you already heard this morning a very powerful one: when we're thinking about oil, when we think about issues of domestic violence. This stuff translates rather easily to those of us who are progressive about our politics into local codes in governments, in municipalities, that restrict, that outlaw, that kind of behavior, number one. Number two, how we translate this into public policy is to reinforce the laws that exist by creating new public policy [to support them], such as when I talked about Bill Clinton in terms of the crime bill. See, black folks should have been speaking about that at the top of our voices. Instead, we were seduced into cooperation with Bill Clinton as opposed to opposing him. That's why I'm saying when Clinton did it—we were silent, including Jesse. [*Applause*]. No, no, no, I've been a friend of his for a long time. He would be mad at me for saying that, but he loves me; I'm a friend of his. So I ain't saying nothing to you I ain't said to him. But what I'm telling you is that when Jesse Jackson stood up and said Bill Clinton's policies are an extension of Dr. King's dream, I got to argue with you on that. Now, his principle, however, is right, even though I disagree with him on individual things.

The principle of public policy means this: what we have to do, then [for instance] is to stop the prison-industrial complex. The very thing that keeps Pookie in jail is not simply the desire to have black men locked up. It's about fueling a local, rural economy. And a local, rural economy—because my brother's been locked up for twelve years for second-degree murder. I believe he's innocent. But I know about Pookie. One brother a professor from Princeton, another brother a prisoner in the prison-industrial complex. So I live that horror in my own family. So for me, I think what's important then is to talk about the prison-industrial complex and its expansion. California's fastest growing industry is prisons. It's being driven by debt peonage-like conditions in American society. So we know we have to deal with that. Public policy says that we've got to stop funding the privatization of prisons.

Number two in public policy [regarding Pookie] is to deal with the disparity in sentencing between crack and powder cocaine. I'm not arguing for affirmative action for thugs. That ain't what I'm saying. I'm saying, however, that if you're going to continue to send people to prison, don't overlook the cat who used to work for Enron up in the suites blowing $10,000 worth of powder cocaine, who gets the same sentence as the brother or sister on the street doing $25 of crack, or rock cocaine. You know this. And Bill Clinton authorized this, with his crime bill. So we have to close that disparity.

Third in public policy [regarding Pookie], is to talk about the death penalty. Because one of the untold consequences of the crime bill that Bill Clinton signed is that now we've got about, what, four or five different ways the death penalty can be enforced, which is disproportionately stigmatizing black and brown people and, increasingly, women as well. So those are just three public policies that immediately leap to my mind in terms of translation.

And fourthly, I think, we need to also understand that politics is not simply about what we do in the parliamentary procedure, although that's crucial. Electing this governor here, electing this senator here, electing this mayor here—that's all crucial. I ain't mad at that. Because I'm working with Al Sharpton on his exploratory committee. Now, I know a lot of people are saying, "Well, dadgum, what about his hair?" [*Laughter*] Right? I understand. I ain't mad, I ain't mad. But I say, if you put a silhouette of Al Sharpton next to George Washington, he looks more like the first president than any other president since. Now, we don't always necessarily have to agree, but I—as well as the Reverend Marcia Dyson—want to be in there giving intelligent thought to public policy formation. And for my money, Al Sharpton has been more progressive than any other politician, especially within

African American politics, over the last five years. His progress has been enormous, his evolution has been consistent. He's put away some of the tragic mistakes he made and has now embraced a very powerful politics of progressive coalition. When I sat at that exploratory committee, I saw women, I saw Jews, I saw Latinos, I saw a whole range of people up there that look much more like America than what we've got right now. I think that what we have to do is to strategically intervene, not only in politics on the official level, but [in the] politics of raising people's consciousness on the local level. Organizing camps for young people; tutoring and mentoring young people. That is political action to me, because you are making better citizens. And when you make better citizens, you are making better human beings and, ultimately, your spirituality is showing in a very powerful way.

10

HOMELANDS, HOMEGIRLS, AND HOMEFRONTS
The Politics of Black Love

with Cornel West; moderated by Amos Brown

In April 2006, Butler University invited me and Cornel West to share the stage in a Diversity Lecture Series. After we each lectured, West and I fielded questions from the audience and engaged in a conversation about the limits, outlines, and meanings of black love in various guises. The conversation was very satisfying, not only because West is one of my mentors, and because he is the towering American intellectual of his generation, but because of his protean rhetorical gifts and his deep sense of humanity. The night reminded me of the part we both played in a historic teaming with Tavis Smiley for "Pass the Mic," where the three of us—men of three different generations—spoke to and engaged mostly sold-out crowds (which paid $50–$60 per person) in major theaters and arenas across the nation for six nights in late 2003. This event, however, was bittersweet for me because I had discovered right before the engagement how gravely ill was my beloved editor and friend, Liz Maguire. She died the next day, and there has been a gaping hole in my life ever since.

Amos Brown: Now we've got a little time—I'm getting old and I can't see like I used to. It's an opportunity to ask some questions of Dr. Dyson and Dr. West. And what I ask you to do, keep your questions short and to the point. You can address them to either one or both. And since I'm old and I'm a curmudgeon, I want to ask the first one. Docs, Indiana is well known for a lot of things–basketball, agriculture, jazz. In twenty-five days, Indiana will be the first state in this union to tell American citizens, either born here or naturalized, who do not have a driver's license by choice, who do not have a photo ID by choice, who cannot find their birth certificate because they never had one, that they will not have the right to vote. Unless a federal board intervenes, Indiana will institute in twenty-five days the most restrictive voter ID law in the nation–only an Indiana driver's license or photo ID card, a military ID, or an American passport are the only identification to vote. Not even a Butler (University) ID will work. How, then, with that kind of oppression, does a community deal with that positively?

Cornel West: I didn't know that. My problem has been trying to get high-quality candidates so people feel as if they have people to vote for. That's on one side. But the backside is [that] now we've had a major movement trying to gain the rights to vote for brothers and sisters of all colors who have committed felonies and who have been to jail. There's over five million fellow human beings in this society who can't vote because they've been incarcerated with a felony. But now, with those kinds of restrictions, I mean, you can just see the fear that went into that kind of bill, trying to restrict and think that somehow you can control and manipulate and insure that somehow things don't get out of *your* control. I just wish that there had been a stronger movement in place to counter that bill. But I don't know the story. But I think that we just have to come up with some high-quality candidates so the folk who can vote feel as if they can organize and mobilize and be encouraged enough to vote for somebody who they think can make a difference, even within those restrictions. Unless you get it declared unconstitutional.

Brown: The judge has been considering how to rule for ninety days.

West: How many days does he have?

Brown: How many days does he have left? Twenty-five.

West: Are we waiting to see what he's going to say?

Brown: Yeah, we're waiting on the initial decision. They've been sitting on this for six months.

Michael Eric Dyson: I think it's also an extension of the kind of politics of surveillance, through the artificial control of a population by means of exclusion. As opposed to expanding, which you were speaking about, the perimeters of democracy and the boundaries of enfranchisement, we're trying to find ingenious ways to snuff out people's potential to be actively engaged in the democratic polity. And the tragedy of that, of course, is that it discourages us, as you said, from trying to find high-quality people to run for office so we will be inspired to vote. E. J. Dionne wrote a book called *Why Americans Hate Politics*. So here we've got the problem, the conundrum, the dilemma of trying to get people to be reengaged in the enfranchisement process; in Indiana, in Indianapolis, [they're] trying to find ways to snuff people out who want to vote from the giddy-up. Backwards and redundant!

Question: Welcome to Indianapolis, Doctors. I'm a local artist—B.F.A. from Howard, M.A. from UCLA in African Studies, and I sat next to many educated brothers in my classes. And there was a lot of tension, often, between the sisters and brothers sitting next to each other in the ivory tower classes. My sisters would often complain that brothers would tell them, "Well, we can be close friends, but I'm going to marry a real woman." And they'd get on a plane, go back to the Continent—Ghana, Ethiopia, South Africa—and get them a woman from over there. Or, of course, a white woman. The question is, what do the Doctors have to say about the decline in marriage among African Americans, especially African American intellectuals, since the civil rights movement?

Dyson: I'll defer to Dr. West.

[*Laughter*]

West: The reason he defers is because he's been blessed with a magnificent wife. Where is Marcia? She must be here somewhere.

Brown: She's in the wings.

West: She's in the wings. Oh, there she is. He's been blessed with a magnificent wife, and I've been blessed with a number, you know what I mean? [*Laughter*] The same Mighty God, you know! [*Laughter*] No, I'm just kidding. But first, there's a very complex dynamic that takes place between men and women, especially men and women of African descent in professional managerial spaces or in [the] middle class on their way to such spaces. Because there's such an anxiety and fear and insecurity that goes hand-in-hand with being at a Howard, or UCLA, or Butler, or University of Pennsylvania and Princeton. They're always wondering whether they're good enough, they're wondering whether they're connected in the right kind of network enough. And so what happens, oftentimes, people either have a tilt toward the trophy option—you're just looking for a trophy companion. It's not the real thing. That's what I mean by living a life of superficiality and peacocking and so forth. So it's just somebody who you think fits in well with your project. But you see, that's empty, and that's not gonna last that long. Second thing is, I think that a free woman, and a free black woman, presents a tremendous challenge to a brother. For many brothers, it's terrifying. Maybe some of the African brothers have to go back to the Continent because a free woman is too much. They get back home, she deferential: "I tell her what to do, she follow through and dictate what I'm saying," and so forth and so on. Now, don't get me wrong: Everybody's got to work their thing out. You only got one life to live. So I don't believe that there's just one model or paradigm as to how persons relate to one another. But for me, most importantly, the courage I was talking about has to be manifest in your emotional life. The courage to love at the deepest, deepest level. And the irony is, you'll only be able to muster the courage to love by being in love, and therefore you have to do it with somebody else, and you have to learn how to do it together with somebody. A lot of folk need three lifetimes for that. But be patient with we brothers, though, be patient. [*Laughter*]

Dyson: I'll just briefly add, thinking back on that very powerful analysis, you think about the fact that black women are both the recipients of enormous cultural attraction and repulsion, simultaneously. So that you got Condoleezza Rice being called a "coon" by a talk show host. You've got Cynthia McKinney being called a "ghetto slut" by another talk show host. And you've got the young black woman who was allegedly raped in North Carolina being called a "ho" by Rush Limbaugh. Now, you combine that with the infrastructure of intimate terror that is visited upon these black women by the rhetoric of gangsta, and broader forms, of hip-hop as well as the dominant culture. It's a convergence. It's where they agree. You're absolutely right—and that's why I've coined this term, *femiphobia*. It's the fear of women. It's not just misogyny—the hatred of women; and it's not just sexism, which is sentiments against women because they're women; or patriarchy, which is the establishing of male norms to dominate women. It's also the *fear* of when a real woman shows up. When a real woman shows up, it just begins to expose some of the holes, the presuppositions, and the fake, inauthentic moments of masculinity.

So as Professor West said, that stuff is mediated in a white supremacist culture that has already assaulted black men—because the greatest threat in a white patriarchal culture is another brother. So black men, bearing the mark on their backs as a target of white supremacy and patriarchal hegemony, come on to the crib, where they feel the black woman's independent authority—*they* have become what *we* want to be—and then they're censured. So we gotta find out ways to both resolve the intimate entanglements that lead to, shall we say, male disharmony and lack of bliss—and I been there and done that—and figuring out ways also, as Dr. West said, to work out a system where we both acknowledge the other, while we mutually and reciprocally support one another. Because at the end of the day, that's what you looking for. Remember Teddy Pendergrass said, "I'm looking for a 50/50 love." You can't find that, Doc. If you get a 70/30 on a good day you rollin' right! [*Laughter*]

Brown: Maybe they're going to fill the vacancies on *The View*. Let's go over here. [*Laughter*]

Question: Hi, Doctors. I'm from West Africa. I have a few questions.

Brown: *One* question. [*Laughter*]

Question: All right. I'll try to ask one question. I want to ask, I never heard the term "European American" before, but since I've been in this country I hear "African American" a lot. Now I want to understand how you two explain the phenomenon of no matter how much educated a black person is in this country, they still call themselves "African American," when we all know deeply, inside of us, they keep us separate, because you call yourself "African American," and I call myself "African." But we still black. All we have separating us is nothing but history. What I want to understand is, how do we keep calling ourselves "African American," and not "Africans," no matter how much educated we are? And I never hear a term "European American."

West: I appreciate that question. One is, we have to keep in mind, that there are a lot of different kinds of black people, brother. There *are* some black people who call themselves "American." They're only about 3 percent, but they're there; we gotta acknowledge them. [*Laughter*] Why do they call themselves that? Because they feel, or aspire to be, so wholly assimilated into American life that they feel they can gain distance from the slavery, the Jim and Jane Crow, the discrimination and so forth, that's part and parcel of American history. Now you move to that other 97 percent, who either call themselves "black American," "African America," so forth, they're saying—in part it's like Malcolm X saying, "You don't put a kitten in the oven and call it a biscuit." They're saying that even though we've been here, we've been in, but not fully of, the nation. You see? So if you don't feel as if you're a full-fledged citizen with the same level of dignity and respect, then it makes all the sense in the world to say we're Americans with a difference.

Now, the thing is, if it's true that so many black folk have generations that go all the way back eight, nine, ten generations, that's longer than many European Americans, in fact, if not most. But [Europeans] can still come in and feel assimilated. So Italian brothers and sisters come in, second generation, they feel that they're American. They're no longer Italian Americans. Irish come in, Jewish come, so forth and so on. I'm just American—capital, capital *A*. And you say, "Okay, you been assimilated," and so forth. Now, you get anti-Catholic backlash, all of a sudden they start saying, "Well, I'm more Italian and Catholic than I thought." Jewish brothers and sisters think they're so assimilated, and all of a sudden somebody starts calling them some anti-Jewish language, and they say, "Oh, I'm actually less American than I thought." For black folk, there's very few of us who are duped, that really believe that we're full-fledged American citizens across the board. And that's a good thing. It means we're in touch with reality, because we're not full-fledged citizens.

Dyson: I'll just briefly add this. That's a powerful point because it's usually only when Americans travel outside the boundaries, either geographically or philosophically, of their own comfort zones that they begin to have reinforced for them just how American they are. So black people are internal tourists. And we're constantly reminded. I mean, what Professor West is talking about is the fact that American culture is a crucible that pulverizes racial and ethnic differences when it comes to white folk. White folk are baptized *into*—black folk are constantly excluded *from*—the American mainstream. So even when we tryin' to assimilate, even when we tryin' to forget, even when we're trying to get involved with the assimilationist project, we constantly are reminded of just what those finite limits of our assimilation are. And as Professor West said, when you're talking about African American, that's a political construct. That's not a natural, national identification. Black folk mean something political when they talk about *African* American. First of all, we're trying to grab hold to the African roots that nurtured us. But roots should nurture, not strangle. So we find out the difference between holding on to those roots and then extending them into America. Because don't forget it—some Africans who come to America become Americanized; start hatin' on Negroes who were born here. And black folk here begin to say, "Don't call me no African 'cause that ain't where I'm from. I'm from Detroit and Chicago and Indianapolis." [*Laughter*] So we got the mutual benefits of white supremacy occupying our heads and not understanding how, internationally and globally, we in the same boat of blackness, and we got to claim that legacy together.

Question: Doctors, thank you for coming to Indianapolis and speaking the truth to power. I wanted to ask a question that neither of you touched on. I was a bit surprised. And that concerns the recent debate over immigration. And it seems that a lot of us have been caught up in a diversion about diversity, so that we keep our minds off of other issues. And I wanted to get your thoughts on that. Particularly, what I'm disturbed by is the many black folks who harbor these same sentiments against immigrants, thinking they're taking our jobs. Rather than embracing each other, as you both suggested, we're hating them too.

West: You want to say a word about that? I'm deeply inspired and excited about these young brown brothers and sisters, Spanish-speaking brothers and sisters, Latino brothers and sisters, who hit the streets—junior high, high school, college. That's a beautiful thing. Just like France. Why? Because the powers that be, who oftentimes are so clever in hiding and concealing the suffering, have to finally take note. See, I wish black folk would take to the streets in those ways. You know what I mean? Police brutality—every black would just take off, take a stand. See what I mean? Bad education in the schools—take off. Take a stand. Right across the board—but then you need leadership, but that's another issue. But the thing is that we do have to acknowledge, though, that there is, in fact, a deeply xenophobic strand in black folk—back to my dear brother's question here. Black people have been Americanized enough to look at Latinos through white supremacist lenses. See what I mean? And they see the stereotype. Latinos Americanized enough look at black people and see white supremacist constructs of us.

So we can't even get at the humanity between black and brown, because the white supremacy mediates it. And you have to have leaders on both sides to try to call it into question. Now, at the same time, you do have folk in the business communities who want to just exploit the labor, 'cause it's cheap. Then you got right-wing brothers and sisters who just want to expel it because they're often xenophobic. And we also have to acknowledge there *are* some real tensions because we're fighting over crumbs. We're fighting over the jobs that so few people want to have, and therefore we get territorial because we're fighting for the crumbs. Well, then you need a leadership that says, "We understand the short-term perception, but we've got to be able to unite against the bosses, against the powerful who love to see us fighting for crumbs, that reinforces this divide-and-conquer strategy and makes it difficult for collective insurgency to take place."

Dyson: What's interesting is some of the arguments of the xenophobic movement, and mood, and polls of many black Americans replicate the same arguments used against black folk in the early part of the twentieth century, when they were brought in as scab workers against white Americans, who felt that "These Negroes are talking our job." That's number one. Number two, when Ray Nagin talked about this as a chocolate city down in New Orleans, what's interesting is that you ain't got to worry about it being a chocolate city—maybe a peanut butter city, with the influx of Central Americans, Salvadorans, and Mexicans who, with jobs bidded out at $60 for Halliburton per hour, they pay the Mexicans $5 to $6, and they pocket the $54 that's left. They create tension between indigenous African people in America trying to live on the margins and the crumbs Professor West talked about—introducing artificial tension between those. Then you got Vicente Fox bragging about the exploitation of Mexicans. "We'll take jobs that even Negroes won't." Don't brag about that. That's a complaint. That's a lament because that means they have to take jobs that are far beneath a living and sustainable wage for anybody. And then finally, what kills me is that they don't understand [that] Latinos have African roots. What are we speaking about? I mean, "us" talking about "them" misses how "they" is "us!" Right. This "us" versus "them" [overlooks] Afro-Latinos. And we know color difference plays a role even in immigrant communities that are Latino. If Elian Gonzalez had been from Santiago de Cuba versus Havana, they'd have given him a Snickers bar and told him to take his black ass back home. [*Laughter*]

Question: Members of Congress are considering allowing illegal aliens to be permitted to eventually become citizens of the U.S., while people here are struggling to receive some of the benefits for American citizens. Could you comment on that, please?

West: Yeah. I actually support trying to bring in and allow people mainstream status, people who are already here. It doesn't mean that we downplay the role of folk who are here and who are still catching hell. But the problem is, if they stay here and they don't have *any* status, it means that you have a significant labor force with no political force whatsoever. And it also means that their children would be mistreated and abused. Now the logic is this—that we must, under all conditions, insure that one's own children are not abused. That's just fundamental—I would think it's human family, and so forth. But from there, you also want to insure other people's children are not abused. And you don't want to, in any way, accent just your folk being abused and, therefore, overlook the ways in which others are abused, too. We've got to keep track of both. What I do disagree with is the guest worker status, which is the second part of that bill. I do not agree with that. And that's another issue.

Dyson: What's interesting, Professor West—think about it this way, too. If the stuff that you think those folk are taking away from you remains in place 'cause you disband them, you still gon' be poor, you still gon' be working for minimum wage and less than. The shift in the political economy, from manufacturing to service industries, means it's a knowledge-based economy. If you're not getting retooled and retrained in an economy—and you can look at this city right here in terms of a postindustrial urban collapse, where education becomes a major export, where certain forms of postindustrial base are real here—then you recognize that even if they ain't here, you still screwed. So it's a red herring for you to assume that they the problem. They ain't the problem. The problem is "they" [the powers that be]— not "them." And we gotta figure out a way to make that distinction.

Question: This question is with the backdrop of Dr. Dyson saying you feel like we're "internal tourists," and like Dr. Cornel West said, that most of us have not been duped in thinking that we are American. The question is: I've heard a lot of comparison between African Americans in America and the religious standpoint of the children of Israel in Egypt being in bondage. And I wondered if the prophesies of the Bible did, in fact—my understanding is that both of you have a theological root—and I want to know if the prophesies in the Bible, could we see ourselves in the extraction of them from Egypt and extraction of them from Babylon? Is there a future for us somewhere outside of America? What's bringing that to mind is that I hear us saying that the conditions we are in are based on the system in which we live, and we're trying to fight a system. Would that be equivalent to the children of Israel trying to fight the Egyptians?

West: Brother, that's a deep question that black intellectuals have been wrestling with for two hundred years—a very deep question. Now remember Henry Highland Garnett said in 1837, he stepped to the lectern and he said, "Black people never confuse yourself with the situation of the Israelites. For us, Pharaoh was on both sides of the bloody Red Sea." In other words, he's saying we between a rock and a hard place. [*Laughter*] What does that mean? You could imagine somebody hollering in the back, "Would somebody sing a song, please?" It's just the music that's going to get you through this mess. And the love *in* the music. That's why music is not ornamental for us. It's constitutive of who we are. That's why Luther matters. That's why Miles matters, Coltrane matters, Sarah Vaughn matters. They're not entertainers. They are spiritual geniuses who allow us to preserve our sanity and our dignity and our humanity. What they also had in mind was, even if we left—where ya gon' go? Africa's still got neocolonial control for the most part, even though they've had independence. Central America's in trouble. Latin America's bouncing back with a democratic awakening, but there's people on the land! You can't just show up when somebody else is already there. [*Laughter*] We did that in Liberia, didn't we? That's the problem. We got to crawl right down the Middle East with Jewish brothers and sisters. They get trashed like dogs and cockroaches by that vicious Hitler. What did they do? They got to jump out the burning buildings of Europe. They had no choice. But what'd they do? They land on the backs of some Arabs. So they've got to learn how to either democratically coexist, or they're going to subjugate them and have a whole new problem. This is a historic problem. It's true of Armenians. You see what I mean? So where do we go? This is a problem. You know what I mean? So most of us say, "Well, we been here for so long, we should sacrifice," and so forth. "We've got to stay here and fight it out." But then, you know, you've got Black Nationalists who say, "You ain't gonna never be free in America in terms of the masses." I'm not talking about the bourgeois Negroes, but in terms of the masses. "You ain't gon' never be free." And you figure, "You've got a point." And you say, "Well, what are you going to do?" "Well, we gon' take over Alabama, Georgia, and Mississippi." [*Laughter*] Okay. But I don't laugh, because it's said out of deep love. When the Honorable Elijah Muhammad said that, he said it out of love for black people. He said until we control our own, we'll never be free. Brother had a strong challenge. I'm sorry. You see the point I'm making?

Question: Yes, sir, I just want to understand. Are you saying that black people have no home? I mean a homeland. If you say "African American," you denote something.

West: I think that when it comes to defining home, vis-à-vis land, for the most part we never have had a home for four hundred years. I'm not just talking about ownership of acres in Mississippi and so forth. I'm talking about the masses of folk having a territory with their own control. So what home have black folk had? It's in their voice, in their bodies, in their song and their music and their movement. That's why we're a people of time rather than space. Rhythm, off the beat, rhythm-and-blues, jazz. We are people of time, tempo, temporality. Because when it comes to space, territory—for the most part we have no control over it. Now, in one sense it's powerful because more and more we live in a culture which is all about temporality, orality. It's about how you stylize your body in space and time.

Therefore, black folk at an advantage. The way people walk and talk in Italy and Russia tend to imitate the young brothers and sisters on the block in Indianapolis. Or the way they *sing* and so forth and so on. But the problem is, it doesn't translate into political power. And it doesn't translate into economic power. You can sing all you want—you don't control the recording industry. See what I mean? I'm sorry to go on and on, on this. I'm sure Brother Dyson—you wanna say somethin' on this?

Dyson: I'll just catch up on the next one. [*Laughter*]

Question: Good evening, Doctors. I am a communications student here, and I will be writing a final paper on the representation of blacks in America as it relates to agenda setting. And I wanted to know if one or both of you can make a brief point about that.

Dyson: Well, that's basically what my man was talking about here, too, I guess. Well, there are many agenda items. Professor West mentioned Tavis—a local homeboy here made good—and his "Covenant with Black America," as a part of the agenda. The National Urban League constantly speaks about focusing its energy on the state of black America, and so on. But, see, one of the things that we have to wrestle with is, when we say "we," who are we speaking about? That pronominal existence—"we"—appears to be a metaphysical assertion. But when you try to nail it down politically and physically, it's very difficult. Because when you say "we"—where we gonna go?—are you talking about Clarence Thomas? [*Laughter*] I mean, as a representative figure. Clarence ain't gon' get down with us. So at that level, there's at least one black person we know ain't heading there. But there are millions more, right? There are millions more. When you say "our agenda," what agenda is that? You see, black America is now so split and fractured along multiple axes. Race is a unifying fiction that gives cohesion to the experiences of individuals that still are significant, that resonates with us. But then, when you start breaking it down in subsections and subcategories and so on, when you talking about "we," black people say, "We down for unity"—until we start talkin' 'bout the gay folk. "Well, we got to purify them 'cause the Bible say they doin' wrong." Already you got a problem. Because no longer is it a unified "we"; it's a fractured "we." It's "we" with an asterisk—everybody *except* the gays and lesbians, transgenders, and bisexuals. Except the poor. Then you start adding all that. Then when you start layering all that stuff, then you begin to see that the complex convergence of multiple strands of black identity demand political allegiances that are fractured along the multiple lines of our identities. Which means, ultimately, that we can have functional solidarity—or what they used to call, back in the day, "operational unity": we agree to come together under one umbrella on this given day for this given purpose to articulate this particular idea. And as much as we can forge alliance and solidarity and agreement around a set of issues, then we constitute black identity at that level. We constitute a black agenda at that level.

But, you see, I think that if it's only about race—Professor West's point in *Race Matters* was, you got to ask the moral content of the identity, not simply the character of the pigment. I would rather side with Ruth Bader Ginsberg on the Supreme Court than Clarence Thomas. If he black all his life and I'm black all my life, it really just don't make no difference. It's not simply the color of your pigment; it's the color of your mind. [*Laughter*] Colored by a perception of what it means to be a citizen in America. When Martin Luther King, Jr., used to quote Arnold Toynbee, the great historian, when he said it may be that the Negro will provide the kernel that will save American civilization—that's what he was talking about. Because he knew, as Professor West said earlier, we had not been ultimately or fatally trapped by the trip of an ethnically exclusive, racially exclusive conception of what it meant to do the right thing. Martin Luther King, Jr., was concerned about right versus wrong, not black versus white.

So when it comes down to it, what we understand at the end of the day is that blackness is how you behave, a certain kind of ethic of regard for the perpetuation of a legacy of freedom struggle against oppression. So that we've always seen blackness to be metaphorical more than literal. Because even when a white brother had an attempt to get down with us, we would rather take John Brown over some elements of Booker Washington any day of the week. So we understood what black was about.

But finally, when you talk about where we going to go. Bro' went to Liberia. We see what happened there: it's a tricky negotiation with identity. You got brothers and sisters from the Caribbean going, "What's wrong with you Negroes?" You be goin', "See, you came from a country where y'all were running things. And so you didn't have to worry about if the oppression was coming to you because you were black; it's just because they were unjust and evil and problematic." Here in America, the singular obsession with race as the dynamic division between the people who are black in America [and others] means that we are constantly trying to negotiate the difference between the injustices we see occurring and the justice we know should occur. So for me, at the end of the day, I think our agendas are determined by the functions and the solidarities that generate when black people who think similarly can come together out of a political project that's progressive. We've got a lot of antiprogressive black folk in America that we can't never say is "we." [*Laughter*]

Finally, let me say this. When I think about agenda setting, I think we have to give up on the fantasy and the fiction that every black person in America is gon' agree about a fundamental objective for us here in America. What it means to be black in America now—Martin Luther King, Jr., couldn't be Martin Luther King, Jr., now. The very success of Martin Luther King, Jr.'s movement makes him impossible. Because what we have now is such a hugely developed, extremely complex, and sophisticated amalgamation of different constituencies within black

America, that there's no longer one umbrella—if there ever was—under which we can operate. Unity was always a fiction made necessary by the division of black folk by white America when we came here. But what it made us forget is that even when we got here, without the fiction of white supremacy, we had different tribes, different understandings, different self-revelations that were predicated upon differences that will never be eradicated by the notion of being "black." That's what I think about the agenda, and I think it has to be much more complex and sophisticated.

Question: This is for both of you. Dr. Dyson, you recently had the black conservative, John McWhorter, on your show, and Dr. West, you've been attacked in his book, *Authentically Black*. I was wondering what you both thought of Dr. McWhorter's works, and maybe you can address the black conservative movement in general.

West: I'm a Christian, so I pray for people who attack me consistently. I really do. You're only as strong as your foes, but when they trash you, you have to have the courage to recognize they have some problems that you ought not be obsessed with because there's other things for you to do in your life. Now, when I turn to Brother McWhorter's recent text, where he says that when I give speeches no one understands a word that I say, because the language that I use is so abstract and oblique, and I just turn to the folk I just spoke to and say, "Do y'all understand a word that I had to say?" So, in other words, he lying, brother. [*Laughter*] The brother's lying. I don't know what speeches he's been to. You see what I mean? Now it would be different if he said, "He does speak in such a way that people understand, but some disagree and some don't." Then he's telling the truth. I wouldn't call him a liar. But then, when I connected to the *spirit* of his critique, the contempt, the *loathing*, the *hatred*, then I say to myself, "Anybody who's wrestling with that kind of spirit stands in need of prayer." The president of Harvard is the same way. They say, "Ah, you're upset with the president of Harvard ['cause he] treat you like a dog?" No. All bullies are unhappy people. They're sad people. They don't have enough joy in their lives, and therefore they got to rule by fear, by intimidation. I don't sink to that level at my best. Now, I do have gangsta moments, but that's all right. [*Laughter*] I want somebody to pray for me.

Dyson: You a gangsta of love, Doc! [*Laughter*] Let me say briefly why I had Professor McWhorter on my show. And I want to have Professor West on my show when I have McWhorter on there again, and I want him to get down like that. [*Laughter*] You know, McWhorter has consistently said nasty stuff about me, too, right? An over five-, six-thousand word essay on my book on Tupac in the *New Republic*. And in the same book [in which he attacks West] he's attacking me, and making all kinds of egregious arguments and so on. The advantage of having a daily talk radio show for three hours a day is that the people who be writing stuff in the academy and abstract stuff—"You know them rings and things you talking bout? / Bring 'em out / It's hard to yell with the barrel in your mouth." [*Laughter*] And I'm unloading it. I'm bringing it fresh. I'm saying, "You gon' write something in abstraction to attack a brother like Professor Cornel West or Michael Eric Dyson? Then get on the radio and defend yourself. Let the people hear what you talkin' about." See, I don't believe in the mushroom theory of letting it grow in the dark. I believe in exposing it to the light of common day. And see, when the folk really see what's going on—'cause he's attacking you for that, he attacks me for other stuff. This is what kills me about people. First of all, they tell us if we don't master the language, we dumb. Then, when we become sophisticated and past masters of it, then we abstract. Well, damn, which one is it? [*Laughter*] Right? Then when we get *too* common, we're barbarically folk-driven. Well, how come we can't be everything at the same time? We gonna give out some shrimp and some chitlins' and some filet mignon and some gravy. You pick up what you need. If you down with "repristinated mimesis," you check that. If you like Derrida and Foucault, you get that. If you like Socrates and Aristotle, you get that. If you like "H to the IzzO, V to the IzzA / Fa shizzle my nizzle / I used to dribble down in VA," you get that. Know what I'm saying? Yeah! [*Laughter and applause*]

Brown: It's a cross between a black hootenanny and a black college bowl. Last question, over here.

Question: I'm Pierre Quincy Pullins and I'm the Democrat running in the Senate.

Brown: Forget the commercial, get to the question.

Question: Sirs, comment on the revelation that President Bush authorized leaks and recalled what he said a few months ago.

Dyson: Well, it's part of an administration that deals with fear and intimidation and believes security is predicated upon the manipulation of information. Scooter Libby has just revealed to us that Mr. Bush himself authorized that. Why are we surprised? This, after all, is the same government that says, as part of a conservative junta, that it's disinterested in letting the government be too much a part of your life—except when it comes to snooping on you. Never forget what Jimmy Carter reminded us at Mrs. Coretta Scott King's funeral: it has been this government which has snooped on us from time immemorial. It snooped on Paul Robeson. It snooped on Harry Belafonte. It snooped on Martin Luther King, Jr. It snooped on Elijah Muhammad. It snooped on Malcolm X. It snooped on Albert Einstein—and any form of radical dissent to the American way of life. [Snooping is] perpetuated by a vicious bigotry, predicated upon an analysis that is thin and ultimately xenophobic. Because they're trying to tell us we're not real Americans.

They're trying to treat us like permanent immigrants in the nation where they've stigmatized us. I think, at the end of the day, the bottom line is this is part and parcel of an American project put forth by Mr. Bush and his surrounding figures, including Condoleezza Rice. Including Donald Rumsfeld. And including Dick Cheney. That triumvirate of terror has perpetuated a legacy that is so fundamentally antidemocratic that the best of the American tradition says we've got to stand up and say it was wrong then, it's wrong now, and what they're doing is morally polluted and politically poisonous.

Brown: As we come to the close of this 2005–2006 Celebration of Diversity Lecture Series and this memorable evening, please join me, all of us, in recognizing our distinguished Celebration of Diversity lecturers, Dr. Michael Eric Dyson and Dr. Cornel West. This was off the hook, off the chain, off the Richter scale. Give up your love! Michael Eric Dyson, Cornel West. [*Applause*]

11

WHERE IS THE LOVE?
Condoleezza Rice and Black Folk

with Meredith Vieira, Star Jones, Joy Behar, Kathy Lee Gifford

For Black History Month, February 2003, I was invited on ABC's *The View* to discuss my book, *Why I Love Black Women*. In the book, I celebrate the spirit, fortitude, intelligence, will-to-survive, and incredible beauty of black women. My chapter on interracial relations provoked heated debate, as did my criticism of Condoleezza Rice. Most of the ladies seemed to think that I should cut Rice some slack because she is smart and successful. Indeed she is, but conservatives and their allies can't have it both ways: denying group identity as the basis of distributing social goods such as affirmative action but claiming group membership in defending themselves against criticism from other blacks. Across the country, a number of black women were angry that my friend Star Jones didn't defend me against Joy Behar's charge—and in fact agreed with the assessment—that I was a racist, a charge made *after* I left the set. In light of Jones's subsequent ouster from *The View*, one can only speculate as to what, if any, role this kind of charged rhetoric may have had in her fall from grace.

Meredith Vieira: In honor of Black History Month, we've invited Michael Eric Dyson to join us. He's a Baptist minister, a college professor, and the author of nine books including *Why I Love Black Women*. But he doesn't love them all. He's got a real gripe with Condoleezza Rice, and he'll talk about all that and more. Please welcome our guest, Michael Eric Dyson.

[*Applause*]

Star Jones: You may pick up your check after the show, 'cause you gave me a big wet kiss in that book, I'll tell you that.

Michael Eric Dyson: I'll tell you, I just love you. And as my wife understands, I'm deeply and profoundly attracted to you as a beautiful black woman, and as a woman who represents so much that's positive in our history. And you defy every stereotype. You speak to a broad audience, you're unashamedly black, but you have multiracial appeal. You understand that you're a full-figured woman and you are sexy, oh man.

Joy Behar: What is this, an infomercial? [*Laughter*]

Jones: Then what's wrong with Condoleezza Rice?

Dyson: Listen, Condoleezza as a human being is a beautiful woman. I just disagree with her politics. We're diametrically opposed. So I love Condoleezza Rice as a black woman, as a human being, but as a political figure, I think that she has compromised the integrity of those people who put her where she is. She says her mother knew one of the four girls who got blown up in the [Sixteenth Street] Baptist church in Birmingham. That's beautiful. Then tell something to George Bush that would make him understand that he can't come out on King's birthday and speak against affirmative action—and for her weak-willed, weak-kneed defense of affirmative action, the very policy that put her where she is. I'm saying, if you're going to play the game, be honest about it. That's all.

Behar: What about her accomplishments?

Dyson: I admire her accomplishments. She has a Ph.D.

Behar: She's up there.

Dyson: She's up there. She's up there. I teach at the University of Pennsylvania; I hope people applaud my accomplishments, but it's not about being proud. It's about once you get in the door don't close it on other people coming behind you. Open the door so other people can get in.

Behar: I don't think she sees it that way.

Jones: No.

Dyson: She *doesn't* see it that way. I don't diss Condoleezza Rice. Look, Colin Powell is a figure whose politics I disagree with, but I understand and appreciate him. Because in the Republican Party he says, "Look, you people have benefited more from affirmative action than anybody else. And even as a black—"

Jones: Let's go to the next one.

Vieira: I'm interested in the fact that you've said that black men who marry white women marry down. What do you mean by that?

Dyson: Oh no. First of all, I cannot begin to tell you the multicultured flavor of the erotic attachments I've had over my life.

Jones: Better known as he done slept with some white women.

Dyson: Lord have mercy, don't tell my wife that. *Every* color. *Every* color.

Jones: The point is—

Dyson: My point is, statistically speaking, sociologically, when black men marry white women they often marry down—status wise. That is, those women don't have as much money or economic security. It's what they call sociological exchange value. What black men get is the unconscious privilege of being attracted to the ideal—which is a white woman in American society. I'm not saying they're not beautiful. But I'm saying in the history of this country they have been constructed as—

Vieira: But when white men marry white women they often marry down. Women do not have the economic wherewithal that men have.

Dyson: No, no, no. When you do the statistics, first of all, in terms of educational attainment—45 percent of black women who are college educated are married to other black men who are college educated. One-quarter of black women marry men who've never finished high school. White women—70 percent of white women who are college educated marry a white man with a college degree. So I'm saying, statistically, in terms of economic status—

Jones: Why do you care that a black man marries a white woman? Why can't he just marry who he wanna marry?

Dyson: You should. I think that love is like that. But I'm saying that sisters have a problem in this country when black men who are visible, intelligent, who are athletes, entertainers, and intellectuals, marry white women because they spurn black women. I don't mind them marrying whoever they want. But they say sisters are too bossy. They're too assertive. They're too nasty. They're demanding too much. I'm saying, "Why are you dissing the very women"—

Behar: I have to go back to Condoleezza Rice, 'cause I see in my notes something that I think is really wrong of you—to call her the "pet Negro" of the Bush administration. It's evil.

Dyson: That's not evil. First of all, that's a quote from Zora Neale Hurston, "pet Negro."

Jones: But you used it, Michael, and I don't get that.

Dyson: Here's what I'm saying. I'm saying to you that Condoleezza Rice, as a black woman, is beautiful, intelligent, and an incredibly capable person. I'm saying her politics don't reflect the widening of opportunity for African American people in this country. That's why I'm saying—

Vieira: Doesn't her getting that position widen the opportunity?

Dyson: You know what it is? It begins to justify people who say, "See, we're against affirmative action, this woman's against affirmative"—or weakly for it—and as a result of that, the very policy that put her in place, she has denied [its] legitimacy.

Jones: Wait a minute, Michael, be clear. Being African American in America should mean you have the ability to have your own thought process.

Dyson: Absolutely.

Jones: And to align yourself any way you want to. It's the same argument that we get with feminism. Feminism doesn't mean you must get a job, you must work outside the home. It means you should have the choice. So what's wrong with Condoleezza Rice saying that, "This is how I think?" Why, all of a sudden, does she become less than a black person 'cause she thinks out of the mainstream? I don't agree with anything she says, but I still think she has a right to say it—

Dyson: She does.

Jones: —believe it and—

Dyson: I absolutely believe that she has the right to say it. But I have the right to say that I think it's wrong! Look, I'm not denying her right to say it. I'm just saying what she says is deeply and profoundly destructive to the tradition of the people who produced her. That's all I'm saying. I'm not saying she's not black for doing that. I'm saying her blackness doesn't make a difference to me. I'd rather have a progressive Jewish person representing that position who's going to [express] the interests of people of color—and poor people—than a black woman who, because of the color of her skin, I should defer to her as an expert on blackness. I say no. I'm saying to you, I appreciate and love her as a black woman. Next. What's the point? What have you done for me lately? If you cannot help black people in that position, get me somebody else who's progressive, who can help out in that position. That's all I'm arguing.

Kathy Lee Gifford: Michael, isn't one of the great problems that statistic I read in your book that blew my mind: there are more black men in prison than there are enrolled in college?

Dyson: You've got almost 900,000 black men in prison, and only about 600,000 black men in college. Look, I have a brother, Everett Dyson-Bey—give a shout out to him—who's in prison, been there for fourteen years.

Behar: Why's he there? What did he do?

Dyson: He was accused of second-degree murder. We believe he's innocent, but he's been there fourteen years. So the point is that I've visited these prisons often. I was in Oakland, California, at a detention center. Fourteen-, fifteen-, sixteen-year-old kids and they're warehoused. Ninety percent of them were black and brown. And that is an incredible thing. That's what I mean. Can't we have people in high places with black faces speaking about issues that average, ordinary people face? I'm saying I don't care what color you are. If you speak for those people, then I'm down with you. And because you're black—I can't be down with you *just* because you're black.

Jones: Fair enough.

Gifford: Yeah, I wouldn't vote for a woman just because she's a woman.

Vieira: Well, we don't agree with everything you say, except about Star. Thank you, Michael Eric Dyson.

12

GENERAL PRINCIPLES
Colin Powell's Compassionate Conservatism

with Juan Williams

Colin Powell gave a remarkable oration at the 2000 Republican Convention in Philadelphia, where he challenged his party to address the "poverty, failing communities, [and] people who've lost hope" that he had witnessed in his travels. Powell encouraged Republicans to confront the racially charged prison-industrial complex that forced a choice upon his mates, "We either build our children or we build more jails. Time to stop building jails." He argued that all children deserved a quality education and suggested the hypocrisy of Republican "cynicism that is created when, for example, some in our party miss no opportunity to roundly and loudly condemn affirmative action that helped a few thousand black kids get an education but hardly a whimper is heard from them over affirmative action for lobbyists who load our federal tax codes with preferences for special interests." I was invited onto NPR's *Talk of the Nation* to discuss with host Juan Williams Powell's speech the day after he delivered it, and while I admired the general's rousing oration, I was unconvinced that his views represented even a significant minority in his party. I haven't changed my mind.

Juan Williams: On the line with us from New York now is Michael Eric Dyson. Welcome to *Talk of the Nation*, Michael Eric Dyson.

Michael Eric Dyson: Thank you, Brother Juan. Thank you for having me, and thank you for that insightful review you did of my [Martin Luther King, Jr.] book. And I appreciate that.

Williams: Oh, you're very welcome. Now let me ask you: what did you think of Colin Powell's speech last night at the convention?

Dyson: Well, first of all, no one in America can deny the edifying eloquence that Mr. Powell phrases his beliefs in. He is a powerful orator who is at the top of his craft. He works with a wide vision of American society. And I was refreshingly surprised by his challenge to the Republican Convention that they should deal openly and honestly with the issue of race. And had they been already doing so, he would not have to have reminded them of doing that.

He also, I think, pressed rather hard about affirmative action, and even went the further step of saying that affirmative action for privileged white people has not been as aggressively assaulted as has the affirmative action of a relatively small handful of African American people. I was distressed by his almost uncritical embrace of Dick Cheney, who, after all, we must be reminded, suggested that Mr. Nelson Mandela should remain in prison under the ostensible reason that the ANC was a terrorist group, but missed the larger and more humane cadences of Mr. Mandela's rhetoric, at least recently, before he was released.

So the point is, I think, Colin Powell did a brilliant job of phrasing challenges to the Republican Party within the ideological orbit that he operates in. I wasn't satisfied with the degree to which he went, but if you're going to be a black and a Republican, you might as well be Colin Powell and not Clarence Thomas.

Williams: Let me ask you, Michael—you are a Democrat?

Dyson: Yes, I am a radical democrat.

Williams: So—a radical democrat. Alright, so as a radical democrat then, listening to what you saw last night, did you think, "Gosh, this is a new-look Republican Party. I might feel comfortable with these people?"

Dyson: Oh, by no means, and not by any stretch of the imagination.

Williams: Why not?

Dyson: Well, because I think that—first of all, I think there was a bit of playing to the gallery, so to speak, with showing the admittedly expanded base of minority voters—or at least delegates—within the Republican Party. That certainly was reassuring and promising, and perhaps the Marvin Olasky/George Bush compassionate conservatism may indeed reach out to African American people. But I think the kind of conservative values that many black people share culturally have not yet translated into public policies, and to political practices, that would make me feel quite safe or secure.

Williams: Well, given that you heard the general [Powell] speak against the drug war, you heard him speak for affirmative action, what's the primary obstacle to getting Michael Eric Dyson into the Republican Party?

Dyson: Well, because I don't think that represents the mainstream of the Republican Party. Colin Powell certainly chose, we are told, not to run as a running mate of Mr. Bush's. Perhaps he didn't want to run as vice president. Maybe he did that to, say, spare his party the embarrassment of having defected in large enough numbers to make it uncomfortable. It is one thing to entertain Colin Powell as an ideal; another to have him in practice. I don't think that Colin Powell represents the heartland of American society in terms of the Republican Party, and he doesn't represent the public policies that they have adopted.

Colin Powell was speaking bravely against the mainstream of Republican values when he talked about affirmative action, when he spoke out against the war on drugs that they have championed almost uncritically, and when he supported the fact that we must make distinctions among people in terms of affirmative action for white guys and for black guys. So Colin Powell doesn't represent, for me, the mainstream values of the Republican Party.

Williams: Michael Eric Dyson, thanks for joining us.

Dyson: Thank you, man.

PART IV

YOUTH AND VIOLENCE

13

DYING FOR ATTENTION
Gun Obsession and American Violence

with Michael Medved; moderated by Bill Press and Mary Matalin

On August 10, 1999, white supremacist Buford O. Furrow, Jr., entered the lobby of the North Valley Jewish Community Center in the Granada Hills section of Los Angeles, opening fire with a semiautomatic weapon and wounding three children, a teenage counselor, and a receptionist. Later, Furrow murdered a Filipino American Postal Service carrier. The day after Burrow's murderous rampage, the day he turned himself in, I appeared on CNN's *Crossfire* with conservative cultural critic Michael Medved to debate the national impact of violence, especially in schools and among the young. We had a substantive dialogue, with hosts Bill Press and Mary Matalin, about the causes, consequences, and possible solutions to the mayhem. In the end, despite our political differences, we all shared the common desire to reduce societal violence, including that perpetrated on—and by—our youth.

Bill Press: Good evening. Welcome to *Crossfire*. Another crazed individual, another assault weapon, another list of victims, another shattered community. Yesterday's shooting at the Granada Hills Jewish community center, just the latest in a fusillade of shootings that has crisscrossed and stunned an entire nation. Pelham, Alabama, August 5, three killed; Atlanta, July 29, nine killed; Atlanta, July 12, six killed; Southfield, Michigan, June 11, two killed; Las Vegas, June 3, four killed; and who could ever forget Littleton, Colorado, April 20, 13 killed. Even before a suspected gunman, Buford O. Furrow, turned himself in today, people from the White House to your house started looking for answers. What's behind the violence? Is it guns? Is it TV? Is it movies? The parent of two students who escaped unharmed yesterday sums it up best.

Shari Weinberg (parent on video clip): I think that we need to take a look and see what is wrong with our nation today, that we can have these kinds of tragedies happening.

Press: Tonight, we, too, look for answers. Mary.

Mary Matalin: Thanks, Bill. Well, while we were ruminating in our homes today, the man in the White House lost no time giving his opinion. Here's what President Clinton had to say today about the latest tragedy.

William J. Clinton, President of the United States (video clip): I can only hope that this latest incident will intensify our resolve to make America a safer place and a place of healing across the lines that divide us.

Matalin: Well, Brother Dyson, is our president looking for answers in all the wrong places? We already have twenty thousand federal, state, or local gun laws. His reference to a safer place is code language for more gun laws, yet prosecution of federal gun crimes has gone down 50 percent in his administration. Do we need more laws or better enforcement of the ones that are on the books?

Michael Eric Dyson: Well, we certainly need greater enforcement of laws that already exist, but I think we also need a kind of reorientation of American society. This society is, indeed, saturated with violence. We're addicted to violence. There's an erotic sheen to violence. And what we need to do is to find a way to move beyond that, and to move, quite frankly, beyond the finger-pointing blame game. I think that stricter enforcement of the laws will be quite necessary. But also, what's interesting to me is that the people who advocate freedom in terms of access to guns are the very people who are at a loss to explain how there's a powerful relationship between owning these guns, possessing these guns, and the enormous violence we see in the aftermath of [such possession].

In the '60s, when Martin Luther King, Jr., was advocating that black people not retaliate in violence against white supremacists who were attacking them, America was behind him. And what we're suggesting is that nonviolence worked then, it will work now. But it can only work in a climate where there's not only strict enforcement of the law, but where the temperature of the society is not so overheated and hyperbolic that we can't speak to one another. What's behind these crimes, it seems to me, a fair deal of them, is enormous forms of hatred, bigotry, anti-Semitic, anti-black sentiments, anti-gay sentiments. And so what we have to do is to confront those larger structural issues in American society along with the enforcement of the laws.

Matalin: So, professor, it's all hatred, it's not just insanity? I mean, you don't think those kids in Littleton were just psychotic, or this hammer-wielding suicidal husband in Atlanta, or this guy admittedly—or it's reported that he's associated with racist organizations—that's just craziness.

Dyson: Sure.

Matalin: You think there's some collective conspiracy of racism still that's behind a lot of this tragedy?

Dyson: Well, I think there's no doubt that racism continues to pervade American society in very destructive ways. I don't think there's a conspiracy to this degree: that someone is sitting in a room somewhere trying to conspire against black people or against gays and lesbians, and so on. But there is a marked, I think, increase in the vituperative ideologies of hatred that have been pervading the society. And people feel freer now to express them. So I don't think there's a conspiracy to the degree that somebody is sitting around saying, "Let's get those people." But the real conspiracy is the pervasive racism and misogyny, and certainly the anti-Semitism that's in American culture, that needs to be addressed.

Press: Michael Medved, before you and I disagree on guns, which I'm sure we will, let me ask you about the bigger picture, and I want to start with the very, very powerful images that we saw all day yesterday. And I don't think that any parent could watch that video of those little kids—there we see it—holding hands, and holding hands with the cops, and being led to safety. I mean, it just tears your heart out, doesn't it?

Michael Medved: It does absolutely.

Press: You've got to think, Michael, that everybody thinks, "That could be my kid." When you see that picture, Michael, doesn't that tell you that something is terribly wrong in American society?

Medved: Well, I'll tell you what it tells me, Bill. It tells me the tremendous danger of drawing big conclusions based on anecdotal evidence. Of course, it tears your heart out, but the truth of the matter is statistics don't lie. The Education Department just yesterday, at the same time this was happening, released figures that show gun incidents in schools have gone way down. They went down one-third in one year. The number of kids killed in school shootings, even the same year as Littleton, was twenty-eight total in middle schools and high schools all across the country. It was down. Murder is down; violence is down across the country. I think what we need is some perspective. We need to stop wringing our hands and making everything into a crisis. We do not, repeat, do not, have a crisis in violence right now in America. We've been doing some things right and getting a handle on the crime rate in this country. We ought to continue.

Press: Well, Michael, clearly the crime rate is going down. Hurrah, give credit to Dick Riordan or Rudy Giuliani or anybody who deserves credit for doing so.

Medved: You bet.

Press: But at the same time, you have seven incidents of multiple shootings in the last four months—not just at schools, at businesses—with thirty-seven people killed, Michael. You're telling me that there's not a problem here?

Medved: No, of course there is a problem. Even one death is too many. But the problem isn't suddenly more guns in people's hands. We have fewer guns in people's hands. Fewer households own firearms today than owned them ten years ago. The truth of the matter is: what's changed? What's changed is the tremendous television focus, the needs of that 24-hours-a-day news cycle. There is too much focus on this material. We went way overboard with Littleton. Yes, it was a horrifying tragedy, and it was great TV, but this tremendous focus again and again. We're sending a message, Bill—and it concerns me greatly—to every loner, to every loser, to every person on the margins who is dying for some attention: the way you get attention in America, and you get a lot of it right away, is you go into a roomful of people and you start shooting. That's a terrible message to send.

Press: Shades of Spiro Agnew, I mean, the last vestige of whatever—I mean, to blame the media. You think that nut yesterday drove to LA [to try to kill] just so he could get on television? Come on, Michael.

Medved: Come on, Bill. I mean, that nut was in violation of his probation by even having a gun of any kind. He was already breaking the law. I want to tell you something. You talk about the blame game. And I think that's a good, good term to use. Right now, there is only one person to blame for this: It's not his mother. It's not his grandmother fighting over him. It's not the media. And it's not guns. And it's not the psychiatric institutions. The only person to blame is named Buford Furrow.

Dyson: Can I jump in here?

Matalin: Professor Dyson, this is a place where you and Michael might agree. Jump in there.

Dyson: Look, when we talk about the blame game, there's enough blame to go around. My concern is that when these incidents are covered, of course, we can blame the media on the one hand—this unseemly avarice, this desire to just have every detail narrated in its full complexity. Now, on the one hand, yes, we can jump on that. On the other hand, let's be honest. What stories get covered are as much driven by what we think is newsworthy and important as others. In other words, there is low-level intensity warfare going on in urban centers across this country. In other words, black and brown kids are dying every day. They don't have the sexiness—they don't have the attraction—as kids in a Jewish community center, or kids in Columbine who are dying. So, I'm saying, let's focus our attention on those kids and the problems they confront. Of course, we can name statistics. We can have a battle of statistics to say that crime is declining, but the violence is very real in American society.

Press: Michael Medved, you want to jump in? Go ahead.

Medved: Yes. I just want to say, he's absolutely right. I mean, the real story in America is the continued unacceptable rates of violence in inner cities in America. And I think it's, quite frankly, quite disgusting that we treat some victims as more sacred than others. That's wrong in the United States of America. Look, I'm very concerned about five kids in a Jewish community center who are wounded. But I'm more concerned about a postal worker murdered by the same guy who, who has gotten not nearly the same attention, because it's not as dramatic on television.

Press: I might add, even the police are saying they're not sure yet that the postal worker was murdered by the same guy. They suspect it; they haven't said that for certain. Mary.

Matalin: All right. Let's go back, Professor Dyson, to the media setting the agenda by virtue of what it is they're covering. Isn't the answer to excessive, collective coverage, individual free will? Just turn it off. If you don't want to watch it, turn it off. That's the answer to that. There's a market for us. But what is the answer? And I agree with you, and clearly Michael Medved does too: the lack of courage for what happens almost every day in minority communities when—this happens in D.C., in my backyard—kids sitting in their front room get killed; kids getting killed over jackets and shoes. Why doesn't that get covered? It barely makes the Metro page. And what should we do about it?

Dyson: Well, first of all, it doesn't make the pages because it's much more difficult to deal with. In other words, when we see these Littleton, Colorado, Columbine situations, we tend to blame the forces in the larger society and not the kids. When it happens in black and brown communities, we tend to blame those communities, we tend to pathologize those communities—"There's something wrong with them; there's something wrong with their daddy or their momma. They didn't have enough resources, morally speaking, to make sure their kids are protected." So, we end up blaming the kids. And I think that what we're at a loss for, then, is to figure out: when this stuff seeps out to suburbia or seeps out to these sanctified and protected communities, what should we do?

The first answer: yes, we can exercise individual will, Mary, but the reality is you can turn the tube off, but you can't turn off the reality that America is still constructing the story in a certain way and the story will continue to be told. If it happens to white kids, it's big news; if it happens to black or brown kids, it's just not as interesting, or we take it to be something they're getting themselves involved in. It's their fault. What my response would be then is to figure out a way that all of us—in media, in the larger political realm, in public policy—can find out ways not to scapegoat people, but to dig beneath the dirt of the common mud-slinging we're doing to each other, and figure out how we can love, embrace, and help each other. And how we can do that, first of all, is by acknowledging the humanity of these people in black and brown communities.

Let me give you one example. In Atlanta, they had a powerful ceremony of hope and reconciliation to celebrate those people who had died, but [there wasn't national attention] until twelve people died [in Littleton], who were mostly white and other ethnicities. The [only] black kid had been taken around by his collar by the man who killed his mother and some of his other family members; he literally saw these people dying. That is as horrible and as terrifying a reality as we can imagine. Can we imagine a way to get beyond the mudslinging, to figure out public policies that don't demonize or attack them? Welfare reform has been devastating in its consequence, and yes, Bill Clinton has become complicit in [mud-slinging] by refusing to recognize how these families are being attacked by public policies as well.

Matalin: Okay. Dr. Dyson, we're not mudslinging tonight. We're trying to get at some of these answers.

Press: Michael Medved, looking for solutions, it seems to me there are two things we could do. I'd like to ask you about both of them. One is do something more about guns, and the second is pass hate crime legislation that's pending in the Congress. Michael, we don't know this man's motive, but we are told that he's linked to white supremacist groups like the Aryan Nation, and we know that he drove to Los Angeles and hit a Jewish community center. If it's proven that he targeted those kids because they were Jews, shouldn't he be charged with a hate crime?

Medved: Of course it's a hate crime. I mean, anytime you go into a child care center and you start shooting at children, you're not doing it because you love them. You're doing it out of hatred. But the point is, why should we treat one class of victims differently? I mean, I think that Professor Dyson was making an absolute point: every child is a child of God. Every child is equally precious. If those children weren't Jewish, if they happened to be just White Anglo-Saxon Protestant Americans, this would be just as serious. The idea that the government should treat the crime more seriously because of the ethnic identity of some of the victims is an obscenity.

Press: Michael, I think you're playing with words, if I may. The question is not why we should treat the victims differently. The question is why we should allow a killer to treat certain classes of people, be they blacks, be they gays, be they Jews, differently, not because of anything they did—

Medved: But, Bill—

Press: Let me finish. Not because of anything they did, but just because of who they are. Isn't that additionally and severely wrong?

Medved: Murder is wrong, period. I mean, are we going to say there was a hate crime when Mark Barton killed day traders, because it was a hate crime against day traders? It's an absurdity.

Press: I don't think they're a targeted group, Michael. You're putting day trade owners on the same list with Jews.

Medved: Bill, what you're trying to talk about, you're saying we're going to take certain groups and we are going to say that these groups deserve and need special protection. Every American citizen deserves protection against monsters like this and against would-be murderers. It doesn't matter what their ethnicity.

Press: Michael Dyson, go ahead.

Dyson: Yes, I think that certainly in principle, and abstractly, Michael Medved is absolutely right. But here's the point: we haven't had a history in this society where day traders have been subjected to forms of acrimony or hatred by people.

Press: Thank you.

Dyson: We haven't had the KKK against day traders. The reality is, in American society, certain groups of people have been targeted viciously by public policy and by the law. So, what we are trying to do is to, in one sense, compensate for that, and to acknowledge our own complicity as Americans in that process, and say, "Hey, let's do something about it."

Medved: Professor Dyson, the reason we had antilynching laws, and they were good laws, was because lynchers weren't being prosecuted. People are prosecuted today. The people who killed James Byrd in Jasper, Texas—one is already sentenced to death. The people who killed that young gay guy in Alabama—both sentenced to life imprisonment already, not based on hate crimes, but based on murder. Murder by definition is a hate crime. To treat one murder more seriously than another, based on the identity of the victim, has no place in an America where we're all guaranteed equal protection of the laws.

Dyson: Well, let me say two things. First of all the law is not equally applied. Even in American society in 1999, the reality is that there's a disproportionate application of the law for specific ethnic and racial groups. I mean, this is one of the great topics of debate for the National Law Association, number one. Number two, again, given the history of American society in its bigotry toward, say, gays and lesbians, we live in a heterosexist culture that privileges the viewpoints of people who happen to be "normal." Normal is defined as those people who are heterosexual. Therefore, there is a particular kind of bigotry that is directed toward people who are gay and lesbian. It is a subspecies—that is the hatred of gays—it is a subspecies of attempted murder and we have to deal with that.

Medved: Professor Dyson, I think it is absolutely wrong if someone goes out and beats up a gay guy. It is no less wrong if somebody goes out and beats up a heterosexual guy. It's the same crime. Punish the act; punish the crime. Don't try to have a research into the motivation. This is a perfect example, because all of a sudden people are saying, "Is it a hate crime or is it not?" And then they find a book in the van, and the book is filled with hatred. Does that make the crime worse? The crime is monstrous anyway.

Dyson: Let me tell you what. As an African American man who has been subjected to racial profiling, who has been subjected to police brutality despite my educational attainments, I can tell you it frightens the crap out of me when I see a guy like that having a book, because what it means is that what is still in this country is a virus so deep and so virulent that it continues to infect the minds of people.

Medved: Do you want to outlaw the book?

Dyson: I don't want to outlaw the book. As Martin Luther King, Jr., said, "I can't make you love me, but I can change the behavior." We can't legislate morality, but what we can do is make sure that the legislation reflects our moral commitment to love and to protect one another as human beings.

Press: All right. Let's jump in just a second. Mary.

Matalin: Professor Dyson, as an African American man, I'm sure you've enjoyed your First Amendment rights to free speech. You wouldn't censor any kind of speech.

Dyson: Not at all.

Matalin: Even hate—even Farrakhan speech or David Duke speech. We all hate that. We loathe it, but we wouldn't censor it. How can you make law that censors thought? You're criminalizing the thought and not the context.

Dyson: I'm not talking about the thought. I'm talking about behavior. When I talk about hate crimes, I'm speaking about the execution of an ill will toward another human being that is against the law. And when we think about the reality of American society, we're talking about people who are going out, like with James Byrd, and dragging him behind a truck. We're talking about incidents that go on every day in this country, where somebody, because of their bigotry—

Medved: Professor—

Press: One at a time, please.

Medved: How much more can someone be punished than the death penalty? The killer of James Byrd has been sentenced to death for murder, which is the right judgment and the right punishment.

Dyson: Yes.

Medved: And the truth is, you know, you say you're an African American male. I've been a synagogue president for years. For fifteen years, I was president of my synagogue. I feel this attack very personally and very directly.

Dyson: You should, yes.

Medved: But I don't believe that these children need extra protection because they're Jewish. They need protection just like all American children do, whatever their ethnicity.

Dyson: But see, that's a false argument to me.

Press: Okay. Gentlemen, you've made that point. Michael Medved, let me ask you before we run out of time, about guns. Again, looking at this individual yesterday, this suspect, he turned himself in. He's got a history of mental illness. He was slammed in prison for threatening some hospital workers with a knife. He told police at the time, "Sometimes I feel like I could just lose it and kill people." Wouldn't you agree he's the last person on earth who should have a gun, any kind of a gun?

Medved: Absolutely, and a condition of his probation was that he was not allowed to have any guns. He broke that law, but he broke a more serious law by shooting at people.

Press: And wouldn't you, then, have to agree, Michael, that the fact that he was able to get his hands, not just on a gun, but on an Uzi and on a lot of other weapons that were in this van, indicates that there's something wrong with gun laws today? Either they're not being adequately enforced, or maybe there are some loopholes in existing gun laws, Michael.

Medved: Bill Press, I couldn't agree with you more. I think the main problem is the gun laws have not been enforced. The enforcement has actually gone down in this administration. We have, as Mary said, twenty thousand gun laws on the book. We should enforce them with utmost vigor.

Press: No, how about the second part, Michael, please, of my question, which is laws that—I mean, loopholes in existing laws? For example—we don't know where he bought this gun—but, for example, no background checks at gun shows, big loophole. Doesn't it make sense to close that loophole?

Dyson: I think it does.

Medved: Let me ask you back a question.

Press: No, no, no, please. On this show, we ask the questions; you answer the questions.

Medved: I'm glad to provide an answer.

Press: You know that.

Medved: My answer is very simple. I don't think when you're looking at people with the Aryan Nations, which is what you're dealing with here, you are ever going to successfully prevent them from getting guns. They will always get guns. I would like that the innocent people in America, the good people of America, have some means for defending themselves.

Press: Go ahead, Professor Dyson, I know you want to get in. You got about fifteen seconds.

Dyson: Well, I think the reality is this, bottom line: we are obsessed with guns in this country. The obsession with guns has led to devastating consequences in American society. When we are we going to wake up and smell the coffee? The reality is the obsession with guns, and the ability to execute violence, is at the very root of the problem we confront in this country.

Press: Gentlemen, excellent debate. We'd like to continue for another half hour—we can't. We're out of time.

14

THE STAKES ARE HIGH
Violence, Hip-Hop, and the United States Senate

with John McCain and John Kerry

In September 2000, the Senate Commerce, Science, and Transportation Committee, chaired by Senator John McCain, held a hearing to investigate the marketing of violence to children. I was invited to testify on a panel that included music executive Danny Goldberg, Motion Picture Association of America head Jack Valenti, and Recording Industry Association of America head Hilary Rosen. I had testified before the Senate more than five years before when Senator Carol Moseley-Braun summoned me to Washington, D.C., to testify before her Senate Juvenile Justice Subcommittee on the impact of rap music on youth. In front of McCain's committee, I offered a principled defense of hip-hop culture and the genre's rhetorical embrace of violence, but which also insisted on getting to the roots of violence for black youth in America. The *Village Voice* insisted that I opened "a can of whup-ass on the U.S. Senate," but most likely they were referring to my lively exchange with Senator McCain in which I suggested that if the nation sought to track how big-money corporations corrupt youth, we'd have to start with the Senate. I also had an interesting exchange with Senator John Kerry about the social impact of rap and pop music, which, as you'll see, ended humorously. And though I disagreed with McCain at points, we shared warm words after the hearing and expressed mutual admiration for each other's gifts and principles.

Senator John McCain: Mr. Dyson?

Michael Eric Dyson: Thank you, Senator McCain. I'm Dr. Michael Eric Dyson, the Ida B. Wells Barnett University Professor at DePaul University and I am honored to be here. Senator Brownback and I have shared time on *Meet the Press*. And though we disagreed, we are committed in common to the future of our children. And Mr. McCain, you—with your blistering brilliance on the campaign trail—really won the imagination of many Americans, even like myself, to the left of you. But we appreciate the fire and plainspokenness with which you negotiated your time in the spotlight.

McCain: Thank you.

Dyson: So I would like to—taking a cue from Mr. Valenti—ask for fifteen minutes to preach my sermon. And then, after the official five minutes, spread the hat to collect money for my sermonizing here today. I'm an ordained Baptist minister as well, but don't hold that against me.

McCain: Thank you, Mr. Dyson. And you make a compelling argument to take the time you need, sir.

Dyson: Thank you, sir. That is dangerous, but I will do so. I think that what we've heard today is very compelling in terms of the necessity for an equally shared responsibility about the violence of American society, and how that violence is packaged, shaped, redistributed on the open market. And the marketing of violence, the seductions of violence, the titillations that are associated with violence, the erotic sheen that often accompanies violence, is something that is deeply problematic to many of us who are parents—like I am of three children—who are concerned about shaping the egos, shaping the mind-set, shaping the perspectives of young people in order to deter them from a life that is fruitless and to redirect them into paths and channels that are very productive.

But the problem I have with so much of the discourse surrounding this issue of violence is that, implicitly, there is a function of censorship. We know that there is no explicit censorship. We know that all of us share in common the development of responses that defend the First Amendment. But there's an implicit censorship that goes on when we begin to give the voice and microphone to some groups of people and not to others. So what I'm concerned about—I'll make three very quick points and end here—what I'm concerned about is the necessity to hear from those young voices, those very powerful voices, sometimes admittedly angry voices, sometimes bitter voices, sometimes voices that are dipped into the deep pools of profanity, sometimes vulgarity. But I'm not so much concerned about the curse words, as the cursed worlds they occupy, and what hurt they experience in order to produce some of the deeply reflective, deeply self-critical, and also deeply problematic lyrics that they put forth.

So I think first of all, what's important about hearing from those young people—a disproportionate number of whom, by the way, happen to be African American and Latino voices—is that they tell truths about their situations that are avoided in textbooks and schools, and we dare say, in the United States Senate at some points, and synagogues and so on. The reality is that the violence is old and it has been around a long time. But the reality also is that we haven't really attacked certain forms of violence as equally as we have others. So that "The Duke" John Wayne would not be brought before a Senate committee to give a mea culpa for the way in which he romanticized and idealized this kind of western machismo that, dare we say, has informed even the Senate careers of some of our colleagues here today. But at the same time, Snoop Doggy Dogg is brought front and center, rhetorically and symbolically, if not literally, to talk about why it is that he chooses to make a living by telling the truth about what he understands. So violence in John Wayne is acceptable. Violence in Snoop Doggy Dogg is not acceptable.

Number two, violence matters most when it occurs in the mainstream and not so-called outside of the mainstream. This is why we applaud President Clinton for having the FTC put forth this report after Columbine. But the reality is violence pervaded America way before Columbine. It struck Latino and African American communities in disproportionate numbers. And yet the rapper L. L. Cool J, by no means a hardcore rapper, released an album yesterday that contained these lyrics, "I don't mean this in a disrespectful way / but Columbine happens in the ghetto every day / But when the crap goes down / y'all ain't got nothing to say." Now this is from a person who is well-received as an actor and as an entertainer in American society, but he understands that there has been a targeting—with vicious specificity—of African American and Latino communities when it comes to violence.

Those forms of violence are seen to be much more pathological and naturalized in a way that is destructive. And the violence of the larger society is not taken seriously until that violence happens in a mainstream white community where now it becomes a national problem, and a public health problem, and a plague. And we have to ask why is it that these voices that have been locked out, that have been marginalized, are seen [by their peers] as a necessity to articulate their understanding of the world, and sometimes violently so, to make a very powerful point?

Number three, if we're really concerned about the lives of kids, then we've got to not shred the safety net in terms of welfare reform, [because it] targets poor black and Latino and poor white kids in very specific ways. Because if there's diminished capacity for providing health care, and providing child care, for your children, that is much more destructive than a rap lyric that may or may not lead to a violent behavior. Also, we have got to stop this war on drugs that really has translated, as Lani Guinier said, into a war on black and Latino youth. And as you know, Mr. McCain, the reality is that a report was issued earlier this year that the human rights of many African American and Latino youth are being violated. A report from Amnesty International was released saying that the American government ought to be ashamed of itself for the way in which it has stigmatized black and Latino youth in disproportionate fashion, leading to their arrest and their imprisonment, and therefore stigmatizing their lives for the duration of their time in this nation.

Furthermore, I heard this morning about the Senator expressing outrage about the video game that deals with the electrocution of a human being. And as repulsive as that is, the reality is, is that in Texas one hundred thirty some odd people have been legally executed on capital punishment for a capital crime. And a disproportionate number of those people happen to be black and Latino men. So I don't want to get rid of a game that may push our buttons in very problematic and provocative ways until we get rid of the very practices themselves that the game points to.

Finally, I think that—

McCain: Mr. Dyson, I would agree with you if we still held public executions.

Dyson: Well, it's not about public executions. It's about if we do them in private, Senator McCain. The horrible shame that is going on in private is not publicly talked about. The horrible shame is not simply the exposure of the execution, it's the numbers of black and Latino men who are being subjected to this form of, I think, racially motivated legal lynching. So I think that, you're absolutely right in terms of the publicity, but the reality is that it's more shameful that it's not made more public so that more people can be outraged by it. Two more points—thank you so much for your indulgence.

Another reason these young people have to be heard from—and we ought to hear their voices—is that they bear witness to the invisible suffering of the masses. And this is what I mean about publicity. We have to hear what they're talking about. We have to be confronted with what they're talking about even if we find it personally repulsive and reprehensible. So that for me, stigmatizing blacks, and avoiding the collective responsibility for the drug war, is something that needs to be talked about. Master P said, "I don't own no plane / I don't own no boat / I don't ship no dope from coast to coast." So we know that the flooding of black and Latino communities—whether intentionally or not, inadvertently or not—with drugs is not talked about as deeply and systematically as it needs to be. And yet the stigmatization of those who abuse drugs, who happen to be nonviolent offenders who end up in jail, needs to be talked about as well. And it's talked about much in rap music.

Finally, in terms of racial profiling, the late rapper Tupac Shakur said, "Just the other day I got lynched by some crooked cops / and to this day those same cops on the beat getting major pay / But when I get my check, they taking tax out / so we paying the cops to knock the blacks out." Now here's a problem for commerce: the subsidization of your own oppression through tax dollars that lead to the imprisonment of your own people. That is something that needs to be talked about, and [often wouldn't be] were it not for these R-rated lyrics—that yes, contain repulsive narratives about rape, murderous fantasies that really are deeply destructive. But what's even more destructive is the environment in which they operate, the world in which they exist, and the world that curses them in a very serious and systematic fashion.

I'll end here. We need to hear those voices because as Mr. [Danny] Goldberg said earlier—and as you've already alluded to very brilliantly, Senator McCain—

many of these young people are disaffected from the political process. And one of the reasons they're disaffected from the political process—we can look here today. They're not being represented. With all due respect to the ingenuity of the Senate, for the most part, Mr. Inouye and others are exceptions, this is a white male club. And if those people felt that they could have their own viewpoints, perspectives, and sensitivities respected in a profound way and [with] a kind of empathy that says that the person sitting across the board from me is really concerned about me because he or she has been through what I've been through, and therefore they know the circumstances under which I've existed, then we would have much more faith in the political process, that [it] would at least alleviate some of the suffering and the pain.

So for me, the reality is this: many of these young hip-hoppers certainly need to be talked to, and talked about, but more importantly, we should listen to them. Because the messages that they often put in our faces—that we don't want to hear because they make us uncomfortable—are the messages that we need to hear. The political process can only be enhanced; the American democratic project can only be strengthened; and the citizenship of America can only be deepened, with a profound engagement with some of the most serious problems that these young people represent—and tell us about. This is why—and I'll end here—Nas, a young rapper, said: "It's only right that I was born to use mics / And the stuff that I write is even tougher than dice." Absolutely true, and the reason it's tougher than dice—because they're rolling their dice in a world where they're taking a gamble that their voices can be heard, that their viewpoints can be respected, and that their lives can be protected.

Thank you very kindly, Senator.

McCain: Well, I thank you very much for a very strong statement and a very eloquent one, Mr. Dyson. That is the intention of this committee—to try to get testimony from, and representation from, young Americans, especially when we're talking about some issues that are coming up such as this business of MP3, and Napster, and the music, and who's going to get what. And what accessibility are young people going to have to that music. But again, I would argue to you, if these young people don't have the $500,000 to buy a ticket—by the way, Mr. [Jack] Valenti, even though at least one of your witnesses couldn't be here, I noticed that he is able to host a big multimillion dollar soft money fundraiser; [he] had the time to do that, but not to appear before this committee—then these young people will not obviously think it matters whether they would take the time or effort if there is no resonance to their views, and their hopes, and their dreams, and their aspirations.

And you mentioned my presidential campaign. The one thing I heard from young Americans all over this country: they don't feel they are represented here.

Dyson: Absolutely.

McCain: So why should they be involved? Why should they take the time to come and testify before this committee when it's the money that—the $18 million that Mr. Valenti's industry has already contributed—

Dyson: They want their money back.

McCain: —to the political campaigns. Well—

Dyson: Can I respond to this?

McCain: —obviously, they're going to keep giving because there are three major fundraisers scheduled in the next few days. So, I don't think they want their money back or they wouldn't be attending these—

Dyson: It's a heavy joke, Mr. Chairman. [*Laughter*]

McCain: Go ahead, Mr. Dyson.

Dyson: I've been a severe critic of corporate capitalism and the way that it has disproportionately affected the American political process. And I think we shouldn't simply point our fingers at Hollywood. My God, if we're going to talk about the ways that corporate capitalism has undermined the best interests of the citizenry, we've got to start with the United States Senate. And not just the Senate, but Congress and local municipalities and governments, because justice is being bought. I think your point is absolutely right, and brilliant and brave, by the way. But this is what I want to say: they're not concerned about—they don't even know about a $500,000 per ticket soiree that might be held—

McCain: I disagree with you. I disagree with you, sir.

Dyson: But I'm—

McCain: I talked to them. They know there's something wrong.

Dyson: No, no. I agree with you.

McCain: They know there's something wrong, Mr. Dyson.

Dyson: They do. They do. But I am saying that about the soirée.

McCain: They may not know that it's $500,000, but they know there's something wrong.

Dyson: No, they know. Absolutely right, Senator McCain. I don't disagree with you. I'm just saying that they don't know specifically the details about a $500,000 soiree. But they do know, as you've said, that money is corrupting the political process. But they don't just simply look at Mr. Valenti. They don't simply look at the recording industry—

McCain: Well, I don't allege that they do.

Dyson: —because the recording industry has given them an opportunity to express their viewpoints, which the United States Senate, with the exception of Ed Brooke and Carol Moseley-Braun, has not given much opportunity for young African American people to have a political career at the highest levels and echelons of representative democracy.

McCain: Thank you, Mr. Dyson. And I appreciate our exchange.

Dyson: Thank you, sir.

[*proceedings continue*]

Dyson: Can I add something to the response, if I may, Senator?

Senator Daniel Inouye: Sure, please do.

Dyson: You know, what strikes me as intriguing, and at least worthy of the same sort of intense scrutiny to which we subject this whole rating system, and music, videos, and movies, is the fact that when we think about television, we can't calibrate the intensity of the psychic violence that was done when, say, back in the '50s—when *Father Knows Best,* which America, through the haze of nostalgia, has acclaimed as the golden age of television and cinema and filmmaking and so on—the reality is that there was so much stuff that was done to devastate the minds of the average American. Including young black kids, young poor white kids, Latino kids, Asian kids, minority kids, gay and lesbian kids. My God! And during the era of *Father Knows Best,* the rates of domestic violence that were intensely expressed in American society were never reflected on television. And what happened through the haze of nostalgia? We romanticized the American family as the kind of *locus classicus* of everything that was good, when indeed there was so much pathology going on.

Number·two, when you think about that era of *Father Knows Best*—in the black and white that we now romanticize—Lassie had a television program, and Nat

King Cole couldn't stay on for a year. Now what does that say to a young person growing up? "I can look at a dog, look at Timmy, and Lassie," sister June [Lockhart], and everybody else that was on that show—because I checked it out. The *dog* had a program and Lassie was worthy of being followed: "Bow wow." "What you saying, girl?" "Bow, wow, wow." "Let's follow her out." But a black man of enormous talent, on whose back Capitol Records was built, couldn't stay on television because of the revulsion for black skin, skill, and talent in one segment [of the culture]. And I'm saying, look at the psychologically violent consequences to young people. So when you begin to try to calibrate—it's not only about the resistance to an Archimedean point of objectivity from which we can look at television and radio and lyrics and movies and say that stuff is bad.

Of course, we have common sense. We know when stuff is destructive and not. But the reality is there's so much more that's destructive that never shows up on the radar screen. There's so much more that does violence to young people who are growing up that has nothing to do with whether somebody said "damn" or "hell" or some other word. It's about the realities that they confront, and the inability to make those realities visible, and to make the United States Congress take those seriously. I think we have to put those in context as well as these other things about which we eloquently discourse here today. . . .

McCain: Thank you, sir. I am unaware of whether Senator Breaux or Senator Kerry arrived first. Senator Kerry?

Kerry: Mr. Chairman, thank you very much. It's been very interesting listening to a lot of this. I apologize that some of us have not been able to be here throughout it. I mean, as I said earlier today, there are some really tricky aspects to this that I know Senator Inouye was particularly sensitive to, and others I think have been. And Mr. Dyson, I was particularly struck—I came in—I didn't hear all of your testimony, but I couldn't agree with you more strongly about the perceptions of young people, and the difficulties of our trying to pass judgment on some aspects of what we hear. Certainly one person's profanity can easily be another person's protest. And that's always been true; it has always been true. And I can remember during the turmoil of the 1960s and early '70s in this country, there was an awful lot of profanity that was part of the political protest. And obviously, it would be sanctioned by the court under the First Amendment. And if I were black or Latino, or some other minorities in America, I could find a lot of four-letter words, and a lot of other kinds of words of powerful alliteration, with which to describe this institution and the political system's lack of response. I mean, after all, 48 percent of the kids in New York City don't graduate from high school.

Dyson: Right, right.

Kerry: There are more African Americans in prison today than in college.

Dyson: Yes.

Kerry: And if I were a young black person growing up in those circumstances in this country, notwithstanding the extraordinary opportunities that there are—and there are, I mean, just amazing opportunities for people. When you look at a person like Deval Patrick in Massachusetts, who came out of the South Side of Chicago, happened to get a great scholarship, went to Harvard, became the assistant attorney general for civil rights. I mean, there are people of enormous distinction who have made it. But the problem is, systemically, there is a sense, still, of much too great a set of hurdles and barriers. You look at what was in the paper, I think it was yesterday or today, that the reports are now—the surveys they're doing on the application of the death penalty—that is showing the same kinds of very disturbing trend lines with respect to race and otherwise. So I would caution my colleagues a little bit with respect to sort of a blanket statement with respect to what we hear. Music has always been a form of expression from the beginning of time, and an enormous political tool I might add. And in many cases it is.

Now that said, it is really hard to find any excuse, and certainly any political redemption, in some of the lyrics that we see. There is, in fact, a particularly onerous aspect to the anger that is expressed in some of the lyrics. It's a kind of anger of domination that is particularly violent against women. And I am a parent, though my kids have now made it through college and seem to be okay, but I had serious reservations about that. And I think any parent has to have serious reservations about what they hear. My question to any of the panelists who could answer this adequately—and then I want to ask Mr. Valenti something about the movies per se. And of course there's a distinction between some of the music, between the software, between the video games, between the movies. There's a lot of gradation here, and we have to also be thoughtful about that.

But with respect to the music, it does strike me that some of what we've heard in the last ten years goes over a line that any responsible corporate entity ought to have second thoughts about sponsoring, notwithstanding some desire in the public at large to perhaps buy it. I can understand maybe pirate companies selling it. I could understand an underground network that makes some of it available. I find it very hard to understand why the most upright, upstanding, respected corporate entities in the country are advertising it, or on it, supporting it, investing in it. And I wonder if it—I mean, isn't there some measure, short of legislation and overreach by a legislative body—isn't there some way for a more adequate and responsible level of restraint to be exercised from the industry itself? Or is that simply, after all these years, asking too much?

———

[*proceedings continue*]

Dyson: Can I add very briefly, in regard to that point, Senator Kerry? I think that—take, for example, what Ms. [Hilary] Rosen is saying. Take for example the first album by Notorious B.I.G., Biggie Smalls. Now on that album, you would find stuff, I would find stuff, all of us, most of us, would find stuff that's pretty repulsive. His song celebrating his girlfriend is called "Me and My B__," and we can fill in the blanks there, even though he means it as a term of affection, and he goes on to iterate how this woman has really helped him and so on and so forth.

On that same album, he's got many other songs like "Things Done Changed": "Back in the days, our parents used to take care of us / Look at them now, they're even f— scared of us / Calling the state for help because they can't maintain / Darned things done change / If I wasn't in the rap game, I'd probably have a ki [a kilo] knee-deep in the crack game / Because the streets is a short stop, either you're slinging crack rock or you got a wicked jump shot / Damn it's hard bein' young from the slums eating five cent gums / not knowing where your meal's coming from / What happened to the summertime cookout? Every time I turn around, a brother's being took out."

Now if you restrict, because of vulgarity, and profanity, and misogyny, and unwarranted sexism, the commercial viability of a particular album, on that same album is an eloquent exhortation for people to deal with.

Kerry: But that's not what I'm talking about.

Dyson: And I'm saying on the same album, though, the complex amalgam of the good and the bad company together.

Kerry: Sure, but that's not what I'm talking about. That's a powerful statement. I mean, at easy blush someone would say there's a—I mean, there's a whole lot contained in that. I don't think that's what I'm talking about. But I don't want to get bogged down here. I think most people—it's exactly what Jack Valenti said. You know, you can't necessarily define pornography, but you know when you see it. People know when they are reading a lyric or a paragraph that has absolutely no value except the shock value. And I think people can do that pretty well. And somehow that stuff finds its way into mainstream marketing. And I think you have to recognize this, and we all know how celebrity works in America, and we know how the marketing and sort of buildup is—you can create a demand for it, and you can create a sense of acceptability to it and build it into something more than any sort of real movement has created. So again, I don't want to get into this business.

Hilary Rosen: That's not really true, with all due respect. You can't buy popularity. I mean, artists get popular because people are attracted to what they say. If you could buy popularity, 85 percent of the records that we put into the marketplace wouldn't fail or—

Kerry: Well, let me say that, you know, you and I are good friends and we don't disagree on a lot. But I will disagree on the notion that, number one, you can't buy popularity. Witness some political races in this country. Number two—

Rosen: Well, in our business you can't.

Kerry: Yes, indeed, in your business you can. I remember when *The Monkees*—

Rosen: You can buy attention.

Kerry: The Monkees were completely created out of whole cloth; completely created out of whole cloth. [*Laughter*]

Dyson: Oh no, not *The Monkees!* [*Laughter*]

Kerry: And they were given a creation and an existence that had no—built on the popularity of *The Beatles,* correct?

Rosen: No, but they were sustained because people were attracted to what was offered.

Kerry: Because it mimicked—of course, because it was a pure mimicking of what was already there. And I can give you—I can create some mimicry and put it out there. It doesn't mean it has legitimacy in and of itself. The original does. But then you create—I mean, I don't want to get lost in this argument, because it's a—

Dyson: Because Micky Dolenz did have skills. [*Laughter*]

PART V

BLACK MASCULINITY

15

MILLION HEIRS
Marching Toward Manhood

with Joe Klein; moderated by Liane Hansen

The Million Man March in 1995 in Washington, D.C., was one of the most significant events in recent black history, galvanizing the black community and thrusting Minister Louis Farrakhan to the front ranks of black leadership. A great deal of controversy surrounded the march. Critics questioned why such a rally was necessary and whether it would be racially inflammatory or violent. The Million Man March proved to be peaceful and successful beyond most expectations, and I appeared on several national television and radio shows, before and after the march, to analyze its importance and impact. One of my more notable encounters paired me on NPR's *Weekend Edition* with journalist Joe Klein, then an editor at *Newsweek*. We dissected and debated the march and the implications for black men after that historic show of black solidarity and spiritual self-reflection.

Liane Hansen: This morning, we continue our series of discussions on the state of race relations in America. Could we hear your reactions, first, Joe, to Lester Sloan's essay [on the Million Man March]? What did you think?

Joe Klein: Well, I have a certain amount of empathy for it, but I find it ultimately depressing, because it mirrors my feelings about the march itself. I mean, I thought the message there was kind of mixed, that it was not a march of atonement but a march of affirmation, where an awful lot of black men were standing there saying, "We reject your stereotype of us. We're infuriated by your stereotype of us." But, at the same time, I think that this was a march about the anger of the black middle class, and it was a march where the answer seemed to be a separate reality. And, I think that that's profoundly dangerous. I think, in the end, you know, the answer is that we're all part of the same country and that we're all part of the same culture and the same society, and that the answers for blacks will come from that culture and that society.

Hansen: Could we get your reaction, Professor Dyson?

Michael Eric Dyson: Well, I think that I agree with Mr. Sloan inasmuch as it was a monumental day. It was a monumental achievement for African American men. It was a day that shall live in glorious remembrance as a ritual of public affirmation and atonement—affirmation of our humanity that has been vilified and demonized in various and sundry ways throughout American popular culture, and in politics and in society. It was an atonement, I think, for some of the plagues that have besieged African American life, that black men, in particular, have become part of. On the other hand, I think that the attempt somehow to focus the energy upon black men is not as Joe Klein worries—and I disagree with his worry about this. It is not a rejection of the necessity of linking our own suffering and pain to the larger American culture in which we exist. It is simply a way of focusing a bright light upon the peculiar predicaments of African American males and trying to come up with resources and remedies for the enormous concern that many of us have, and for the problems that continue to besiege us. So I think it was an attempt both to say that if democracy is to be real for African American men, there is both a political remedy and a spiritual one. And this was a march for spiritual renewal, linked to political transformation, that could have powerful consequences for all Americans, but especially black men.

Hansen: Was it, indeed, a coming of age?

Dyson: I think so in many regards. It's a coming of age because it was an attempt of black men in public, in a global audience, to say that we are not what so many have deemed us to be. Unfortunately, some elements that I wanted to see there—such as the atonement for, if you will, the sin of patriarchy and sexism that all men share, but particularly African Americans toward black women—I wanted to see some specific remedies for that coming forth from the leadership, which I think was painfully absent. And, as well, [for] homophobia—some kind of atonement for the vicious ways in which homophobic passions have been unleashed within African American society, which can scarcely afford those [passions] since we are already [viewed as] marginalized "others" in American culture.

Hansen: bell hooks mentioned the whole idea of patriarchy when she was on our show last week. Joe, I want to give you a chance to respond to what Professor Dyson is saying.

Klein: I think we need a little bit more patriarchy in the black community, and also in the white community. When you have out-of-wedlock birth rates of over 80 percent in the inner cities, what you have here is the absence of responsibility, not the taking of responsibility, and I think we need a little bit more of that. The concern I have about this moment is this. This was a middle-class march, and there is agony in the black middle-class community, some of which we've heard the professor speak about, which has to do, in large part, with white blindness. But it also has to do with the embarrassment about the behavior that we're seeing in a lot of these communities—the anarchy, the disintegration of families. You know, I like to think about what John Edgar Wideman wrote about in his book *Brothers and Keepers*. I think that his metaphor is the submerged metaphor of this march, which is, "My brother is a murderer." The brothers of those who were on that mall on Monday, many of them are criminals, many of them are murderers, and it's very hard for people to figure out how to deal with that.

Hansen: Professor Dyson, you wanted to say something?

Dyson: Well, I wanted to say that it wasn't simply that these were middle-class black men coming together to affirm themselves and to lament the failures of their brothers and uncles and sons and cousins who had not measured up to the moral standards that they so precariously observed, or tenaciously observed—or in an attempt to somehow say that they were different than these other brothers. What they were affirming, first of all, is that most black men are living lives of dignity and intelligence and moral circumspection against the vicious diatribes that have been launched toward them from both politics and pop culture. So, I think that those black men were there and, at least, I was there, to affirm that, "Yes, on the one hand, regardless of our social station and class in life, we are often treated negatively. We can't get a cab in New York, we get treated poorly by the police, and there are a whole range of ills, from the lower class to the upper class, that black men are commonly subject to."

Hansen: Let's talk a little bit about remedies and solutions, and I'm not quite sure they're the same thing. I want to take you back to 1964 and the Civil Rights Act, where we heard people like Dr. King calling it a "cool and serene breeze," but someone like Malcolm X was a lot less optimistic, saying, "You cannot legislate good will. The only thing that will eliminate discrimination and segregation is education, not legislation." Let's start there. Where do each of you think the role for government is in affecting solutions and maybe differentiate, in your mind and to us, what you consider to be the difference between a solution and a remedy?

Klein: Well, I don't think the word games are as important here as what actually happens on the ground. I think that there are ways that government has hurt the racial reconciliation in this country and ways that it could help it in the future. I have been very much opposed to writing race into law in remedial fashion. I think that it's served to further divide us over the last thirty years. I think that taking the turn toward affirmative action was a wrong turn. I've also been very much opposed to the bureaucratic welfare state, as it has delivered services and enslaved the poor in this country, and I think that there is an area where we can begin to make major changes, and we have a moral responsibility to make major changes to become much more active in the lives of the poor in this country.

Also, a very important issue here that the professor made reference to is the problem of the police. I think that it's become very clear that over the last ten years in this country, the quality and number of police in this country has declined precipitously. We have to break this kind of blue mentality, this cult-like mentality, that we have among the police, and there's a way to do it. There's a program called the Police Corps, in which young people would be given scholarships in return for service of four or five years as a police officer. I don't think anybody should serve as a cop for more than four or five years unless they're a genius, and then the geniuses could be the ones who manage, who become the sergeants and lieutenants further on. We need to have a different class of cops. Service should be something that each of us does for a short period of our life rather than something that we pay other people to do for all of our lives. And, if that were the case, we would have a much more caring and much more interconnected society.

Hansen: Professor Dyson, your reaction not only to what Mr. Klein had to say but your thoughts on whether government can legislate this sort of thing, and your own thoughts on remedies and concrete solutions to these problems?

Dyson: I don't think that the solution is, "Well, let the government step aside because it's flunked for the last thirty years." It's not so much that the government has flunked for the last thirty years—and I'm not one to defend the programs of the Great Society uncritically because I think that we have to learn from our past failures. On the other hand, I think that study after study, social scientific treatise after social scientific treatise, has come up with an amazing relationship established between people who have employment and jobs, and people who are able to do well in that society. I'm not reducing morality to economic infrastructures, but I am suggesting, to paraphrase Dorothy Day, "I want to work toward a world in which it's possible for people to behave decently." And the possibility of decent behavior is incredibly strengthened by people who have food in their stomachs, education for their minds, clothes for their backs. It's not simply saying, "Well, can the government legislate morality?" What's important is how can the government aid in the moral and spiritual reconstruction of these communities, but more importantly, using political and economic measures to encourage growth in these cities.

Hansen: Mr. Klein, I'm going to give you the last word.

Klein: I think that, you know, Professor Dyson says—and I agree with him—that we are enslaved by stereotypes in this country to a very great extent. We have to start looking and recognizing the vast majority of blacks who don't fit into the stereotypes that we see in the media, that we in the media promulgate. But we also have to recognize that the vast majority of whites don't fit into racist stereotypes either. A great deal of progress has been made.

Hansen: Okay. Both of you, thank you very much for joining us.

Klein: Thank you.

Dyson: Thank you very kindly.

16

IN HIS OWN HANDS

Black Male Intensity and Latrell Sprewell's American Dream

with Len Elmore; moderated by Ray Suarez

In 1998, Golden State Warriors basketball player Latrell Sprewell attacked his coach, P. J. Carlesimo, choking him, and then attempting to rush him again after he was separated from Carlesimo. The incident earned Sprewell an unprecedented suspension for the balance of the season, after which he was traded to the New York Knicks and emerged a bigger star by helping to lead his team to the NBA championship series the next season. The incident was widely discussed, and in June 1999, I joined lawyer and former pro basketball player Len Elmore—now a television analyst for the sport—on NPR's *Talk of the Nation* for a wide-ranging and insightful discussion about black male angst and racial identity, the difficulties of saying "I'm sorry," and professional sports and violence.

Ray Suarez: It was just a moment ago in time when sportswriters were talking about the NBA as Michael Jordan and three hundred supporting players. Michael Jordan was a guy team owners would gladly welcome into their foursome in an otherwise restricted golf club. While they sometimes seemed uncomfortable with the young generation of spinning, dunking, trash-talking showboats from city school yards now festooned with tattoos, the moaning and wailing over the departure of Michael Jordan was a neat counterpoint to the departure and the return of Latrell Sprewell, who attracted attention far beyond the practice court of the Golden State Warriors when he wrapped his hands around the neck of coach P. J. Carlesimo.

By attacking the coach, trying to take another whack at him a short time later, and then remaining only as repentant as he had to be to save his career; heading into suspension; and then reemerging with the New York Knicks, Latrell Sprewell forces an uneasy encounter between mass America and what it wants in its celebrated players. Between the dreams we project onto these young millionaires and a group of real flesh-and-blood men making a fabulous living while they can. Sprewell is a streaky, aggressive, serious player. He's not Mr. Congeniality. He somehow got through the truncated, poststrike season as a sub, but made no secret of his belief he should start. The playoff season that took the Knicks to the championship round has also made Sprewell a hero in New York. Okay, it would have been a better story if three games later, that desperation shot at the buzzer had dropped. But Latrell Sprewell's still a pretty interesting story. What does it mean when such a player moves from being a poster child for everything wrong with professional athletes to someone advertisers are ready to embrace again?

Both my guests are in New York. Michael Eric Dyson is the Ida B. Wells-Barnett University professor at DePaul University in Chicago and the author of *Race Rules: Navigating the Color Line,* and the forthcoming *I May Not Get There with You: The True Martin Luther King, Jr.* Welcome back to the program.

Michael Eric Dyson: Thanks, Ray. It's good to be here. And congratulations on your new book.

Suarez: Thank you. Len Elmore is with us also from New York. He played in the NBA for ten years with the Pacers, Bucks, Nets, and Knicks. He's an attorney specializing in sports and entertainment law and a college basketball analyst for ESPN. It's great to have you with us.

Len Elmore: Thank you very much, Ray.

Suarez: Well, Michael Eric Dyson, it's not new that there should be a tension between almost, oh, flip-side, mirror-transposed images of each other, of the black man, in society, whether it's Sonny Liston [and] Floyd Patterson, or Cassius Clay and Muhammad Ali being a mirror image to himself almost.

Dyson: Right.

Suarez: So what should we make of Latrell Sprewell?

Dyson: Well, I think Latrell Sprewell is a rather interesting and powerful metaphor for the complexities of black male identity. On the one hand, Latrell Sprewell represents, to many Americans, everything that is horrible in the post-Jordan era. That is to say, an athlete who is so egocentric and so focused that he can't subordinate his own concerns for the concerns of the team—i.e., he wants to start—[and] that he wears his hair in a braided form that is antithetical to the clean-shaven dome of Mr. Jordan and others. And furthermore, that his willingness to choke his coach in order to get his point across celebrates a kind of barbarism that is well-nigh disrespected in the hallowed halls of basketball.

But I think that Latrell Sprewell is much more interesting and powerful. I love his new commercial where he says—you know, on the And 1 commercials—"You say I'm an American nightmare; I say I'm the American Dream. Others say that I'm not worthy of this kind celebration; I say I'm a three-time All-Star." I think that Latrell Sprewell's rehabilitation, if you will, is symptomatic of how desperate the situation is for young black men who bring a hip-hop aesthetic, a certain style, to the formerly white and powerful halls—both in terms of corporate power, but in this case in terms of the basketball game.

Even though the basketball game has been, for a while, a black man's game, this new generation is representing a powerful challenge to even Charles Barkley. In the comparison [between] Charles Barkley and Latrell Sprewell, Charles Barkley now looks like a kind of high-school player compared to Allen Iverson and so on. So I think that Latrell Sprewell, however unfortunately, has revealed something else that's quite pernicious; that is to say, there is still a very powerful racist understanding of black men. Let me give you an example. Kevin Greene, a white defensive player for the Carolina Panthers, lost his cool at the end of the 1998 season. He attacked his defensive coordinator, and yet, you could hardly find anything in the media about this equally barbaric act as Latrell Sprewell's.

So I think that, again, Latrell Sprewell bears the brunt of some unfortunate and nasty consequences of the stigmatization and demonization of young black males' style and what that represents. What he did was not good. But what he has done to rehabilitate himself—one year, you're choking your coach; the next year, you're trying not to choke in the NBA finals. That's the American Dream. That's what it's all about, and he represents that powerfully.

Suarez: That was all about playing, though. I mean, he had a hard time saying the words "I'm sorry," at one point famously saying, "Well, it's not like I killed anybody or anything."

Dyson: Right.

Suarez: I think given the chances, people want to continue the illusion, like, "Here, just say something nice enough so that we don't have to be concerned about this anymore. Help us put this away." He wouldn't.

Dyson: Yeah. Well, Bill Clinton and Latrell Sprewell have so much in common. I think that the interesting reality, of course, is that it's difficult for a whole lot of people to say "I'm sorry," and Latrell Sprewell certainly is not immune to those human inclinations to be unwilling to acknowledge your error. Even though he has, time and time again, acknowledged that, and time and time again said, "What I did was wrong." I think that if you catch him at a different stage, he said a different thing. Here's my point, though: In terms of his own personal deport-ment, let's be honest. Many people outside of basketball didn't know who Latrell

Sprewell was until this unfortunate incident. He was an extraordinarily highly re-garded guard, a two-guard in the shadows of Michael Jordan, but a very power-ful figure. He was well-regarded for his intelligence and his intensity. So this one incident does not sum up his life. You know, we have to judge people not by one isolated incident that reveals what we think is character. Character has to be as-sessed over the space and time of a player's or a person's life.

You've got to look at the entire box score, not just one night's game. You've got to look at his season, and for most of his career, Latrell Sprewell has been a pow-erful influence in terms of bringing a certain kind of style and aesthetic to the game of basketball. And his own streakiness, his own intensity, his own fierce determi-nation to win on this New York Knicks team has certainly elevated their game. And I think the reason why many New York fans have embraced him is because they see in him the kind of scrappy, the kind of willful, the kind of persevering fig-ure, who was emblematic of the working-class aesthetic—over against these whin-ing, high-paid superstars who refuse to get down in the trenches and do the nasty work. And Latrell represents, both in his personal life, in terms of his rehabilita-tion, and in his playing style, a powerful determination to fuse those two.

Suarez: Well, Len Elmore, one person who wrote this program suggested it's all about winning. If he didn't have a great season, if the Knicks didn't make it to the finals, people would still be harping on the deeds of the past and not even giving him the shot at rehabilitation he's getting now.

Elmore: Well, absolutely. And let me preface my remarks by saying I agree with a lot that Michael just said. I think the latter point, though, needs to be drawn out a little bit. Latrell Sprewell obviously had a tremendous season. He comported himself almost in model citizen terms. But what it does, it points up, once again, the dichotomy that we've had since, really, professional sports in America, both individual and team sports. And that's that perceived black superiority in sports with the mainstream, or white male inferiority complex, regarding that, and try-ing to reconcile those two versus the need to root for a team in that greater iden-tity. And I dare say Latrell Sprewell, for all that he's done, had the Knicks gone out against Miami in the first round, we probably wouldn't have been able to build this momentum working towards him being some kind of New York City hero. I think that if Latrell Sprewell had played for Miami or some of these other teams, I think the press in New York, as well as the fans, would have been on him unmercifully.

I mean, the bottom line is—I've been one of those people in the past that when Latrell Sprewell committed the act against P. J. Carlesimo, I thought that he should be punished and punished severely—not necessarily taken away from the game, but having an example made based on his conduct. But now that the pow-ers-that-be didn't feel that that kind of punishment was necessary and he's un-dergone that punishment, suffered the consequences, and has come back, I say it's now time to move on. Let's begin to judge him from today going forward. And, yes, he has been contrite in this situation, but I don't think right now it's probably a good thing to make him out to be a saint. Because you haven't done anything in the last couple of months doesn't exactly exonerate you from your conduct before. But I do say it's a step forward and let's continue to watch.

Suarez: I would imagine that he has—win, lose, or draw—from now on, a very tough row to hoe as far as how to present himself to the public. There's a constant spotlight on you. He is a very tightly wound fellow. He is not a jocular, easygoing, glib-with-the-press kind of guy. And there's this microscope that sometimes a guy like Latrell Sprewell gets under where, even if he doesn't mean anything by it, his body language, the way he composes his face, is all being examined in such a way that people will ascribe to him a dark personality. Or they'll call him an "angry black man" instead of just a basketball player.

Elmore: Ray, I disagree a little bit. I mean, I've watched him fairly closely, and what you see is an extremely intelligent, very introspective young man. He understands the position that he's in. He chooses his words very carefully, at least from what I've seen. Regarding a tough row to hoe, I mean he's got a pretty sizable shoe contract right now, a national television commercial. There aren't a whole lot of NBA guys that have all of that. So I wouldn't think that he's exactly facing a lot of obstacles going forward. I think his greatest obstacle is in facing himself and recognizing, "Who is it that I want to be?"

Dyson: I think I agree largely with what Len just said, but let me make this addendum in coda. I think that to the degree that Latrell Sprewell is a highly intelligent, deeply introspective black man, he contradicts the stereotype of what black men should be. He's not a happy darkie, so he's not on TV smiling and jockeying and shuffling and sniveling and high-fiving. He's out there to take care of business. He's executing this as the most serious thing when he's in that game—for those forty-eight minutes or so—as the most serious thing on earth, and that kind of dedication and that kind of intelligence brought together are formidable. But in the arsenal of black masculinity, those are formidable tools that get turned against you. So now he becomes surly, he becomes churlish, he becomes diffident, he becomes distant when, indeed, he is introspective.

Think about Dick Allen, who used to play baseball. Think about some of the other black figures who were not willing to speak to the press or who understood that the media was about manipulating your image for their own good to sell their papers. He refused that. He resisted that. So Latrell Sprewell, I think, as Len said, has ingeniously parlayed his misfortune into an expanded portfolio upon which he has been able to project his own personality, and indeed make a whole lot of money at the same time, exploiting, if you will, the controversy in the most powerful and palliative way.

Suarez: Well, Michael, you might have just said it better. What I was getting at was that, in fact, if he just goes out and plays ball, people will ascribe motives to him that he maybe never even thought of himself.

Dyson: Right. Right. Well I think you're right onto something there. And you know what? This is why I think Latrell Sprewell represents so much more powerfully than even a figure like the hallowed Michael Jordan, the average working black man. Michael Jordan had gotten to a level where people were worshiping him, genuflecting before the shrine of his great and global fame. Whereas Latrell Sprewell represents the brother who can't get a break no matter what he does. Mess up one time, can't forget it. Do something wrong and the society will always forsake you, never acknowledge what you've done. And you've got to keep on proving yourself time and time again, whereas, when I mentioned Kevin Greene, the white player for the Carolina Panthers, this guy has not nearly been subjected to the same kind of problem. Let me give you another example. Look at Lawrence Phillips, the football player who has had troubles both in college and now in professional sports. His own teammate, Christian Peter, who had a far worse record, never got the kind of public and vehement denunciations that Mr. Phillips sustained. So I think it is a racial differential that we have to acknowledge.

Caller (Roger): Yes, Ray, see, I can look at this very objectively because I'm neither white nor black. And I do agree that white athletes are being maligned much less for what they do, like one of your guests was saying, Kevin Greene—you can [cite] a lot of examples. Even [when] they bump the referees, bump the coaches, you know. And what about in the hockey games? Every day there's a fight. What about that kind of violence? And those are the black athletes that come from very bad backgrounds and [have] to accomplish much more than the white athletes to get to the level where they're at. So like one of your guests was saying about the black inferiorism today, what about the white superiority complex? And that is why they are always maligned much more for the same deed they do as a white athlete. The other day, John Daly, in the golf match, he was hitting the ball where he should not be hitting it and it came back. What about that? You know, all kinds of things happen for white athletes, but when a black athlete does that same thing, next day when there is no other issue, all the talk show hosts, one hundred stations, they all catch on to this and malign the black athlete like anything. And it's a race issue and it should not be done at all.

Dyson: Well, I agree. I think that there's a double standard going on. And the interesting point that I think Roger made about hockey is just fascinating. I mean, hockey has been accepted as a ritual sport of violence for masculinity in American society, so you can go in there and beat each other's brains out and then emerge as a greater hero. It's the testosterone politics of the ultimate expression of masculinity; whereas in the relatively free zone of contact, if you will, in basketball, you know, the kinds of things that those athletes do there are magnified beyond all proportion. And I think that we have to pay attention to that. Now people will immediately say, "Well, that's hockey. That's what they're supposed to do." Well, the thing is that in basketball and in football—basketball's 85 percent black; I think football's something like 60 to 65 percent black—these are sports, again, which have been imprinted by black male style, and black masculine style has to be controlled, contained, and, in some senses, surveilled in ways that protect the larger society from this violence. Because the real subtext of Latrell Sprewell and Lawrence Phillips and other black athletes is if these highly paid figures can act like this, boy, what can the average black person that you don't know about do? So there's a powerful subtext there that is always being thrust upon the black athlete, a further layer of representation from which he is not easily discounted.

Elmore: And Roger kind of misinterpreted what I stated regarding superiority, inferiority. I talked about black superiority in sports as perceived and as perceived white male inferiority, and the need to try to reconcile them, and usually the control of the media more than anything else kind of balances that out. I think an interesting point does go back to hockey. Now that hockey is becoming more and more integrated, we've seen when the combatants are interracial, all of a sudden, now the N-word pops up, accusations of racial discrimination in taunts, etcetera, have surfaced. And people want to try and sweep that under the rug. But that is what we're going to face as we continue down that road, if we continue with viewing white athletes more sympathetically or black athletes less sympathetically. Let's try and view them equally. Michael Jordan, if he doesn't win, he doesn't receive the ardor that he's received over the years, and that's really the fact.

Suarez: Well, Roger brought up John Daly, the golfer, who has been battling a terrific problem with alcoholism. If you contrast the way his very public, dramatic working out of all his problems has been understood, talked about, versus Darryl Strawberry, has there really been that much of a difference? Is there more indulgence for John Daly?

Elmore: I think—

Dyson: Well, go ahead, Len.

Elmore: I was going to say, remember, once again, the common denominator is—quite honestly, winning is the thing that brings everything together. If Darryl Strawberry had continued in his difficulties—and notwithstanding the cancer that he suffered—if he continued his difficulties and didn't play for a world champion,

I wonder if, in fact, people would view him that way. And history will prove me out that there are many instances of guys who struggled with substances over the years that were pretty much written off as thugs, as antisocial in their behavior, and "Why can't he come off of this stuff?" where, once again, John Daly, playing the ultimate mainstream sport in America, is viewed as a guy who's struggling along, and rightly so. You know, my point is you've got to be able to view each instance equally regardless of race. A guy who has a substance problem with cocaine is no different than a guy who drinks himself under the rug, day in, day out. They have a disease and it's time to recognize it.

Dyson: I think Len is absolutely right, except like there's a difference in the judicial system where crack cocaine will get you a much harsher sentence than powdered cocaine—or it takes a lot more powdered cocaine to do something wrong in the eyes of the law [while it only takes] a little bit of crack cocaine. The reality is that drinking is seen as a kind of white boy's sin, whereas cocaine and other substance abuses are seen as a black boy's problem. So the reality is there's even segregation in that arena. But look, John Daly can write a book—I think he's the author of the book *A Good Walk Spoiled*—where he can rhapsodize, you know, the—

Suarez: No, that's John Feinstein.

Dyson: John Feinstein, Okay. Well, wasn't there a book about John Daly? I'm thinking there was a book about John Daly.

Suarez: Yes, there is a book about John Daly.

Dyson: Right. So the point is we can rhapsodize about his very powerful struggles in the public sphere with his own alcohol—he's battling this problem and he's got to conquer it. So his own battles become a metaphor for his own sport; his own sport becomes a metaphor for his own personal struggles. So there's a kind of rhapsodic, elegiac celebration of his heroic struggle against these odds that is seen in mythic terms, whereas the black athlete is reduced to the individual. John Daly is seen as representing an entire culture struggling for its own right to exist against these certain diseases; whereas I think black men become very victimized by [an] individualistic ethic. They are problems themselves. They don't represent the black ghetto. Latrell Sprewell and Allen Iverson don't represent the tremendous odds against which they've struggled all of their lives, as well as millions of other black men. So I think there's a very powerful segregatory element that we have to talk about.

Suarez: Well, for someone who's never talked about it, didn't one of the Knicks players refer to a slave revolution during the finals? I mean, when you're talking about trying to raise high for a tip-off there, I mean, that's some pretty elevated language to use for a basketball game.

Dyson: Well, you can say that, but look at—what did Marge Schott say in, what was it, '96, that she had million-dollar "niggers" working for her, and she'd rather have a trained monkey working than a "nigger"? So if you think that a black person doesn't have the right, then, to appropriate language that has been used to denigrate him, which seems hyperbolic in the least, the reality is we're living in a culture where Marge Schott owns black men and owns them to play the game, or formerly did. And I think the reality is that, as Len says, as long as those young black men are winning, they're great. But I've been in the stands when as soon as they make a bad play, they're a "nigger"; as soon as they mess up in their personal lives, "You can't do anything with those people." When they're winning, they are exceptions to black people. When they're losing and failing, they represent all of black people. And I think that either way, it's unfair, but the reality is, the representational burden that these young black men bear is extraordinary.

So I can understand them being "slaves" even if—and I know Len wants to jump in here—even if we think it's impossible for slaves to make millions of dollars. That's the first thing white people say, "Wait a minute, back in the day, you didn't make any money. Now you're making millions of dollars." Well, millions of dollars doesn't make you exempt from the kind of prejudice and bias and bigotry that people can project onto you. Malcolm X says, "What do you call a black person with a Ph.D.?" You call them a "nigger," the same thing as a person who makes a whole lot of money for putting a basketball through a pair of nets or hitting a white ball.

Suarez: Len Elmore.

Elmore: The interesting point about Larry Johnson's comment [about being a slave] was that it just floated right past folks. You know, I think we've gotten to a point now where people understand the metaphor, and a lot of people may not agree with it but they understand it. And we've got to go back to the point once again of personal identification. The mainstream has a very difficult time identifying with African American athletes, regardless from where they've come. And quite honestly, that's where the sympathetic view comes. John Daly—he's everyman for the mainstream, and that's why they can identify, they can look in their families and see a John Daly there. And you can see that in hiring in professional sports, where owners will hire guys that they look at as maybe their sons, and it just permeates the sport itself. As soon as we get away from this identifying with our own, and having the ability to reach out and identify with people with similar experience, identify with character, quality, etcetera, etcetera, then we're going to be much better off.

Suarez: Let's go to Tempe, Arizona. Tiari is with us. Welcome to the program.

Caller: Hi, Ray. Thank you for having me on. First, I'd like to say that I think it's wonderful that DePaul has an Ida B. Wells professor. I think that's great.

Dyson: Well, thank you.

Caller: I want to say that I think the theme of this conversation so far has been double standards, and I wanted to point out another one. It seems that usually in American culture, we think of rich people as people who don't have to take crap off of people because they are rich. But when it comes to athletes, people think that they should endure insult and disrespect because they are rich. For example, I can't imagine someone hearing that someone has done something very rude to Bill Gates or some other rich person, and people say, "Well, you know, he's a millionaire. He should expect that people should be in his face." It seems like they want the athletes to be just grateful and grovel every moment for the money that they have, although they earn lots of money for the teams. You have to think about it—that some team owner makes enough to pay all of them. And I'll take my response off the air.

Dyson: Well, first of all, I'll applaud DePaul for naming the first named professorship after a black woman. But secondly, I think she's absolutely right, that there is this double standard in terms of the perception of how these athletes should act. Look at the lockout. The very brilliant and powerful lawyer, Billy Hunter, who is now the representative for the Players Association there, made a very powerful and sustained attempt to honorably carry forth the demands of the players in a way that respected the integrity of the game, while also arguing for the integrity of the players to share more equitably in the revenues that were being generated by this globally accepted game. And yet, he and the other players were denigrated constantly for, in one sense, griping and whining and bemoaning because they were rich. And on top of that, that these rich players had no right to expect to be treated fairly, to get a greater share of the revenues. To expect that integration would not only happen on the basketball court—but, as Tiari alluded to—happen in the front offices, or in the managerial spots, or even in the coaching spots where the power is distributed. So I think her point is absolutely right, that Bill Gates and other rich people do not have to suffer the calumny or insult that is heaped upon these athletes as a matter of course.

Elmore: Well, the Bill Gates situation, certainly he has had his share of ridicule. Lord knows that he probably wishes that he didn't, but the bottom line is with that kind of money, you expect that type of attack. The difference is Bill Gates's economic system is far more complex for the average person to understand and recognize as opposed to sports, where most people perceive the economic system in sports as: "I'm a fan, I pay to watch you play; therefore, I am paying your salary; therefore, you deserve anything I can dish out." Obviously, that's not the reality, but that's the perception, and that's why many people, combined with this lack of identification with these athletes, and the inferiority complex—that necessarily has to be reconciled. That's why they feel that they can say anything or do anything to these athletes. Charles Barkley is a magnet for people who feel as though, because they buy a ticket to a game, they can say or do anything that they want to [him], and that really underscores the lack of respect for these young men as individuals and for what they do.

Dyson: And let me add something else to what Len said. Look on the college level, where it's even more difficult, however. When you look at Pat Ewing—Pat Ewing made about $4.5 million for Georgetown in terms of ticket sales, in terms of television, in terms of publicity, in terms of revenue that was generated. But he got something like $48,000 for a scholarship for that school. So the reality is on the college level, where these extraordinary athletes are making millions and millions and, in some cases, collectively, billions of dollars for the public education of American society, they are not rewarded in anywhere near the proportion to which they've invested their own lives and careers—and often don't even get a good education. So on the professional level, that works, but on the college level, the investment that they've made, and the blood-sweat equity that they've put forward, is not nearly rewarded at the level it is in professional sports, and I think that's something we have to take a look at as well.

Suarez: Arthur writes from Palm Beach Gardens, Florida: "Give me a break. All-star or not, the man's [Sprewell's] behavior is criminal. He needs to be locked up. If he wants to be an example to up-and-coming young black men, then let that be it. If you act in a criminal way, you're punished. And all the dreams you had and potential you had goes down with it." Steve writes from Dallas: "Why isn't Latrell Sprewell in jail for battery? Battery is criminal, not civil offense. Latrell Sprewell committed battery in front of at least twelve witnesses and admitted to committing the crime on *60 Minutes*. On *60 Minutes*, Lesley Stahl didn't bother asking the district attorney why they weren't prosecuting the case. She did, however, on behalf of a friend, ask Latrell Sprewell for his autograph. Whatever happened to the hard-hitting *60 Minutes* pieces of the past? I am a sports fan, but I did not attend or watch one NBA game this season." Sally writes from San Antonio: "What about the good guys in the NBA? I could not believe I had to hear about Sprewell. What about David Robinson, Avery Johnson, Tim Duncan, and the rest of the Spurs? These are some fine examples of men with good morals who are involved with their community for the betterment of everyone. The media is at fault for not showing more fine, strong, upstanding black men like them. Why not more publicity for the good guys?"

And Susan writes: "From a Spurs fan in San Antonio, please tell Mr. Sprewell

thank you for being such a joy to watch and for being a gentleman. I was all prepared to despise him, but he's won an admirer. He deserves a second chance and
has proven he will make use of it." Mike writes from Sag Harbor: "The guy's a
basketball player who happens to be good. As written in the *New York Times* this
past weekend, 'If Slobodan Milosevic had an outside shot, we would forgive him,
too.' How many other players have gone after their coach? How many have gone
after P. J. Carlesimo? How many of these incidents have been reported? I believe
Latrell Sprewell is the American Dream." And finally, Everett writes from Port-
land: "Gentlemen, why don't we just call this what it really is, another example of
racism American-style? White players have done despicable things, from raping
people to being blatant bigots, but have never been held to account the way black
and other players of color have been. The fact that he's not crying and whimper-
ing before the great white hope, the American people, makes him perceived as a
threat. Yes, what he did was wrong. Who hasn't done wrong? Let he who has no
sin cast the first three-pointer. What we have here is a country full of majority-
population guys who could never play any type of sports, who get very upset
when they see a person of color get paid good salaries for a sport."

Elmore: Let me go back real quick to a couple of those who wrote in regarding
the criminal element. First of all, it's my belief that it was a criminal act. The problem was P. J. Carlesimo did not want to press charges. He had his own reasons
for doing that, and he wanted the league to take care of it. Now recognizing the
relationships between coach and player—and a bad relationship at that—maybe
that was the right thing to do. As I've stated before, I didn't think the NBA went
far enough in punishing him for that act, but now that the punishment has been
served, I think it's time for people to start moving on and recognizing that you
judge the guy from this moment on.

Suarez: Jeremy is next in Oakland, California. Hi, Jeremy.

Caller: Hi. I really want to take issue with Reverend Dyson's panegyrics of veri-
table Bible-thumping glorification of Sprewell's thuggery. It's not like he only
messed up one time. He previously threatened to bring a gun to practice, and
after he was suspended, he was found—and I live in Oakland so this is something
that barely broke the news barrier here, but at least we did hear about it. He was
found in his car at 4:00 in the morning by a policeman, and upon waking up, he
started screaming racial epithets at the guy. I mean, it's amazing to me that he
didn't go to jail for that, which shows you something about the power of celebrity
to get you out of jail. Also while he's been in New York, he's continued to refuse
to ever pass the ball. He never showed up at practice. I mean, he's obviously, you
know, an incredible athlete, so he can get away with that sort [of thing], but there
hasn't—I mean, I'm offended at your attempt to recuperate somebody. I really
don't see how this could be called messing up one time. And also, the John Daly—

Darryl Strawberry opposition was offensive, too, because Strawberry also beat his wife. I mean, what we're talking about here is violence, and I really don't think it's all right to excuse it.

Dyson: Well, thank you. I've rarely been put in my place as eloquently as you did there. Let me say a couple of things. First of all, in regard to Latrell Sprewell, we're not here to debate whether or not Latrell passed the ball. That's something for his coach to decide and for his teammates to impose. And his particular style of play has to be regulated within the context of the defense and offense that is put forward by the New York Knicks. Obviously, they relied upon that because they were looking for him to take the last shot in the game [that counted] most in their season. Number two, in regard to the attempt to recuperate, or even alternatively, to rehabilitate Mr. Sprewell, the reality is if we're going to use beating a woman—that is, domestic abuse—as the litmus for legitimacy within sports, then get ready for [a bunch of] guys to hang up those cleats and the spikes and the shoes because a whole heck of a lot of them have done that and far, far worse than Mr. Sprewell was accused of. I don't even exonerate [Strawberry] on that score and even try to justify and legitimate what he did because I take domestic abuse seriously. And if that's the case, then all of sport has to take that much more seriously. Thirdly, when Latrell Sprewell put those black fingers around that white man's neck, that raised a kind of fear in American society. The collective unconscious—the psyche—was struck boldly by that, because it was a metaphor for how black privilege was overstepping its boundaries and then getting uppity in a serious way. And so many racial epithets are tied in with that. I don't want to go there.

So let me say three final things. First of all, to tie your comments into the other comments, number one, the Spurs are being celebrated, and other figures like that. That is very fine—Tim Duncan, David Robinson, and so on. But let's better ourselves. Grant Hill, in his book, *Change the Game*, said this: that he was satisfied that one sportswriter said, "Can Grant Hill save the game?" But in the same article, he saw Grant at a party where some black guys in fur coats came up to him and hugged him, and then they called him King of the 'Hoods. We have to be serious here. Tim Duncan, David Robinson are [perceived as] "good Negroes, passive Negroes," who never raised a question—not only about their so-called criminal behavior, but about the reality of racism and lack of opportunity in American culture that Latrell Sprewell taps into.

Finally, look at this. We have come from the black athlete, from Muhammad Ali, who was protesting a war and gave up at the height of his career all of his earnings, or had that snatched away from him, down to athletes who represent now a brand in a commercial entity. We've gone from Nam to Nike, and the reality is that the black athlete has historically been connected to the representation of his race, or her race, in order to further the race, in order to further opportunity, in order to make America understand the plights and predicaments of African American people. Today's athletes owe a loyalty mostly to brands, not to communities, and when they do speak about racial issues, they are branded as up-pity Negroes who are unwilling to subordinate their interest to the better interests of the NBA and their team.

Suarez: But wait a minute. When you say that the individual athlete is more aligned to a brand than to the community, I think you can make a fairly deep case for that and use a lot of examples. There are counterexamples, but you can make a case for that. However, to say that anybody who isn't actively and outspokenly resisting the racial regime in this country is somehow a collaborator to oppres-sion—putting that on the shoulders of Tim Duncan, who is a fairly young player and didn't even grow up on the American mainland, I think that's pretty wild.

Dyson: Here's what I'm saying, Ray, and I know that Len wants to jump in. What I'm suggesting is that—you're missing a part of the argument. The very pos-sibility that they have to exercise their craft in American culture is not because of the largess of larger mainstream society. It is precisely because of the struggles of people like Jim Brown, and Muhammad Ali, and Joe Louis, and a whole range of figures who were willing to [struggle]. We didn't hear white America complain very bitterly when Joe Louis struck a blow for democracy against Max Schmel-ing. Not only was he representing the articulation of black masculinity at a very powerful point; he was striking a blow for the freedom of the American way of life. So when those interests are being defended that represent the mainstream, it's fine. It's invisible. But when it is struck for the interests of African American com-munities—Tim Duncan couldn't even come here from a Caribbean island to enjoy the American sport of basketball, much less to play it, without Muhammad Ali, without Jim Brown, without Hank Aaron and a whole range of figures, Althea Gibson and so on and so forth, who made it possible for him to do that. I am de-manding that they at least be conscious of that lineage and conscious of the con-nection between the two.

Suarez: Len Elmore.

Elmore: Well, I was going to say exactly what Michael said with regard to the Joe Louis situation. You take Joe Louis and then compare him to Jack Johnson, and Jack Johnson struck everyone that he came in contact with in the ring and did his job. But because it's out of the ring, he wasn't able to [represent like Joe Louis did]; we all, myself included, we all owe a debt of gratitude. That's the legacy that African American athletes have to deal with as opposed to white athletes, and anyone who will say, "Well, I don't owe anyone anything," is really deluding themselves, because the reason why they're here is based on the suffering of oth-ers and going forward as leaders. And that's what they are. They're economically and financially very well off. They have the work ethic. They have the persever-ance, innate intelligence, and the opportunity to do some wonderful things. And if you essentially abdicate that responsibility, you're essentially letting that legacy down. And I've maintained that, even as an agent with athletes that I've had. That's the responsibility of black athletes, and there's absolutely no reason for any of them to forget that.

Suarez: Oakland, California's next. Sandra, welcome to the program.

Caller: Thank you. I listen often. I love your show.

Suarez: Thank you.

Caller: I've heard Mr. Dyson from the pulpit, and Mr. Elmore, I work with one of your former clients. I'm wondering at what point is enough enough for Latrell Sprewell? Has he not been vilified enough by both his hometown press in Wisconsin, the Oakland press, and the national press? And I also wonder has anyone ever taken a third-party opinion? And what I mean by that is those players who played alongside with Sprewell pre- and post-Carlesimo. Has anyone ever asked them: "What were the signs leading up to the choking incident?" Because I hear there were many and [they were] often provoked by Carlesimo and his ill-treatment of Mr. Sprewell.

Elmore: Well, let me address that real quickly and say there probably were. P. J. has an acerbic way of dealing with players. I'm sure he's toned it down since then. But if you understand what were the signs leading up to that—and I don't think Latrell was the only one—why didn't the other players react in the same way? And that's the point that I'm making with regard to the conduct. When is enough enough? I've said it before. I didn't believe in the punishment, but now that the punishment has been meted out—I thought it was too lenient. But now that it's been meted out, it's time to move on. He's essentially served his time, done his punishment, and now we have to judge him. I'm not ready to put laurels on [his head] yet, but the guy has conducted himself thus far as a model citizen. And we all make mistakes, and it's time, really, to start judging him on his actions now. You don't have to forget, but you can certainly forgive.

Suarez: Sandra in Oakland, thanks a lot for your call. We have time for another one? From San Antonio, John, welcome to the program.

Caller: Hi. I'd just like to ask a question. I'm originally from Boston, transplanted to San Antonio, so I get a boatload of this "What a great citizen David Robinson is," and I think most of it comes out of the Christian athlete vein, but that's a whole 'nother subject for another day. What I wanted to ask: You've got Antoine Walker and Ron Mercer up in Boston. I don't know if you guys follow the game. They're kind of off the mat right now. But when I go on the Web and read about

Antoine Walker, I read about how they hate the Walker Wiggle, how they hate how he celebrates, how they hate how he trash-talks. You know, Larry Bird, one of the greatest trash-talkers ever, came from that town. Ron Mercer, on the other hand, actually is considered a better player by many fans because he is soft-spoken. And also I'm wondering if you think it has to do with the color of his skin, the fact that he's lighter skinned and soft-spoken?

Dyson: I think that the caller has tapped into a very powerful vein of racial sentiment that is barely produced above the surface. People don't want to confront this. I think Larry Bird, one of the greatest players of all time, had an enormous reputation for trash-talk, and I think the calumny that Antoine Walker has suffered as a result, I think, of his trash-talking, is partially racially coded, and in terms of the bodacious style that he brings to the game and his self-celebratory kind of jiggle after he makes points and so on. And Ron Mercer—I think you've brought in something else here: the black, darker athlete, brown skin, representing the behemoth brutality of black masculinity versus the lighter black man who is closer to the ideal representation of white culture. So I think you've tapped into something yet again that black communities have struggled with from the very beginning.

And finally, let's be honest. Bill Russell just recently had the second retirement of his jersey there precisely because when he first retired, he didn't think that the sentiment of the Boston community was genuinely in his corner. So only recently was he able to be celebrated by the very people for whom he worked for so long in his life to bring them nine championships in eleven seasons. So I think that there is a deep racial bias, again, in basketball, even in the way we perceive the behavior of these athletes and what's acceptable and not acceptable. That's why when you see the body typing, and the kind of tattoos and so on and so forth, and the wearing of the hair—that is again the articulation of a different aesthetic than [the one] Michael Jordan embodied.

But let's not forget this about Mr. Jordan. When Jordan first came into the game, he was viewed also in suspect terms. Zeek—Isaiah Thomas—and Magic Johnson kind of distanced him because he was the arrogant, upstanding rookie who was trying to get in their business and get in their game. And now Michael Jordan—we've forgotten all about that because, as Len said, now that he's won, we have a kind of Afro-amnesia. We forget what he's done in terms of the negative, and now we celebrate the positive. And we've got to put those two together.

Elmore: Ray, let me be real quick—

Suarez: Len, we have about a half a minute left. Go ahead.

Elmore: Well, if Antoine Walker and the Boston Celtics start to win in the year 2000, they'll name a tunnel after him.

Suarez: Oh, really? Well, everything's still dug up, so why not get one started right now? John in San Antonio–

Dyson: Well, for Ted Williams and Bill Russell both, huh, right?

Suarez: Right. John in San Antonio, thanks a lot for your call. Thanks to everyone who called and wrote this hour. Thanks especially to my guests. Michael Eric Dyson, good to talk to you.

Dyson: Good to talk to you, Ray.

Suarez: Len Elmore, a pleasure to have you here.

Elmore: It's always a pleasure for me, Ray.

17

IS DAVE CHAPPELLE CRAZY?
The Price of Fame and the Paranoid Style

with Keith Murphy

Actor-comedian Dave Chappelle had it all: a thriving career with arguably the hottest comedy show in the land on cable's Comedy Central Network, admiration by fellow comics and the nation at large as a comic genius, and a lucrative contract that would pay him millions to do what he loved best. Then suddenly, in 2005, Chappelle walked away from it all, with rumors quickly spreading that he had suffered a nervous breakdown and had fled to South Africa to check himself into a mental health clinic. As it turns out, Chappelle felt that he was being pushed into comedic directions that obscured the line between parody and reinforcing the racial stereotypes he had expertly lampooned. Of course, Chappelle isn't the only black man to "go crazy" and unravel, self-destruct, or choose a radically different path in public. That number includes boxer Mike Tyson, fellow comic genius Martin Lawrence, and music legend Michael Jackson. *Vibe* magazine's Keith Murphy interviewed me for an article about Chappelle and these other figures—and musical genius Prince. Murphy interviewed me simply to get a couple of quotes for his story, but his questions provoked me to explore some of the contradictions and paradoxes of famous black men and the tribulations they endure.

Keith Murphy: We've seen these public meltdowns by the likes of Mike Tyson and Martin Lawrence and, more recently, Dave Chappelle. How heavy do you think is the burden of celebrity that is placed on black men largely by white dominated society?

Michael Eric Dyson: Well, it's huge, obviously. The demand for black men to meet the historic requirements of all men—that is, to show up to work to support your family, to be able to provide a means of comfortable living for the people you love—is hard enough. If you add the problems black men face in an often hostile white world, the problems just multiply. Black men have been fairly pulverized in the public eye; we are either portrayed as heartless criminals, or shuffling and jiving good-for-nothings, or coons. There's some space in between, but in the public realm, things are awfully limited as to what roles black men can successfully adopt. Our complexity is always being compromised by ready-made images of black masculinity that we are either forced into accepting or seduced into cooperating with. We are allowed to sing and dance, or play sports—in other words, entertain white folk and ourselves. But if we step outside of that box and begin to challenge some of the stereotypes that black men struggle against, then we're certainly at greater risk of meltdowns. It's not that hard to lose a sense of reality and balance.

You mention Mike Tyson, Martin Lawrence, and Dave Chappelle. Mike Tyson's been unraveling over a painfully long period of time. I remember wincing when I saw him on that Barbara Walters special, where Robin Givens, his wife at the time, is sitting on the couch next to him, sending all kinds of signals that this guy is nuts. It's as if she were pleading, "Please free me from this brutal and violent animal." Now I'm not saying that she didn't have reason to fear Tyson; I'm saying she wasn't clean either, and that her gold-digging and otherwise exploitative reputation may not have been entirely unearned. Not that she deserved the physical punishment she may have received either, but she surely wasn't Little Miss Innocent being put upon by the "massive monster" she married. It was just so tragic to see them tangled in webs of deceit and entrapment on either side. And to see Tyson in such horrible shape was painful as well.

I also think about Mike's bizarre meltdown when he was facing, I believe it was, Lennox Lewis. His words are still haunting. "I'm the best ever. I'm the most brutal and most vicious and most ruthless champion there's ever been . . . My style is impetuous. My defense is impregnable, and I'm just ferocious. I want your heart. I want to eat his children." And then, like one of these rappers thanking God after winning an award for a song or video that demeans women, Tyson ended his tirade with "Praise be to Allah!" And then we recall Tyson twice biting the ear of heavyweight champion Evander Holyfield during a match. Mike Tyson was performing in public the ritual unmaking of black men that the white public seems to demand—or at least accept—as the price for either extraordinary achievement, or for challenging the dominant culture. Having said all of this, I must tell you that I've still got love for Tyson; he's one of the most brilliant fighters ever to live, and not just brilliant in the ring. He knows the history of the fight game like few other fighters have ever known it—including obscure fights and fighters, stats about how many punches they threw, what kind, and where on the body they placed them. His genius only makes his suffering—and he's openly admitted his struggles with bipolar disease—that much harder to witness.

Martin Lawrence melted down on a street corner while making the film *Nothing to Lose*—an ironically titled movie in light of his troubles—with Tim Robbins. He lost a sense of balance and a sane perspective about his own life. He seems to have temporarily lost sight of how to manage the demands of superstardom and domestic life. In Dave Chappelle's case—even though some critics and comedians played it as an instance of "He just couldn't handle the pressure"—he seems to have been struggling with questions of vocation, identity, and integrity that, quite frankly, make him look a lot better than how he has been portrayed in the media. At some level, I think it's hard not to say that Comedy Central was forcing him to make choices, aesthetically and artistically, that ran counter to his beliefs about how black people should be presented on the small screen. So, yeah, the joke was that he went to South Africa because he lost his mind, but what is far more significant is that he chose not to cave in to what some elements of the dominant white media culture wanted to see from a black man on television.

He drew the line when it came to them asking him to wear a dress—a gesture which appears to be the rite of passage for well-known black male comedians. They seem to have to defrock themselves, or should I say, re-frock themselves in women's clothing. Black male comedians are often asked to adorn themselves in the dress of another gender to challenge the patriarchal codes of masculine strength by feminizing the black man. Now that's different from the choice that some black male comedians make to cross-dress, and the sexual politics of heterosexism that they're bravely choosing to confront. In many ways, that's what's going on with Tyler Perry and his character Madea. That's a separate issue.

In the patriarchal codes of American society, *forcing* black men to dress as women is not simply a take on Robin Williams dressing in drag to play *Mrs. Doubtfire*. In the case of black men, it's a ritual reenactment of the feminization of black men in order to keep them in their place by, oddly enough, putting them out of their place. They're no longer men, but women. That's not a progressive affront to patriarchal politics; that's a not-so-sly reinforcing of patriarchy's power by de-masculinizing black men, by arbitrarily assigning them a gender value based on the social subordination of women to men, to bring comfort, or comic relief, to certain white men's psyches. The threat of the black stud has been contained by symbolically remaking the black man as a dickless caricature. It's an act of comedic castration.

And finally, man, the theme that runs through all these troubles famous black men are having is the notion of mental illness. One of the things that black people have been afraid of is admitting that some of this stuff can make you lose your mind. You know, we have songs, like the one by DMX with the famous refrain, "Y'all gon' make me lose my mind, up in here, up in here." But the reality is that there's a great deal of mental stress for black men who want to fulfill the demands of a dominant culture that tells us to walk and then cuts our legs off. Black men are often left in tiny spaces to negotiate our psychic pain. That's why our suffering often opens up as wounds in the public for the world to see. We don't get much private therapy and relief from the agony. We don't often turn to another brother to seek counsel and wisdom and direction. There are few spaces for everyday black men to do that. There appear to be even fewer spaces for well-known black men to heal from punishing situations.

Murphy: Now, Doc, there was one statement that Chappelle made that was just so glaring and so on point. He said, "What is a black man without his paranoia intact?" That was one of the statements he made to Oprah, when she asked "Why did you feel fearful of what was going on with Comedy Central? Did you think they were trying to hurt you?" And Chappelle responded, "Well, that's just life, because I'm a black man. You know, you're always going to think that." What do you think about that statement?

Dyson: Well, the tragedy of that statement is that in many ways, it's absolutely true. A black man without skepticism and suspicion may be in for heartbreak. A black man has always got to have his nose open for the possibility of the putrid. He's always got to have his eyes alert to the possibility that he might be being tricked. He's always got to have his ears open, or at least to the ground, to hear the rumblings of discontent in ways that are hardly ever truthfully told to him. Now, you can write that off as paranoia, but black men who aren't duly informed or righteously skeptical about the claims of dominant society have often been taken advantage of. The trigger was often pulled on us when our heads were turned or our eyes were averted. So I think that, in one sense, it's tragically true that to be a black man is to be in a constant state of forcible paranoia. Or, at least, in a low-grade intensity of paranoia, which could be healthy skepticism—although sometimes it can turn into paralyzing suspicion. But in any case, a black man without a willingness to subject things to the smell test will often be tricked and mistreated in America.

Now, that doesn't mean that black men ought to cave in to a collective delusion about white intentions or powers. And we've got to be careful not to internalize the myth of the white boogeyman. But let's be real: conspiracy theories, and some forms of paranoia among African American folk, are ways that we use our instincts and intuition to render moral judgment upon unfair circumstances and unjust conditions. So paranoia and conspiracy theory are grassroots judgments on powers that range far beyond our capacity to control. You'd think that a famous and wealthy guy might have a better chance, but he's a bigger target and he's got bigger forces to contend with.

Murphy: The same was true with Mike Tyson. It seemed like he really started to crumble when his championship defined him as a man. He was no longer a man because he was a human being; he was a man because he was a champion. And once the championship got taken away from him, and he was heavily scrutinized, it was like he freaked out.

Dyson: Well, there's no question about that. Mike Tyson was a champion the moment he emerged as a black man able to wield his fists against opponents in the boxing ring rather than killing somebody on the street. That was a victory right there. Remember, Tyson lived under harsh and brutal circumstances—he was abandoned, and he was precociously criminal as a child—before being adopted by legendary boxing guru Cus D'Amato. The fact that he could transform his rage and anger into huge wealth and fame was simply remarkable. But the problem is that the very thing that freed him from financial worry also vexed him: Tyson was suffocated by his celebrity. He could barely breathe in the depressingly small cultural and psychic spaces in which even famous black men are often forced to thrive.

And once Tyson challenged the box the culture had him in, and once he began to resent his fame and to do destructive things that kept him from making money—especially for the white corporate structure and, in Tyson's case, for Don King, a poster child for both black self-determination and hideous forms of black capitalist exploitation—then he was of little financial or cultural value. And once he lost the heavyweight championship and he was no longer feared as the baddest man on earth, he was at a loss to define his masculinity. Mike Tyson exorcised his demons in public—since the absurdly famous have precious little privacy to reflect or retreat—and a lot of folk shied away from him. Many folk feared him, thinking that if they tried to help him, he'd only end up hurting them. So it was tragic all around.

Murphy: And, Doc, it was so funny, with Chappelle, people were more worried and more shocked that he turned down the money for his well being.

Dyson: Well, the bottom line is that he looked like he was crazy because he made a sane decision: "I will not allow money to define my maturity or my mental health. I will walk away from $50 million before I will sacrifice my integrity." And people thought he was crazy because he turned the money down. They didn't think he was sane because he made a choice that he would not be a servant of the very thing that alienated him from his craft. You don't have to be a Marxist economist to understand that if you're alienated from the work that you love and produce, then you're alienated from yourself. Chappelle simply wanted to reconnect to his art and the spiritual inspiration that motivated him to create in the first place. If a brother steps up and says, "Look, I ain't gonna be a slave to a contract, but I want to be my own man, my own comedian, my own artist, and I want to stand up and represent as best I can," he shouldn't be thought of as crazy. But that just shows you how difficult it is for black men to be accepted for making morally mature, mentally sound choices in our culture.

Murphy: My next question is about Michael Jackson, who's had what I term an arrested development meltdown that's been going on for several decades. It's not something that just happened—boom! I mean, we've seen it from the '80s on. What can we learn from that?

Dyson: Well, Michael Jackson's a complex case. Because on the one hand, Michael Jackson represents all that young black men have yearned for: to turn their enormous talent into capital and celebrity that frees them to pursue their lives with all their might. He is one of the great prodigies of world musical history. You'd have to turn to a cat like Mozart for a parallel figure who, at six or seven years old, is already at such an advanced level of mastery of his craft. When you look at those films of Michael Jackson when he's seven or eight, it's clear that he's a genius of both sound and movement. He's already emulating James Brown's most technically sophisticated moves, with some Jackie Wilson thrown in for good measure. And vocally, he's already tapped into William Hart, the lead singer of the Delfonics. That's quite impressive for a youngster to understand Hart's genius as the lead singer in a group. He had to seek him out musically, so to speak, since that's not an obvious vocal choice. Jackson's prodigious talent was extremely marketable because he was a chocolate, cherubic-faced boy with an Afro halo; thus, both artistically and aesthetically, he represented the aspirations for authentic black style of a generation that came on the heels of the civil rights/black power movement era. He put an entire generation of urban black people on his vocal chords for a while at such a young age and carried them, symbolically, before hip-hop emerged as the vox populi.

Michael Jackson's music expressed an urban yearning for the American dream. He embodied the hope that one's talent could carry you far beyond the outlines of even desperate situations like those in the city of his birth, Gary, Indiana, a city that exemplified the postindustrial urban collapse that black folk in the ghetto confronted daily. Gary symbolized the restructuring of the economy, the deindustrialization of urban labor forces, and the misery of grappling with the shift from manufacturing to service industries—and the quest for black political power with the historic election of Mayor Richard Hatcher. Jackson and his family symbolized the struggle of black folk in the transitional economy: patriarch Joe Jackson working in the factory; Joe spying the talent of his children as a marketable commodity and honing their talents to fulfill a service niche in the entertainment economy; and Michael's piercing voice summoning the bright entrepreneurial and spiritual hope of the young, gifted, and black. Even the name of their first record label, *Steeltown Records*, captures the economic and existential forces [that] they had to contend with and, by extension, that all of us who grew up in the urban jungles of America had to face. That's easy to forget now that Michael is seen primarily as a freak show.

And then as a solo artist, he has obviously done miraculous things: sold all those records, created all those dance moves, and changed the way pop music is sung, produced, and consumed, especially with his pioneering role in music video. Michael Jackson, at his best, with all the changes he's been through—some remarkable, some ugly and tragic—is an example of the willful transformation of the self as an artifact of one's own imagination. I mean, that's a deep thing: Michael Jackson made it apparent that the black self, collectively speaking, is a work of art, an experiment of self-remaking. Michael experimented with his face, and it changed dramatically from an identifiably black visage to a curious racial caricature of Caucasian shade and sculpture. Michael's face was monstrously deconstructed of its African identity; his face became a geography of distorted possibilities, a fleshly region of racial ideals invaded by spooky European features that rendered him ethnically opaque. It might sound clichéd to say so, but Michael Jackson embodied all of the malicious demons of identity that black people struggle with. The question we constantly face is how do we fight the demands of a white society that tells us that black identity, black skin, black features, are dark and unromantic and wrong and out of favor, and should be demonized and cast aside?

Michael Jackson's scary alteration of shape and color is emblematic of the colossal struggle in millions of other black minds and bodies for black self-love, self-determination, and self-definition. His actions force us to ask what our identities are about, and if we can withstand the constant onslaught of a white supremacist culture that punishes us for our blackness. Michael Jackson seems to have cut a Faustian deal with the pigment devil. And even if he does have vitiligo, a chronic disease that causes a loss of pigment, as some have claimed, the way he's managed it by bleaching himself to whiteness is a dead giveaway as to his racial trauma. And he becomes a laughingstock to many people, obscuring his earlier genius.

Now, with allegations and suspicions that he's a child molester, Michael is trapped by his seeming inability to grow up—or to at least grow out of his pose of perennial childhood, and get free of being a stymied adolescent, a menacing Peter Pan. But let's not forget that Peter Pan turns out to be a white myth, not a black one. The inability to grow up will never be ceded to Michael Jackson to explain his apparently troublesome behavior. Even though the culture wants to infantilize black men, it never allows them to be young or innocent. See, Michael's going against the notion that black men can even have a childhood worthy of empathy. For the most part, black males begin to get criminalized in childhood. They are rarely allowed the innocence that all children should be granted. And then, at the other end of the spectrum, Michael's a grownup who demands his childhood, but out of order. And because his insistence upon his childhood becomes the mark of his manhood, it eviscerates that manhood. It empties it out of all of its nuance and complexity. And that obscures his genius as an adult and forces folk into nostalgia about a Michael Jackson childhood that only *we* enjoyed; in many ways, it was hell for him.

Murphy: So, Doc, critics say that this is about the black man not being able to live up to the pressure. What do you say to that?

Dyson: Well, we've got to ask ourselves: Is it the normal pressure that everybody else faces? You know, black men are facing multiple pressures simultaneously.

They're trying to live up to the demands of American manhood. Black men are already being viewed skeptically through the prism of dominant culture as to whether or not they're able to step up to the plate and strike the ball out of the park, so to speak. Can they just show up? Can they have a job? Can they take care of their families? Can they *not* beat their women? Can they *not* bruise their children? Can they *not* abuse their loved ones? So the deficit, the negativity against black men—the stereotypes and mythologies that ring their necks like an albatross—is a huge weight they've got to shake from the start.

The famous black man, even more, becomes peculiarly representative, because his struggles become the struggles of the race. A famous black man has to deal with his individual space, the psychic challenges and distortions that must be overcome in his mind, and then he's got to work these out against a dominant culture that often denies him—and surely his brethren—legitimate standing as an authentic embodiment of pure and virtuous manhood, right? White guys get a crack at that. But brothers rarely do. Brothers have to transform themselves. They have to bleach themselves literally, like Michael Jackson, but more likely symbolically, like O. J., in a pool of whiteness, to prove they can be part of the dominant culture. Michael Jackson says, "it doesn't make a difference if you're black or white," as he gets whiter and whiter and whiter. And if Michael's face was bleached, then O. J.'s image was bleached, and he achieved another milestone of sorts for those obsessed with white acceptance when he married a blue-eyed, bleached-blonde white woman, which is the ideal embodiment of beauty in America. So black men face enormous odds to begin with, and famous black men have even more obstacles, along with, of course, undeniable advantages and opportunities. But like the late great Notorious B.I.G. rapped, "more money more problems."

And heterosexual famous black men have to overcome other obstacles—like the culturally supported doubt as to whether their own women are beautiful and wonderful enough to be chosen to share their lives and build a family with. Then there's the corrosive myth among black men of all sexual orientations and levels of fame that other black men are not worthy warriors with them in a fight together against societal oppression and cultural obstacles. They end up paired off against each other like they were in a gladiatorial spectacle, where black men must defeat other black men in order to remain *The* Black Man. It's the pathology of exclusivity that stalks black men and drives a competitive ethos that has turned tragic and bitter, because we fail to acknowledge each other. That's why black men, especially in the hip-hop generation, can't fundamentally acknowledge each other beyond their "boys," their circle of intimates.

It's interesting indeed how so much of black masculine mutual recognition is sexualized, even homoeroticized. "Naw, I don't wanna ride his dick. I don't wanna get on his nuts. You know, I want to go up and tell that brother how much I love him but I can't do that, so I'm gonna say, 'Yo, what up'"? And not only is the failure to positively recognize other brothers sexualized, but it's gendered, too, in the worst possible ways. That's why you hear famous male rappers declare, "I don't want any male groupies." To harken back to early Ice Cube, "Get off my dick and tell your bitch to come here." All in all, for a lot of famous black men in the public sphere, we see the ritual reenactment of individual black male upward mobility against another brother.

Then there's the familiar problem—but no less painful because it's common—of what James Baldwin called "the burden of representation." That's an even more keen duty for the well-known black man, the unspoken pressure to be, or to become, representative of the race's best contributions to humanity. That's a hell of a lot of pressure! And let's be honest: it's enormously unfair, but still, it's real, in a nearly material sense. So now you can't simply be an artist or a person seeking to live out the true meaning of your own talent and finding the level that your gift will rise to. Now you're accountable to the race—which can be quite confining, even stifling, and sometimes downright fascist in how it works out, given the polarities, prejudices, and purities that beset the collective black folk mind on any given day.

But, on the other hand, you've got to deal with a white culture that is suspicious, sometimes even afraid, of black masculinity. They don't want you to be *too* black, and God knows that's a dicey act of definition and negotiation. So you've got to strike the right balance between being perceived as threatening by the mainstream and then not strong enough, not black enough, for your own people. You're between a rock and a hard place, and that's enormous pressure. I think that the troubles of Mike Tyson, Michael Jackson, Martin Lawrence, and Dave Chappelle all prove the enormous price to be paid by famous black men.

And then let's not discount the black community's taboo on seeking therapy and strengthening our mental health. "All you need is Jesus," they'll say, or "Just pray to Allah." I like to Dysonize the story of Jesus coming down from the Mountain of Transfiguration, where he was met by some of his disciples who were stumped by their failure to deliver a poor soul from his spiritual affliction. "Lord, why couldn't we cast out this demon?" they asked Jesus. And Jesus said, "Oh, this kind comes out only by prayer and fasting." And I like to add, "and Prozac." I tell folk, "Naw, you need to send that Negro to the psychiatrist. Jesus gave you enough sense to understand that—and blessed the therapist with some healing advice." For too many of our folk—and let's not lie, in the broader culture as well—therapy means that you're weak or that you're not sufficiently spiritual. The hurtful myth that religion alone will sustain you has kept many a brother from tapping into alternate forms of help and alternate narratives—like self-examination in therapy—that might be able to keep him sane in a culture and country not designed to do that.

Murphy: Well, the irony is a person like Prince seems to have survived it all, and come back to his sanity.

Dyson: Isn't that interesting? Michael Jackson and Prince were our leading musical geniuses in the '80s—both could sing and dance and perform to the hilt. But Prince has always been distinctive because he wrote all of his own music. Back in the '80s, Prince was on the postmodern tip of deconstructing sexuality and embodying an omnivorous sexual appetite that often made him androgynous and omnisexual. He certainly transgressed against cultural norms, and settled sexual mores and social boundaries; to his detractors and some of his devotees alike, he looked as if he could, and would, have sex with who- or whatever. Of course, Michael Jackson was seen as increasingly bizarre with his Howard Hughes bent for germ-free environments and his honorary tragic mulatto status because of his white-/light-skin problems. But it looked as if Prince might edge Michael in the unacceptable weirdness quotient. [There are acceptable forms of weirdness—like the idiosyncrasies and superstitions of ball players who sleep in the same drawers before each home game.]

What's not often talked about is how Prince has gained a new lease on adulthood by taking up the religion of Michael Jackson's childhood and youth. Prince is now a Jehovah's Witness—legendary musician Larry Graham helped to convert him. Michael Jackson was reared a Jehovah's Witness, but after troubles with the occult overtones of his music video "Thriller," Michael eventually left the faith behind. In one reading of things, Michael Jackson had a religious crisis, and chose commerce over the narrow demands of his religious communion, and ultimately parted with the deity that defined and designed his dream and early life, at least through the religion of his mother.

Prince has integrated himself within that religious narrative, within the mythos of a religious community where God now reigns, not as sexual orgasm, but as spiritual communion. So he taps back into the psychic dimensions of a religious myth that Michael Jackson spurned. And Prince's fortunes have gone up as Michael has suffered, though I'm not arguing a relation between Jackson's rejected religious affiliation and his troubles. And now Prince becomes one of the most elegant embodiments of the religious narrative and the spiritual communion that are the hallmarks of historic black community. Go figure.

PART VI

CATASTROPHES

18

THE EMPIRE KEEPS TRACK
9/11, Race, and Religion

with Jeremy Earp

September 11, 2001, is a day that, as Franklin Delano Roosevelt said about Pearl Harbor, will "live in infamy." The evil and terror directed on that day against America is indisputable. However, the Bush administration and other conservatives have shamelessly politicized the event and exploited our fear and insecurity as a nation to their ideological advantage. Graduate student Jeremy Earp traveled to Philadelphia in 2004 to interview me for a documentary produced by talented media scholar Sut Jhally about the conservatives' manipulations of 9/11 and the administration's ideological warfare against civil liberties and progressive politics. Earp's questions encouraged me to reflect at length on the ominous consequences of empire, the religious elements used to justify the politics of fear, the racial undertones to 9/11—and the neglected racial wisdom of black folk who have suffered terror for centuries.

Jeremy Earp: Can you talk about your own personal reaction to the 9/11 terror attacks, and your immediate reaction to how it was dealt with by the Bush administration?

Michael Eric Dyson: On 9/11 I was in Boston, on my way to New York. I was supposed to have been at the World Trade Center the day it was attacked, signing my new book about Tupac Shakur, which was then being released. So it was an eerie feeling. But because of a conflict in my schedule, I had to make it for the next day. Needless to say I had a sense of extraordinary fate and destiny—and empathy for the people who were there. People from every race and ethnicity, and people from all over America and the globe were there. There were people from the highest level of the so-called economic food chain and those who were on the ground. It was a devastating example of evil; it was a vicious act in the name of a profound and longstanding anger. But nothing can justify the level of malevolence and acrimony that were directed at those people. 9/11 reminded me again that even when we have just causes, as Martin Luther King, Jr., reminded us, we must prosecute them in a just fashion. And so for me, 9/11 was unequivocally a problematic example of what happens when people who are understandably outraged seek unrighteous means to prosecute their particular ends.

I think the Bush administration has been problematic in its exploitation of this event. There's no question that 9/11 was a ruinous occasion and one that, in many senses, changed America forever. The administration's response brought us into closer contact with people who deal with terror and violence at the hand of the American empire—at least through its secret agencies. I was on a book tour starting on 9/11 and I didn't get off the road. I was in Boston and then I came to Philadelphia. From there I went on to New York and then to Atlanta. I traveled mostly by train. It showed me that many black people have been dealing with slower forms of terror, domestic forms of terror. I consider racial trauma and violence in American society to be a form of terror. And not to be hyperbolic, but when you think about the fact that people have been subject to arbitrary forms of violence, similar to what occurred on 9/11, for no other reason than their skin color, you'll know that we have been dealing with issues of terror in this country for some time. Unfortunately it took 9/11 to make other Americans aware that there are other forms of violence that people are subjected to that are relatively invisible, and now we can understand and empathize with them.

Unfortunately, the Bush administration has exploited that to the nth degree. It has now made people feel unsafe and as a result of feeling unsafe—which terror of course always makes us feel—I think the Bush administration has exploited that sense of terror for its own political advantage while saying that it's ostensibly committed to not politicizing this issue. It has crassly politicized this issue and it has done so on a number of different levels. Take the Patriot Act, for example, which of course is intended to somehow shore up the boundaries of American democracy when in one sense it has repelled those very principles. What else are we fighting for in this war against terror except our security and the ability to tell the truth as we see it as American citizens, regardless of the political choices we make or the ideology that we align with? So if one of the main reasons for fighting the war on terror is defending the possibility that we, as Americans, can speak up, we can't at the same time be angry at those people who see a nefarious relationship between domestic policy and foreign policy. We should not be told that we are un-American if we express these views. We saw that in our nation's history before. Martin Luther King, Jr., faced that in Vietnam; progressives have faced that time and time again when they've spoken up. So for me, the Bush administration has exploited an unfortunate act of evil on American soil. And, in that sense, America on 9/11 joined the modern world. This is how people in Israel live; this is how people in Palestine who own land live; this is how people in Ireland live. This is how people in all parts of the globe live. Now we have been forced to join them.

Earp: When you say the Bush administration exploited 9/11, what exactly do you mean? Are you talking about exploitation of fear?

Dyson: Right. When we think of how the Bush administration has specifically exploited the fear and paranoia and sense of conspiracy that in the wake of an act of terror as colossal as what happened on 9/11 inevitably occurs, I think we can point to at least one thing and maybe more. First, all the heightened sense of security and the colors we assign somehow suspiciously coordinate with parts of the domestic agenda that the Bush administration wants to see either focused on or deemphasized. So when the debate is concentrated on the sluggish economy in the face of the Bush administration's inability to stimulate it, there have been curious and suspicious correlations of heightened forms of alert. More particularly, I think, the exploitation of fear has come out with the Patriot Act. That is to say, we are told, "Look, you'd better be very careful. If we don't clamp down on what happened here, you will be subject to a virulent form of terror, the likes of which you have never seen." So now, the fear that somehow a terrorist is lurking around every corner means that we ought to get past our own suspicions about the Patriot Act.

In a sense, that rallies the troops by saying that we can go into Muslim brothers' and sisters' homes and collect them, or we can detain people at Guantanamo without giving them due process of law. We can also put down certain acts of civil disobedience. And Mr. Ashcroft has been quite vocal about his belief that even to speak up as an American, and to be critical of the Bush administration, is to side with Osama Bin Laden. These kinds of rhetorical manipulations comport well with what happened in the earlier parts of the twentieth century when Joseph McCarthy was at his height. This kind of neo-McCarthyism that you see in American society is in direct relationship to what's going on with the Bush administration. Of course, we have new ways to scare up the public. We have new forms of surveillance that we can deploy against these "enemies" of America. Some of those forms of surveillance have, in the past, been used against some of our leaders, including Paul Robeson and Martin Luther King, Jr.

I think that it's very important for us to see the relationship between the two—McCarthyism and neo-McCarthyism—and to see that the kind of fear-mongering that has occurred in the aftermath of 9/11 has been harmful to American society because its advocates refuse to acknowledge that civil liberties are the lifeblood of American democracy. Now, we don't mean "civil liberties" in the straw-man way our opponents have used the issue to paint us as naïve political idealists. Our opponents portray us as being incapable of discerning the difference between necessary safeguards to assure as wide a protection as possible and the use of extraordinary circumstances to justify old-style injustice and social tyranny. Most of us would say, "Yeah, we don't mind going through extra checks at the airport to make certain that we are all safe." Regardless of our ideology, our commitments, and our beliefs, we're willing to do what's reasonable to be safe. We don't mind doing that, but we do mind chucking fundamental civil liberties. We don't want to say, "I am willing to give up the freedom of speech and the ability to criticize the Bush administration." That kind of demand I identify exclusively with the Bush administration. That is totally ridiculous, and I think that bullying has made people quite suspicious—and rightfully so—about the manipulation of American fear in the aftermath of 9/11. In its wake it really creates much bigger problems.

Earp: Within this context of cultural politics, one of the things we're interested in with this project is the gender gap, specifically the male side of the gap, which very rarely gets talked about or examined head-on. Do you have any explanation for why white working-class men have moved steadily toward Republican candidates when we know that on most issues the Republican Party is not exactly friendly to the interests of these guys? Is there something the GOP understands, something the Bush political operation understands, about race and masculinity that shores up this gap? Or do you think that issues are enough to explain the white working-class male flight to the GOP?

Dyson: There's no question that to me there's an ideological consistency between Bush the elder and Bush the younger in terms of prosecuting their war on all fronts, so that cultural conflict becomes the war on terror by other means. What I mean, more specifically, is that all of this brouhaha occasioned by civil marriages versus gay marriages, for example, just serves to ratchet up an atmosphere of paranoia which seems to say, "You had better watch out because the terrorist that lurks outside is also the kind of cultural terrorist that looms large domestically. Those who support a gay or lesbian living next door to them are the same people who were telling this country to be critical of the Bush administration. They want to reject your evangelical Christianity or your conservative Judaism. They're now assaulting you." So I think there's a concerted ideological effort to create an environment of paranoia around cultural values and to link that cultural fear to political fear. That kind of ideological illusion is brilliant, but I think it's ultimately perverted.

There was a focus in the early administration of the elder Bush on the Willie Hortonization of American political discourse, which sent a convenient signal to suburban America to "Watch out because these people who are Democrats and liberals and progressives are soft on crime and, as a result, they're going to unleash this terror of crime on you." In this day and age, it's about gays, lesbians, and transgender and bisexual people who are now part of the so called "progressive" agenda. The fear is, "They're going to be unleashed on you." I think that it is very critical for us to see the relationship between the politics and the culture because the same agenda of fear and conspiracy and paranoia is operating. I think such a state of affairs allows the Bush administration to divert attention from a lousy economy. It also makes it easier to dodge tough questions about domestic policies like those on education. The president says, "We don't want to leave any child behind," yet he refuses to give sufficient money to support the educational uplift of these same people. In many senses, then, domestic issues are obscured by attention to terror. The threat of terror creates a kind of political tabula rasa: "We're going to clean the slate," they seem to be saying, because the war on terror allows them to justify and legitimate a whole bunch of things that I think are pretty frightening for many citizens.

Earp: What do you see going on in Bush's camp that has led to such success with the white working-class male?

Dyson: I think there's a convergence of at least three issues. I think there's the issue of race and the kind of identification that reflexively takes place with other white guys in control—even if they're white guys who you don't think are doing the best job. But the alternative is implied in the following way: "Other folk will come in and take over and then we'd really be at a disadvantage." Number two is the gender issue. These are white guys, so even if you're not part of the male movement, where you're beating the drums on the floors on the weekend, you're at least beating the tom-toms of a kind of militarism that reinforces a sense of security. There's a very gendered way in which the Republicans have ingeniously created the sense that this is about "real men." They seem to be saying, "It's time for real men to step up to the plate. Enough of this namby-pamby stuff, because George W. Bush represents the reborn American male. He is one of us. He doesn't speak very eloquently; he was a C- student at Yale. I mean, the guy was drunk by his own admission until he was forty and got a job. He might not drive a pickup except on his farm when he goes home to the ranch, but that guy's one of us." So there's a real visceral identification with him, even if those who admire him most don't necessarily have the same circumstances as George W.

Thirdly, I think there's a class dimension here. I think the Republicans have ingeniously exploited working-class and working-poor, but especially middle-class, white men, who feel that they're under assault. In their minds, affirmative action has beaten back the interests that they have; women identify with it, black and Latino people identify with it, so in one sense white men feel under assault by affirmative action. This is an extension of the same kind of resentment that someone like Timothy McVeigh could tap into. I'm not suggesting that these people are fellow travelers with Timothy McVeigh, but there's no question that when even Howard Dean said that "we have got to win back the Democratic party for those guys out there who drive pickup trucks and fly the Confederate flag," that was Dean's attempt on the Democrat side to tap into the pool of resentment that the Republicans, by and large, have had their way with. So I think those three things together allow them to exploit their natural market.

Earp: You mentioned Bush's religiosity, his evangelicalism. Can you talk about that a bit more, especially whether or not you see it infusing his policies and his political approach to problems?

Dyson: There's no question that the evangelical Protestantism which Mr. Bush is party to has had a significant influence on his understanding of foreign and domestic policy. I think he has a sense of divine calling to make sure that all of the values that we have as Americans will be protected. In one sense, then, there's a collusion between ideology and theology here, and we're not entirely certain that the theological would outweigh the ideological and, if it did, whether there would be any advantage because the theological has been so deeply and profoundly informed by a sense of missionary zeal to join with the pursuit of empire. There's an old story that many people tell throughout the world that was recently told by Bishop Tutu of South Africa: "When the Americans came they brought the Bible and we had the land. They asked us to pray and when we opened our eyes, they had the land and we had the Bible." That kind of missionary impulse, one that deploys theology and, in this sense, feeds evangelicalism, depends upon conversion. "I have to get the message of Jesus to you. And in order to get the message of Jesus to you I have to first convert you. In order to convert you, however, I have to tell you the truth about what I see is going on in the world." There is a strict relationship between politics and religion; and in that sense, I think Mr. Bush has been profoundly and deeply influenced by this missionary impulse to go forth into the world and to preach the gospel of Americanism.

How this manifests itself culturally is pretty scary because there's a Manichean distortion going on, an "us versus them" mentality. Bush's evangelical theologizing—and his sense of history, too, conjuring World War II's Axis powers, including Nazi Germany—is especially clear in his conception that Iran, Iraq, and North Korea make up an "axis of evil" that "threatens the peace of the world." But what's interesting is that there are other dimensions of his religion that can be turned against him. Any good evangelical theologian or layperson could say, "Look, what about the notion of sin being in us and not just in them? How about the fact that all of us have fallen short of the glory of God? How about the fact that when we think about evil, it's not just something out there, but it's something in us that we're tempted by as well?" There's none of this self-reflection or self-criticism in Mr. Bush's rhetoric, and unfortunately he has been able to ingeniously exploit not only his evangelical religious beliefs but the conservative civil religion that millions find appealing.

Moreover, a lot of citizens seem willing to suspend their skepticism and deny the legitimate fears they may have, and allow Mr. Bush to cultivate in national life his religious views in very scary fashion. They believe, as Bush believes, that this battle is black and white: It's between forces of good (us) and evil (them); between those seeking to destroy our country and our way of life and those seeking to protect our country and uphold our way of life. I think he has been able to take advantage of the fear that people naturally have in the aftermath of 9/11 and use it to push a religious agenda, sometimes in subtle fashion and sometimes in a quite explicit way.

Earp: How would you respond to someone who makes the link, as a lot of people have, between that kind of evangelicalism and Americanism? People might say they're the same thing, that this is a God-fearing nation, it was built that way, and any critique of Bush's religiosity, along the lines of the critique you just gave, is actually a critique of America. Do you see some countercurrent, some other way of conceptualizing America without losing religion?

Dyson: The mistake that many people often make is that they blur the history of American religion and American empire. For instance, if you take a close look at Thomas Jefferson and Benjamin Franklin, these are not Christians in the sense that we would understand Mr. Bush to be. Bush believes in divine revelation; they believed in practical moral guidance. This is not a Christian nation in the sense that people think. The founding fathers were not promoting Christianity to evangelize the culture. Benjamin Franklin said, and I'm paraphrasing, "Hey, whatever religion there is, if it is good for the nation because it brings us together and creates a kind of political consensus for us to be able to do our business, great." He was not promoting a particular version of Christianity. And by the time Thomas Jefferson cut and pasted what he believed should be extracted, and what should remain, from the scriptures—Jefferson slashed the miracles and mystery of the Bible and reduced it to reasonable propositions—most evangelical Christians would have been appalled. They wouldn't even recognize their Bible afterwards. So we've been hoodwinked by some of the right-wing members of the evangelical branch of the church to believe that this is a Christian nation, when it simply is not.

Furthermore, the founding fathers for the most part believed in a mechanistic deism. They didn't believe God was involved in human history; they believed God wound the world up and now it's operating on its own energy. God kicked it off, but God doesn't get in on our side. None of that, "We want to thank Jesus for helping Notre Dame to win; we want to thank God for being on our side of the war versus those evil people." Many of the founding fathers did not even believe in the kind of personal God involved in human history, at least not the way believers claim today. So, just as a matter of historical emphasis, many conservative Christians have snookered the rest of us. For those believers who do subscribe to the belief that God operates in human history, there are many other thinkers who provide countervailing theological and political arguments, people like Martin Luther King, Jr. King offered us a language of civil disobedience and civil rights that were available to all people, whether you were Jewish or Christian or Muslim. He didn't want to recreate a Christian nation. He used his Christian beliefs to create a *just* nation. For Martin Luther King, Jr., and others of his ilk, justice is what love sounds like when it speaks in public.

Unfortunately, there are other evangelicals who want to remake the nation in their Christian image, and as a result of that, they're trying to police the world for images that are empathetic to God. That's why Americanism has been collapsed into evangelicalism in many ways. It didn't just start now; it's been going on for a long time. When we think about manifest destiny, even slave owners were going out into Africa to save these "heathens" from their own non-Christianity and bring them over here—to become slaves! So there's always been this collapse between American ideology and American empire. The expansion of American dominance in the world has always had a religious justification. In the present, the evangelicalism promoted by Mr. Bush and other conservatives fits the bill to a tee. It is a narrow slice of evangelicalism that has to be acknowledged; it's only one slice, though, because there are many more progressive evangelicals who challenge the powers-that-be, and who warn against identifying the Kingdom of God with the social or political order or the state, including America. This notion that America is God's chosen nation is not only politically harmful, but it's theologically heretical. Such a claim involves the sin of ideological exhaustion, as if one form of state completely captures the will of God. Unfortunately, the more cautious and critical voices just don't get heard as much as the shrill right-wing voices in our society.

Earp: You've used the term "American empire" several times. It's a contested term. There are a lot of people out there who say there's no American empire, that this is a simplistic and gross misreading of the nature and history of empire. Can you explain why you say the United States is an empire, and explain what that actually means? Also, would you argue that we face a special danger with this empire, as it's now being advanced via the so-called Bush/Wolfowitz doctrine, or that this is nothing new, just more of the same?

Dyson: When I say that this is an American empire, what I simply mean is that forces of domination fuel the nation with a sense of "justifiable" outrage against the enemies of America. American empire suggests that we are the bully and the cop throughout the world. We often impose a moral viewpoint on other nations in the name of a self-righteous perspective. What I mean by a self-righteous perspective is that we feel that given our protection of the principles of democracy, we are justified in making sure that anti-democratic principles throughout the world are opposed, and when we see manifestations of them, it is our responsibility to wipe them out. So for me, empire is both the ability to impose your will on the rest of the world and the desire to do so in the name of a "justifiable" self-righteousness.

The brilliant deception of an empire is in part that its advocates and beneficiaries can deny the fact that, in this case, America is imperialistic. One of the rudimentary conceptions of empire is the ability to have plausible deniability: "We are *not* an empire. We're a nation that's interested in loving our neighbors. We're join-

ing with other figures and other nations throughout the world." Plausible deniability of empire is similar to the interesting dialogue about whiteness that's going
on now in the nation: that when you're in a dominant culture and you're white,
you're often not made to reflect on that whiteness. It is not until something challenges that—until blackness, brownness, redness, or another ethnicity begins to
show what whiteness means—that you even acknowledge that A) you're white; B)
you have privileges associated with that whiteness; and C) that you have to do
something actively to interrupt such a situation; otherwise you're extending the
dominance of whiteness. Now, substitute "empire" for "whiteness" and you see
how empire works. First, you are already part of an empire when you have the
ability to deny it, and second, plausible deniability is linked to extraordinary
forms of privilege that are rarely questioned. Third, since 1945 when we emerged
as the primary superpower, America has felt justified in speaking for, and against,
less powerful nations, as our interests motivated us. For me, empire is about the
colossal concentration of power and the ability to impose one's political will according to a moral vision.

Now is that different than what happened before? Well, the circumstances have
made it different. This is neo-imperialism, so I suppose, technically, this is a neo-
empire. The circumstances of globalization have thrust discourses about empire in
a different mode now because we're living in a world that is much more intimately connected as a result of the Internet, shifts in global capitalism, and the
collapse of local economies. You now have multinational corporations and con-
glomerates, such as German companies, owning American book publishing, so
there's a kind of ideological promiscuity occurring. In that sense, globalization has
brought nuance to the notion of empire. But such developments haven't stopped
America from being an empire, especially because of our military. The bottom
line is that if we see something that we don't like, we're willing to go to war to
eliminate it. True enough, this new doctrine of preemption is not exactly the
American isolationism that critics worried about earlier in the twentieth century.
But we're willing to go it alone and willing to say that if we think something is a
problem, then we're going to strike first by anticipating an attack *before the case*—
which is an act of stunning hubris, because it leaves no room for error on either
side. After all, we could be wrong about some nation's potential assault on us, or
they could change their minds. This is a high-stakes, no-margin-for-error-game,
and it's utterly deadly. This marks a profound shift in American foreign policy in
intellectual, ideological, and ethical terms. And to be frank, it makes us no better
than the people who we claim to be evil, who are, by our preemptive and imperial logic, simply responding to what they perceive to be *our* threats to their national security.

Earp: You've just placed the concept of empire within the racial context, and I'd
like to do the same now with Bush's domestic political rhetoric and imagery. If
you go to Bush's Web site, you'll find a number of photo galleries dedicated to

specific themes of his presidency and candidacy: foreign policy, national security, etcetera. One of these galleries is called "compassion," and in virtually every one of the pictures featured Bush is shown posing with people of color, mainly African Americans. In none of the other photo albums do you see so many black faces, if any at all. What do you make of this conflation of compassion with race?

Dyson: Mr. Bush and his aides would most likely defend themselves by saying, "we're reaching out," especially since Republicans have rightly been accused of being insensitive to Latino and African American interests. That's the positive, charitable interpretation. The negative, suspicious interpretation, which is mine, is that there's condescension there. And not only is there a manipulation of race, but there's a ghettoization and segregation of black people. It's almost as if you can hear white conservatives say: "Black people are good when we want to talk about compassion and when we reach out to them in order for them to be better as long as we control the Republican Party and the means by which that compassion can be distributed." The problem with that, of course, is that it doesn't leave any wiggle room for those black people to, one, dissent against the kind of compassion that is distributed to them, and two, to express their legitimate interest in foreign policy and national security and the like.

When Martin Luther King, Jr., moved from speaking about civil rights and began to talk about domestic policies in relationship to poverty, or especially when he began to speak out against the war in Vietnam, there were people who felt he was overstepping his boundaries and ranging beyond what is normally associated with "the Negro." Once Dr. King became irreverent when he spoke out on foreign policy, he was no longer Dr. King—he was an irascible preacher who didn't have any expertise on such matters. In 1964 he won the Nobel Peace Prize, so that may have given him some moral authority to speak out against what he understood the war to be. This politics of compassion among conservatives seems to reproduce elements of that scenario.

These compassion politics are similar to the 2000 Republican Convention, when you had this kind of Negro parade: "Let's get all of the black people we know and put them up on stage—they won't have any serious effect on domestic policy, except for Colin and Condoleezza." But when we think about the manipulation of the symbolic politics of race versus more substantive racial politics, we are reminded of the phrase Mr. Bush first used at the 2000 Republican Convention and has since endlessly repeated: "the self-bigotry of low expectations." I'm afraid that was an inadvertent autobiographical statement about the president's politics when it comes to race.

Earp: How has Bush been on race, substantively speaking, in your view? Do you see his [presidency] as markedly different from past presidencies in confronting issues of race in this country?

Dyson: I'm sure that, as a black person, if you were to live next door to Mr. Bush, he would be kind. He would help you take out the trash and shovel your snow. I have no question in my mind that as a human being he's a good-hearted guy. But that doesn't make a hill of beans of difference when it comes to social or public policy. For Mr. Bush to announce his strong opposition to affirmative action on Martin Luther King's birthday in 2003 suggests that he is willing to manipulate the politics of racial compassion for his advantage, but doesn't care a great deal for the core political interests of most African American people. On King's birthday, Bush's administration revealed its true colors in the brief it filed siding with the plaintiffs from the University of Michigan who wanted to turn back the clock on affirmative action. Bush's harsh personal stance in opposition to affirmative action is especially galling since in school he benefited from every form of special pleading that one might imagine.

His personal skills are enormous, but his social and public policies when it comes to race are atrocious. This is why, by the way, most African American people feel that we can be proud of Condoleezza Rice as a human being who has achieved a Ph.D., or Colin Powell as a general, but still be critical of their public stances on racial and political issues. There's little question that Rice's perspectives are far more troubling. But many people outside of black communities insist that black people should somehow give Rice a break. "Aren't you proud of her?" Well, we're not proud of people who extend repressive policies; we're not proud of people who are in the White House but who are incapable of preventing the president from speaking out on Martin Luther King's birthday against affirmative action. We're not proud of people who manipulate their race when it is convenient for them and who declare that they're about race-neutral forms of democratic government. I think that Mr. Bush has seized ingeniously on Colin Powell and Condoleezza Rice as the figureheads for his racial policy, but such racial seizures have not meant anything substantive for the advancement of African American people. I think in that sense he joins Bill Clinton's manipulation of the symbolic politics of associating intimately with blackness (though he lacks Clinton's racial flair that grows from familiarity with black life) to his father's failure to do anything serious about race. In that sense George W. has ingeniously benefited both from the politics of Clinton and the politics of his father, Bush the elder, and the combination has been especially destructive to black people.

Earp: Just today Bush gave a speech about proliferation, about the global spread of weapons of mass destruction. What would be your response to someone who said, "Hey, look Professor Dyson, it's all well and good to talk as you are, all very nice, but whether you want to recognize it or not, the world's a dangerous place. Fine, 9/11 allowed us to push through an aggressive foreign policy agenda, but we had that agenda for a reason. If you'd have listened to our line before, maybe 9/11 wouldn't have happened; maybe we'd be safer today." That's their argument. How would you respond to that?

Dyson: When we understand people's responses to their fears—you can imagine a lot of folk saying, "I don't like the Bush administration's politics but I understand their impulses; they just want to protect us"—I can understand why people might find such a response rational. The problem with that response, of course, is that this stuff has tremendous blowback. It would be one thing if you could quarantine the consequences of our foreign policy to foreign lands, although that would still be problematic for me. But even for those that want to cut Bush some slack and suggest that he and his administration are basically doing what is good for America don't realize the tremendous ideological boomerang. The more you begin to plant that stuff in foreign soil, the more it begins to show up here in domestic soil. And so the Patriot Act is just part of that blowback. And the fear and paranoia being whipped up by the Bush administration to justify what it did is also part of the blowback. The manipulation of facts is a part of the blowback, as is the arrogance of their approach. The Bush administration can't even admit they made a mistake.

The question we as Americans must keep asking is, "When does the lying stop?" If the U.S. government uses preemption, for instance, to invade your home, suggesting it is an appropriate measure, would that be fine? Or many of Bush's allies argue: "You cannot speak out against the Bush administration, and if you do, we'll harass you. Your tax returns will be audited. We will look at you differently and cause other citizens to do the same. If you go to the library to check out the *Nation* magazine, we're going to haunt you. If you side with those people that are to the left of our politics, you're going to pay a price for that." It just gets real invidious. This is why we must ask the question, out of national self-interest, "What is the ideological blowback from the notion that we must do whatever it takes by any means necessary to protect the boundaries of American democracy?" And I think when ordinary Americans hear that, they become naturally suspicious, and they begin to say, "Hey, if they make me look like the enemy, then they're not protecting me from the enemy; they become the enemy."

This is similar to when black people say, "We're not against police. We're against police being unable to make the distinction between us and the bad guy. And when the police show up at our home, they shoot us. When they see us in the street, they arrest us. When they arrest us, they brutalize us"—"us" being average, working citizens who ask the police to help us. But the failure to make a distinction between the good and the bad, so to speak, is the same thing operating here with the Bush administration. They can't make distinctions among citizens that are outraged by the excesses of the Bush administration which, in the name of securing democracy, polices the boundaries of speech and tells us what we can and cannot say. And they're calling everybody evil who speaks against them. We want to live where it's safe for us to protest and rebel in civil fashion. That's what we seek.

I think when that ideological blowback hits us and we begin to feel the heat and the pressure, and we witness the Bush administration's indiscriminant assault on our rights and ability to speak up, that is when it gets scary. And as an African American in this country, I'm awfully afraid right now. I'm afraid of an administration that sees me as a vocal opponent to its policies. I'm more afraid of a government that is now so paranoid that it will do virtually anything to shut people up than I am of the terror that looms in the broader world. And that's a shame.

On 9/11, I think America felt for the first time the ugly intensity of black vulnerability. Since black folk have valiantly combated racial terror for so long in this country, the question the nation must ask is whether it will behave like those African American heroes who pressed their righteous cause against a white supremacist government that hurt us. Did we try to blow it up? No. Did we try to subvert the process of justice? No. We created more justice by loving the hell out of our enemies. So we hope in the aftermath of 9/11 that the American government, which praised Martin Luther King, Jr., when he encouraged his followers to be nonviolent, can duplicate the wisdom and logic of Martin Luther King, Jr., and say that they want to make the world a safe place for democracy. And if that's the case, then we have to make it safe by protecting the world from *us!* And what America so often fails to do, especially in times of crisis, is to interrogate its practices and ask serious questions about its moral character. Instead, it sees people who raise those questions as anti-American. But that's a long, old, seedy tradition in American society, and it's one we've got to guard against.

19

WHO'S TO BLAME?

Victims, Survivors, and Agents in Hurricane Katrina

with Juan Williams; moderated by Lynn Neary

Hurricane Katrina, one of the most destructive disasters in the nation's history, exposed for many the brutal underbelly of poverty, economic inequality, and class oppression endured by millions throughout the nation. The suffering of the black poor in New Orleans was particularly highlighted in the storm's aftermath. Despite a strong speech from President Bush—after he finally made his way to the region—little of what he promised has come to life for the largely forgotten and invisible poor. On the one-year anniversary of Katrina, I traveled to New Orleans to participate in ceremonies marking the loss of life and the continuing quest for relief for the most vulnerable. I took a walking tour of the city's blighted Ninth Ward and attended a ceremony of memory and hope with NAACP head Bruce Gordon; I moderated a panel on housing for the New Orleans branch of the NAACP; and I broadcast my nationally syndicated daily talk radio show live in front of Harrah's Casino. Finally, for NPR's *Talk of the Nation*, hosted that day by Lynn Neary, I debated journalist Juan Williams, who sat in D.C., about the meaning and significance of Katrina. Williams gives passing recognition to the structural problems faced by the poor but plays up the role of the poor themselves in the poverty that crushes them. It is an argument that rests on conservative notions that exaggerate self-help and personal responsibility—ideas that most Americans agree with—far beyond their possible impact on the lives of the poor. In the end, Williams does little more than blame the poor for their condition. As I stated in our debate, lashing the poor for their "victim" mentality often makes them victims all over again.

Lynn Neary: This is *Talk of the Nation*. I'm Lynn Neary in Washington. In the weeks after Katrina hit land and the world watched as the poor and black of New Orleans were stranded in the flooded city, a new conventional wisdom began to form. Race and poverty, the pundits said, were no longer back-burner issues.

Katrina had reopened an old wound, and a new national conversation about race relations seemed ready to begin. But a year later, that conversation seems to have died down to a murmur. And the questions that Katrina raised about the intersection of race and poverty no longer seem as pressing. What lessons, if any, did we learn about race and poverty in the aftermath of Katrina? And to help answer those questions, we are joined now by NPR senior correspondent Juan Williams. He has a new book called *Enough: The Phony Leaders, Dead-End Movements, and Culture of Failure That Are Undermining Black America and What We Can Do About It.* And Juan is with me here in Studio 3A. Good to have you Juan.

Juan Williams: Nice to be here.

Neary: And joining us now also is Michael Eric Dyson. His latest book is *Come Hell or High Water: Hurricane Katrina and the Color of Disaster.* And he joins us from member station WWNO in New Orleans. Thanks for being with us.

Michael Eric Dyson: Thanks for having me.

Neary: You know, I'd like to start with both of you where we just left off in that conversation. And that is this issue of trust and perhaps lingering suspicions on the part of the black community first of all in New Orleans, but also nationally, as a result of watching what occurred in New Orleans and attitudes towards the government and feelings that the way the government handled the situation in New Orleans showed a kind of institutional racism that still exists. Juan, do you have any thoughts about that?

Williams: Well, clearly there was a very immediate, almost knee-jerk response I think coming from some in the black community. I remember the rapper Kanye West saying that George Bush doesn't care about poor black people, and this was the thought that you heard Jed Horne just, you know, express again—that if this had been some ritzy neighborhood, maybe people would have responded more clearly. That was the thought that went out. I think there was a degree of concern that so many poor black people were on television because the TV cameras were all located in New Orleans, so that's where the focus of the media attention was. And who was seen there in desperate conditions slogging through waters but poor black people?

Later it turned out that just wasn't true, that FEMA had failed not only poor black people, they had failed rich white people. They failed everybody. They proved to be inept, incompetent, to people in Mississippi as well as Louisiana.

Neary: Michael Eric Dyson, what are your thoughts about this? Is there a lingering mistrust?

Dyson: Oh, absolutely. I think there's a righteous skepticism about the effect of government and its intent for poor people. I think Juan is absolutely right that the storm was racially neutral in terms of its attack. But it was not racially neutral in terms of its consequence, and I think we have to draw a distinction there that is both logical and ethical. Furthermore, I think the lingering suspicion among African American people is wholly justified. One need not buy into wholesale theories of conspiracy, where the government blew up the levees or some other malicious force imposed its will through dynamite. The intent of a conspiracy theory is to communicate a moral vision. That moral vision is: black life just doesn't count as much as white life in this country. So I think that when Kanye West made the statement, what he was trying to suggest is that the government—he doesn't know George Bush individually. George Bush is the face of the government.

How is care measured in political terms? The distribution of critical resources to vulnerable communities in a timely fashion. And in that sense, the folk who are black and white [and] able to take care of themselves are going to do well after the storm. Even though it affected them in a vicious fashion, they were able to gird up their loins and gather their resources and move forward with the goodwill of their communities. African American people, and other poor peoples, by the way, are much more vulnerable and therefore less likely to be able to recover in the aftermath. That's the racial difference that we have to account for.

Neary: What would you say we learned in the aftermath of Katrina about race, if anything? Did we learn anything?

Dyson: Well yeah, I think it's absolutely clear that we have refused to engage in an edifying conversation about the convergence of race and class. We've got some language for race in this country. We have less language for class, less analytical acuity, less clarity, and less willingness to engage these issues [both] within these communities and between communities. And I think that it appeared early on, with the outpouring of charity, that Americans were willing to gird up their loins and put their resources squarely behind African American and other poor people.

What it turned out [to be] is that we got charity but no justice. Justice is about dealing with the structural realities that have to be contended with, and why poor people had been left behind long before the vicious winds and violent waters of Katrina descended. And the vicious consequences of racial difference have to be acknowledged.

And finally, I think that when you look at the stuff that Jed was speaking about earlier—the terrible rates of concentrated poverty—that means you live in a terrible neighborhood that has a lot of other poor people. You have poor schools. You have a terrible infrastructure. You don't have great levels of incentive to push beyond the immediacy of the horror, and as a result of that, prison becomes your destiny—and a date with a prison cell is nearly guaranteed by poor schools. So when you look at that all together, we just don't have the will to confront that.

George Bush gave a great speech in the aftermath of Katrina. Had he matched it with public policy, we would have been further along one year later than we are now, and I'm afraid we just don't have the will to do so.

Neary: What happened to that national will that seemed to be there, Juan, a year ago? I mean, if nothing else, there seemed at that moment—in this terrible moment of Katrina—that people were saying, "All right, we've been ignoring race now; we've been ignoring poverty. We're going to start talking about it again. We're going to start looking for solutions to this." And a year later that conversation doesn't seem to be going on really.

Williams: Lynn, I think you're right on target. You know, to my mind we had what Dr. King might have referred to as a moment of conscience, because I think we were called upon, you know, ten years after the Clinton effort at welfare reform, welfare to work, all that—here was an opportunity for us to say, "Well, really, what is the consequence of national policy with regard to poverty, and how does it impact when you consider that so many of the poor disproportionately are people of color, and specific[ally] African Americans?" And instead what we did was we got locked into a polarizing racial conversation, with black people, as I said, having the kind of reaction that suggests conspiracy theories, blown up levees and all the rest, and the Republican white man in the White House doesn't care about black people.

And then you saw a response from the right that said, "Oh look at all the looters. These people are looters and not worthy of our sympathy." And look at the allegations of rape and slaughter in terms of the New Orleans Superdome and Convention Center. So much of that turned out to be fables. I mean absolute madness—not true, and that's what caught us in the mud and didn't allow that moment of conscience to truly flower.

I think back to, you know, Michael Harrington, who was writing about "the other America" early in the '60s and then leading the Johnson administration towards a Great Society program. I think we had that kind of moment there, but we got lost. And even to this day people want to make the case somehow that, you know, it's about race. But, you know, if you looked at what people have done in terms of the studies subsequently, Lynn, what they find is, you know, 28 percent or so of New Orleans is made up of white people, but 33 percent of the people who died in New Orleans during Katrina were white—so [their death rate was] even larger than their proportion.

You think about the damage to property. You heard what Jed Horne said: There were areas in New Orleans East—black millionaires wiped out. But whites were damaged as well. It's not just the Ninth Ward, but it's also St. Bernard

Parish—overwhelmingly white. And yet the opportunity for the national conversation to come together in the way Jed Horne was talking about, people on a local level saying, "Hey, wait a minute, we've got a crisis here. We're all from New Orleans. We've got to build together." That conversation hasn't taken place on the national level because people I think have been trying to exploit it for political reasons or to make some larger point that's self-serving.

Neary: Where should the conversation be now? What should we be talking about now, a year later?

Williams: Well, you know, again, it's such a rich moment—the Katrina story. Because what you saw there were real solutions to poverty. You look at it: deeply entrenched poverty in New Orleans. You know, a poverty rate overall of about 23 percent, but 35 percent in the black community. If you talk about black children in New Orleans, over 50 percent living in poverty—deeply entrenched poverty, generations of poverty.

What happened during Katrina? We saw church groups go in to try to help people. We saw extended families say, "Hey, you can come live with us for a while." We saw neighboring states say, "We will help you with the displaced population." We saw big business say, "There are jobs elsewhere in the country." We saw educational institutions say, "Come here to continue your education."

If you talk about basic prescriptions for dealing with poverty, this doesn't only apply to Katrina. It could apply to the poor anywhere in America. Remember, a quarter of African Americans live in poverty, Lynn. You have a higher concentration in New Orleans—a 70 percent black city at the time. It was deeply entrenched, and yet no one was dealing with these issues of poverty. No one was saying, "You've got to graduate high school." No one was saying, "Don't have babies when you're teenagers and not ready to be a parent." No one was talking about getting into the job market as opposed to thinking, "I can slide by with this hustle and that hustle." That kind of conversation was not taking place in terms of really saying this is how we can end poverty in the United States in the twenty-first century.

Neary: Michael Eric Dyson, do you think that the discussions about race so far have been—the discussions that have taken place, and as we have been saying, perhaps they've tapered off now at this point—but were they too polarizing? I think, Juan, you seem to be indicating that you felt that maybe the discussion was polarizing. Do you think that they were polarizing?

Dyson: Well, unavoidably. But polarization is never a litmus test for the legitimacy of the argument. It was polarizing when Martin Luther King, Jr., took arm and flight against the vicious forces of white supremacy. It was extremely polarizing to communities. But ultimately the moral suasion that Dr. King brought to bear was able to convince America of a critical point in our trajectory of democracy that this was the right thing to do.

So polarization can never be the litmus test of whether it's authentic or legitimate or a good thing to pursue.

However, I think that—I'm afraid that the haphazard formulations that Mr. Williams has put forth, in regard to what some of those solutions might be, may be part of the problem that perpetuates a legacy of such divisive thinking. For instance, it's not either/or. It's not either that people assert personal responsibility as the predicate for removing the barriers, the impediments, and the obstacles that block them from the path to success. Nor is it about ignoring the fact [of] structural features—low wages, severely depressed economy, the service economy, which has been extraordinarily exacerbated by tremendous political tensions. All of that stuff together means that people don't have the opportunity to exercise responsibility.

Let me give you an example. I'm here in New Orleans, where I've been since last Friday, arguing, speaking, and participating in events. And I've taken tours of the Lower Ninth Ward. Home after home, I see young black people and working black people saying, "Look, we have trucks out here. We want to go out and remove cars. [What happened is that the government gave $100 million no-bid contracts to big corporations—be they Halliburton or Bechtel or Shaw or the like.] They bid out the jobs, they prevent us on the local level from exercising our autonomy, much less our responsibility." So those who want to exercise personal responsibility are prevented by structural features like no-bid contracts, [factors] that prevent them from maximizing their potential. So that, to me, is writ large against the canvas of our racial lesson here. And that is to say that we will never be able to solve the problems of poverty unless we engage in less demonizing and stigmatizing of the poor, and [begin] focusing on the structural features, as well as the personal habits, dispositions, and behaviors that may perpetuate self-destructive behavior.

Let me end by saying this. Mr. Williams spoke about Michael Harrington. Michael Harrington, who was a democratic socialist. Michael Harrington, whose famous book inspired the Johnson administration to indeed attack the poverty in this nation. There has been a shift, a very subtle but very powerful one, from a war on poverty to the war on the poor. And the war on the poor that's being prosecuted, I think, is itself so deeply and fundamentally flawed that unless we renege upon our commitment to it, we will only perpetuate the devastation for the poor. Unless we're willing to say, "Hey, it's both/and, not either/or," we're not going to have a very enlightened conversation about this.

And white brothers and sisters who feel resentful here in New Orleans about Mr. Nagin's comments about "chocolate city," that's understandable if they felt they were being precluded from participating. But what Ray Nagin was saying is that this city was 67.9 percent black before the storm. It looked awfully chocolate to me. And the reality is we have to talk about how we can resolve some of the tensions that Juan Williams is absolutely right [to address]. Long before this storm, we didn't deal with the pathologies inherent in governments that ignored people, both black and white, and I think that's the fundamental issue we have to confront.

Neary: All right. I just want to remind our listeners that you are listening to *Talk of the Nation* from NPR News. And we are going to take a call now. We're going to Wally calling from Allentown, Pennsylvania. Wally, go ahead.

Wally: Hi. Thanks for taking my call. I couldn't agree more with Mr. Williams's and Mr. Dyson's comments. You know, I think the issue is far beyond race, but it comes out in race. The issue is really poverty in that many people who live in poverty don't have an advocate. And so a wealthy person, black or white, in New Orleans might have savings or resources or the ability to hire a lawyer or things like that to help them find solutions to their problems. With people in poverty, they either don't have the educational background or the financial resources to even begin to find help or get help.

And beyond Katrina, even in the justice system, you know, if you're poor and you're wronged, you have little recourse. You know, justice is for people with resources.

And even in Allentown, where I live, there was a whole issue with predatory lending, and it was for poor Hispanics. And on its face it looks racist, but really it's just targeting people who don't have the resources to get a regular loan, and so they find themselves trapped in these situations. And I think across the country it's poor people who either lack, you know, education or resources, to even begin to address some of the injustices that they face every day.

Neary: So, Juan, Wally was sort of reinforcing this idea that we've been discussing, which is that race and poverty are just inextricably linked, it would seem. These two issues, you can't really discuss one without the other, and yet that we seem to have gotten away from even talking—we said we didn't get into the conversation—

Williams: Well, I think we get confused, Lynn. I mean it's just confusing. For example, when Michael Eric Dyson says that there are people with trucks who want to haul stuff out and, you know, they can't exercise personal—look, that has nothing to do with race. If you're white, you can't. That's the law as established by the government for all people. So that's a—you know, all of a sudden, you make it into a racial issue. It's not a racial issue. It's a matter of government regulation and the government taking steps that some people may now disagree with or in hindsight say was absolutely wrongheaded. But it's not about race. I mean if you—

Neary: What about what Wally said? He said something interesting, and I wanted you—which is—he said you can't have justice unless you have resources.

Williams: Well, absolutely. But that means that you've got to deal with poverty. You know, I think the big divide—you know, what Du Bois famously said about the color line being the struggle of the twentieth century—I think that the issue here in the twenty-first century is becoming very clear: it's the class line becoming more sharply demarcated in American society. And people who are on the wrong side of that line, disproportionately people of color and young people in American society, are being left behind at such an alarming rate, it's harder to get on that ladder of upward mobility and to then try to reverse that cycle, [that] downward cycle.

But to come to this point, Lynn, it's not about race always. Because, for example, in the aftermath of Katrina, questions were asked by Pew about racial attitudes, and here's what they found. "Are the poor overly dependent on government?" Two-thirds of black people said absolutely. Seventy percent of white people agreed. When the question was asked, "Do individuals have the power to succeed?" Sixty-five percent of black people, yes. Seventy percent of white people, yes. "Are blacks moving ahead? And the ones who aren't moving ahead, are they creating their own problems?" Fifty-six percent of black people said black people are moving ahead better than ever. When it came to, "Are the black people who are not moving ahead creating their own problems?" About 50 percent of blacks said, "Yes, that they're not helping themselves, not taking the opportunity to be self responsible, self-reliant."

Dyson: First of all, in regard to the Pew poll. You know, we have to ask a lot of questions about polling: What size is the sample? How many people? Was it representative? Is it scientific? And the lot. And the self-reporting is one thing. People self-report and say, "Yeah, I voted for the Democratic guy," and it comes out that the Republican guy wins. So self-reporting doesn't have to have scientific, and one-to-one, correlation to the actual, empirically verifiable, results. So we got to admit that.

Now, but beyond that, I think that the caller made an interesting point that Juan at least tipped his hat to but failed to wholly embrace. And that is the fact that, yeah, it doesn't always have to be about race, but it's about race a lot of the times. And the fusion and merging of these two characteristics, race and class, is what makes things intriguing. It's true that race is a central factor of many aspects of our lives, as well as class, but I think race makes class hurt more.

Even in the concentrated poverty of New Orleans, white brothers and sisters who are living in poverty don't live in the same kind of concentrated poverty that African American brothers and sisters live in. Which means, then, that there are some effects that are exacerbatory—that make it harsher for African American people who live under the ostensibly same conditions that white brothers and sisters [live under].

And then, finally, I think the caller said this, that, "Look, if you're poor, you can't get the same kind of justice because you don't have the resources." The point I made about the trucks, true enough, Juan is absolutely right. There could be some white guys who, because of the restrictions, don't have trucks. But all the guys owning the corporations that *do* get the bids happen to be white. And when you talk about that, there is a high degree of correlation between the contracts being distributed by the government [and] the largesse economically that is accruing to those who have businesses which are owned. And preexisting contracts are the basis for the distribution of the resource at first. That is to say, if you already have a relationship with the government and you get the contract, you have a higher likelihood of being able in a crisis to respond. Those are overwhelmingly 99 percent white Americans.

So I think it would be silly, and insidious, and just cutting off our nose to spite our face to suggest that race doesn't have a huge role in who gets the resources, how they get distributed. And finally, as the gentleman who called said, the advocates for the poor are barely as loud and abrasive as those who are willing to stigmatize them and those who defend the interests of the dominant society.

Neary: All right. Let's take another call now, from Darryl. And he's calling from Georgia. Hi, Darryl.

Darryl: Hey, how you doing?

Neary: Good, go ahead.

Darryl: Yeah. I would like to make a comment. I think that the only thing the Katrina storm did was televise the blatant discrimination and prejudice that everyone in America knows exists. And I don't think it'll disappear in my lifetime or my children's lifetime. I think it's all-Americana. And I'll take my response off the air. Thank you.

Neary: It's all-Americana?

Williams: Well, race is part of the American picture. I don't think there's any getting away from it. And racism, you know, as long as I've been alive, I think has been a daunting and sad feature of the American landscape. And it's not going away. My point is if we are truly looking for this moment—you know, Katrina even a year later—to be instructive, to allow us to be productive in dealing with poverty issues, Lynn, then we have got to say: "Where is the consensus for action?" How can we say to people across racial lines, "this is a shame," when we in

America look and see these people in desperate conditions not being helped by our government? That's wrong. How can we take action? And that's why I come back to the idea that if you look at the poll numbers, these polls done by Pew—Pew is a very legitimate, reputable organization—if you look at it, what you see is that black people—remember, 25 percent of black Americans live in poverty—when you ask black people basic questions about whether or not the poor are overly dependent, they're saying yes.

When you ask them basic questions about whether or not black people who are not moving ahead are creating their own problems, black people who live next door, whose, you know, family, friends, neighbors are sometimes poor black people, are saying yes. I think that would give people a sense: "Well, wait a second. We can get beyond the 'you're-the-blame liberal guilt, all that.'" Let's get to the real heart of the matter. What are the steps, what are the prescriptions that we can take in order to alleviate poverty in America today? And that's the conversation I'd like to have rather than the finger pointing.

Neary: Well both of you, the two of you, seem to be representing two sides of—not two sides, but two lines of thought that have crystallized in this debate. You, Juan, sort of talking about personal responsibility, the need for personal responsibility; and you, Michael Eric Dyson, talking about the fact that there's institutional racism, that this is part of our culture, and that the government response we saw in New Orleans perhaps reflected that. Isn't that sort of the debate that was going on before Katrina—

Williams: It's the same old stuck-in-the-mud debate, and there's just no evidence, for example, that FEMA's response, the government's response, was racism so much as ineptitude.

Neary: Mr. Dyson, is it the same old debate? Can you change the discussion now? Has Katrina changed the discussion or is there a way to change the discussion? Michael Eric Dyson, you there? I think we've lost Mr. Dyson, unless he may have had to go, and we didn't get a chance to say goodbye. Okay, we're seeing if he's still there. [*Technical difficulties*]

Juan, the same old debate? You're saying that it—but this question of personal responsibility which you are articulating, that's something that people have been talking about for a number of years now as well.

Williams: Oh, it's in the tradition of black leadership in the country, but it hasn't been in this generation. Instead I think there's been this focus, this tremendous focus, on victimization, to my mind, and I think it's a real lost opportunity. Because what it does is it breaks down—you think of, Lynn, the glory of the civil rights movement as a movement that was trying to establish equality and justice for all. It was to kind of move us beyond race. That's why you had people, you know, without regard to race or religion coming together to form what was the greatest social movement the country has every seen. At the moment, instead we have people in our community who want to focus on victimization, who want to make it about race instead of saying, "Wait a second, how is it that we as Americans can act on this problem?" That's what I'm trying to say. Where is the consensus, and in fact—

Dyson: Can I—

Neary: Mr. Dyson?

Dyson: Yes, ma'am.

Williams: —as the polls had indicated, the consensus exists, although some people don't want to mention it.

Neary: Mr. Dyson is back, and I know you have to leave shortly to make a plane, so let me—

Dyson: No, no, I'm going to stay until the end of the show. [*Laughter*] I didn't hear all of what Juan had to say, and I apologize for that, but I think I got the gist of it. You know, the reliance upon the language of victimization assumes that black people are *not* victims. So we stigmatize the notion of victimhood [for] those who are actual victims. If you've been subjected to cancer and you say, "Well, we're against people who call themselves cancer survivors or cancer victims," well there's a deleterious pathogen in your body that is eating you away cell by cell. So those who have been literally victimized by the forces of oppression are now re-victimized because they're denied access to the very language that could express the horror and the tragedy of what has occurred to them.

But beyond that, Juan's own polls contradict the very notion of victimhood's wide and pervasive spread among African American people. First of all, black people have always been bifocal. They look at the fact that we must be responsible for our lives and that the dependence upon government is something we should be discouraged from. Marcus Garvey was about that, Booker T. Washington was about that, Frederick Douglass was about that, Martin Luther King, Jr., was about that, and so every leader worth his or her salt—Ella Baker, Jo Ann Robinson, and the like—have discouraged us from being overly reliant upon the government.

But they have not shirked from demanding that the government be responsible for what they are to be responsible for, so that we are victims, survivors, and agents at the same time. The same group of people who have been victimized by historical legacies of white supremacy, social injustice, and economic inequality have to have a resonant language to articulate their blight and their predicament.

But at the same time, they have exercised extraordinary responsibility in arguing against the very premises that would deny them legitimacy, you know, in American society.

And finally what's interesting to me: It is not that people are going around as African American people crying "victimhood, and we can't do anything." I've been down here on the ground in the Lower Ninth, and people have been nearly heroic in insisting that despite the fact that their government will not show up, A) they need for it to show up, B) what we don't talk about is that these African-American people by and large have demanded of themselves a level of accountability and responsibility that the government has not nearly begun to match. If George Bush was as responsible as the average black person I have seen down here on the ground, this government would not be besieged by ineptitude, by extraordinary cronyism, by corrosive cynicism about the possibility of the government responding to the issues of African American people.

And let me say this finally. When it comes to the notion of victimization, the truth is that African American people have lived in a society where their legitimate rights and claims upon the state have rarely been acknowledged. So I think Juan would be naïve—and it would be naïve for the rest of us as African American people—to dismiss that. Martin Luther King, Jr., whom he has quoted, said the night before he died, "All we say to you, America, is be true to what you said on paper." Let's close the difference between your preaching and your practice. Let's march those words from parchment to pavement—and that demands accountability and responsibility of the government.

The poor are always the easiest marks. African American people are always the easiest marks for people to pour their venom upon. The real question is can the American government live up to its historic demand for responsibility and accountability so that as that woman said when she wrapped herself in the flag down in New Orleans—

Williams: Can we jump in here? [*Laughter*]

Dyson: —I am an American citizen, and as an American citizen—

Williams: I'll tell you what, man. I'll jump in since no one's interrupting this rant. But let me just say this. If you're talking—

Dyson: I wasn't nasty to you, Juan.

Williams: —responsibility here. What we're talking about is people saying, "Wait a minute. You can wait for the end of racism for all time. It won't save you in this generation. It won't help your kids in terms of getting them an education." What we're talking about is 25 percent of black Americans living in poverty, to come back to the topic of this show, especially in the aftermath of Katrina, in a city

where we're seeing a 35 percent level of poverty among black people, disproportionate. What you're talking about then is how can these people be helped? And
one of the things that we have learned I think from Katrina is they have the power
to help themselves, but when you understand–

Neary: But with the help of government, would you say, Juan?

Williams: It would be wonderful if government would come in. But I'm saying
to you, Lynn, at this point the government hasn't done the job. And not only that,
oftentimes you look at who's in charge of government in New Orleans–black
people. Ray Nagin is there, right?

Dyson: But why do you let them off the hook, Juan? Why don't you hold them
responsible? Why don't you hold them accountable?

Williams: Hold on a second. The point is that–

Neary: Juan, you're going to have to wrap this up because we're running out of
time.

Williams: Okay, so the point, the larger point is here we have the opportunity to
say to people, "Here are steps you can take to help yourself and to get out of this
poverty, 25 percent." And yet there are people who want to instead talk about,
"Oh that's blaming the victim." To the contrary, that's trying to help people and
say to them, "Here are steps you can take to put yourself in a better position."

Dyson: As long as there are structural barriers to prohibit people from engaging
in self-help and responsibility, all that talk is mere theory. On the ground here it's
about negotiating the possibility where poor black people can engage in full citizenship and be protected by the government that should be held accountable–
black, white, and otherwise.

Neary: All right, thanks to both of you for joining us today.

20

THE HUMOR IN THE HURT
Politically Incorrect Reflections
on Hurricane Katrina

with Stephen Colbert

During Black History Month, 2006, I was invited to the television show *The Colbert Report* for a debate of sorts about Katrina with host Stephen Colbert. I say a debate "of sorts" because Colbert's shtick is to imitate a conservative talk show host while engaging the issues of the day. His wildly popular show grew from his stint on Jon Stewart's successful and influential *Daily Show*. However, as the old black folk say, you can be "crackin' and fackin'," or joking, but telling some truth at the same time. I tried to roll with Colbert's humor while inserting my brand of truth into the conversation. Through his humor, Colbert probably represents a lot more Americans of a certain ideological persuasion than one might suspect. I found him funny and witty, and thus was able to address some of the beliefs he articulated with humor and honesty as well. If nothing else, my engagement with Colbert proved that you can bring humor and politically incorrect views to a serious subject without insulting or belittling the victims of an extraordinary disaster.

Stephen Colbert: Tonight's guest is a leading African American scholar, and the author of *Come Hell or High Water,* a new book about New Orleans, which, if the index is any indication, has nothing about "Girls Gone Wild." Please welcome Dr. Michael Eric Dyson. Brother Dyson, thank you for coming.

Michael Eric Dyson: Thank you for having me, Brother.

Colbert: Testify.

Dyson: Alright. You know what? I'm glad to be here. This is an extraordinary program and it's wonderful to have the opportunity to talk about some very serious issues on your show.

Colbert: I couldn't feel the same way more. [*Laughter*] Now you've got a book, it's called *Come Hell or High Water: Hurricane Katrina and the Color of Disaster*. What do you mean—"Color of Disaster"? I don't understand.

Dyson: Well, I'm talking about a disproportionate number of those people who bore the brunt of what we saw in Katrina happen to be people of color. We know poor people in general—poor whites, some poor Latinos, some poor Asians—but the majority of African American people bore that. And it was a natural disaster, but [also] an *unnatural* disaster. Race, poverty, and class converge in a very destructive fashion to make the lives of those people hell. So I wanted to talk about both of those issues.

Colbert: How is New Orleans doing, by the way, right now?

Dyson: Well, it's in bad shape.

Colbert: I've been there once. I went to Bourbon Street. Okay. Is that still there?

Dyson: People are still drinking bourbon. Bourbon Street is still there. The French Quarter is still there.

Colbert: So what's the problem? [*Laughter*]

Dyson: Well, the problem is, the people can't consume enough of inebriating, toxic liquids in the French Quarter to get down to the Ninth Ward, where you've got a lot of poor people, a lot of devastation, a lot of unreconciled issues for those people. They can't get schools, hospitals; they can't get enough jobs; they can't get enough work. And as a result of that, they're suffering a second storm, if you will.

Colbert: So are you saying there's some sort of racial component to this? [*Laughter*] The reason I ask is because this is very distressing to me. Because when I was a kid, in the late '60s, early '70s, I heard a lot about race, okay? And then I didn't hear a lot about it for years and years. Now suddenly, everybody's talking about it again. Doesn't that just make the problem worse? [*Laughter*] If we stop talking about race, maybe we'll forget that we're different races.

Dyson: Or what race you're in.

Colbert: Right. I'm color blind. People told me that you're black. Okay? People say I'm white. I accept that. I don't see us as different races.

Dyson: Well, bless your heart. You're one of the few Americans who's got the ability to do that. When I talk about race here, I'm talking about race as an atmosphere, race as a set of expectations that leads you to say, "If Natalie Holloway disappears, you go looking for her. If a black woman disappears, you don't." Whatever that has to do with–that reality–that's what happened down in New Orleans. I'm not suggesting that white people sat back and said, "Aha, a bunch of Negroes, let's not go down there." It's more subtle than that.

Colbert: They prefer African Americans. [*Laughter*] That's what I understand.

Dyson: I certainly prefer it. Absolutely. But did they say, "There's a bunch of Negroes or black people down there, let's not go down there?" No. Although that happened for some people, what happened, more likely, is that the president and other people in the administration just didn't get the same kind of cues. If a nation of Barbara Bushes–

Colbert: Are you Kanye West-ing it now? Are you Kanye West-ing it? You saying George Bush doesn't like black people? I'll play Mike Myers if you are.

Dyson: Well that would mean you'd have to be quiet. [*Laughter*] But what's interesting is that I'm suggesting that if a nation of Barbara Bushes were down there, I'm not saying they could have gotten there any faster, but ignorance–

Colbert: Oh, if only. A nation of our Barbara Bush. [*Laughter*]

Dyson: Look, ignorance and ineptitude were critical, but they should have tried harder. So I am suggesting that Kanye West wasn't talking about George Bush the individual. He doesn't know him. He's talking about George Bush, the face of the government; the institutional identity. And he says "care." How do you measure care in political terms? By delivering resources in a timely fashion to vulnerable people. That's how you measure care.

Colbert: Okay. Two quick questions. One is, on a scale of one to heck, how good of a job did Brownie do?

Dyson: Sub-heck. Sub-minus, brother. He was awful. He did a terrible job. But I'll tell you what–Michael Chertoff was really responsible. He should have been the first person to make the call; then he should have called Brownie in. So don't just back up on Brownie to make him a scapegoat. Let's look at Michael Chertoff as well. And God knows, let's look at the president.

Colbert: Well, isn't really the problem here FEMA? That it exists at all. I mean, it's a crutch. [*Laughter*] If people know that safety net's there, of course they're going to allow hurricanes to wipe out their town. [*Laughter*] They're waiting for all those $2,000 little credit cards they got.

Dyson: Oh, yeah, really pimping that hurricane. [*Laughter*] But here's the point—

Colbert: Do we need FEMA anymore? I mean, they got celebrities out there, who'll do telethons.

Dyson: Yeah, I know what you're saying. But here's the point.

Colbert: Do you really?

Dyson: FEMA only developed in 1979, under Jimmy Carter—

Colbert: And we got rid of Carter but we kept FEMA. I don't understand.

Dyson: Well, because FEMA got better, under certain people. Under President Clinton it did well. Under Mr. Bush it's not doing so well. So the point is, it's not [that] the problem is FEMA; the problem is cronyism. If you get your boys, your posse, it's like Snoop saying, "Come on boys from Long Beach, let's go in and do our thing." Mr. Bush called all his boys from Texas to come in. They had no experience, no skills. They had no ability for disaster mitigation or emergency relief. So, as a result of that, you've got a guy who ran the International Arabian Horse Association being in charge of disaster relief. That doesn't make for a very pretty picture for FEMA. It's "the soft bigotry of low expectations."

Colbert: I've heard that. Now, this is Black History Month. You saw the Reverend congratulating me on the work that I do. [*Laughter*]

Dyson: You know what? You're one of the outstanding black people in this nation. [*Laughter*]

Colbert: Thank you very much. I've always said that. I've always said that, until someone told me I wasn't black. [*Laughter*] Let me ask you this. Bush right now is at a 2 percent approval rating among African Americans.

Dyson: Wow, that high? [*Laughter*]

Colbert: What can he do to get that to 3? [*Laughter*]

Dyson: Probably bring Colin Powell back.

Colbert: All right. You know, he is willing to take one for the team.

Dyson: There's no question about it. You pointed that out. So many of us have taken one for the team. And unfortunately, taking one for the team means that you bleed for the team but the team doesn't bring you back in when you've done your job. And that's part of the tragedy. That's what black history teaches us, and I'm glad to have an African "Scaremerican" like you, on television, speaking about these issues. [*Laughter*]

Colbert: All right. Please come back next Black History Month.

Dyson: All right. [*Laughter, applause*]

21

SORRY SEEMS TO BE THE HARDEST WORD
Apologies and Reparations for Slavery

with David Horowitz; moderated by Bobbie Battista

David Horowitz has become a right-wing darling because of his caustic views, his mixture of half-truths and facts taken out of context, and his ad hominem assaults upon his political and intellectual opponents. I have been the victim of Horowitz's tactics, especially his witch-hunting pursuit of progressive intellectuals, by being cited in his book, *The Professors: The 101 Most Dangerous Academics in America*. On college campuses across America, Horowitz has attacked advocates of affirmative action and reparations. I have debated him a few times on television, including our June 2000 encounter on CNN's now defunct *Talk Back Live*, hosted by journalist Bobbie Battista. Horowitz's mean-spirited demeanor only reinforces his bitter opposition to civil rights and anti-racist activism. I think it is *Horowitz* who is most dangerous to open dialogue and healthy debate in his rabid desire to undermine the influence of liberal professors in contemporary higher education. On *Talk Back Live*, Horowitz and I debated whether the United States should apologize for slavery and offer reparations to the descendants of slaves, one of the most controversial racial issues today.

Bobbie Battista: Should the U.S. apologize for slavery? What do we owe the descendants of slaves? Last week, a large group of African Americans gathered in Washington to celebrate what is called "Juneteenth." It was on June 19, 1865, [that] the last slaves in the United States learned they were free. Congressman Tony Hall, a Democrat from Ohio, chose that day to call on Congress to apologize for promoting and sustaining slavery and its legacy. Well, let's bring our other two guests in. Joining us now is David Horowitz, president of the Center for Popular Culture, and editor-in-chief of its online magazine, www.frontpage.com. He is also author of *Hating Whitey and Other Progressive Causes*. Also with us is the

Reverend Michael Eric Dyson, a Baptist preacher and communications professor at DePaul University. He is the author of the book *I May Not Get There with You: The True Martin Luther King, Jr.* and *Race Rules: Navigating the Color Line.* Welcome to both of you.

Michael Eric Dyson: Thank you.

Battista: David, an apology seems like an easy thing to do. Why not?

Horowitz: Well, let me just say, I've spent fifty years fighting for civil rights for all Americans, and for African Americans in particular. Like many Americans, I have flesh-and-blood family that is black. And like almost all Americans, I abhor racism and of course slavery. The problem here is that this is not going to heal, that this is really part of a divisive movement, I think, to keep the race issue alive in America. In the first place, it's the wrong government. If you want an apology, you want it from the Confederate government. It was the United States government that ended slavery. We had slavery in this world for thousands of years, and there never was an antislavery movement until the British and the Americans started one, and it was the United States that helped to end the slave trade and then to end slavery itself.

And when I hear statements like the gentleman before who said blacks have been given nothing, you know, what about the trillions of dollars that's been transferred to inner-city communities by the majority of Americans? What about all the race-based scholarships and job opportunities that have been given to African Americans in this country? It just looks like another scam and another attempt to raise much higher the sense that everybody needs to express a feeling of guilt toward African Americans. There are so many injustices in this world, and if you go back in time—I mean, forty acres and a mule, one hundred fifty years ago—it'll be just absolutely endless.

Almost all the people in this country, maybe 90 percent, are descended from people who came after slavery. You know, if I look at my ancestors, they were being oppressed in some ghetto in, you know, Eastern Russia, at the time there was slavery in America, and if you look at the Irish, or you look at Mexican immigrants, recent ones, or Vietnamese boat people. You know, the time is to look forward now, not to look back at the past.

Battista: You're bringing up a lot of issues here, David. Hold on, we've got an hour, so let me bring Michael in here. And Michael, is it possible this sort of thing could end up being more divisive than [helping] to build community?

Dyson: Well, inevitably and unavoidably, initially it might be divisive. It's divisive now because America has refused to collectively confront its racial history and its own past and the responsibility for that. Mr. Horowitz makes some interesting points but let me respond to just a couple of them. First of all, he says that the wrong government is being asked to take responsibility for the issue of slavery. Well, it evolved into, and metamorphosed, if you will, into the government we have today. We can make intellectual distinctions and academic ones between the Confederate and the Union and what government we have now. The point is, this is the American government. The United States, as a collective entity, is responsible for something that all of us benefited from. Even if they were not slaveholders themselves, people benefited from that slave society.

Number two, Mr. Horowitz makes the point that many people, 80 percent, as high as that number, were not here—[the] people who produced them weren't here when slavery was in existence. And now that they are here, they shouldn't be held responsible. But the reality is, those Italians, those Polish brothers and sisters, those Jewish brothers and sisters who immigrated here in the late 1800s and early 1900s were able to take advantage of what we now know as white skin privilege. And that white skin privilege permitted them to be able to engage in a whole set of practices, business-wise, entrepreneur-wise, education-wise, employment-wise, health care-wise, and so on, that allowed them a more rapid ascent up the scale of mobility than it did African American people who had been here, indeed, who had fought for this country in many of its wars, and who had still been turned back with their aggressive demand to be treated equally.

So I think that the issue of reparations, as Martin Luther King, Jr., understood, was about fairness and justice and compensation for things that have been done wrongly, and explicitly, and evidently, against African American people. You know, a minister, Rev. Manuel Scott, Jr., preached a sermon once when he said there are three phrases that can help any relationship: "I love you; I'm sorry; forgive me." The fact [is] that America has been incapable of putting those phrases on the table, first of all, by acknowledging its own wrongdoing, and secondly, not simply acknowledging the wrongdoing but doing something about it.

The congressman earlier said: If you've got a relationship with somebody, your friend or wife, and you do something wrong and you don't say you're sorry, the relationship will be soured. Absolutely right. But more than that, if you've stolen money from this person, if you've stolen human resource, or capital, or the possibility of working in gainful employment, you've got to not only say you're sorry, you've got to make real restitution. And in American society, the issue of reparations has been extended to a range of other people but not when it comes to the most wounded and the most victimized people of all, African American people.

Battista: I think one of the hardest things about the issue of reparations is that it logistically seems overwhelming. I'm not sure how you would determine who gets exactly what.

Dyson: Look, that's a legitimate point, but let's look at it this way: that's not reason enough to keep us, or prevent us, from doing the right thing. It's as if [we're] saying: "I've done a wrong, but making the thing right now would be so overwhelming I can't do that. So I don't know where to begin." Well, begin by acknowledging A) it happened and it was wrong, and B) as the congressman said, there are many routes to racial redemption that can be worked out. There are many reparations that can be dealt with.

Martin Luther King, Jr.—and I quote this on page 28 of my book, *I May Not Get There with You*—said the following, a very short quote: "No amount of gold could provide an adequate compensation for the exploitation and humiliation of the Negro in America down through the centuries. Not all the wealth of this affluent society could meet the bill, yet a price can be placed on unpaid wages." And I'll skip down very briefly: "The payment should be in the form of a massive program by the government of special compensatory measures which could be regarded as a settlement in accordance with the accepted practice of common law. I am proposing therefore . . ."—last sentence—". . . that just as we granted a G.I. Bill of Rights to war veterans, America launch a broad-based and gigantic bill of rights for the disadvantaged, our veterans of the long siege of denial."

Battista: Let me get David.

Horowitz: Bobbie, yes, look. We've already done that. There's two or three trillion dollars [that] has already been spent on programs for the disadvantaged. The idea that, you know, this white skin privilege, this is a very left-wing idea. I—it is—

Dyson: Left wing or right wing, deal with the subject—

Horowitz: Excuse me, you know, people like Rev. Dyson, you know, need to think about their own attitudes towards America and a certain amount of gratitude for the fact that America did free the slaves and the fact that American blacks are the wealthiest blacks on the face of this earth. If your ancestors—if you are black and your ancestors were not kidnapped and brought to America, you're probably earning twenty to fifty times less than you do from having been brought to America. This is not to say that it was a good thing that you were kidnapped.

Dyson: That's exactly what you're arguing.

Horowitz: No it isn't. There needs to be an attitude—if there's going to be a healing, there needs to be an attitude on the part of those in the black community who are pushing this, of gratitude, the way other people who live in this country have [gratitude] for this country and what was done.

Dyson: I'm certainly going to respond to that.

Battista: Michael, hold on.

Horowitz: We have acknowledged that slavery is bad. We have a monument to Lincoln, who freed the slaves. Martin Luther King has the only national holiday devoted to an American—to him.

Battista: I've got to go to break. Michael, you can respond when we come back.

[Commercial break]

Battista: In 1994, the Florida State legislature agreed to pay $2.1 million to the survivors and relatives of those who lost their lives and property when a white mob destroyed the all-black town of Rosewood in 1923. Let me go to Michael quickly, and then I'll try to get the audience in here. Michael.

Dyson: Sure. I think the thinly veiled vitriol—I think, really, contempt—that is boiling beneath Horowitz's rhetoric is remarkable, and it speaks to this point. This is typical white paternalism, saying to black people that we should be grateful that America released us as slaves, when indeed, initially, it was wrong for America to enslave us. Number two, this attitude of gratitude, so to speak, is something that's preached Sunday after Sunday in many churches across this nation, where millions of black people listen to this. So [the lack of] gratitude hasn't ever been our problem.

But then we join that gratitude to an analytical prism that says, "Look, we know what's going on. It's been wrong. We have to deal with it." An offended white conscience puts forth its own wounds as the basis for backing up black complaint. Here's the point: you can't expect black people who have been harmed, who have been wronged, who have had terrible things done against them, to all of a sudden be grateful. We are—you don't even know the attitudes of many black people—we are enormously grateful that America has given us the privilege to expand and to grow and to argue for democracy. But we refuse to be grateful for injustice and unfairness. And we will continue to put in the faces of this society, including other African American and other minority people, the claims of African American people that are just and that are fair. And I think that's the thing we've got to contend with here—

Battista: Let me get→

Dyson: —not simply asking black people to be grateful for what white people have done, but to be honest about what the injustices have been.

Battista: Okay, hold on just a second.

Horowitz: Michael Eric Dyson doesn't speak for black people any more than I speak for white people. I mean, that's just the way we think racially now in this country as a result of movements like this.

Dyson: I speak for those people who think I speak for them, David.

Horowitz: There are lots of black Americans who, when they speak, understand what this country has given them. And I'm not just talking about freeing the slaves. This is an argument about something that happened one hundred fifty years ago. America today is a place of enormous privilege for all Americans and especially for black Americans. You look at those Haitians who risked their lives to try to get here, who come across in boats that are as cramped as the slave boats once were, and cross, you know, dangerous waters and die in the passage just to get to America for the privileges it will give them as black people. And I just, you know—I'm as capable as anybody else—

Dyson: But that's not the point. That's not the point we're dealing with.

Horowitz: I listen to Michael Eric Dyson and people like him—

Battista: Let me try to get some other opinions in here, you guys. There—this is—

Horowitz: —and I don't hear that ever.

Battista: This is a volatile subject and I want to try to get some other folks in here from the audience.

Horowitz: Sure.

Battista: Let me go—because I don't think I have that much time—let me go first to Kenny up here in the audience.

Kenny: Well, I have a problem with the money that they're seeking because they could spend their efforts on working at educating the people of today, their minorities, their African Americans, to be entrepreneurs, to get out there and learn to make a buck today—not what happened one hundred fifty years ago. You're out—

Dyson: Well, but the reality is that that's not against what African American people have done. And black people have always been about upward mobility; black people have always been about seizing opportunities that are available to them. What we are speaking about is the systematic and structural prevention of people to exercise their opportunity about what you speak. So, it's not that black people are lazy, or inefficient, or don't want to work, or don't want to be educated. Black people have an enormous drive to be educated. But if you have structural features in place that prevent you from realizing those goals and ambitions, then you have to deal with that.

Number two, I think African American people have always understood that American society, contrary to what Mr. Horowitz is arguing, has been a place of enormous opportunity. But to acknowledge that enormous opportunity doesn't mean on the other hand we can't acknowledge that there are still barriers remaining that disallow black people to realize their best goals and ambitions as rightful citizens of American society.

Battista: Joe in the audience.

Joe: I think that this issue runs deeper than folks realize. I think the state of the black community now can be looked at in terms of how the state and the police department treated blacks. When you went in and beat blacks and this, that, and the other—blacks today won't support the police department. That is the reason we have a lot of crime. [Some people think] it's okay to kill, steal, and rob, and we can't live in our neighborhood. The next issue: My education today is not the same as what my counterpart's would be, because I didn't have the supplies, I didn't have the tools. My parents didn't have the education to help me. They didn't have the skills that the whites had.

Battista: Now hold on. I will come back to you in just a second, Okay. I have to share the mike here. Jason from Ohio on the phone. Go ahead, Jason.

Jason: Okay, I had to agree with the gentleman out in California, and pretty much with what he was saying. Of course, I can see both sides of this situation, but I don't feel that—there shouldn't be an apology, for one thing. It was something that the ancestors, our ancestors, have done, and we have no responsibility for what they did.

Battista: You know, let me ask you something. Because you say that you don't agree with an apology or reparations, but you say you can understand?

Jason: I can certainly understand, yes I can. I can understand exactly how both parties would feel, the black communities and the white communities. But I grew up kind of in a poor situation myself and I made the best of my opportunity. Of course, I am not a millionaire, as far as that goes there. But I think here in America, everybody has the ability to progress along, and I have got black friends and I have white friends. And I think that it's a cop-out, basically, is what I am trying to say.

Battista: All right, Jason.

Dyson: Can I respond to that? Can I respond to that?

Battista: Okay, go ahead.

Dyson: I think that what's interesting is that many white people say, "We are not responsible for what happened a hundred years ago; that was my ancestors." Here is the reality: we are not suggesting that individual white people be responsible for [the decisions] that individual white people made back then. We are talking about corporate and collective responsibility. We have to clarify that. We're talking about as a nation we benefited—as white Americans, as African Americans—from policies that were put in place a hundred years ago. We weren't here when the Constitution was written. We weren't here when the Declaration of Independence was drawn up. But you can be sure the people going to court right now against Bill Gates and Microsoft are using words that were not even written when he was alive. They were written years before he got here, yet they have a contemporary effect.

Number two, many white people benefited from policies that were put into place long before they came along. They are not making any more land. They are not giving out any more land in America. Martin Luther King, Jr., and other civil rights leaders say, "Look, the very economic floor that undergirded white immigrants who came here from other lands was predicated upon the slave labor that black people had contributed to this society." So even immigrants who arrived here after slavery's demise benefited from the slave labor that black people contributed.

Three, when you say you weren't responsible, the reality is, if you benefited from that in terms of education, in terms of employment, and in terms of the kind of riches that you have received historically, you have to face up to that collective responsibility as a nation, not just [on an] individual basis. This is not about finger-pointing at individual whites to say, "You are racist." This is about assuming collective responsibility. This is about America doing what it says to black people.

Battista: Let me—

Horowitz: This is such—

Dyson: They say to us, be responsible for what you have done. All we're saying to America is, "Be responsible for what you have done collectively."

Horowitz: This is such a bad idea. Look, black people have benefited enormously from whatever happened a hundred years ago, as I pointed out.

Dyson: From slavery?

Horowitz: Yes, black people in America make twenty to fifty times what the black people who were left in those countries of Africa which they were taken from. This is an endless argument. In the next generation, people can say, "Well, blacks received all of this, you know, welfare money, and all of this money from racial preferences, and all these privileges, and therefore black people should, you know, make a gift to other people."

Dyson: That's ridiculous.

Horowitz: But the reality is that in America today and for the last fifty years, the opportunities to black people have been huge, and there has not been structural obstacles, as the professor says—

Dyson: Racial profiling is a structural obstacle.

Horowitz: Excuse me. You know, I didn't interrupt you, Michael.

Dyson: Certainly, okay.

Horowitz: —to black people's advance. There is a huge black middle class in America. It is much larger than the underclass. If you have to pick one obstacle to black advancement in America, it is the 80 percent out-of-wedlock births in the inner cities. If you have one parent, it doesn't matter if you are white or you are black, you are six times more likely to be poor. The problem with this movement, and it has been shown in this discussion, is that the mentality it creates among African Americans is one of grievance, of hostility, of thinking that white people don't care about them, which is obviously wrong. White people do care about what happens to black America. And it is looking for another handout and that is not going to help people. It's going to set them back.

Dyson: Well, that's—

Battista: Let me go to John in the audience here.

John: Well, I think the reasoning that this guy gives—and I want to just call him a jerk—the reasoning that this guy gives is very representative of the masses of people in this country. And I would call this guy an ally of John Rocker just based on the statement that he made, and that stuff permeates the American community. And with that kind of guy's thinking, who really represents the majority of this population, we can forget any consideration. I think we are here in this country. We are going to have to make the best of it. And where we find obstacles, we are just going to deal with them.

Dyson: Well, look at the–I think–look at the parallel between–

Horowitz: You know, excuse me.

Dyson: –what Mr. Horowitz has said and what we might consider in regard to our Jewish brothers–

Battista: Let me interrupt. We have breaking news.

[Preempted by breaking news]

[Commercial break]

Battista: In 1988, Congress acknowledged that treatment of Japanese Americans during World War II, particularly the one hundred twenty thousand confined in internment camps, was wrong. The 1988 Civil Liberties Act provided for reparations, for which about eighty thousand survivors applied. Most were paid $20,000 each under the restitution law, which expired two years ago. We're back, and we had a little jam-up with our e-mail thing here, but we're starting to get some. Linda in Illinois says: "My people came to central Illinois from Germany in the 1820s as dirt farmers. None of my family ever owned a slave. I lost two ancestors in the Civil War fighting to free the slaves. How much are they willing to pay me for my loss?" Do you want to address that Michael?

Dyson: Well, yes. I think, again, I've said before that of course many white people were not here literally, but they have taken advantage of it–been benefited by the practices of white supremacy, Jim Crow law, apartheid, which didn't make distinctions, by the way, based on what ethnic origin you were, except if you were black or white. So the people who came here as immigrants weren't disadvantaged as a result of their coming here; and in fact, they were advantaged by their white skin.

Let me address two things David said very briefly. First of all, he said that black people should be grateful because we have a higher living standard here than in Africa. That's like saying to our Jewish brothers and sisters, 2.5 percent, at most 3 percent, of the population here in America, they should be grateful because they're living much better than Jews were faring in Germany, so shut up and quit griping about anti-Semitism, and let's not talk about compensation for the Holocaust, by the way, to which they were meanly and evilly subject.

[Secondly], this comment about Africa I think reflects, again, the inability of many white liberals and white conservatives to understand the visceral impact of oppression on African American people. It's not simply that we were slaves and then we were freed, and therefore we should move on, because we've now been able to reap the benefits of American society in the twentieth and twenty-first centuries. The reality is, there are consequences to slavery.

Look at the interruption of the breaking news story about a black convict being put to death in Texas. If we need any more sharp example of how the impact of slavery continues to manifest itself—before he makes a ludicrous leap in logic, I'm not suggesting that slavery is responsible for the bad choices that black people made to murder. What I'm suggesting is the disproportionate number of black men on death row, the way in which this society continues to impugn the integrity of young black people. A report came out in April that said that young black and Latino men—

Battista: I've got to share here. I've got to share the airtime, Michael. Go quick. David, go ahead.

Horowitz: Yes, okay. The lady lost two ancestors who died to free the slaves. Her question was, what do you, Michael, owe her?

Look, let me just say, Bobbie, people like Michael talk one way. Black people in America—you know to distinguish between what people say—

Dyson: People like Michael talk one way, but black people talk another? As if I'm a different species or some other? I'm an African American.

Battista: Hold on. Hold on.

Horowitz: As if you're a left-wing troublemaker is what I'm talking about. If black people really believe that America was so horrible to them, there would be a lot of blacks who would migrate to Canada and other countries where they can be treated better. The reality is, there is no black emigration out of this country, and Haitians and other blacks are risking their lives daily to try to get here. That's the reality that we need to sit with. That's the reality that we need to look at.

I think that this is a very destructive movement for African Americans, and even for the gentleman who called me a jerk. I will sum it up this way: When Martin Luther King, you know, had a movement to end discrimination in America, it was supported by 85 percent majorities in the Congress and by the vast majority of the American people. Now, this congressman who's putting up this bill is having a lot of trouble. This will be very divisive. It will isolate African Americans, and the African American community should think about that.

Dyson: That is absolutely not right.

Horowitz: Stop picking the rules of the past—

Dyson: [Martin Luther King, Jr.,] was opposed tooth-and-nail by the Congress and by many white people.

Horowitz: And the difference between Japanese Americans and Jewish Americans, where we say reparations, is that they're the ones who actually suffered. They were in the camps. This is about something that happened one hundred fifty years ago. And nobody can show that slavery has been an obstacle to black people living today succeeding. Oprah Winfrey was the daughter of a sharecropper.

Battista: I've got to go. Guys, I've only got about thirty seconds left, so I've got to take the mike back, so to speak. A couple of more e-mails. Dale in Tennessee: "If anyone needs an apology, it's the Native Americans. They are still being treated very badly." And from Steve in California: "An apology is the first step in healing a nation that has been malnourished by the spoiled fruit of slavery." That will have to do it for this show today. Michael, thank you very much for joining us. David Horowitz, to you as well.

22

STILL SOME JUICE LEFT
O. J. Ten Years Later

with Ofra Bikel

In 1995, O. J. Simpson's murder trial bitterly divided the nation along color lines, and his acquittal by a largely black jury only deepened the racial differences. The nation's obsession with the Simpson case, one that I fully participated in, reflected both our fascination with celebrity and the downfall of legends and heroes. Ten years later, Simpson's case still ignited strong feelings about his guilt or innocence and underscored the persistence of the racial conflict the case revealed. Ofra Bikel came to my home and interviewed me, seeking a few comments for her PBS documentary to be broadcast on the tenth anniversary of Simpson's acquittal. I reflected on Simpson's meaning, probing the social and racial elements of his descent to infamy. In November 2006, Simpson sparked fresh outrage by writing *If I Did It*, a book featuring the fallen icon speculating about how he would have committed the murders he was acquitted of. Public outrage resulted in both the book and its accompanying Fox TV special being pulled. Unsurprisingly, Simpson remains nearly as divisive and controversial a figure a decade later as he proved to be when he famously sought escape from his troubles by being driven down an L.A. freeway in a Bronco. It wasn't the first time he used a white vehicle to escape a black reality.

Ofra Bikel: How important was the O. J. trial?

Michael Eric Dyson: Well, the O. J. debacle of a decade ago was extraordinarily important for race relations in America. I think it was a racial earthquake, so to speak; a race quake. It didn't create racial tension; rather, it revealed the fault lines of bigotry and bias that trace beneath our common lives together. But it did reveal to white and black America that, first of all, we see things enormously differently. There are contrasting and almost contradictory viewpoints that animate black people and white people around the issue of race, and O. J. revealed that in the sharpest of terms.

Bikel: How did African Americans view the trial?

Dyson: Obviously, when you think about many of the African Americans who were on the jury, I think they reflected the viewpoint of many African Americans in the broader culture, and that was it's not that we couldn't conceive that O. J. would be guilty. The question is, one, can you legally prove that the man did what it was claimed that he did? Two, did the prosecution make a compelling case to substantiate their claim that Mr. Simpson was guilty? And three, there's a difference between being innocent and not guilty. So black people are not naive enough to think that the proof, or the lack of proof, of guilt suggests that somebody is innocent. It means that the prosecution didn't meet its burden of proof—to prove the guilt of Mr. Simpson.

So black people believed—when they looked at that racism of Mr. [Mark] Fuhrman, and his promiscuous use of the "n" word, when they looked at the history of justice being doled out to African American people in L.A., and the refusal of the police system to reform itself, especially under Daryl Gates, who infamously headed the LAPD—when you put all that stuff together, there's no question that black people saw the O. J. Simpson case through the lens of race. And that lens had been colored by their immediate experience, and the texture of their lives certainly influenced what they understood was happening in the O. J. Simpson case.

Bikel: What if O. J. had been a white man, or Nicole [Brown Simpson] had been a black woman?

Dyson: Well, if we change the facts of the case, if O. J. Simpson were a white man—say if he were Robert Blake—and Nicole was a black woman, to be sure it would have been an enormously different outcome. First of all, we wouldn't have had the cultural brouhaha. It's not that had Mr. Simpson been a white man and Nicole been a black woman that there wouldn't have been enormous interest by the media. But given the history of race in America, there's a strange dynamism between a black man and a white woman. We saw it more recently with the Kobe Bryant incident. And I think the O. J. Simpson case reaffirmed the reality in America that interracial sexuality between black men and white women, specifically, harkens back to D. W. Griffith and 1915['s] *Birth of a Nation,* where it was socially put forth in that film that black men are marauding, peripatetic phalluses with a desire for their denied object: white women. So seeking to inseminate white women, seeking to rape them, is a major narrative that is a strong undercurrent in the story of American race relations. O. J. fit into that pattern. Nicole was a blond-haired, blue-eyed, voluptuous white woman that was the ideal representation of beauty in America. O. J. Simpson was a thickly muscled, legendary celebrity who played football and who gained a powerful position in the pantheon of American heroes. So when you put that stuff together, it's enormously chaotic, and it's enormously controversial.

But at the same time, the death of a white woman ranks higher in American society than does the death of a woman of color. On the same day that O.J. was alleged to have murdered Ron [Goldman] and Nicole, there was a black woman thrown to her death several stories down in a building in New York, and yet there was hardly any media mention for this heinous crime. And daily, women of color go to their deaths in equally vicious fashion, and yet they don't make the front page of the newspaper.

Bikel: And yet O.J. wasn't really perceived as being black.

Dyson: Well, there's no question that O.J. Simpson had been a substitute white man in America. He had gained honorary white status. He was not viewed by many white Americans as black. He was not seen as the African American athlete who was rebellious: Jim Brown, Muhammad Ali, Hank Aaron. He was accepted in golf clubs that were very tony. He was accepted into the elite circles of white society. He fit in. He didn't raise a ruckus. He didn't make white people feel guilty for their historic legacy of slavery. He didn't point out white supremacy. He didn't talk about Jim Crow. He didn't talk about racial inequality. O.J. hardly spoke about race at all. He confessed himself, when he was in jail, that for the first time in many years, he was forced to confront his own racial reality and the fact that he was still a black man in America. And white America dissented from their views about O.J. They left them behind once he was charged with murder. He was reblackened. He was rechristened in his African American identity. He was dipped again in the healing water, some would say—others would say the troubled waters—of race, and once again he emerged full-fledged as a black man in America.

Bikel: Why do you think the public had such strong feelings about the outcome of this case?

Dyson: I think the O.J. Simpson case conjured all the paranoia, the racial anxiety, but also the racial fatigue that America has endured over the last half century. After all, O.J. was the ideal type character from central casting. If we're going to get a black guy who will conjure empathy and yet produce controversy about race in America, he's got to be a black guy whom white people love and that black people in the past have identified with and at least respected. So his exploits on the athletic gridiron gave him a sense of cachet in black America and white America. His refusal to provoke issues of racial consideration gave him carte blanche, so to speak, in white America. Here was the ideal guy.

Only a guy like O.J. could both appeal to blacks and whites to see race in a specific fashion. And the reason we invested so much passion in this is because black people had for years been trying to say to white America, "The justice system is broken; you've got to fix it. Here's our best chance to tell that story with a guy that in the past you've been sympathetic to. You'll never hear it with a person for whom you have no sympathy, but you'll hear it in the case of O. J. as much as you're willing to hear it." Many white people believed, "Look, we're going to show you that we are trusting, and we have reached a high plateau in race relations. We're going to treat O. J. like we treat any other white person in America. If he's guilty, we're going to send him to jail. If he's innocent, we'll let him go." So he was the ideal person to bring out these contrasting viewpoints, but it all broke down.

Bikel: Broke down how?

Dyson: Well, it broke down because O. J. refused to follow suit, and black America refused to follow the script, and white America then saw that all bets were off.

O. J. refused to follow through because he claimed his blackness again in a way that was troubling to many white Americans: "Wait a minute, O. J. You haven't talked about blackness in our circles for years, indeed for decades. You've never made us feel uncomfortable about the issue of race. All of a sudden now you're claiming your allegiance to black people? You're identifying publicly with black people." Black people themselves had to squeeze and squirm. They had to re-inscribe O. J. into the black narrative. They had to baptize him again into the community; they had to accept him. Black people are typically, if you're willing to say you're sorry, always [willing to welcome you back] with open arms: "Come on back home, Michael Jackson. Come on back home, Kobe Bryant. Come on back home, O. J. Simpson."

And then white America said: "Well, wait a minute. We had granted you honorary status, which means you have to play by our rules. You have to accept the reality that race doesn't exist. But now you're saying it exists. You have to accept the reality that race is no longer hugely significant, and it no longer rules America. But now you're saying it does. Well, if you say it does, then we're going to go back to our ways as well." All bets were off with O. J.'s acquittal.

Bikel: Most liberals thought that by the 1990s, race was no longer much of an issue, but with the O. J. trial, race was suddenly front and center. Was that hard for them to accept?

Dyson: Sure. Especially for white liberals in the O.J. Simpson case, it was even much more difficult. Right-wingers, or conservative brothers and sisters in America who happen to be white, perhaps had concluded from the very beginning that O. J. was likely to have committed the crime, whereas white liberals were willing to suspend judgment until such point it was proved in the court of law. But also, what was revealed was this kind of liberal white racism, which we're not used to talking about. We're used to talking about conservative white racism. We're used to speaking about right-wing white racism, but even commentators like Gloria Steinem, the remarkable, formidable, and heroic defender of women's rights in

America, went on *The Charlie Rose Show* and was outraged that black people might deem O. J. innocent, not understanding that it wasn't simply about the fact that race trumped gender; that the concern over race outweighed the concern over whether or not O. J. abused his wife. What she failed to understand is that as a white privileged woman in America, she benefits from her white skin—even as a white woman—in ways that black people don't in general, and specifically black women don't.

So I think that white liberal guilt, and white racism, have never been sharply attacked in this country, and they came out in the O. J. Simpson case. One of the reasons we can point to, to suggest why this was such a powerful case, is because so many people had staked their lives on believing the world operated in a certain fashion, and O. J. came along to challenge it. O. J., in the technical lingo, provided a paradigm shift. O. J. forced a new theory about how the racial world operates, and many white people had not been used to thinking about that.

Bikel: What was the new theory?

Dyson: Well, the paradigm that prevailed was that race is a deck of cards, and that people arbitrarily, or willy-nilly, pull out a race card at their discretion to be able to put it down on the table to defend themselves or to cut through and do something distorted. Well, O. J. proved that "Wait a minute, there's no such thing as a race card being played by black people not already dealing with the race deck that white America has put on the table." So maybe the metaphor of race as a deck of cards doesn't work. Maybe you have to have a new paradigm because Johnnie Cochran, the great lawyer for the O. J. Simpson case, proved that when he spoke about race, all of a sudden he was dealing with the race card.

No, the race card was there the moment the prosecution chose Christopher Darden as a member of the prosecution team. The race card was being played the moment [prosecuting attorney] Marcia Clark chose the jury based upon what she thought would sail with black women, who would feel offended that a black man had murdered this woman. So the race card was already being played, but white America refused to see it. That's what came out in the O. J. Simpson case.

Bikel: So the race card was connected to Johnnie Cochran?

Dyson: Well, the prosecution tried to pretend and commentators in America tried to pretend, many of whom were white, that Mr. Cochran is the one who deleteriously played the race card and that O. J. Simpson venomously appealed to racial passion. No. Race was thick in the O. J. Simpson case from the very beginning, but it wasn't [necessarily] evident. And I think the O. J. Simpson case revealed that there is subtle race, and there is sophisticated race, and there's evident and observable race. The undercurrents of race often go by without being witnessed, but in the O. J. Simpson case, they were exposed for everybody to see.

Bikel: But wasn't O. J.'s money more important than his race in getting an acquittal?

Dyson: Well, that's a very powerful point, to suggest in America that a black person actually has the wherewithal to defend himself, or herself, when the government says you are wrong. We expect Martha Stewart to have millions. We expect the people from Enron to have money, massive armies of lawyers to detail their being injured by the state, but not a black person—not even a black person who has worked for twenty-five and thirty years as a legend or at least a visible celebrity in America. How dare he have the means to protect himself. And how dare he suggest that the criminal justice system has been racially corrupt from the beginning.

And how dare he, a rich man, become a symbolic representative for millions of black people who don't have cash or visibility but whose lives are similarly assaulted but without the ability to say so. So O. J. Simpson, whether he wanted to or not, became a representative. And often for black people, we don't get a chance to choose those who end up symbolizing us. We had tried to get a 747 to represent us—Martin Luther King, Jr., Malcolm X, Ossie Davis, Harry Belafonte—but lo and behold, a broke-down, rickety-old secondhand car named the O. J. Simpson case became the carrier of our dreams. And so many black people invested in that broken-down car because that was going to get the message across.

Bikel: Doesn't that depress you?

Dyson: It's very depressing that some of the most eloquent, brilliant, insightful figures in America who have happened to be African American, or for that matter white, or Latino, or Native American, or Arab, or from across the ethnic and racial spectrum have tried to discuss race in empowering and enlightening fashion, but their words have for the most part fallen on hardened ground. But O. J. Simpson cut right to the matter. O. J. Simpson dug a deep wound in the collective psyche of America and planted the information that America had been trying to repress for most of its history. And now, in the face of O. J., it couldn't avoid it. So yeah, it's kind of depressing in that sense, because O. J. was not necessarily the best vehicle to discuss the subtle nuances and the complex images of race that we need to deal with if we're going to have a complete and complex understanding of how race operates in America.

Bikel: Was race the most important force at work in this case?

Dyson: Well, when one thinks about the O. J. Simpson case, race is the most evident and observable and obvious difference. But there were many other differences tracing beneath: one, the level of celebrity in America—that if you're a celebrity and you've got face recognition and you've got high visibility, you're just simply going to get a different brand of justice than the average Joe Schmo. Number two, I think issues of gender were extraordinarily important in this case, that is to say that women, who often don't receive a fair brand of justice in America, had hoped that with this O. J. Simpson case that that issue could come to the fore. Unfortunately, I think many women who were white didn't understand the degree to which their black or brown or red or yellow sisters don't often receive the same kind of notoriety or infamy that Nicole Simpson did in order to get their cases heard and broadcast.

Number three, the issue of gender justice in America certainly is not [a] high [priority], and yet it did get some hearing in the O. J. Simpson case. We know that there are thousands, perhaps even hundreds of thousands, of women who daily toil under the brutal oppression of sexism or misogyny or other forms of sexual assault, whose cases are never heard, whose voices are never listened to, and whose bodies are mangled and maimed, and yet we don't see them. So in that sense, there were many issues that were converging in the O. J. Simpson case. Race was the most evident face of it, but the body of consideration was much broader.

Bikel: What if it had been O. J.'s first wife, a black woman, who was murdered, and not his second wife?

Dyson: Well, one thinks about the fact that had O. J. been married to a black woman—of course, his first wife, Marguerite, was a black woman—and allegedly Mr. Simpson engaged in some domestic violence with her. But the reality is that the body of a black woman doesn't rank as high on the totem pole of social consideration as does a white woman.

Bikel: Even within the black community?

Dyson: Well, certainly in the black community there's consideration for the black female. On the other hand, there's tremendous gender injustice in black communities, where women's bodies just don't count as much as men's bodies. If Mike Tyson is accused of raping Desiree Washington, many black people rally around him. When Mike Tyson was accused of biting the ear of Evander Holyfield, it was seen as outrageous. So the ear of a black man counts more than the body of a black woman. That's in black communities as well, so I think that there's no question that the gender imbalance is very powerful here as well.

Bikel: What do you think about the accusation that it was the prosecution who initially introduced the issue of race into the trial?

Dyson: Yes, well, I think the prosecution from the very beginning used race. Marcia Clark admits that she stacked that jury with black women because she felt that black women would be sympathetic to Nicole, who is a battered woman, especially since, as Marcia Clark understood, so many black women had been abused. But what she failed to anticipate was that so many of those abused black women had never received the consideration from white women like Marcia Clark. So she didn't anticipate the kind of resentment of a white woman, Marcia Clark, now trying to manipulate race and gender to defend her point of view while not being sympathetic to O. J., and the way in which these black women understood that they're going to be discriminated against first because they're black, not because they're female. Or at least they're going to receive an equal amount of bias and bigotry for their race as for their gender. And so in that sense, Marcia Clark was playing the race card from the very beginning. When Christopher Darden feigned outrage that the use of the "n" word would so indelibly be inscribed on the brains of the jury that they could never overcome hearing that word, because it's associated with Mark Fuhrman—come on. This is the use of the race card as well. This is the manipulation of racial passion as well.

Bikel: Was Darden right about the power of the "n" word?

Dyson: No, because to believe Mr. Darden's notion that black communities would have been outraged or at least incapable of recovering from that epithet is to deny what black people feel on a daily basis. Black people hear that word on a daily basis. Black people are assaulted with that word in far more common fashion than we are willing to acknowledge in America. So Mr. Darden again was doing some racial gerrymandering there, trying to use his own color as a badge of authenticity to the judge and to the jury. He was trying to say, "Look, I'm a real black man, too." But in the stakes of the "real black man," he got trumped by Johnnie Cochran. Johnnie Cochran brilliantly deployed the notion of authentic black man in a way that Christopher Darden never had access to.

Bikel: How do you explain the apparent joy many African Americans felt about the verdict?

Dyson: Yes, well, Johnnie Cochran should be accorded an enormous share of responsibility for the utter ecstasy that many black people expressed on that day when the verdict came down. But one mustn't gainsay or underestimate the fact that it could have been a by-rote lawyer standing up there, simply by the numbers, and had that verdict come down, there still would have been enormous jubilation because it is exactly this case: "We did it by playing by your rules, playing the game the way you said we should play it. And now that the verdict has gone against you for what you perceive to be the first time in a major case, you want the rules changed. Slow down. These are your rules." As they say in the ghetto, "Don't hate the player; hate the game." If you don't like the rules, then change the game itself. Don't be mad at the player like Johnnie Cochran.

Many white people were upset with Johnnie Cochran, outraged at Johnnie Cochran. Why be upset with Johnnie? He's taking your rules, playing by them, and he won. And that's why black people were so happy, I would suggest, that day.

Bikel: Why? Because so many innocent black men had been condemned by a system that had set many guilty white men free?

Dyson: Well, yes. There's no question that O. J. got the benefit of all of the righteous anger that black people had over cases where we knew that a white guy like Byron De La Beckwith, who was eventually charged with murdering Medgar Evers, had gotten away with murder. Which is why black people said to white America, "You can't be simply upset that somebody got away with murder, because then you'd be concerned about the four little girls who got blown up in the church in Birmingham. You'd be concerned about Medgar Evers's murderer, who was going around bragging that he had killed him. So if you're upset, be upset at that. You can't be upset at O. J. He's not the first person to get away with murder." So a hidden message in that was: "See, this is what we've been saying all along, white America, that even when you said that the rules were being played by, you knew [the system] was immoral. So now you need to reexamine the legal system to see if it can be improved. And if it can be improved, it should help black people as well."

Bikel: But did the African Americans rejoicing at O. J.'s acquittal really believe he was innocent?

Dyson: Absolutely not. I don't think we should make the mistake of believing that black people who celebrated A) thought O. J. was innocent, or B) were even concerned most about O. J. as opposed to their Uncle Charlie, or Bubba, or their sister Shanaynay, or their Aunt Jackie, who had been screwed by a system that never paid attention to them.

Again, O. J. was beyond his body. "O. J." was a term that represented every black person that got beat up by the criminal justice system: "And now we have found some vindication, and guess what, white America? It was with a black man that you loved. It was with a black man that you said was better than us. It was with a black man that you said wasn't like us. He was different than we are. He wasn't a troublemaker. He didn't cause racial consternation, or he wasn't controversial. Ha, ha, ha. The very guy you thought was so perfect turns out to be the one who turned the tables on you." That was a delicious irony of the victory as well.

Bikel: So it was payback of a sort?

Dyson: It wasn't on its face bawdily payback, but yes, there was a sense of vindication and justification. There was a sense of "You know what? We've been trying to tell you this for a long time, and you have not awakened." So much less
than revenge or payback, it was a kind of wake-up call to white America: "This is
what *we* have been dealing with, and now how do you feel? Multiply it a million
times. Then you'll begin to understand how we feel." So it's: "Let's let them stew
in this just a little bit to understand just how messed up, how terrible, how awful
we felt after justice was not given to us and after a verdict came down that we
knew was wrong."

Bikel: What about jury nullification? Was it possible that the jury knowingly set
free a guilty man in order to send a message?

Dyson: Well, if that's the case—let's just even grant the benefit of the doubt that
the term is legitimate and applies to the behavior of people—then my God, white
juries have been practicing jury nullification forever. If that's the case, how do you
account for the fact [of the] kangaroo court where Emmett Till's murderers were
not brought to justice, and everybody there knew they were guilty, and yet they
were not convicted? That was jury nullification. The history of white judicial
practices toward black people has been a history of jury nullification. So again,
spare me the acrimony and outrage because you've never had that kind of acrimony and outrage for millions of black people who have been subjected to ridiculous levels of nullification by white juries for the history of this country.

Bikel: Were whites angry because the jury deliberation was so short?

Dyson: Well, I think that what white America failed to realize with that quick jury
deliberation, [is that] black people had been deliberating far longer than the O. J.
Simpson case; that similar cases had taken place in America, not with equal
celebrity, not with equal acrimony because of the introduction of sex and gender
into the case, but in clear instances, where black people were innocent and yet
white juries failed to find them innocent, or they were not guilty and white juries
found them guilty. Black people have been collectively deliberating for a long
time, and if what I say is true, that O. J. was bigger than his body, so was this
case, and the jury was dealing with unavoidably the influence of that history of injustice toward black people. So the quickness appeared in the O. J. Simpson case,
but it took about two hundred fifty years to come up with that jury verdict.

Bikel: Was there no other likely outcome for this trial?

Dyson: I think most black people sitting on that jury would have voted similarly.
Even if they felt in their hearts that Mr. Simpson was guilty, they knew that the
prosecution was so contaminated with so many extraneous biases and bigotries

that there was no way that they could reasonably conclude that the prosecution A) had met its burden of proof and B) that they had proved that Mr. Simpson was guilty.

Bikel: How much did the outcome of the trial have to do with the Los Angeles of the 1990s?

Dyson: Well, when one thinks about what occurred, one remembers the social context of race in L.A. in the late '80s and early '90s. Daryl Gates had been at the helm of the Los Angeles Police Department, and he was notoriously indifferent, at best, to the interests of African American people, and some claimed [he was], at worst, callous and racist in his treatment of black people and certainly [in] his refusal to respond to the outrage of black people about police brutality. Furthermore, Rodney King was a symptom of Mr. Gates's out-of-control police department. Here is a black man being pummeled by four white policemen, who when they go to trial are found to be not guilty. And then the Rampart division in the LAPD proved to be so corrupt in the meting out of justice, especially cops lying and fabricating evidence in regard to black and Latino defendants. When you put all that stuff together, there was a powder keg of controversy waiting to explode. What happened in that case was symbolic of the enormous racial tension that occurred in L.A. during that time.

Bikel: So it wasn't surprising that evidence in the Simpson case was contaminated given the history of the LAPD?

Dyson: What is surprising is that many white people were surprised. What is remarkable is that many white people were caught off guard. [They were] not listening to [the lyrics from the N.W.A. song]: "F– tha police / Coming straight from the underground. / Young brother [sic] got it bad 'cause I'm brown / And not the other color so police think / They have the authority to kill a minority." That's a rap song [from] 1988, '89. And you're surprised? Right in L.A. they're making rap songs about this several years before the Rodney King situation. So I think what was remarkable to many African American people is that so many white people were racially naive. They were like ostriches—symbolically sticking their heads in the sand and pretending that the world of racial acrimony didn't exist. This is why the O. J. Simpson case opened the eyes of white people to the reality that black people confront on a daily basis.

Bikel: Is there any point in revisiting this case now, ten years later?

Dyson: Many people think that, ten years later, why are we looking at O. J.? What's the big deal? Many white people have written him off as a pariah. Many black people have seen that O. J. came to a black restaurant or two after he got out, and now he's playing golf for most of his life. He's irrelevant to black and white people. And yet it is important ten years later to see just why we were so invested on both sides. And I think both sides need to rethink their jubilation, or their acrimony and hostility. Black people had to deny the fact that O. J. hadn't been black for a long time, and white people had to lie about the fact that O. J. wasn't black and had been a substitute white guy. So both sides had to juggle and fiddle and fudge with O. J. because he was such an imperfect "perfect" carrier for the aspirations of white and black America, which is why he's so important, which is why a figure like that continues to arrest our attention. Because he is, and remains, hugely controversial precisely because he failed on the black side to tell the truth about black identity, and on the white side finally he failed to fully fit in. That's the perfect example of what race can do and mean in America.

23

WEAPONS OF MASS SEDUCTION
The War in Iraq and Inside US

with Ann Coulter and Dennis Miller;
moderated by Bill Maher

Bill Maher is one of the bravest and most brilliant social critics we have in the after-math of 9/11. Not only is he willing to challenge received wisdom on political prac-tice and public policy, but he is capable of self-criticism, a rare trait among contem-porary pundits. In this debate, which took place on Maher's HBO show, *Real Time with Bill Maher*, I argue with Ann Coulter and Dennis Miller about American empire, democratic institutions, the squelching of dissent by the Bush administration, and the wars on terror and in Iraq. Despite my profound differences with Coulter and Miller, I find them to be smart people and worthy opponents. I have hosted my friend Coulter on my radio show, and we have waged serious debate without falling prey to vicious ad hominem attacks like those favored by David Horowitz. I have appeared on Miller's now-defunct cable show, and admire his rapier-like wit and vast knowledge. The warmth of our rapport—despite the fierceness of our disagreement—shows when Miller praises me for being "the Marvin Gaye" of rhetoric. Many may find it strange that I could be on such good personal terms with folk with whom I fundamentally dis-agree, but I suppose it is as much a sign of my Christian refusal to demonize my op-ponents as it is their humanity.

Bill Maher: Let's meet our panel. First up is U Penn Professor of Humanities and author of *Open Mike* and *Why I Love Black Women,* my friend Michael Eric Dyson.

Her old book, *Slander,* was the number one bestseller. She's now mellowed—her new book is *Treason.* It is in bookstores on June 23rd. My drinking buddy Ann Coulter is here. And a friend of many, many years. He will be at the Paris Hotel. Wow. As much as you hate the French—still playing the Paris Hotel. [*Laughter*] Ac-tually they're on my shit list.

Dennis Miller: Paris, Texas.

Maher: No, it is in Las Vegas. His stand-up special is so great I had to watch it twice. *The Raw Feed* is currently on HBO. Dennis Miller is back on the show.

Now, let me pick up a little bit where I left off last week. I was saying that the Bush administration won this war. We will see what's going to happen now. And liberals who are against the war cannot now work backwards from the premise "I hate Bush. Let's find out what he's doing now is wrong." However, I have to say, this week when they found Abu Abbas—this is the guy who pushed Leon Kling-hoffer into the drink—okay, you couldn't get a more evil guy than someone who pushes an old person in a wheelchair into the water. We know that. However, for the conservatives to be saying, "Now, see? See what we told you? That's why we went into Iraq, because he's harboring terrorists." Yeah, but this guy is a terrorist who did his last thing in the '80s. Aren't we just clutching at straws here?

Miller: Hey. Listen, I still think Peter Max's art is shit, and he did that in the '80s. [*Laughter*]

Ann Coulter: No one is citing that.

Maher: Sure they are.

Coulter: No one is citing it as if that was the sole reason we went in. I mean, just last week a poll was taken, and a majority of Americans support the war in Iraq, even if there are no weapons of mass destruction. The point is liberals are saying he's not harboring terrorists. Well, here is one.

Maher: But that's like saying I'm harboring Olympic athletes because Bruce Jen-ner's sleeping on my couch. If that's the best they can do—

Coulter: That's not what the point was. The point was to say that liberals were wrong. Not that this was the point for the war.

Michael Eric Dyson: That doesn't prove the liberals are wrong, because first of all, they had an amnesty agreement between Israel and Palestine. They've been knowing for a long while that he's been living in Baghdad after he moved there in 2000, so it's been an open secret. But number two, I think this again shows the conservatives have been duplicitous in the sense that they refuse to admit that this war—if it's not about weapons of mass destruction, and if it's not about proving the relationship between Mr. Hussein and bin Laden, then what the heck are we there for? The point was, this was the reason for the immediacy of the invasion. And to find an old-style terrorist—and, again, he was evil—but to talk about that as the proof that now what we've done is correct I think is [a stretch].

Coulter: But no one's citing it that way. And the other thing it proves—

Maher: The conservatives want it both ways.

Coulter: No, the other thing conservatives [say] is this is the second time we've caught him. We caught him once before. The Europeans had him and they sent him back. And now we want Europe involved in the rebuilding of Iraq. I think we can do this without their help.

Miller: Wasn't Abu Nadal cut down in Baghdad too? I mean, how many Abu's you gotta find? What you gotta find Abu Ragley? Is that who we're looking for? They're two big Abus. [*Laughter*]

Maher: Okay, Saddam Hussein, of course he's a bad guy. Of course you turn over a rock and you're going to find some maggots. But the whole thing was about making us feel safer. Do you feel safer that the terrorist old-age home has now been raided?

Miller: No, but I feel safer [now] that I know the rest of the world knows that we can be real motherf—ers when we're pushed too far. [*Laughter*]. We've got an awesome military machine, and I guarantee you Syria, North Korea's coming to the table now. Syria's over there thinking, "Christ, we're at least not going to be hassled 'til they get these three hundred thousand kids out of here."

Dyson: The problem with that, though, is that first of all, wielding a superpower military is undeniable in terms of its legitimate effect—or at least, the fact that it has a huge effect. But the point is, to say that because we're a superpower and we're beating some people down, then we'd have to really invade the entire Middle East. We'd have to go from Syria to Jordan to Egypt; we'd have to go across the board wiping them out.

Coulter: No, we don't have to—

Dyson: That's bad foreign policy, but it's also bad for the notion of American democracy. This is why, again, people are in Iraq saying "No, we don't want Hussein. You're right; he's a thug. But we don't want America, because of what you've done historically and what you continue to do to ignore the legitimate creation of the role of democracy there." We're trying to *force* democracy onto people.

Miller: People always come up with this imperialistic thing. And if you think anything about going into these sh—hole countries and getting them right feels imperial in any way, shape, or form, you're missing the point. Why don't we just start ascribing regal status to the kid who walks up to private booths at Show World? There's nothing imperial about this for Christ's sake. [*Laughter*]

Dyson: I agree. But you raise a very good point. The point is that imperialism rests upon the denial of the legitimate goods and spoils to the average, everyday people. So we've got people in Iraq right now who are fighting the war. They're not the son of Rumsfeld; they're not the son of Bush. They're the sons of everyday, ordinary working people who bear the brunt of what's going on.

Maher: Let me ask, why is it that they have found nothing? And why is it, if this guy was so bad, with such bad weapons, he didn't use them when we were knocking right on his door?

Coulter: I can answer that.

Maher: Yes please.

Coulter: First of all, we won this war in three weeks. Give 'em time to find weapons of mass destruction.

Maher: Why didn't he use them while we were there?

Coulter: He didn't use them because Rumsfeld said anyone who deploys these weapons is going to be tried as a war criminal.

Dyson: Oh, yeah, that's a real threat. [*Laughter*]. That's a real threat. You've got weapons of mass destruction and you're worried about an old guy [threatening you?]

Coulter: Apparently it was, because he didn't use them—

Miller: —saying that to his underlings. I think they knew it was going to collapse really quickly.

Coulter: Right. They also didn't fight very hard. I mean, Saddam himself isn't the one who's going to set off these weapons of mass destruction. He needs everyone around. And they did crumble pretty fast because they knew the regime was going to collapse.

Dyson: I think they're not there. I think, number one, they said they're looking for them. I stand to be corrected. But the point is if there was a huge cache of weapons of mass destruction, by now, with all of that sonar scanning and ability to survey, we would have found them by now. So, first of all, they're not there. Secondly, they didn't show a relationship between Hussein and bin Laden, and now, in the name of the very imperialism about which Mr. Miller speaks eloquently [*laughter*], the reality is that America wants to whip behind over there without the justification that sent us there in the first place. And I'm saying, "Pardon me for asking for logic, but what's the relationship between why you went there and what you're doing there now?" Just because you happened to find a good booty while you're over there doesn't mean that the reason you were sent over in the first place is right. I think it's ridiculous and baloney.

Miller: He's saying we found Jennifer Lopez in Iraq? [*Laughter*]

Dyson: No, no, no. I'm talking America "backing that thang up," brother! [*Laughter*]

Maher: Let me introduce this into the discussion. I think we need a couple of new terms here because of what's going on in this country. One would be "patriotically correct." Now, we all remember "politically incorrect" and what that meant. I think that was more the fault of the left, that you couldn't step on certain verbal landmines without being blown up, as John Rocker and many people found out. Now we have "patriot correctness." It seems like if you do not show this blind Bush love, that you lose your job. They try to get rid of you. You get Dixie-Chicked. [*Laughter*] This is the other term I think we need.

Dyson: You can get Robbin-ized or Sarandon-ed as well. I mean, that's the real deal, too.

Maher: Well, Tim Robbins made a speech this week at the Press Club in Washington and I think he made a couple of interesting points. He said that when Clinton was in office, and they were bombing Kosovo, he spoke out against Clinton and Kosovo and the war there, and he was never called a traitor then. It was not treason then.

Coulter: Nobody heard him that time.

Maher: Of course they heard him.

Coulter: I don't remember it. Where did he say that?

Maher: I don't remember. But you know what?

Miller: I think it was the seventh anniversary of *Bull Durham*. [*Laughter*]

Dyson: I actually wrote about "patriotic correctness" in a column I wrote for the *Chicago Sun Times*. Here's the point. It is such a tyrannical atmosphere right now that if you don't toe the line according to what a narrow, conservative regime thinks about what is American, then you're un-American. I resent that, because so many people have paid the price with their blood, with their sweat, with their tears to build this country, and ostensibly the reason we go to a foreign nation to deploy our weapons against them is to protect the very right to speak out against what we think is wrong. And if we can't protect free speech here we can't protect it anywhere else.

Maher: Why do conservatives, why do they get so upset? Sometimes I read something that an actor says, that I don't agree with, but I turn the page of *People* magazine. I don't start an e-mail campaign.

Miller: Yeah, but Bill, think about what a tenuous grasp anybody has on any-body's approval in the showbiz world. I mean, for God's sake, there are people who won't go to people's movies 'cause they don't like the way somebody looks. So to think that people are expected to overlook the way people *are* is a little sim-plistic. Listen, I think the Hall of Fame made a horrible decision not having those two people there to speak. [The Baseball Hall of Fame snubbed actor Tim Rob-bins and actress Susan Sarandon, his longtime partner, by canceling a celebration of the fifteenth anniversary of their baseball film, *Bill Durham,* because of their an-tiwar activism.] But the simple fact is, there's a lot of people in America now who are simply going to dislike Tim Robbins and Susan Sarandon. And they don't want to see their movies anymore. And it's going pretty far to say, "Listen, you should be able to dislike them and still fork out your money." That's just not the way people work.

Dyson: But that's your choice. The Hall of Fame has no more right to tell them they can't come to their—

Miller: It's stupid, man. I'm really with—that was really bad.

Dyson: It's different if you vote with your pocketbook and say, "Hey, I won't go to see another Susan Sarandon and Tim Robbins movie." That's fine.

Miller: Well, that's all that's gonna happen.

Dyson: Well, but I don't know. No, there's more a sense of intimidation because it can happen to them. This is what people are going to say: "Dadgum, if it can happen to Susan Sarandon and Tim Robbins, what the heck will happen to me, Joe Blow, average American on the job, if I dare speak out? And then I'll have some right-wing fascist junta deployed against me because I'm not American the way they say so." I think that's rather ridiculous.

Miller: I say that the chill wind that Tim's worried about will meet the global warming that he's worried about and everyday will become 72. It'll be cool. [*Laughter*]

Dyson: I'm afraid of who has his hand on that barometer, brother, that's what I'm afraid of.

Miller: Can I say, I don't agree, but I love the way you speak, my man. Isn't he beautiful?

Maher: That's why he's here Dennis. Only the "A" team here.

Miller: This guy, he's the Marvin Gaye of ideology. You are beautiful, man. Smooth, very smooth my man. Annie, where you been tonight, you're the angry young colt. Where have you been? Dive in here doll! [*Laughter*]

Coulter: Yes, I'm trying. I think liberals are a bunch of whiners. [*Boos*].

Miller: Hey, hey, why so preemptive? [*Laughter*]

Dyson: Proving a point.

Miller: Yeah, right. That did look bad.

Coulter: Every time newspapers, publishers won't publish me, newspapers or producers fire me, no one says that's censorship. They say, "Don't call that censorship." They say, "That's not the government. They can do whatever they want." It happens all the time to conservatives. Now suddenly, you know, it's private enterprise; I don't care what the Baseball Hall of Fame does.

Maher: You are the only conservative I ever saw lose a job since 9-1-1, okay? You cannot usually say anything—

Coulter: Right, but look, nobody would publish my last book, which was the number one book all summer. No one would publish it. And everybody said, "It's not the government, not the government."

Maher: But somebody did.

Coulter: Okay, for six months no one would publish it.

Dyson: But [some liberals] been trying for six years. But here's the point, too. [*Laughter*] No, no, no, I'm not dissing you.

Coulter: Wait a second. Gosh. Okay, go ahead. I'll just sit back.

Dyson: What I'm saying is this. You know what? This amazes me. I haven't seen any progressive, left-wing, left-liberal voices of reason on TV. I think it's been all closed out. Even the major networks are basically the propaganda arm of the government. I don't even see any cracks in the armor. I don't see any kind of tincture to the armor that says, "Look, we have a progressive viewpoint that's [dominant] here" because the right wing has it sewed up. So it's moved so far to the right that even the center looks like it's suspiciously left. And I think that's really problematic.

Maher: I remember when I was on Howard Stern defending myself after September 11th. And Howard Stern said—well, I was defending my crazy comment—he said, "I think we should drop a nuclear bomb on a Muslim country. I don't care which Muslim country. It doesn't matter, just any Muslim country, just drop a nuclear bomb. Throw a dart at the map and drop a nuclear bomb." That's okay.

Miller: Now, Jackie wrote that for him. [*Laughter*]

Maher: So *you* [Ann Coulter] speak. You're grumbling over there; you're not getting to talk. This is your field. You were the one who—I think the thing you got thrown off, where was it, the *National Review* fired you for saying that we should kill more Muslims—

Coulter: Actually it was the next column.

Maher: —and convert them to Christianity.

Coulter: But that was a very popular column.

Maher: What would you say to this sort of dichotomy between Jesus being Mr. Peace and Love, and this war being so backed apparently, according to the Republicans, by Jesus. How do you reconcile that?

Coulter: I haven't heard anyone say it's backed by Jesus.

Maher: Well they seem to invoke Jesus a lot. When, really, it's a lot more Old Testament stuff that seems like we've been coming to. A lot more about "smiting evildoers" and so forth. Jesus never seemed to say anything about—

Coulter: That's true. He doesn't.

Maher: So how do they reconcile—how come Mr.–

Coulter: I have not heard anyone say we're fighting this war for Jesus. We're fighting this war because of 9/11.

Dyson: But they do invoke Christian values. And you don't have to mention Jesus specifically to talk about Christianity. As a Baptist minister myself, and this is Good Friday, I certainly feel a proximity to this issue. But the thing is, I think that the Crusades themselves—as is the contemporary crusade—are backed by an implicit reference to Jesus okaying this. And so not only do you have "patriotic correctness," you got "Christian correctness" now. Because if you're not on the right side of the war, which means that Jesus stands behind it to justify and legitimate missionaries, in the name of God, going over there. "By the way, we're going to give them some food and help them out, but if we happen to mention God and conversion from Muslim faith to Christianity, it's alright." And as a Christian minister, I find that reprehensible. Because imperialism *has* been draped not only in the flag but in the cross. And we who are Christians must stand up and be voices for those who are oppressed, and those who have been maligned, and those who are being put upon. I think that's the real role for Christians here.

Coulter: You know, this concern about George Bush referring to this as a crusade or denouncing this as some sort of crusade. I note that General Dwight Eisenhower's memoirs about World War II were called *The Crusade in Europe*. That didn't get people inflamed.

Maher: But in Europe we weren't fighting Muslims. We *did* fight a crusade against Muslims.

Coulter: It's only when we go against liberals' favorite cult, the religion of peace, that you're not allowed to talk about a crusade.

Maher: Please. You know this as well as I do: A crusade against Nazis is not the same thing as a crusade against people who we had a religious crusade against.

Coulter: It is exactly the same; it is exactly the same. They have a vicious regime and we're going to go in and change them.

Maher: The Crusades was a series of wars between Christians and Muslims.

Miller: I've got a great joke when you're done with this s–. [*Laughter*]

Dyson: There's a huge difference between politics and religion.

Coulter: We're not going to be killing people if they don't convert to Christianity. What do you think the crusades were?

Miller: This isn't a crusade, it's a jihad! [*Laughter*] That wasn't the great joke. [*Laughter*] That was a segue to try to get it back.

Dyson: There's a huge difference between politically being opposed to persons in war and in the name of religion trying to wipe out your enemy who happens to be religious—whether it's between Protestants and Catholics or, now, between Christians and Muslims. I think it's a huge difference.

Coulter: You think that's what we're doing?

Dyson: I think absolutely that's what we're doing. Look at your president, I mean, who bows his head to God, and prays to God, and says, "Because I have God's love—"

Miller: At least he's not bowing his head to watch an intern blow him. [*Laughter*]

Dyson: You know what? I ain't mad at him, either.

Miller: So what's wrong with praying, for Christ sake? The world's going to hell in a handbasket.

Maher: He was getting blown, for *Christ's* sake. [*Laughter*]

Miller: We're *praying* to get blown. [*Laughter*]

Dyson: Here's the problem. That's not what's happening. We're praying, and then we're *blowing* stuff up. That's the real problem. I think that, as a Christian minister, I believe in praying, but I'm saying what do you do—not pray, p-r-a-y, but p-r-e-y, is the problem. In the name of religion we're going over exploiting people and [saying] God's backing us up. And this is what ticks me off. People always point to the civil rights movement. "Well, Martin Luther King, Jr." Martin Luther King, Jr., did not want to make this a Christian nation. He was a Christian minister who believed that the disestablishment clause of the amendment was very critical to establishing every religion having its right to say, which means none should be officially enshrined. When the president and Rod Paige, the Secretary of Education, says that it's good to have Christian schools, the administration is really shredding that line between separation. And I think that's problematic. It shows in education, it shows in the war, and it shows across the board. So as a minister, I'm offended by that. Let's keep God out of this madness that we're doing and this militarism that we're engaging in.

Coulter: After both World War II and the Korean War we specifically sent in Christian missionaries. And we got a Christian country out of Korea–[*Laughter*]

Miller: Just trying to get tabula rasa there. Come back and get in the game. Go ahead.

Coulter: McArthur offered to convert all of Japan. That was a country that was not a Christian country that we conquered and occupied and turned into a country that is producing–is beating us in small electronics and cars now. I think that is a fine example. McArthur didn't explain that the military doesn't convert people, but he put out a call for Christian missionaries. They poured in, Bibles poured in, and now there's religious freedom in Japan. And South Korea *was* converted.

Dyson: This is what Archbishop Tutu said. He told a story. When they went to South Africa, the Christian missionaries had the Bible and the South Africans had the land. They said, "Let's pray." When they opened their eyes, the South Africans had the Bible and the Christians had the land. That's the deal. That's the history of imperialism in America.

Miller: Listen, there's a lot of troubles in the world. That's the least of it.

Maher: Speaking of crusades, I want to talk about this smoking thing because I'm going to be in New York very soon. I'm going to New York to do Broadway. Thank you very much.

Miller: You're not doing that part in *Grease* are you?

Maher: No, no, no. [*Laughter*] No, I am doing my stand-up, my one-man show.

Miller: I'm still at Governor's out on the Island. [*Laughter*]

Maher: So I'll be spending some time in New York. And I notice now that they have a smoking ban. And somebody got killed over it last week. A bouncer threw a couple of smokers out of a club and they stabbed him to death. New York is the old New York.

Miller: The biggest Lower Manhattan stabbing since Norman Mailer got Jack Henry Abbott out.

Maher: Jack Henry Abbott, right. [*Laughter*] So I'm wondering what you think of the fact that a Republican mayor is forcing upon the citizens of his city something that is pretty far from a libertarian sensibility.

Miller: Listen, I saw Bloomberg talking this week, telling people not to take SARS too seriously, which cracks me up, to say, "citizenry should not panic about SARS." But somebody having a smoke in a building four streets down is a f–ing calamity to man, you know?

Maher: What is up with that? You still smoke?

Coulter: He's a Democrat. I mean, he converted to run as Republican so he didn't have to run in the primary. He had been a Democrat his whole life and, in fact, he's as bad as I think Mark Green would have been. It's stunning that he's doing this. It's especially stunning, I think, during a very bad economy, especially for New York. I've been in New York for the last two weeks. You go around to restaurants now and they're absolutely empty. And restaurant owners come out and they point around and say, "This is unbelievable. It's killing us." And I also note–it occurred to me recently, and I don't think this is a phony point to make– it really is sort of discriminatory against poor and middle-class people in New York who don't have enormous mansions like Bloomberg where you can invite people over to have a dinner party and smoke. That's where we *entertain*–in bars and restaurants.

Miller: Isn't Bloomberg sharing that mansion with Donna Hanover still? They been able to pry her out yet? [*Laughter*]

Dyson: It makes the smokers look bad if they end up killing–"ah, it's a nicotine withdrawal or whatever"–but killing somebody for getting thrown out of a club for smoking–

Coulter: Interestingly, the bouncer's family blames the smoking ban as well. The victim's family blamed the smoking ban.

Dyson: I can understand it, but I'm saying it makes the smokers look bad. I mean, can they go outside and smoke? I don't know what the deal is.

Coulter: No, they can't, actually.

Dyson: They can't go outside and smoke?

Maher: You mentioned the bad economy. I did want to bring up the tax cut that was in the news this week. Now that the war has apparently been won, President

Bush is back to his first love, giving rich people money. People, I think, would maybe like to know the details of this. He wants a $550 billion tax cut, after the tax cut that we had already, which was $1.35 trillion. A third of the people will get nothing. Half the people will get a $100 or less. Two-thirds will get $500 or less. Two hundred and twenty-six thousand people—two hundred and twenty-six thousand—will get the same amount from the tax cut as a hundred and twenty million who make less than a $100,000 a year. So those two hundred twenty-six thousand people, they're the ones who are going to stimulate this economy. They'd better, 'cause they're getting all the money.

Miller: Might they just get a percentage back when they've paid more in? Isn't that the deal?

Maher: Well, yes they have. Of course.

Miller: So you're talking about reallocating wealth, because then we're in Sweden and we're all killing ourselves. [*Laughter*]

Maher: You know what? It's something between Sweden. We are always reallocating wealth.

Dyson: Well, it's going upward, but it's not going downward. That's the point. And I think here, you can tack onto that—that tax cut—you can tack on Bechtel, 35 million, maybe standing to make up to 600 million. We're already giving up the spoils in a post-Hussein economy. I mean, the redistribution of wealth is critical but not upward. Downward! How about trickle down? How about wash down? How about flood down? And I think this is another example, again, of [this] kind of gross insensitivity. What about those people on the front line who—they can't even get a proxy to file their taxes, and when they do, they get penalized? I'm saying to you, if we want to make the economy get stimulated, why don't we help those people who need the most stimulation? Those who don't have the cash.

Miller: These kids can't get a proxy for their tax return over there? I hadn't heard of that since the Democrats didn't let kids vote in Florida.

Maher: Really, is this going to stimulate the economy? Cause that's what it's sold as. It seems not likely. It seems like rich people who don't need the money are just going to put it in the bank.

Coulter: For one thing, to talk about tax cuts being for rich people, the rich we shall always have with us. The rich are rich. The tax cuts are for middle-class people.

Dyson: No way. No way.

Maher: How can you say that?

Coulter: Because you have to pay taxes to get a tax cut. I'm sorry about that.

Dyson: Everybody's paying taxes, though.

Miller: Will everybody make up their mind what they want me to pay, and I'll pay it. I'm just getting sick of the left telling me what a f—up I am, and then in the next breath asking me for 48 percent of my f—ed-upedness–[*Laughter*]

Dyson: I'm in there with Bush taking my money too. I understand what you're saying.

Miller: Take what you want, but get off my f—ing back already. [*Laughter*]

Maher: I've seen your house. If I had your money, I'd throw mine away.

Miller: Yeah, but you only saw it on the tour. You've really got to see it.

Maher: I loved the gift shop, by the way. [*Laughter*] Let's take some questions from our audience. We'll also go to the phones and we have some e-mails. Yes, sir, right over there. What is your question?

Question: My question is for Mr. Miller. I get the impression that you used to be more of a liberal but obviously now are more of a conservative. So if, indeed, that is true, what brought about that change?

Miller: Mislabeling Hitler brought me around. I remember I had so many friends, I'd go to New York and they'd tell me, "You know, Guiliani"–this is before Guiliani proved himself to be a pretty mensch-y guy–I used to go to New York and it looked cleaned up, and I'd say to friends, "Wow, this city's really start-ing to run right." And they'd go–"Guiliani's f—ing Hitler." And I'd go, "Really? Hitler? You think Guiliani's Adolf Hitler?" And then Ashcroft was Hitler. Then Bush was Hitler.

Maher: Everybody knows Saddam Hussein is Hitler.

Miller: Exactly. Everybody to the left–everybody's Hitler, except the foreign guy with the moustache who's throwing people into the wood chipper. You know, everybody else is Hitler–except him. We can't agree on him. So that's when I re-ally started to turn.

Maher: We all do to a degree.

Miller: I don't. I think there's only been one Hitler.

Maher: No, I mean move to the right. Because I think—remember somebody once said, if you're not a liberal or radical when you're twenty, you have no heart. And if you're still a radical when you're fifty, you have no brains. [*Laughter*]

Miller: One other reason I'm more conservative is, I'm not certain enough of my guesswork to be a liberal anymore. You have to be absolutely certain about your guesses. [*Laughter*]

Maher: We have on the line Richard, in Michigan. What is your question?

Caller: Yes, I wanted to know—Alaska has so much oil. We got a pipeline built back in '72. I wanted to know how come we're bombing Iraq and eventually conserving what we already have?

Miller: This guy's scaring the sh— out of me.

Maher: I didn't get the gist of the question, but I must say that I've heard a lot this week about how come we let them loot the museums but we guarded the oil? Let me just say, the oil *is* their treasure, a lot more than the museums. I feel bad about the museums, too, but it is kind of yesterday's news. And oil is what is going to allow this country to have a future. It *was* the right thing to guard the oil before the museums. I don't know why they couldn't have done both, but I'm much more concerned about that zoo and that lion. Throw him a steak.

Dyson: But it doesn't have to be an either/or. The reality is that what we know now as Baghdad is also Babylon back in the old days. So a sense of history, an appreciation of ancient reality that shows up in what's going on in the country, it's not either/or. It can be both/and. The oil can be protected while you're protecting these ancient manuscripts and these artifacts that imply something about our human journey. I think that's critical as well.

Miller: Seems to me that Baghdad hasn't moved from square one since they were the cradle of civilization. I mean, that was their high point, and it's been a JDS Uniphase chart since then. [*Laughter*]

Maher: Not to have a history lecture, but Baghdad was not part of ancient Mesopotamia. That came along with the Muslims, later on in the AD era.

Question: My question is, considering that we have so many people in this country now, and the catchphrase being "majority rule" for democracy, why are we still using a system as outdated as the Electoral College when every other issue is voted by majority rule—governors, mayors, city ordinances. But the president's office is left to this Electoral College.

Miller: You're right.

Dyson: Amen.

Miller: Yeah, we all agree with that.

Coulter: I wouldn't really care, as long as you know what the rules are before the election is run. But I, in fact, probably would vote to keep the Electoral College. You want different regions of the country represented.

Maher: All right, we have a call from Ann in Tennessee.

Caller: Christian missionaries going into Iraq—I want to know how the Christians in America would feel if we had the Muslims going into our schools under the pretense of teaching our children, when they were actually wanting to convert them to Muslim. That is what the ones who were taken captive, the Christian missionaries who were taken captive, that was the way they were getting to the children, to convert them to Christianity—by going under the pretense of teaching them.

Coulter: As a Christian, I can tell you we're not happy with what they're doing in the schools here right now. And it doesn't take the Muslims to do that.

Dyson: But her point is, the genius of the American system, to me, is the fact that we say, "Hey, everybody can participate because nobody can be officially enshrined." So if you're trying to get it in the back door, or in the side door, or in the front door, it's ridiculous. And I think we would feel offended if we were forced to be converted to a particular religion.

Coulter: It's not like a Christian Scientist comes to your door and gives you a pamphlet.

Maher: That's what missionaries do, whether it's in Iraq or elsewhere. They feed the poor; they take advantage of you at a moment when you're down. They come in after there's been an earthquake and they go, "Boy, your God sucks. Would you like a sandwich?" [*Laughter*] "Whoa, whoa. Who's God—who's God?"

PART VII

ANATOMY OF A CONFLICT: WHY BILL COSBY IS STILL WRONG

24

BILL PAID
Philanthropy or Social Justice?

with Debra Dickerson

My debate with Bill Cosby about the black poor has continued several years after his assault on them in a 2004 speech, and long after the 2005 publication of my book, *Is Bill Cosby Right? Or Has the Black Middle Class Lost Its Mind?* As I suggest in my debate with Debra Dickerson on C-SPAN's *Afterwords*, the purpose of my book was to offer a principled defense of the poor while answering Cosby's bitter critique of their values and behavior. Dickerson and I engaged in a vibrant exchange over Cosby's belief that the poor had brought their suffering on themselves and that they were to blame for the stalled black progress toward the goal of social equality. I argued that Cosby's lack of practice in the skill of publicly parsing the meanings of race makes him a bad candidate to examine the complex lives of the black poor. I argued also that Cosby's undeniable and incredible philanthropy is no reason for us to refrain from just criticism of his positions or to suspend the quest for a brand of social justice that will never be replaced by charity.

Debra Dickerson: *Is Bill Cosby Right, or Has the Black Middle Class Lost Its Mind?* That's quite a title. The first question's got to be: Why did you write the book? What did you hope to accomplish?

Michael Eric Dyson: Well, I wanted to write the book because when I first heard Cosby's comments—of course I realized, having been a victim myself, that your words can be taken out of context—but I was still disappointed in the level of animosity and acrimony that I think Mr. Cosby visited upon the heads of the poor. So I made comments about him that were critical in the *New York Times*. We had a chance to talk [for] about an hour-and-a-half. He sent me the entire speech. Then I was outdone. I wanted to write a book that responded to, specifically, the points he raised. Not in a general broadside, or an assault, on Mr. Cosby or what he had to say, but to pick it apart, so to speak, and look at the constituent parts and see if it made sense, both in their elements alone and in abstraction. But, more especially, as they came together to form a unit of thought that was critical of the poor. To see what was good, what was bad, what was something worth keeping and not worth keeping. So I wanted to defend, in a principled way, the perspectives and lives of those poor people over whom [we fought].

Both he and I, of course, have been poor, and you've had your struggles as well. So we come at it from different perspectives. And I wanted to put [forth] a different perspective to get a dialogue going, to get a debate going, and to engage him—rather pointedly—about the particular issues that he let loose on. And I have no romantic inclination to defend poor people as sort of recipients of God's grace in abstraction from other people who struggle similarly. But I also believe that poor people don't deserve to be hit up and deeply, profoundly assaulted without being able to have a counter voice. I don't claim to be the voice of the poor. I'm the voice of one formerly poor person whose critical engagement over the years has at least touched on many of the subjects that Mr. Cosby lighted upon that infamous night. So that's why I wanted to write my book: to spark a discussion, at least to have a countervailing argument against what he said. Because so far, it's been Bill Cosby onstage, remonstrating against the poor, without a significant and substantive dialogue from somebody else who had an equally strong opinion in the opposite direction.

Dickerson: But would you say there's been quite a lot written about it? Now we're talking about people who have access to media. But you say that he's sort of onstage alone. But hasn't there been a lot of commentary, at least, about it? I know I wrote something about it.

Dyson: Sure. You did. I read that piece. Cosby reborn as Shelby Steele, I think you said.

Dickerson: Well, it has to be read. But there's been quite a lot of talk in the black press about it. And how would you characterize that?

Dyson: I think, for the most part, it has been supportive of what Mr. Cosby had to say. Some, I think, medium modification; some argument against—some very strong. But that has been quite rare.

Dickerson: Mostly it's—

Dyson: Mostly, I think, the black press, and the black writers in the white press, have been largely supportive of Mr. Cosby, with [a notable] exception. I think William Raspberry of the *Washington Post* took issue with the tone and style of what he had to say and, consequently, some of the substance of his remarks. Others, like Clarence Page, have been extraordinarily supportive—intelligent and insightful in their defense of what Mr. Cosby had to say. And across the board—Leonard Pitts and others—even those who had picked bones of contention with small subsections of his speech have, in the main, supported what he had to say.

I was quite disappointed in the black press in that sense, and in black writers in the press, for no other reason than to maintain your authenticity and credibility as the fourth estate, the estate willing to engage people in significant and substantive dialogue. Caving in to, genuflecting before, the altar of black celebrity on the one hand, at its worst, and on the other hand simply believing that what Cosby had to say was overdue and about time: [the black press should] at least hold out the possibility that there are prevailing viewpoints that are against what he had to say or at least suggest that he could add more shade and nuance and context. I happen to believe that the substance of what he had to say was equally as opprobrious as the style he adapted to say it. However, I think that it is incumbent upon the press, even if they agree with him, to raise serious issues that might at least suggest that the countervailing viewpoint has some legitimacy. Or we should air it just for the sake of having fairness in the press.

Dickerson: But all of that drove you to write this book, though. So it's achieved that purpose, to stimulate serious discussion in the community. I mean, you've got enough of a following that I would imagine there's going to be major interest in this. One of the things I am interested in: You talk about the black press and black writers in the white press. Have you had any response from this community? The poor blacks. And I would imagine the only way that could really happen is maybe through some ministers' groups, or maybe through the hip-hop community. Is there any way to know if this conversation is even being heard by the folks who are reading the stuff?

Dyson: That's a great point. And, yes, to answer that, in some of the ways you've already mentioned: in church groups where I've preached before thousands or before hundreds. On the street when people stop me, "Yo, brother, I'm just glad you represent a different viewpoint." Even among people who might agree with some of what Cosby said but felt the tone and tenor were overwhelmingly negative. They at least admire me, or at least congratulate me, or at least suggest that I should be supported in putting forth an opinion, because there should be a lively debate and not a one-sided assault and a wallop delivered rhetorically by Mr. Cosby. And I've also had a few book signings already, about four or five, where hundreds of people have come out. I've been able to engage them at each book signing—and with people who disagree with me substantially and who defend Mr. Cosby's ability to say what he said, as well as the substance of what he said.

And I don't disagree with his ability to say so. I'm not one of these people who thought the airing of dirty laundry was an opprobrium that we had to dispense with immediately. No. I think it's very important to put stuff on the table. Because some of this not airing dirty laundry–having conversations among black people–was radically anti-democratic and didn't invite the masses of black people to the table. Intellectuals like myself, and yourself, were invited. All the leaders were invited. But in the main, [not] the masses of black people, with their cantankerous complexity and their radical diversity. There's a heterogeneous voice out there; it's not a monolithic, homogenous voice. *Even* among the poor–some of whom *agree* with what Mr. Cosby had to say. When I see the signs of those everyday people–many of them have been in support of at least having the dialogue.

Dickerson: That's a very important point. There's so many–it's going to be really hard to get to everything. You frame this in a class type of way in your subtitle: *Or Has the Black Middle Class Lost Its Mind?* But as you mentioned, but maybe in my mind didn't spend enough time with, [is] this notion that what he said would be applauded in many corners of the black community. I come from the black working class, as do you. And people I know back home have no problem [with Cosby], even when you give them the full text of the speech. I really only read the absolute full text of the speech in your book, and I have to say it was quite a speech. Especially the "God is tired of you."

Dyson: Yeah. Or the DNA card: "You're going to soon have to have a DNA card in the ghetto to determine if you're making love to your grandmother." Because, he said, "If you're twelve years old, and you have a child at thirteen, you could be [a grandmother] at twenty-six." It is a vicious kind of biological determinism in blackface–

Dickerson: I wonder if he doesn't regret the life that speech has taken on. And if he might not have chosen his words more carefully had he known that you were going to pick up on it. There's so much I want to get to. What about this notion that a lot of people in the black community–there's a lot of anger in the black community, a lot of unresolved intergroup tensions. He talked about black kids getting shot for stealing Coca-Cola or pound cake. They were likely to have stolen that from a neighborhood store.

Dyson: Oh, absolutely. Or a neighbor. Of course black people are fed up. They always are. Those who are most vulnerable to criminals are the very ones who are most outraged by their activity. That's always been the case. That those same poor black people, unlike Mr. Cosby, essentially want, when the police come to their neighborhoods, not to have a blur of stereotypes that leave them incapable of distinguishing between the criminals and them. And so often when they're reaching for their wallets, and police, with these projected stereotypes, think they're reaching for a gun, end up assaulting these people. That's the reality these people live with as well. So I would never deny that, number one. Number two, when it comes to class, black people have never been strictly about a kind of Weberian conception of class, or a straightforward sociological analysis that says, "What you make in your job is the sole determinant of class." Class has always [also] been about style. So you could be a millionaire ball player, and they say, "Oh, you're just so ghetto." Or you could be a person walking down the street, without any means, and they say, "Mmm-hmmm, she actin' seditty." Or, "Yeah, she gon' be climbing—you can tell." There's critique, there's implication, there's suggestion, there's signifying, and there's appreciation. All that comes together with black people—

Dickerson: Within the same family. Among siblings, you've got laborer, and you've got Wall Street banker.

Dyson: No doubt. In my case, prisoner, professor. And from what I understand, not simply "there but for the grace of God, go I." I also understand that there are very complex circumstances that lead people to make choices that are self-destructive or others that are creative. My talent was more easily recognized in my family earlier on in a way that allowed me to be nurtured in the womb of black celebration by teachers who identified my gift and, therefore, encouraged me. Whereas my brother didn't have nearly as smooth a path to recognize his internal genius, so to speak, and as a result of that made some self-destructive choices. Even though I believe he's innocent of the charge for which he now serves life in prison, I do know that he had some self-destructive choices along the way. So I'm not here to romanticize poor black people.

Dickerson: So let's stay there for a minute. Bill Cosby in this whole critique is not denying the existence of systemic racism and institutional racism—

Dyson: He didn't mention that in his speech.

Dickerson: But in some of the things that you quoted, because you were juxtaposing some of his earlier pronouncements—

Dyson: Sure.

Dickerson: And I found some interesting contradictions in there.

Dyson: Oh, sure. But he made those, especially, in three [places]: the *Playboy* interview of 1969; *Black History: Lost, Stolen, or Strayed?* I think in 1968 or '69, [a CBS special] which was scripted for him; and his doctoral dissertation for his Ed.D. degree, which he received in 1976. So in those three significant moments—

Dickerson: But he had a change. Listen to this. I guess this is back in the *Playboy* interview, which is 1969—

Dyson: Right.

Dickerson: "I don't think people can arbitrarily be put into neat categories of violent or nonviolent. I can tell you that I don't believe in letting black people get pushed around when they're in the right." I think that's continuity there. And another example that you use—he talks about European immigrants coming here and immediately becoming bigots. He says here, "There's no lamp"—in juxtaposing that. "The Statue of Liberty welcomes them but it doesn't welcome the man who was born here, the black man. There's no lamp lit for him, so the black man has to climb up there and light it himself." That speaks to a consistency.

Dyson: No, what that speaks to is an exceptionalism in Mr. Cosby's ideological trajectory. What do I mean by that? That this was an interview given—and something like the racial Holy Ghost got up in him, and he began to speak in many black tongues. So the point is, if you read that entire interview, it was remarkable for the intensity of its ideological commitment to, "By whatever means are necessary," for black folk to gain their freedom. And he supported a wide variety of options for black freedom, both violent and nonviolent. Now, that was an interview that was given. Mr. Cosby has never, *even* at the beginning of that interview, suggested that he would *publicly* make these statements. Now, we know that *Playboy* is a public venue. But there's a difference between print media and Mr. Cosby standing onstage alongside, say, Harry Belafonte—or later on, Danny Glover, or other figures within his own comedic, or his own thespian, community—who had made similar stances in defense of black people on a variety of fronts. Mr. Cosby has never been willing to put his face where his place is.

Dickerson: What about his CBC speech?

Dyson: His CBC speech in 1971. Even then, besides his liberal use of the n word, which is quite remarkable, and his cursing, two of the things he railed against at Jesse Jackson's forum at PUSH—"our dirty laundry gets out every day at 2:30, and it's cussing and calling each other the 'n' word"—that CBC speech was, again, quite interesting. You talk about consistency: [Cosby was] speaking about the necessity of black people supporting their own; of not blaming the Jews, or the white folks, for problems that you have to deal with on your own. So even there, there was a kind of creeping conservatism.

Dickerson: But he talked about systemic racism.

Dyson: But what you're doing [is] you're pulling at single threads in a larger fabric that Mr. Cosby has woven. What you didn't quote in the book, interestingly enough, and you might want to point to now, is where Mr. Cosby says, "Why do I have to give all the black statements? White people don't even consider me a

Negro, and that's an advantage. I like that." When he said, "Look, when a black person falls out of a chair, it's the entire race; when a white person falls out, it's an individual [act]. I'm tired of representing black people. Look, I'm not an expert on race; I'm not an expert on blackness. I will not do what the civil rights leaders demand that I do. In fact, I will not speak about race in my comedy. I believe you can bring people together by speaking about their similarities and not their differences." So what is interesting, but unknown to most people, is that Mr. Cosby has resolutely refused to step up to the plate of racial representation and take a swing at the systemic racism that he acknowledges in asides.

To be sure, he said in Detroit the other day, "We all know about systemic racism." But he moves very quickly. Wait a minute—rest there for a minute. What does that mean? How does it interplay with the demand for racial responsibility? Now, look, there have been—as you well know, given your profound understanding of black history—black leaders [who stressed responsibility] from the very beginning: Frederick Douglass, Booker T. Washington, W. E. B. Du Bois, Marcus Garvey, down to Dorothy Height, Ella Baker, Joann Robinson, Martin Luther King, Jr., Jesse Jackson, Louis Farrakhan. Black leaders worth their salt have always spoken about personal responsibility. And let's be honest, Jesse Jackson at some point and others as well have been even more pointed in their critique of black people than was Mr. Cosby that night—though not full of the same rancor and the disdain for the poor.

They have been equally as demanding of the poor, but they have always juxtaposed it to the call for responsibility of the dominant white supremacist society, or a society that practiced varieties of forms of inequality, and to the demand that it provide the opportunity for black people to maximize their good behavior. They told black people in ashrams and temples, and especially church sanctuaries, get your stuff together. "Don't tell me about the white man. Don't complain to me about what he's doing to you. You've got a responsibility to lift up the race, based upon what those people who have died for you [showed you] to do." I know, I've made that speech myself.

And at the same time, [I was] making a speech, not in fear of contradiction but in continuity with a broad ideological spectrum that says, "We can be simultaneous." So in the white situations, spaces, and places, we say, "Look, you have prevented the flourishing of a certain kind of ethical virtue that needs to flourish." And as a result of that, to paraphrase Dorothy Day, "I want to work toward a world in which it is easier for people to behave decently." Mr. Cosby's got the black self-management down. What he lacks is a corollary viewpoint that allows him to espy, upon the horizon, the reality that these obstacles and impediments that are systemic are still pervasive. And despite the fact that he, as an individual black man, probably is not subject to them in such arbitrary fashion as the masses of black people are, they nonetheless have a great impact.

So the danger of his speech is that it now reinforces beliefs, especially among the white right wing that I talk about in the book, who say, "Aha! For the first time we got a black leader to speak out." Where you been, bro? We've been speaking about this for a couple hundred years. But secondly, it reinforces, as you well know—and I write in the book—this tradition of the notion of racial self-uplift. That meant that in the nineteenth century, after Emancipation, the black elite—what I call here the black Afristocracy, the black aristocracy, folks who, by virtue of birth or good fortune or God's grace, were able to climb the ladder of upward mobility. But they had to prove to white people that they were worthy, ironically enough, of citizenship, and prove that they were human. Even to white people who could not pass the very litmus test that these black aristocrats evoked to themselves or to the black poor. But one of the ways they proved that they were worthy of that consideration is to dis them, is to degrade them, or to invite them to be integrated and assimilated into the larger circle of American values and mores.

So I think, in that sense, we have to say to Mr. Cosby, "You ain't the first person to talk about self-help." In one sense, he's a racial Johnny-come-lately, because he's refused to speak about race for forty years. I'll end by saying this. In 1985, Mr. Cosby, on the *Phil Donahue Show*, rudely and abruptly remonstrated against a woman who asked him a question about race. He says, "Look, I am not an expert on race. Why are you asking me a question as if I know something about that? Why don't you let me be a h-u-m-a-n b-e-i-n-g?" Now I'm saying, Mr. Cosby, you've not been practiced in the fine, delicate art of parsing the nuances of race in public—and it takes a certain kind of skill. Don't tell me that, "Well, what he said was said on every corner and barbershop." Well, your uncle ain't on *Nightline,* and your grandmama ain't on C-Span. So it takes a particular kind of skill. Black people are not interchangeable. What Debra Dickerson does with the word is what very few people have managed to do with the [same] force of eloquence and the rhetorical style. That takes years to develop.

So let's not pretend that what somebody on the street corner said could be as powerful and impactful as what you have done and certainly what I aspire to. So let's not pretend that blacks are interchangeable parts of expression. What black people do on the corner is great. I laugh at it. I go get my hair cut at the barber shop and sit up there and just crack up. But I know that, in one sense, the self-taught, the autodidact, always is broad in terms of shooting at subjects but not necessarily very deep in peeling back the layers of analysis that need to be heard. And I think, in that case, Mr. Cosby is like that crotchety old uncle who got a bull horn and, God bless him, it's a very difficult thing to abide such shallow analysis and stereotypical thinking. And the irony is, Mr. Cosby has worked brilliantly and generously in his career to oppose stereotype. But on that fateful day, May 17, 2004, he capitulated with a gravitas that still resounds and, of course, provoked me to write my book.

Dickerson: Please take a sip of water. I'm thirsty just listening to that. I guess there are a couple of major areas in which I have a problem with your analysis. One of them is: Bill Cosby never claimed to be saying something new. And anybody who said that he was saying something new was just either very dumb or had some political purpose. You talk about that a lot.

Dyson: A lot of people said that.

Dickerson: Well, they're dumb, and they need to be educated. They're wrong and they need to be brought up to date.

Dyson: Well, I confirmed the latter, that they need to be educated. I don't know if they're dumb.

Dickerson: Yeah, that's probably willful. And this notion that he's a racial Johnny-come-lately, I'm very troubled by this. He's—what is he, seventy-some odd?

Dyson: Sixty-seven.

Dickerson: He doesn't have to fight the race war the way you would fight it. And I'm interested in your willingness to critique his approach to his art. He said—and Bernie Mac said something very, very similar, when the networks pitted Damon Wayans and Bernie Mac against each other in a time slot, Damon Wayans tried to start this thing, "Let's get together. They're not going to do this to the black people." And Bernie Mac was, like, "I'm an artist, and we're competing, and we're not going to approach this this way. I'm not gonna do that. There's this crutch. Either I'm funny or I'm not funny." Bill Cosby is saying the same thing: "Either I'm funny or I'm not funny." And to this notion of using race as a crutch, you may disagree with it, but how can you feel so secure in telling him that that's wrong? Because he wasn't the kind of racial leader that you wanted him to be back in the day, now he can't be any kind of a leader.

Dyson: No, no, no. And if I believed that, you'd be absolutely right. But that's not what I believe. It's a misstatement of my perception. Look, this is what I think. First of all, Cosby's comedic genius is extraordinary. But don't overlook the fact, and don't neglect to tell the people, that he began to experiment early on with being Dick Gregory. And we're using a code word here because he said, "I don't want to use race as a crutch. I want to get rid of race." Because somebody came to him and said, "Look, brother, if you had to get rid of race tomorrow, you'd never be funny." Which was a tremendous challenge to him, and he took it up, although it was a rocky road finding his own comedic voice. But he began, and the *New York Times* took notice of him, as a kind of young, angry Dick Gregory. We know Dick Gregory came along and had the broadest white audience imaginable. [He] shifted from his comedy as social critique, to social critique as comedy. By the end of the '60s Dick Gregory had basically given up being primarily a comedian and had become a social analyst who used comedy. And by his own words he admitted that.

Cosby initially wanted to be Dick Gregory, but he found his own voice—like we all do when we're young, trying to find ourselves by finding other people first and then discovering our own voice ultimately. So he was taken notice of by the *New York Times*; [they noted] his own kind of angry, acrimonious, internal racial jokes that he then gave up on because he wanted to find who Bill Cosby was. That's beautiful. I don't have an argument against that. I think Bill Cosby has done improvisational comedy that borrows from jazz in a way that has been remarkable, both for the passionate intensity with which he pursued his craft and for the length that he's been able to sustain himself in American society. Right now he can fill audiences of people who come to see his comedy. I don't have a problem with that. I don't even have a problem, as I say in the book, with Mr. Cosby making certain choices about the kind of comedy he preferred. That is to say, unlike Richard Pryor after him and Dick Gregory before him, he chose to be race neutral. That's fine.

I'm saying that when you've made those kinds of choices—and partly what it has to do with is refusing to "contaminate" your comedy with color consciousness—and then you begin to make statements about race, when you have had no practice—my point and bone of contention with him is not the modus vivendi he adopted to express his comedic genius. My problem is [Cosby] not having the skills of practice over forty years. If you are Richard Pryor, you've been talking about race a long time. If you're a Dick Gregory, you've been speaking about race a long time. You've got those kinds of skills. I'm a public intellectual, and an author, and a scholar. If I got up tomorrow trying to be a comedian, I haven't developed those kinds of skills—even though some people think I'm unintentionally funny.

Dickerson: But the CBC wouldn't invite you to address their convention if you tried to become a comedian tomorrow. The folk who did the *Brown v. Board* event [where Cosby spoke] wouldn't invite you to entertain at that as a comedian. They invited him because of the person that he is. And the audience applauded.

Dyson: And they were giving him an award, he and Mrs. Cosby, for the extraordinary generosity they've expressed over the years. That's great. He got up and gave a statement, a kind of off-the-cuff rant, about poor people. They expected him to give a little typical speech—"Thank you very much, we appreciate it, we've got a long way to go," and so forth. And as the brilliant comedian he is, and as the powerful, disturbing figure he is, he threw a pebble into the water whose ripples continue to be felt. So I have no problem with that. The problem is when you begin to speak about things that you don't have a significant, substantive grasp of. I'm saying he's not practiced, not that [he should] agree with me.

In other words, it could have been Thomas Sowell, although he's a scholar and not a comedian. It could have been Dennis Miller. Dennis Miller, who's very conservative at this point, but a well-spoken person, who's gone through his own particular positions and thought about them in ways that are substantive because he's been trying to confront public policy for the last decade. I'm suggesting to you that the issues about which Mr. Cosby spoke that night—he is not practiced in, either in his comedic armature, so to speak, and neither has he been publicly speaking about these issues. So I'm suggesting to you that the lack of practice in engaging these issues in a complex and substantive fashion is my problem. Not me trying to announce to Mr. Cosby what's appropriate and inappropriate for him to speak about. God forbid. Because I don't want him to try to tell me what kinds of books to write.

Dickerson: That's a really good point. Why don't we pick that up after the break.

Dyson: Alright.

[Break]

Dickerson: Your last point was an extremely good one. And I have to say, I didn't get that from the book. When you talk about him being a Johnny-come-lately I thought you were saying, "You can't start talking now. You had to have been making comments all the way along." If that's your argument, that's a much more sustainable argument. You know, but—

Dyson: I'm talking about the practice, the skill, the ability—when it could have counted for black people, when your face could have shown up on the front line. This is what people usually say to me in response, "Well, look, the man has given millions upon millions of dollars." There is no question about that. Even though I do have a footnote in there about the philanthocracy—the rule, reign, and tyranny of those who give huge amounts of money that, therefore, squeeze the possibility of dissent. And in this case I think that's very true. I think that Cosby's philanthropy, and his world-historical, Hegelian, Brobdingnagian—let's join Jonathan Swift and George Hegel here together—presence in the culture bestriding, like a colossus, both sides of the racial divide. This man is just huge to take on and it's hard to even talk about him in a negative fashion—and understandably so, because he's been so good and positive and powerful for the issues that many find resonant in the culture. On the other hand, we can't allow Mr. Cosby's philanthropy to silence us if we disagree with him. And I'm saying—

Dickerson: But I think that's a misinterpretation.

Dyson: No, people say that to me directly.

Dickerson: But the reason the philanthropy is raised is to say that this is a person who does care. He's not just sitting back and saying, "Oh, I hate poor black people–"

Dyson: Right, right.

Dickerson: One of the best points you make in the book was one of the simplest. When you talked about Shaquille, Condoleezza, and Keyshawn–

Dyson: And Oprah.

Dickerson: Oprah. And you talk about the consumerism. And I need to read more about–because that's a prevailing belief, about the $200 sneakers and all that sort of thing.

Dyson: Yeah, he called them $500 [sneakers], but they're $250, but we knew what he meant. And he said, "They don't buy *Hooked on Phonics*." They do buy *Hooked on Ebonics,* he believes. But *Hooked on Phonics,* of course, has been proven not to do what it claims to do. So maybe those black–

Dickerson: But that's–

Dyson: Wait a moment now–

Dickerson: He's talking about education. He's talking about going the extra mile for your kids. He just used *Hooked on Phonics* as an example.

Dyson: Oh. His mama went the extra mile for his education.

Dickerson: Absolutely. She did.

Dyson: So wait a minute. So let's assume people talkin' 'bout yo' mama. And if they talkin' 'bout yo' mama, they talkin' about a whole bunch of poor black people. Most poor black people I know go the extra mile for their children. And this is my point about Mr. Cosby: he is so deeply adrift in stereotypes that he fails to see the complex specificity of poor people's lives. Most poor people I have encountered–and I continue to encounter them in many and various forums, as I'm sure he does–most of these poor people want the right thing for their kids. They want [them] to speak the King's English to the Queen's taste. They want their kids to speak better than they do. Now, that's one thing to say, and let's be honest about it: You don't start by attacking anti-intellectualism by looking at Snoop or Shaquille or Bey-Bey or Man-Man or Versace or Lexus or whatever interesting consumer product after which black people nominate their kids. The point is, start at the White House. We have a president, in office, whose bum-fumbling, idiotic, idiosyncratic expression defies literacy at a high level, and certainly it is a quite conscious choice, made by Karl Rove et al, to suggest that Mr. Bush is a hail-fellow-well-met, everyday man with whom you could have a beer—

Dickerson: But—

Dyson: Let me finish. And as a result of that, he obscures his own privilege by pretending he didn't go to Harvard and Yale, and he plays up this kind of dum-dum mentality when anti-intellectualism is writ large across his face.

Dickerson: He cares about the black community. He doesn't care about George Bush. He's trying to make a difference in the black community.

Dyson: I'm grateful for that. But I'm saying—you said a critical word: care. You know, if somebody comes up to you and just reads you up and down the riot act, and calls you out of your name, and disagrees with you because your book said *The End of Blackness*, "and you're now trying to be a tool for the white man," you know, that's simplistic. You have a complex argument in your book. Even though I disagree with many elements of it, I understand, first of all, your command of the language itself demands attention. And even if one disagrees with the substance of your facts, you're putting forth a viewpoint that has to be encountered. And we have to presume your intelligence in order to acknowledge your argument, in order to engage it. Now, I'm telling you, Cosby ain't having much care and compassion for these people when he's talking about how people name their kids. That ain't none of your business, first of all, 'cause you ain't in they crib paying child support. Step out of their business. Number two, in terms of consumer culture, let me see—Mr. Cosby sold Jell-O, Ford, Coca-Cola, E. F. Hutton—

Dickerson: That was another good point.

Dyson: So let me finish. So my point is, here's a man who's been a supreme pitch-man for American corporate capitalism, who has been in the business of creating artificial desire in people—desires they're not born with—to have consumer products that they have perhaps overspent [for], and out of greed, reached for, that he helped create. *Now* he is going to malign the people who have fallen in line with the very desire he has helped to artificially create? *Now*? If he came along now, with those expensive sweaters he had—you couldn't find those at Target or J.C. Penny. You have to have some know-how to know how to spell that Italian designer, whoever he was, to do that. So my point is that Mr. Cosby, at that level, is just being disingenuous. Because now, had he come along, he might have been selling Reebok or Nike or some other product. Or some rims that spin like Sprewell's mind.

Dickerson: You call it his blame the poor tour.

Dyson: Yes.

Dickerson: Where did he go? Where were his stops? What is he saying? Has there been a change in his rhetoric?

Dyson: Well, he's gone to some places like Cleveland—he had to cancel Cleveland, actually, because the allegations that are against him were lodged on the same day he was scheduled to go to Cleveland. But he's been to Detroit—he's been to maybe six or seven cities. Most recently he was in Dallas, Texas. And, no, he's not changed his tune. In fact, he's reinforced it. He's dug his heels in. He's fallen back on his haunches and said, "I am going to reassert the validity of my initial opinion." Now it would be different if Cosby said this, "You know what? I had a few drinks that night; went off on poor people. Dadgum. You know, sometimes you just get frustrated." Because, let's be honest, the kind of talk he shared that night, some people probably have said that—some poor people who are mad at other poor relatives in their own house. So I would never be a hypocrite about Mr. Cosby. But the point is, context is critical. And if he made it in public, he could have said, "You know what? I'm so sorry. Yeah, I might've felt this way. I felt that way at the moment, and maybe there's some legitimacy to what I said, but the approach I had is so devastating that it disallowed people to respond in dignity." Look, if you make a criticism of somebody, leave them a ledge upon which to stand, to respond with human dignity to improve themselves. But if your criticism is so devastating that it wipes out the ledge upon which they can stand to dignifiedly respond to you, then you've not done something constructive; you've done something destructive. And my argument with Mr. Cosby is that—have you heard the speech? I have. The bitterness—

Dickerson: I've only read it.

Dyson: Reading it is like reading C. L. Franklin's sermons. It's one thing to hear, "You better not fight the Lord, umh, humh. 'Cause if you try to fight the Lord, er uhh, the worms will get you." Uh, "You better not fight the law-w-w-d. Because if you try to fight the Law-w-w-wd, the w-o-o-r-r-ms will get you." Now it's very different reading that and hearing that. That wasn't C. L. Franklin; actually that was C. A. W. Clark. But the point is, it's like reading a sermon in the black tradition: you just missing the point. And when you hear Cosby's bitterness, the tone of voice, the condescension, the virulent disdain, one cannot help but conclude that this man is not compassionately engaged in loving these people. He has what

Barack Obama has called an "empathy deficit." He has a lack of critical compassion for these people at this point.

And this speech has resounded so profoundly in the culture because it reinforces prevailing stereotypes and vicious beliefs about who poor people are. And I say to Mr. Cosby, they're so much more complex than that. Yes, they be messing up. Yes, they're doing things. But if you claim that poor black people are the ones who have let us down in this movement—no, blame us, blame the upper middle class. Blame the black middle class. Blame those Negroes who get into high places and then sit there and close the door behind them on other people. Blame those black people who sit on the Supreme Court. See, Pookie might steal your car. But Pookie ain't gonna write a judgment against you to affect the lives of millions of black people with one stroke of his pen. Condoleezza is doing much more damage than Sheneneh.

Dickerson: This is one of my major problems with some of the animating logic behind the book. This notion that it's obvious what the common good is. And Clarence Thomas is ipso facto wrong. Condoleezza Rice is ipso facto wrong.

Dyson: No, I'm looking at their behavior. I'm not saying [they're wrong] a priori—if we're going to sling around some Latin words—goin' in the doe'. I'm [not] saying we don't give them a chance—

Dickerson: I'm saying, they have their politics. And you don't accept that their politics are authentically black.

Dyson: Oh, they're authentically black. They are authentically corrupted in terms of progressive politics for me.

Dickerson: So they have the wrong politics.

Dyson: No, no. They have politics with which I disagree. I don't say that they're inauthentic. Clarence Thomas is a black man. Condoleezza Rice is a black woman. I don't debate their authenticity as black people. They can be authentically black; they could be authentically wrong.

Dickerson: But you're saying that their politics are antithetical to the common good of black people.

Dyson: To the common good of black people.

Dickerson: This is a major problem here.

Dyson: I'm looking at what they have done, not what I think that they done ideologically.

Dickerson: People disagree. He has different politics from you. She has different politics from you. You can't determine what's good and bad for black people. You have your opinion—

Dyson: Oh, sure, I do. Let me tell you what. I have the responsibility to point out what I think is edifying and helpful and that which is destructive and not conducive to argument and leadership. Let me tell you something. I wrote a book on Martin Luther King, Jr., that *many* black people found *reprehensible*. Came up to me—

Dickerson: I gave you a positive review. And I know you checked it out.

Dyson: You certainly did. You know what? I appreciate you for that. And so the thing is, is that people say, "Look, you did the white man's job for him." I am used to taking heat for being willing to go against the grain. So you're not talking to a person here who buys, and toes, the line that's politically correct. I'm saying to you that I'm not arguing that Clarence Thomas and Condoleezza Rice, a priori, have politics that are so corrupted that they're incapable of being authentically black. I'm saying they're authentically black. She's from Alabama. He's from Pin Point, Georgia—wherever he's from. And they are as authentically black as cornbread and collard greens. The problem is that, like some soul food, they have a high salt content that raises the blood pressure of the body politic of black people. Now, I'm saying to you that Clarence Thomas and Condoleezza Rice, because of my analysis of the product of their politics, have been antithetical to the best interests of black people. I have the right to say that. Because I don't believe in this kind of unified black front, or black solidarity, that says: "It is because of our skin color that we must be brought together."

I believe in the moral substance of one's identity. I have more in common with Ruth Bader Ginsberg, and I have the right to say I forge connection with her. I leave behind skin nationalism and bowing at the altar of black political reality that is predicated upon pigment. I don't worship at the epidermis level. I worship at the epistemological, that is, the knowledge base. I worship at the level of the ethical: "What is the basis of what you're doing? Is it destructive or constructive?" King said: "It's not black versus white; it's right versus wrong." I've got to make a decision about what I think is right or wrong. I at least have to do that as a human being and as a public intellectual.

Dickerson: But the point I'm making—let's take another example. The way you analyze *The Cosby Show*, again, I find problematic. What was not black about *The Cosby Show*?

Dyson: I didn't say *The Cosby Show* wasn't black. Listen here. And I quoted Henry Louis Gates—it's interesting, why don't you use his quote there? Early Gates, 1989.

Dickerson: 'Cause I pick my own quotes.

Dyson: I ain't mad at you, know what I'm saying? But let's just be representative in the quotation department. That's your right; you the host! What's interesting is that Gates said there, in 1989 in the *New York Times,* that one of the negative consequences of *The Cosby Show*—he praised it, I praised it. I wrote a piece on Cosby around the same time, praising him for that show. Most of it was glowing praise. And so I don't have a beef with *The Cosby Show* qua *The Cosby Show*. But the undeniable consequence, as Gates pointed out, could be that many white people thought that the Huxtables represented most black people and, therefore, now it's about what you're willing to do as an individual black person to get over in society and to lift yourself up by your bootstraps. And so Gates says—and I agree with him—that it then redounds negatively on most black people because it makes it appear that when we fail to succeed, it is because of the lack of individual initiative versus the ongoing structural impediments and obstacles that are in place. And all he was arguing is that *The Cosby Show* reinforced that viewpoint. And I agree with him. I think *The Cosby Show* was incredibly important—and resonating and signifying. But it also had this other side. Why can't we have complexity and recognition of that?

And what's interesting to me is that when people step to me [*sic*] and say, "Hey, you're being kind of critical of Bill Cosby. Are you attacking him?" And I say, "Did you listen to the speech?" Very few people are willing to admit that Cosby assaulted and attacked the poor. If the black middle class wants to be self-critical—not critical of black people who are poor, but self-critical—[it should detail] the five biggest faults of the black middle class. What are the internal demons that we have to expunge in our own experience that need to be addressed? Could Mr. Cosby have stepped to that podium and done something brave? Not pick on the poor and defenseless and vulnerable, but pick on somebody his own size. Harry Belafonte went on the *Larry King* show—whether you agree with him or not—and called Colin Powell out. He used some rather rough and tough and straightforward language, and some people thought it was offensive. I understand. But the point is, he took on somebody his own size. Could Cosby have gone up against them?

And let me make a stronger point. Cosby has refused over his career to speak nearly as powerfully, directly, venomously, and viciously against white supremacy, social injustice, and economic inequality as he has against poor black people. That was my argument. Forty years you haven't spoken about race, and then the first opportunity you have, you use one of the brightest spotlights in the culture, which extends across the media and, indeed, around the globe, to assault poor people in a way that reinforces the enemies of those poor black people rather than lifting them up? Let me tell you what Jesse Jackson told me once. He said, "When you're in a ditch, you're either going to get a shovel or a rope. The shovel will dig you deeper; the rope will allow you to be pulled out." I think that Mr. Cosby threw down a shovel. I'm trying to let down a rope.

Dickerson: I think, then, the purpose of this show today should be dedicated to the proposition of bringing you and Mr. Cosby together. Because I continue to believe that we're all on the same side and that he was speaking off the cuff. I don't know the man. I've never met him. But I'd be willing to bet he regrets that speech. There's no way he thought it through. He thought he was in the barbershop, because he was at a fiftieth anniversary for *Brown v. Board.* Having read the full text I don't think I actually want to hear it. But having read it, I know it's a pretty rough thing. And I'm almost positive he regrets it. So, Mr. Cosby, if you're watching, we need to get y'all together—

Dyson: I would love to.

Dickerson: —to talk about these issues.

Dyson: I don't think he wants to, though. I don't think Mr. Cosby is interested in dialogue. I think he's interested in thundering down from the pulpit in apodictic statements, speaking ex cathedra like the Pope of Blackness—

Dickerson: But he's been reminded—

Dyson: Why would he change his mind? You said he's regretful. Why does he go out on tour and reinforce what he said? And he says, "Not only did I talk about dirty laundry, your dirty laundry gets out every day at 2:30 and is calling each other the 'N' word and it's cursing." When I show that *he* cursed and called black people the "n" word—it was fine for him, because he was exempt from that same moral purview that now castigates and casts aspersions against black people.

Dickerson: I think he was using the "n" word in that instance for effect.

Dyson: Wait a minute, now. Tell me P. Diddy or Nas or Jay-Z or 2Pac haven't used it for effect.

Dickerson: He was basically saying, you all are members of Congress, but you're "niggers" when you leave here.

Dyson: Right. And you know what? His ability to say "nigga"—and he didn't say "nigger," the white supremacist epithet hurled with lethal intensity—he said "nigga."

Dickerson: We didn't say that back then.

Dyson: Look, we've been making a difference since the field slave days, when the slaves—

Dickerson: I've been pronouncing it wrong.

Dyson: No, no, no. They've been making a distinction between "the field nigga" and "the house nigga," and using the word "nigga" to suggest to them that there were some people who were down with the master and some people who were down with the people. As Malcolm X said, the "house nigger" would just pray for the wind to cease, and the "field nigger" would say—

Dickerson: That's a little oversimplified.

Dyson: Of course it is.

Dickerson: Doctoral dissertations have been written on that—

Dyson: No doubt. But all I'm saying to you is, he did say "nigga," and let's deal with that.

Dickerson: And this is good. This controversy is good. And I think that somebody's got to go the distance and make it okay for Mr. Cosby. This is my opinion about Clarence Thomas. We have *no* relationship with this man because of our attacks on him. So I think he marches off in a much more conservative way than he wants to because we have no relationship—

Dyson: Make a safe space? "Oh poor black millionaire and oh poor black Supreme Court Justice, without any recourse or ability to engage."

Dickerson: They're human beings who're afraid to go out to a black gathering.

Dyson: Oh, my God. Well, imagine how [Cosby and Thomas] have rendered those poor black people who are afraid to show up anywhere because of the vicious context and consequences of [their] words. Shame on [them].

Dickerson: So let's make it so Bill Cosby can't go anywhere black. That would fix something.

Dyson: He's not afraid of that. Not at all. You know what? I would love to debate Mr. Cosby. Do you think Mr. Cosby would actually want to debate me? I don't mean me individually. I'm saying to have a conversation and dialogue.

Dickerson: I've read your book. He's not a dialogue—

Dyson: I would love to have a dialogue. I don't have to debate him. I want to dialogue with him.

Dickerson: What we're all concerned about here is the black community.

Dyson: Oh, no question about it.

Dickerson: And there's got to be mutual ground, and places to come together. You made some points that he can't refute. You made some points that can be refuted. I think it could be done [with] Jesse Jackson. Let's go back to *The Cosby Show*. You said, not in speaking of *The Cosby Show*, but in your book, you wrote, "He has flatly refused to deal with blackness and color in his comedy." And then you go on to say, "Cosby was defensive, even defiant, in his views, as prickly a racial avoider as one might imagine for a man who traded so brilliantly on dimensions of black culture in his comedy." How can both of those things be true?

Dyson: Oh, here's how. You can have the substance of the reality without acknowledging it in public. That's what I'm saying, is—

Dickerson: But if you're black, you're black—

Dyson: You just said that blackness was complex, and difficult, and diffuse, and not monolithic. We can't have it both ways. It's not like if you're black, you're black, and a priori blackness is understood instantly by everybody. That's not true. Because people have different regions and—

Dickerson: It was on, for what, ten seasons?

Dyson: Eight seasons.

Dickerson: It was [on] every week, for eight seasons.

Dyson: All I'm saying to you is that you can trade brilliantly on blackness and, at the same time, not acknowledge the source of that blackness. Or give some consideration in public to the virtue and the complexity of what that blackness is all about.

Dickerson: How can you say that he didn't do that every week on *The Cosby Show*? Or with *The Cosby Kids*? I remember the fact that he had that Harvard professor, Alvin—

Dyson: Alvin Poussaint.

Dickerson: Poussaint. I found the show to be a little tedious sometimes. Because they put so much effort into making everything be so racially—

Dyson: Correct.

Dickerson: Correct. Well, I remember one show where, specifically, Denise went to ask the boy—

Dyson: Theo.

Dickerson: —Theo, for help with a math question. And I remember reading that Dr. Poussaint said, "See, because that's showing—"

Dyson: Right.

Dickerson: So how can you say that's not black?

Dyson: Well, listen, I'll tell you what—

Dickerson: —that he's trading on it. I think these are irreconcilable: Brilliant on dimensions of black culture—

Dyson: That's not what I'm saying. I'm saying to you that Mr. Cosby's refusal to take on race head-on was a result of his own politics of race, his refusal to acknowledge blackness in an explicit fashion. Of course it was implied. Of course it was signified in the Varnette Honeywood art on the wall. On the [anti-]apartheid [sign in Theo's room], for which he gave a great stand. He said, "If that [anti-] apartheid sign has to come down, I'm going to stop doing the show." He took principled stands in defense of his conception of blackness. All I'm arguing, again: his blackness is inferential. It's implicit. It's not explicit. I'm not judging him for that.

But I'm saying, *now*, why are you being explicit about racial politics and your assault on the poor? Why not be inferential and implicit to the same degree that you were in deploying the ingenious elements of blackness in your art before? That's where the contradiction that *you* fail to point to exists. I'm not demeaning Mr. Cosby for his approach. I'm saying your approach is inconsistent. And the reason you're willing to break *faith* with it in regard to poor black people is because there is the vulnerability of the poor and the ability to make *them* the *heel* and the *butt* of all of our animus, our insecurity.

And our venomous assault on the poor represents, in the final analysis, such a lack of compassion that we are giving up the incredible analytical acuity that we have generated over a couple of centuries now in deference to our ability to feel good about ourselves as upper-middle-class black people, just to be able to assault [the poor]. And I think that's problematic. I'm not arguing with Cosby about his ability to present blackness in the fashion he finds most comfortable. I'm suggesting: do it the same way with the poor black people as you do it with the middle-class black people and the upper-middle-class black people. Do it by inference. Do it by implication. Do it by signification. If you break faith with that, we have a right to ask as to the reason for the disjuncture between past history and present practice. That's all I'm saying.

Dickerson: You mentioned Chris Rock, very quickly and positively in the book. Do you have a positive impression of Chris Rock?

Dyson: Oh, absolutely.

Dickerson: There's a difference in—

Dyson: Oh sure, and here's the difference—and I'm glad you asked that. The difference is, Chris Rock is doing a comedy routine when he says, "I love black people but niggas gotta go." And black people got that, in terms of the signifying. But here's the beauty of Chris Rock: Chris Rock is both within "Bring the Pain"—that comedic routine—and later, with his most recent comedic routine, skewer[ing] white society with equal intensity as he does the internal contradictions of blackness. You see, ultimately Mr. Cosby doesn't like the newer black comedians because they are willing to engage in what I term "edifying irreverence." I think the point of art is not simply to coddle people, to make them feel good. You oughta be in somebody's face sometimes. You ought to challenge them. Real art should be independent. You have a responsibility as a writer not simply to embrace, but to embrace with a kind of critical edge, to force us to think in new and fresh ways about issues that have been sitting on the shelf for so long.

Dickerson: I disagree that I have to do that. I think that you can write for *Reader's Digest* if you want to. Again, I think you're denying him the legitimacy of his own artistic choice.

Dyson: No, no, no. I'm saying to you that one of the functions of art is not simply to embrace and to pacify. It's also to prick and to raise consciousness.

Dickerson: Not everybody has to do that.

Dyson: Of course not. And I'm not saying every artist should do it. I'm just suggesting you be consistent when you want to do it for purposes that you think are redemptive within your race, for upper-middle-class and black people, and to defend your modus operandi when it comes to race. And then, when we call you to account, when we call you to responsibility—your favorite thing, Mr. Cosby—

about why you have chosen to leave aside a forty-year history of how you've dealt with race, to now do it differently–Debra, that's my job to ask why you've made that decision.

Dickerson: That's a good point. I think the other good point you made is–

Dyson: Well, thank God I got at least two of them.

Dickerson: –I think maybe your best point–because this is a hobby-horse of mine, so you know everything sounds brilliant if you agree with it–

Dyson: Absolutely.

Dickerson: –is this notion of intergenerational conflict. And I think that's been a huge failing of the civil rights generation. And I'm a forty-six-year-old person–

Dyson: We're the same age. You just look better.

Dickerson: I have a hard time with the piercings and the baggy pants–

Dyson: That's cool.

Dickerson: –and all that stuff. But that's the future. And I do think there is an extent to which Mr. Cosby–I think I have a lot of sympathy for him because he's sixty-eight years old, he thought the race was going to be won now–

Dyson: I hear you. Look at all the empathy you have. This is beautiful. And I feel the same way. But look at this. The sympathy, the empathy, the love we feel for him–all we're asking him [is to] use that sympathy for poor young people. When Tupac says, "Somebody wake me, I'm dreaming, I started as a seed, the semen, swimming upstream, planted in the womb while screaming / On the top was my Pops, my Mama hollering stop, from a single drop this is what they got? / Not to disrespect my people but my Poppa was a loser, only plan he had for Mama was to f– her and abuse her / And even as a seed I could see his plan for me, stranded on welfare, another broken family." *Listen to that,* Mr. Cosby. That's a cry for help. That's from the belly of angst. That's an anxiety that is more deeply pathological and incredibly powerful.

Dickerson: You don't think he feels that?

Dyson: Listen to the speech when he dismisses all these young people. "With names like Shaliqua and Taliqua and Muhammad, and all that crap–and all of 'em are in jail." No, I don't think he feels that. I think what he feels–

Dickerson: I think he does. I think so many of us—

Dyson: —I think he has a tremendous disdain for hip-hop that has blinded him to any possibility of—

Dickerson: —I think so many of us can see that in him, whether we're wrong or right. I think that's why so many of us in the black chattering class have defended him.

Dyson: But you've got to project it on to him. You know what you're doing now? You're doing a faith leap. You're doing leaps of faith. You're saying, "In the absence of textual evidence we're asserting the Spirit's presence."

Dickerson: Textual evidence?

Dyson: Textual evidence, empirical evidence. He didn't say it.

Dickerson: So the words should be taken at face value?

Dyson: No, no, no. The words should be spoken, and the action should be consistent with the words that have been spoken. I'm talking about textuality in the postmodern sense *and* the literal sense. I'm saying to you, there ain't no empirical evidence to substantiate your claim. You've got a Kierkegaardian leap of faith going on here. And I'm saying to you, I'm from Missouri—your state—"Show me."

Dickerson: Well, on that note, we should probably leave things where they lay, and hopefully there'll be some opportunity for Mr. Cosby to, not back off from his words, necessarily, because that's not a position that leaves him face. But maybe he would like to recapitulate them. So hopefully, if that opportunity presents itself, I hope you'll—

Dyson: Without question.

Dickerson: —take each other up on it.

Dyson: You know why? Because I love him as a man, as a human being, and as a great figure in our community. I don't have personal animus against him. This is a principled disagreement between two black men who love black people, who have differing views about the route to racial redemption.

25

RESPONSI*BILL*ITY
Cosby's Conservative Turn

with Shelby Steele; moderated by Ted Koppel

Bill Cosby's insistence that personal responsibility is the magic key to unlock the future of the poor flies in the face of everything we know about how poverty is caused by low wages, dramatic shifts in the economy, chronic underemployment, job and capital flight, downsizing, outsourcing, and crumbling inner-city schools. And as evident here in the arguments of Hoover Institution intellectual Shelby Steele, Cosby's views square easily with the ideas of conservatives who deny the structural forces that clearly shape the lives of the black poor. As I point out in my debate with Steele—carried out on *Nightline*, hosted by Ted Koppel—it's one thing to say that personal responsibility is crucial to our survival, but it's another to pretend that it's the only, or most important, thing that matters.

Ted Koppel: And joining me now, Michael Eric Dyson. He's the author of the recently published book *Is Bill Cosby Right?* He is a professor of humanities at the University of Pennsylvania. And Shelby Steele, a research fellow at the Hoover Institution, who specializes in the study of race relations, multiculturalism, and affirmative action. Michael, let me, if I may, begin with you, since you were more critical of what Bill Cosby had to say. The essence of your criticism is what?

Michael Eric Dyson: Obviously, all of us want to talk about social responsibility and personal responsibility. I think that the speech Mr. Cosby gave could have been repeated effortlessly in numbers of sanctuaries, temples, mosques, synagogues, and wherever other black people gather to concentrate on their ethical, and their moral, propriety. But the point is that he emphasized, or overemphasized, personal responsibility to the exclusion of looking at a society that disallows the flourishing of that personal responsibility. We're not against people taking care of their children; people dealing with their own educational status; people looking for upward mobility. The question is, how do we account for concentrated effects of poverty? People are not poor because they simply want to be poor. Most of them don't want to be poor. And it's not simply self-destructive behavior that leads to concentrated poverty.

Koppel: Let me interrupt you because I'd like to get Shelby Steele in on this conversation, too. Basically, I find it hard to disagree with anything that Michael has said, Shelby, because he's simply saying the responsibility is broader than simply what Bill Cosby was talking about. But then, I didn't get the impression that Mr. Cosby was attempting to be all-inclusive.

Shelby Steele: No. I think the whole phenomenon that Cosby's comments generated came precisely because personal responsibility, individual responsibility, was the sort of, the elephant in the living room that everybody for the last forty years has been looking away from. And we've been looking so much at social responsibility and at the responsibility of the larger society, white America, to reach out and make things better for black America that we have ignored entirely— we've made it a taboo to use the words "black" and "responsibility" in the same breath. And I think that's the sort of furor that Cosby ignited. He said we can literally go no further without personal and individual responsibility, quite apart from whether or not the larger society intervenes on our behalf.

Koppel: Michael—

Steele: And I think he's right.

Koppel: I must say, Michael, it just seems to me that those who were listening to the speech seemed to get it. There was, as I say, the laughter of recognition. There was applause throughout the speech. People understood what was being said. And if I say to you, I can't imagine that Bill Cosby thought he was summarizing everything that has caused the tragedies that we find in our inner cities today, but was simply pointing out there's an element that isn't getting the proper attention, would you still disagree as much?

Dyson: Sure. I think that's a straw argument. I don't think that I have to either believe that Mr. Cosby was summarizing social theory over the last fifty years or that he was focusing on something that had been neglected. I disagree with Shelby. I think that if you go to any church on any given Sunday morning or to a sanctuary on Wednesday night Bible study, you will see the emphasis, and reemphasis, upon personal responsibility: "Don't tell me about the white man. Don't tell me about your momma. Don't tell me about what your children did or did not do. You be front and center accountable for your own lives."

Koppel: Let me get in a word just for a second because it's too good an opportunity. What you're talking about *defines* preaching to the choir. We're not talking about the folks who are in church listening to that message. We're talking about folks who aren't going to church.

Dyson: But look Ted, he wasn't speaking to the poor people. He was speaking to upwardly mobile black people who were gathered there. Had he been interested in getting the message out beyond the choir, to the people who needed to hear it, he would have had to [have] gone on-site to those communities which are poor. And he would have heard some raucous agreement and disagreement. So I'm not denying the necessity for that. I'm just simply saying to you, Cosby wasn't speaking to the poor. He was speaking for those other black people who are outraged by what they consider to be the ethical lapses of the poor. And Ted—

Koppel: I'm trying to keep the time a little bit equal here. So, Shelby, come on in.

Steele: Well, I think there's another truth here. And I think that the real mistake, not by my lights but mistake probably by Michael's lights, that Cosby made is that he said these things in ways that white America could hear them; could hear a famous, well-off black man asking black people to be responsible for their lives. And the one thing that we know is in black America, we are asked by our leadership to constantly wear a mask which says that white people are responsible. And if you ask black people to be responsible, you're blaming the victim. And so, we never let white people see us talk about responsibility in relation to ourselves. Cosby crossed that line. And when white people begin to hear it, when white people hear something, we become accountable to it. And so, what Cosby did was make us accountable to larger America for being more responsible. And that's the problem that he got into.

Koppel: Michael hold on—

Steele: And others of us have made that same mistake and have paid for it. And I'm glad to see Cosby sort of join this issue.

Koppel: It is an interesting point, one that cries for a response, which you, Michael, will have a chance to give in just a moment. But first, we have to take a break.

[*Commercial break*]

Koppel: And I'm back with Shelby Steele and Michael Eric Dyson. Before the break, Michael, Shelby was saying it's not so much *what* Bill Cosby said but that he said it in a forum which could be heard by white Americans.

Dyson: Well, I disagree with that. Look, I have myself washed dirty laundry in public. I wrote a book on Martin Luther King, Jr., that, besides calling him the greatest American who ever lived, talked about promiscuity and plagiarism. So, I am used to black people who were offended by my reach into the politically incorrect territory of black self-reflection. What I'm suggesting here to Shelby is that this is not the first time that white folk have heard black folk talk to each other about personal responsibility. What Shelby misses is that many of the themes and accents that Mr. Cosby underscored were borrowed from white America. What I'm telling you is that Mr. Cosby, in one sense, reinforced the very right-wing conservative values that have assaulted the integrity and the individuality of African American people who are poor. You see, white America that is conservative wants to emphasize personal and individual responsibility when it's to their advantage. But they impose *group* identity on African American people when it comes to reinforcing certain biases and prejudices. If we really allowed people to be treated as individuals in America, then we would have a broadening of the understanding of what it takes. We can never correlate class status and moral achievement.

Koppel: Shelby, you have to jump in here. If you wait for Michael to take a breath, you're gonna be waiting all evening. Go ahead.

Steele: Yeah. I'm trying to be polite here. But look, the point remains, Michael, that in America, whites are threatened with being stigmatized as racist if *they* say something to the effect that blacks should be more responsible. Blacks who say this kind of thing as Cosby did are going to be immediately called black conservatives and right-wingers and so forth. And so we have this repression that both races observe and live by that has kept us from saying the simple truth, which is that you cannot get out of poverty unless you take an enormous amount of personal responsibility for doing so, even if you were the victim of racial oppression. Being a victim does not spare you—

Dyson: But I don't think that's—

Steele: Let me finish, Michael. Being the victim, and suffering, does not spare you from responsibility. In fact, responsibility is one's greatest hope for overcoming poverty in the United States.

Koppel: Let me if I—

Steele: My point is, we need to get to the place where we put this repression aside. We stop calling each other names, naming things right wing and left wing. The fact of the matter is, in the human condition, responsibility is power. And it's the last thing in the world we ought to be hiding from black Americans.

Koppel: Hold on one second, if you would. Let me make an observation. And, Michael, let me begin with you. I'd like to propose that it shouldn't be either/or. It can be both. What Bill Cosby had to say has resonance, has truth to it. But it doesn't, I think, as I said at the outset, presume to be a reflection of the entire picture. Why can't it be that *and* all the other things that you have referred to?

Dyson: It certainly can be, Ted. What I'm suggesting is that Mr. Cosby, in his own emphasis and overemphasis on personal responsibility, to the exclusion of understanding the structural and the social, has neglected a wise lesson of judicious black leaders who have always—and intellectuals—who have always emphasized the fact that you *cannot* live in a society where you are prohibited from enjoying the fruits of your labor as a group and then, therefore, be expected that your individual responsibility will overcome those barriers. It can be both/and. It's simply the fact that Mr. Cosby—

Steele: That's where we disagree.

Dyson: But Mr. Cosby was so bitter and acrimonious and vicious and name-calling, the very thing that we think we should avoid, it couldn't be helped but believed that it was part of a centuries-old tradition of the black elite looking down their noses and being embarrassed and ashamed by black people. As opposed to holding upper-middle-class black people responsible. When Mr. Cosby said, the poor are the ones who have let the civil rights movement down, I disagree. It is people like me, black middle-class and upper-middle-class black people, who have gotten into the door, gotten into the room, closed the door behind them, [and] refused to reach out and to help those who are poorer than they are. And felt that their own success was due to their individual effort and not the collective enterprise of the struggle for black freedom in this country. That's why it's both/and.

Koppel: Shelby, you get the last word.

Steele: Thank you. I think the problem is the fact that almost all racial policy since the 1960s has been designed to have larger America give things—whether welfare or affirmative action or whatever—to blacks, and has failed, absolutely, to *ask* anything in return. Why do young people get a preference to a university and that preference is not contingent on performance? Basically, America has said to us, "There's no amount of failure that's too much. We will just give and give and give." Everybody in America, blacks and whites, knows that what Cosby said is absolutely true: the only hope for black America is individual responsibility. Responsibility *is* opportunity. And because you have suffered—we have to get over this idea—because you have suffered does not in any way mean that you're spared from opportunity. In fact, it unfairly gives you a heavier burden of responsibility. That's the existential reality in which black Americans live. And black Americans who take responsibility thrive in this society.

Koppel: Somebody had to have the last word. Shelby Steele, you've just had it. Michael Eric Dyson, thank you. Shelby, thank you also.

26

SHOCK (JOCK) THERAPY?
Bills of Right

with Bill O'Reilly

I have appeared on Bill O'Reilly's cable talk show, *The O'Reilly Factor*, several times, and despite our sometimes heated debates, I have always maintained cordial relations with him. In this debate, O'Reilly and I explore Cosby's beliefs about the black poor. But what may be most surprising is that, while O'Reilly sides with Cosby's ideas, he also questions why Cosby refuses to come on his show to share his interpretation of the black poor. In the end, O'Reilly is not sure that Cosby's intent is to help, rather than scold, the poor. Even if we concede Cosby's desire to help the poor, I think there is little doubt that his harsh methods and ill-informed approach will do little to relieve the vulnerable of their suffering.

Bill O'Reilly: "Back of the Book" segment tonight. Comedian Bill Cosby being sued for some alleged misbehavior. We don't care much about that, as all celebrities are targets these days. But Cosby's campaign to confront misbehavior within the African American community is of great interest. With us now is Michael Eric Dyson, the author of the new book, *Is Bill Cosby Right? Has the Black Middle Class Lost Its Mind?* Dr. Dyson also teaches at the University of Pennsylvania. Now, you've been a critic of Cosby's. What's your main objection?

Michael Eric Dyson: Well, a couple of things. First of all, nobody denies the necessity for responsibility. I'm a Baptist preacher. We preach it every Sunday. So that's not the point. The point is: Mr. Cosby distorted the way in which black people who are poor operate. There are vicious stereotypes, I think, in his own mind that cluttered his own imagination about how they can respond ably to their condition, number one, and, number two, what they can do about it. My second problem with Mr. Cosby is that he's unwilling to acknowledge that there's any virtue in the lives these people live. So if you beat them up for how their parents named them, that's not their fault. What are they going to do? Secondly, we should get over the bigotry. Oprah is unusually named. Shaquille O'Neal is unusually named. But if we love the person, we accept the name. I think the black middle class has historically always waged war against poor people. And Mr. Cosby is part of a long history. That's why, in my book, I discuss the racial uplift doctrine of the nineteenth century, where what I call the Afristocracy, the ruling elite of black America, tended to look down on their poorer brothers and sisters because they wouldn't adapt themselves to the whiter world.

O'Reilly: Okay. But what you see as looking down some might see as his challenge.

Dyson: Sure.

O'Reilly: His challenge to ask African Americans to reject out-of-wedlock birth—

Dyson: Right.

O'Reilly: —reject drug use, profanity—

Dyson: Yes. Yes.

O'Reilly: —Gangsta rap.

Dyson: All the things you've mentioned, absolutely right. And most black people—I would wager 95 percent of black people—say absolutely right. So the question is, why is Mr. Cosby being viewed as kind of a moral hero to black America when, first of all, he knows better than to suggest that most black Americans don't embrace those values? And number two, even among the poor themselves, the deep, inherent conservatism, morally speaking, of those black communities, even when they're politically progressive, is often underannounced.

Number three, here's the interesting part: Mr. Cosby for most of his career has disavowed the necessity for being explicit about race. He says, "Look, I'm a racial healer. But I don't speak about race. I'm not an expert on blackness." All of a sudden, after forty years of an extraordinary career, Mr. Cosby has now remonstrated against poor people without having a great deal of [balance]. Every great black leader we know, from Frederick Douglass to Marcus Garvey to Martin Luther King, Jr., down to Jesse Jackson, has always said: "Get on your game, stop blaming anybody but yourself." But at the same time they talked about impediments and obstacles in the broader society that we have to hold *them* responsible for, as well.

O'Reilly: He might be just doing shock therapy. Just listen to me. He might—look, it's obvious that the carrot and the stick approach has been mixed. Some blacks get the message, some don't. Would you agree?

Dyson: Yes. Some people agree. Some people don't.

O'Reilly: He's using shock therapy. He's Dr. Huxtable who everybody thought was this kindly grandfather–

Dyson: Right.

O'Reilly: –now getting in your face, saying, "Look, you have got to stop yelling obscenities. You've got to support your babies. You have got to stop the nonsense." Maybe there is some value to that. Why do African Americans have to be coddled?

Dyson: They don't have to be coddled. Here's the point: You can say that to a whole class of people. Not just the poor black people.

O'Reilly: That's his cause, though.

Dyson: But look at this: there are a whole bunch of people who are rich in this country. What's Paris Hilton's excuse? What is the excuse of people who are rich, who have money, who have means, who have made moral mistakes? The point is: not only the poor are the ones who are messing up.

O'Reilly: But that's his target group.

Dyson: Of course.

O'Reilly: I think the guy is sincere in wanting to help people. You don't think he's sincere?

Dyson: Of course. But here's the point: I think he's sincerely wrong in his approach. I think his substance is wrong–and his approach. But let's just say you thought his substance was right. If you beat on somebody and call them names, Bill, what business does Bill Cosby have to do with some kid being named Shaliqua and Taliqua or Muhammad? Shaquille O'Neal is a great superstar. Oprah is one of the great beloved figures of American society. Condoleezza–that ain't no regular black name. Her mother made it up when she heard a musical signature on her score. So my point is: let's not have the bigotry and violence and bias directed against poor black people who are already vulnerable. Let's lift them up. Jesse Jackson said something. I'm sure you'd appreciate this: "When you're in a ditch, do you want a shovel to dig you deeper or do you want a rope to dig you out?" I think Mr. Cosby has thrown down a shovel.

O'Reilly: I disagree with you. I think he's given them a rope. But it's not a kind rope. He's saying–

Dyson: It's a noose then. If it's a rope that's not kind, it's a noose.

O'Reilly: I said to you, Doctor, I can't get a handle on Cosby. I can't. I have asked him fifteen times to come in here. He won't. He is obviously afraid to come in. I can't get a handle on him. You could be right. I'm hoping you're not. I'm hoping he's sincere and not trying to denigrate poor people. But anyway, your book is very provocative. Doctor, it's always a pleasure to see you. Thanks for coming in here.

Dyson: Thanks for having me.

27

POOR EXCUSE
Cosby and the Politics of Disgust

with Damian Bruce

In this dialogue with writer Damian Bruce, I explore at length my intellectual and political disagreements with Cosby. Initially slated to appear as an interview in *Sister 2 Sister* magazine, our encounter never saw the light of print. Bruce's questions elicited substantive responses from me that detail my resistance to Cosby's haphazard formulations about poverty and his tragic mischaracterizations of the black poor.

Damian Bruce: How did you first hear about Mr. Cosby's comments?

Michael Eric Dyson: Well, a reporter, Felicia Lee, called me from the *New York Times* and sought comment from me on Mr. Cosby's controversial comments. We discussed them. She read a few of them to me, and then I responded that I thought Mr. Cosby's comments were elitist, that they were rooted in generational warfare, and that they would do little more than hamper the quest for a solid and secure expression of black humanity in the larger white world. And then she put those comments in a story she did in the immediate aftermath of Mr. Cosby's speech at the NAACP. And after I made commentary on his remarks for my slot on Tavis Smiley's *NPR* show, I had the occasion to speak to Mr. Cosby.

Bruce: What were the circumstances?

Dyson: Well, we were talking about his comments.

Bruce: I mean, on the phone or in person?

Dyson: Oh, yeah, on the phone.

Bruce: You called him or—?

Dyson: I reached out to him, and he returned my call. And we spoke for an hour and twenty minutes. And it was a very genial and cordial conversation. And Mr. Cosby expressed to me his beliefs about poor black people and the problems we confront in our community. And his passion and his disgust in varying degrees were quite apparent. And when he told me that his wife believed that he was being a bit harsh about the poor, I saw that as an opening to suggest an alternative perspective and to forge solidarity with her by agreeing with her sentiments, while at the same time trying to strike out at the issue that vexed both me and Mr. Cosby. He then suggested—and he had his publicist, David Brokaw, on the phone with us during the entire conversation—that I hadn't heard his entire remarks. So he sent me both written and audio copies of his remarks. And when I received them, I knew immediately that I would have to make a sustained effort to respond to Mr. Cosby's comments, because I felt that they broadly generalized the condition of the black poor. They fatally mischaracterized the complex conditions that [the poor] confront. They viciously assault the integrity of the lives of poor black people.

And furthermore, I felt that his comments would have a deleterious effect on a conversation in America that needs to take place about the poor, but without the blinders of bigotry that often keep us from seeing them in their full and contradictory humanity.

Bruce: Right. And simplistic?

Dyson: Yeah, yeah. Well, it was severely simplistic. And I think, for all of its simplistic nature, it was also widely influential. And that's a dangerous combination.

Bruce: Now, all along, from the first call from the *Times* reporter to this conversation with Mr. Cosby, had you had a visceral reaction to this—or all along was this simply an intellectual response where you just needed to set the record straight?

Dyson: Well, I'm sure it was a bit of both. You know, obviously I have an intellectual disagreement with Mr. Cosby about how the poor have been characterized, and about how we've got to delve into the extraordinary amount of work that has been done by scholars, thinkers, critics, social analysts, and other commentators over the years—especially in the last twenty-five years—that has marked a significant change in how we comprehend the complex and contradictory lives of the poor, especially in this case, the black poor. So I felt that his comments dishonored that work, and willfully ignored the difficult circumstances that poor black people must confront in order to negotiate their way in life.

Bruce: Has he really? I mean, he is from North Philly. You're in Philly. You know how bad North Philly continues to be. I'm from Philadelphia.

Dyson: Right. Well, it is a willful ignorance of the scholarship that has been done. It takes more than growing up in North Philly to understand what's going on in North Philly. It takes more than me growing up poor and black in Detroit to understand what's going on in Detroit. Because I experienced it doesn't necessarily mean I can explain it.

Bruce: Point taken.

Dyson: Which is one of my recurring themes, especially when it comes to celebrity commentary on black life: whether positive or negative, whether edifying or degrading, it takes more than an experience with a particular circumstance to completely unpack its contents and skillfully examine what lies within. So, for me, it's crucial to have a personal, and even an existential, relationship to a terrain that one might study. That's very important indeed. But it takes more than that. That's a necessary condition, perhaps, of understanding, but it's not a sufficient condition, as the philosophers would say.

Bruce: I agree. Because we're talking about fifty years ago, pre-crack, they were gang warring with zip guns and so forth. It's a whole different thing.

Dyson: Exactly. And if you don't pay attention to that, you're going to miss some of the nuances and complexities of black poor life. And you're going to discount the fact that when Mr. Cosby—who's sixty-seven years old—was poor, that's different than a person like me who was poor, and I'm forty-six years old. And it's certainly different than those who are poor now. And as you've said, [they face] the political economy of crack, the devastation unleashed on our communities when crack gangs began to distribute this rock-like substance of cocaine that altered the terms of relationship between the older and younger blacks, and between those who were attempting to be gainfully employed and those who were closed out of the legitimate economy, and therefore sought a livelihood in the underground economy. And then you compound all of that with the shift from manufacturing to service industries in America, where black people, who were working poor, who were made even poorer because they no longer had access to low-skilled, high-wage jobs that prevailed when the steel industry was at its height and when the automobile industry was flourishing. So those jobs all but disappeared, creating an enormously difficult economic situation, where the bottom fell out for those in the legitimate economy, making those who were their children, or peers, much more vulnerable to an illicit life of crime, to an underground economy that could generate sufficient capital to provide sustenance for one's family. So when you put all that stuff together, it's much more complex than the simplistic nostrums that Mr. Cosby offered.

Bruce: You've written ten books in ten years. Was this simply another opportunity for you to continue exploring, or was this something that really hit hard at you?

Dyson: Well, it was both. Certainly I'm motivated in my work to try to explain as clearly and eloquently as possible the convergence of simultaneous truths in black life. By which I mean that truth is not serial to me. It's simultaneous. In serial versions of truth, one thing is true until something else comes along to displace that. Then that's true. No. Truth is simultaneous to me. That means stuff that is contradictory and conflicting can be true at the same time. You can believe in your mind that O. J. was guilty, and you can also believe that Mark Fuhrman tried to frame a guilty man. That's complex truth. You can believe at the same time that Michael Jackson should be held accountable for his own particular behavior, and at the same time understand that a racist white D.A. could pursue him with a vigor that he would never display for other potential criminals. So truth is simultaneous to me. And in that sense, in my books I attempt to get at the complex simultaneity of truth in black life which always avoids simplistic and reductionist arguments, on the one hand, that thrive on stereotype. Or on the other hand, it seeks to avoid the romantic edification and uncritical celebration of black life. It's a critical engagement that establishes the basis for black virtue while also relentlessly pursuing black vice. And those things that are helpful and those things that are destructive at the same time have to be engaged.

And in my books—in this book on Cosby, and in my book on *Pride: The Seven Deadly Sins*—I try to make clear the basis for understanding and comprehending black culture in a way that does honor to those who argue that black culture is complex. You have to look at it from within and from outside. You've got to examine it from multiple perspectives at the same time. And you've got to have a kind of principled humility in the face of black life. You can't assume, because you were born black, you know everything about black culture. You have to have enough self-regard for the race to take seriously the obligation to study as rigorously and vigorously as you can the conditions under which black people have existed and continue to exist, and the intellectual and spiritual and moral themes that have occupied them over our history.

Bruce: I'm glad you mentioned about being born black because that's a good segue for me to ask you, what is—if it can be defined—authentically black?

Dyson: Well, that's a complex issue. Authenticity depends upon who's defining it and what constitutes the authentic in your particular philosophy. For me, authenticity is not necessarily a positive or negative thing. Somebody can be authentically black and just authentically terrible. Authenticity never resolves the prior ethical dilemma that one must decide whether a version of blackness is not only real but valuable and worthy of emulation, or if it should be subject to criticism.

The things we think are terrible about black life—that we must acknowledge don't contribute to our uplift or, furthermore, undermine our determination to live as nobly as possible—could be authentic, but they're authentically horrible. And we've got to do something about them. So the quest for authenticity, while an understandable preoccupation, especially in this younger generation where the "keep it real" mantra rings with deadly consequence, sometimes, in our postindustrial urban centers called ghettos and slums, is not one that they plucked out of a cultural vacuum. They pulled it out of the trick bag of race in America where white supremacists had tried to tell us for so long what was authentically black. And in the white supremacist mind, what was authentically black was clear: the vision of blackness as dumb, and backward, and savage, and volatile, and violent, and anti-intellectual, and incapable of having moral beauty.

Bruce: Sounds like Nat Turner. The same time you had Nat Turner, you had Frederick Douglass. And you had Marcus Garvey, you had Father Divine. You have the NAACP, you have MOVE.

Dyson: Well, no question. That's the depth, the breadth, the height, and the full measure of our blackness. But the point is that when you think about black authenticity, the white supremacist tried to tell us what was black and we tried to resist that, because you begin with a stereotype. A stereotype is the lazy person's way of engaging the other. But what black people did is combat these vicious stereotypes and the quest for black authenticity by putting forth our own archetypes. We said, "No, we're going to define for ourselves what's positive, what's powerful, what's black." But it became obsessed in a couple of ways.

First of all, it became obsessed with the positive versus the negative. Then it became obsessed with the edifying and the beautiful that was linked primarily to what we thought was appropriately black, and therefore authentically black. And that usually ended up being a class-divided definition. Because the poor black got excluded from what we thought was positive and what we thought was authentic. Now, the obsession with the positive is problematic because certain things that we think are positive may be good for some and terrible for others. There's a huge debate now raging about whether gay or lesbian people have a rightful spot at the table of black identity and black politics. And for people who are in black churches, it's negative to talk about homosexuality and lesbianism. And yet those are our brothers and sisters. So to resort to positive-versus-negative never resolves the moral dilemmas that we confront.

And finally, we move from an archetype, because we exclude ranges of poor black people, while others—the pimp, the mack, the ho'—become celebrated in the antitype, which is the third type of quest for authentic blackness. Now, advocates of the antitype say, "We're going to go against type." And that's not just all the pimps and the hoes and the hustlers and so on; it's also, ironically enough, those who are gay and lesbian, those who believe in black irreverence—that is, they're going to transgress against the received norms of blackness. So there's quite a space in that irreverent antitype. But the point is that the quest for black authenticity unleashes these quests, unleashes these different stages of blackness—the stereotype, the archetype, and the antitype. And for me, then, the question of authenticity never resolves the ultimate question that lies behind it, which is the question of whether or not we're going to have simplistic-versus-complex versions of blackness. Not positive-versus-negative. And when we have simplistic-versus-complex, what that means, then, is we're willing to say that even when stuff doesn't look positive to some black people, it might have a very powerful long-term effect.

For instance, some black people didn't think it was positive that Martin Luther King, Jr., went into communities trying to open them up beyond their segregated history. They said, "Look, we get along with the white folk. He's doing a negative thing." So positive-versus-negative can never ultimately address the dilemmas of blackness in a satisfying way. And only when we have notions of complex blackness versus simplistic notions of blackness can we get anywhere. I happen to believe that what Mr. Cosby did on that fateful night was a simplistic version of blackness. I'm trying to put forth a complex version of blackness.

Bruce: In Cosby's speech, when he says that poor black people don't know anything about Africa, isn't he overlooking how when they name their children, [names like] Shaniqua, that they are, on their own, trying to make a connection? Even when you look at the film *Rise,* you see the way these kids are dancing and painting their faces, [and compare it] with [the] footage from Africa, with young black males almost doing the same thing—painting their faces, and even the kind of dance movements they're doing. There's a connection.

Dyson: Exactly. David LaChapelle's film, *Rise,* highlights a specific kind of dancing that their inventors call "Krumping." It grows out of L.A. street culture. A cat named Tommy Johnson, known as "Tommy the Clown," developed a unique dance form, which he called "Clowning," in response to the 1992 L.A. riots, as an aesthetic form of highly skilled, athletically charged, speed-driven movement viewed as an alternative to gang warfare. One set of movements exchanged for the other, so to speak. "Clowning" morphed into "Krumping," and it definitely draws on African tribal rituals.

I think what you're raising is very important. And that's why I argue at length with Mr. Cosby on this issue in particular in my book. Because black naming practices, again, are complex. Let's not have a simplistic version of black naming practices that Mr. Cosby had, where he said, for instance, that you name your kids "Shaniqua, Taliqua, Muhammad and all that crap. And all of 'em are in jail." So now this simplistic assault on poor black people happens to reinforce some of the most vicious stereotypes of white supremacist culture. In essence, what Mr.

Cosby did that night, in parts of the speech, was to legitimate white supremacist discourse and racist rhetoric about poor black people. But he gave it a sheen of authenticity and a glimmer of appeal because it came through a black throat and tongue. I think that's why it's especially destructive, and why it is necessary for Mr. Cosby to be vigorously opposed.

Now, when we take the issue of naming that you brought up—black people from the very beginning have had problems with naming. As you've already pointed out, Africans from the very beginning, who were enslaved in America, attempted to resist the authority of the plantation owners' naming them, and the overseer's calling them, by their European Christian American names by maintaining their African names in private. So they would answer to their European Christian names in public, but in private, among themselves, they would maintain the African name that they were given by their parents. Number two, Africans attempted also to resist dominant white culture's assault upon them by giving them vicious names, for instance, names of donkeys, like Postilian and Jumper and Bossy. And they also signified on black intelligence and morality. For instance, if they thought black people were especially dumb, they'd give them the name of Plato or Aristotle to just be ironic. And then, on the other hand, if they thought they were especially promiscuous—and how hypocritical was that given the fact that white men had unlimited access to black women's erotic treasures—they would give a black female the name Diana, as in Diana the Love Goddess. So the point is that white folk misnamed us constantly. And any attempt of black people to control their self-naming is an attempt to resist the forces of white supremacy. Mr. Cosby ignores that.

Thirdly, even now, with the trend to have these "pseudo-sounding African names," as you've already indicated—at least it is an attempt to take back, syllable by syllable, the priority of self-naming and governing one's identity with the names we give. So, fourthly, it is hypocritical for us to not understand that the struggle over naming has gone on from the very beginning. This is not the first generation, by the way, to name their kids after Alize and Moet and other consumer products. We did it earlier—Eldorado and Cadillac. We did it earlier than that with Hershey Bar and Cremola and Listerine. Black folk always name their kids after stuff they want and can't have: Lexus, Mercedes, Good Loving! Whatever it turns out to be.

And finally, how hypocritical of us to ignore the fact that those black people who are using these so-called pseudo-African names to take back their dignity have logic in their use. We unfairly demand of them, "You don't even know what your children's name means, so therefore give them a name that means something." Most of us, when we're named with American names, don't know what the heck they even mean. I don't know if my mother knew that Michael meant "one who is like God," or Eric meant "great," when she named me. You know, most of us name our kids after events, people, situations, and circumstances that we love and admire. That's what Africans have always done. If your name is Akua, your name is Wednesday. If you named your kid, back during slavery, Sambo—now it's been, of course, transformed into something negative because of an overseer who made it an epithet—but Sambo was simply the second born son of the Hausa. So when you look at the traits of African identity and the way they have been communicated and expressed through the rituals of naming, and the attempt to be self-governing and self-determining by choosing the names we give to our children—all of that is so much more complex than what Mr. Cosby made it.

And I'll end here by saying, on this point, that look at people who have unusual names, like Oprah. Oprah was the misspelling and the mispronunciation of Orpah in the Bible. And yet she has risen to an unprecedented height for a black woman in America. Look at Keyshawn Johnson, a great athlete. Look at Shaquille O'Neill. You know, Cosby ain't going to say nothing to him, because he will say, "I will beat you down and then score forty points after that." Or, my God, Condoleezza Rice. Where did that name come from? I'll tell you where it came from. Her mother, like Dr. Rice herself, was an extraordinary musician, and she loved the Italian musical signature *con dolcezza*, which means "with tenderness" or "with sweetness." That's how she named Condoleezza. That's like naming your kid *Adagio,* or "a slow tempo."

So the point is, that's what Africans do—take stuff we like, and then name our kids after it. Seasons, time of the year, the day of week, the month of the year. This is all part and parcel of what Africans have done. And, truly, when Gwyneth Paltrow names her daughter Apple, or when Miss Hilton's parents name her Paris, or when white folk name their kids Brandy—what's the difference in us naming our kids Chardonnay? So the point is that we have to have linguistic tolerance and moral patience, and a huge bit of humility to understand that poor black people have tapped into some complex characteristics of African identity that we need to study more than attack. And I think Mr. Cosby got caught out there on the branch of bigotry without having tapped into the deep and profound roots of wisdom that he needs to study.

Bruce: Speaking of names, this is another perfect segue, because family, friends, and mentors are very important to the readership of *Sister 2 Sister* and to myself as well. Along with many others, two names come to mind that I'd like to ask you about—Mr. and Mrs. Everett and Addie Dyson. Are they still with us?

Dyson: Everett Dyson, Sr., died in 1981, at sixty-six years old, a hard-working, incredibly industrious, diligent man from whom I have inherited my work ethic. And Addie Mae Dyson grew up very poor on a farm in Alabama, the youngest of five children, the daughter of people who were formally uneducated. And my mother picked cotton. She is a noble, beautiful, intelligent woman who, with my father, fearlessly reared five boys in the inner city of Detroit and who, by virtue of her keen intelligence and profound wisdom, transmitted these values to me as well. They shaped the person I am. As you mentioned, there were also other figures, mentors, who influenced me, many of whom my parents provided me the chance to meet. Those figures were extremely important in, of course, making me who I am. Like my pastor, Dr. Frederick Sampson, who had unquestionably the greatest influence on me of any person that I have ever met. Martin Luther King, Jr., and Malcolm X, and another man, Kenneth Cockrel, who was a radical black lawyer in Detroit, whose oratorical ability and whose penetrating analytical acuity made me want to use words as weapons in defense of the vulnerable.

And then there were my teachers in Sunday school and my teachers in elementary school, especially Mrs. James, my fifth-grade teacher, who was enormously influential because she taught us black history at a time—in the fifth grade, in 1968, in a segregated school in Detroit—when even the black teachers questioned the value of her sharing our history with us. She taught us about the great figures and forces in our community. And it is because of her that I have a love of black history and an appreciation for the pride and dignity and self-esteem, as well as the self-critique and the self-examination, that are critical to black communities and peoples. Then there were my junior high school teachers—Mr. Burdette, who first encouraged me to explore my oratorical skills through the Detroit Optimist Club oratorical contest, where I wrote my first speech at eleven and delivered it at twelve, so he set me on that road. Mrs. Click was my typing teacher who influenced my values a great deal, and Ms. Stewart was my seventh grade English teacher, who also took an interest in my development. They were all very important.

And then, after that, of course, there were my teachers in high school—Madame Black, who taught me French and so much more, because her husband was an intellectual who gave me a sense of what one could achieve with the life of the mind. And Mrs. Sutton, my English teacher, gave me a sense of the essay and the virtues of writing, and Mr. Cleveland gave us a sense of both the literary and practical dimensions of drama and debate. All of these people have been enormously influential in shaping my psyche, in molding my persona, and in giving me a sense of what black people who were on the quest for excellence could reasonably achieve.

Bruce: So you're standing on the shoulders of people whom you knew, some inspiration from the greats of some earlier era.

Dyson: Oh, there's no question I'm standing on the shoulders of those who were powerful and insightful, as well as the examples of those who Mr. Cosby insulted—the working poor and black poor. Not simply because I come from them. My father worked for thirty-three years, until he was laid off. And then, refusing to go on welfare, started a business—the "Dyson & Sons Grass Cutting and Sodding" business. And we also hustled on the streets—we painted houses, we collected steel and took it down to the city, in downtown Detroit, to weigh it and get money. He was a hustler in the finest and most noble sense of that word, and he taught me to hustle in the same way. That is, to do whatever it took to support one's family. In our case, it was quite legal. And no job was too low and no aspiration was too high in order to fulfill our obligation as men and as black folk who loved our families. And that model continues to gleam for me. But there were so many other working poor people that I observed growing up in Detroit, that to answer the second part of your question posed a few questions ago [about what drove my Cosby book]: it was not only intellectual, it was also existential. It was personal for me because I knew that Mr. Cosby was slighting the incredible work ethic and the enormous diligence of those whose efforts remain invisible to all but the most careful and conscientious chronicler.

Bruce: Which, of course, continues today as you make plain in your book. There's still the working poor. They're still working below a real living wage, but they're working! We see them going to jail, and we see them with the plastic hairnets, and all that stuff, but that's just the media's imagery.

Dyson: Oh, of course. And that's a very good point. Many of the people about whom Mr. Cosby spoke that night are working. They are not lazy. They are not without a work ethic. They are not without the desire to do the right thing. Many of them find their work crushing. And many of them are crushed by a desire to work but can't find reasonable work that will allow them to provide for their families. I mean, these processes of the American political economy have been documented in book after book. And not just dense academic treatises, but readily available *New York Times* best sellers. Like *The Working Poor* by David Shipley. And Barbara Ehrenreich's book, that was on the *New York Times* best seller list for a long time, *Nickel and Dimed*. So the point is that Mr. Cosby had access to this literature that would have told him that it's not a matter of failing to take personal responsibility as to why most people are poor. It is the structural features of the American political economy, the concentration effects of poverty.

And poverty has to do with the reason some billboards promote higher nicotine cigarettes, or liquor ads are in poor black communities but not in rich white communities—or black ones, for that matter. It's why wealthier white and black kids come in from suburbia to try to get their "drink on" by going to the local liquor stores which dot the landscape of our communities like churches do. So it's about having a lack of political power to keep eyesores out of your community or zoning laws that allow broken-down edifices and horrible houses to occupy your community. And then it's the downsizing and outsourcing and the capital flight, and the loss of nearly eight million jobs in the manufacturing industry. The exploitation of indigenous workers in foreign lands who will work far beneath a minimum wage as corporations flee the cities of our country in search of cheap labor and tax breaks on foreign soil. So when you put all that stuff together, you have a much different picture of the poor.

Plus, when you're poor, you can't afford a washing machine. So you try to go to the laundry to get your clothes clean. But some people can't even afford the transportation cost to get to the laundry, so they get these rent-to-buy machines that are so costly. And yet, they're not cost effective. But more people are caught betwixt and between. They don't have a ride to the grocery store, so they have to ride with somebody else by giving them money. They can't take public transportation to do their most necessary deeds socially. So the thing is, when you put all that stuff together, the plight and predicament of poor people makes them so vulnerable—and they're buffeted by all these economic and social forces. Of course, personal responsibility is critical; good behavior is its own reward, because it gives you a sense of doing the right thing in the world. And most poor black people we know behave right. But good behavior will not address all of the other factors that keep people poor and that make them poor to begin with. And this, again, is an obnoxious consequence of Mr. Cosby's unfortunate focus on personal responsibility to the exclusion of all of these structural features which reinforce poverty.

Bruce: You've been stating facts quite clearly. I'm going to go into the realm of opinion for just a moment. Of course that could be dicey—no pun intended. But Cosby's—as you characterized it—bash the poor tour—

Dyson: Blame the poor tour.

Bruce: I'm sorry. Blame the poor tour. As I understand it, from what I've been reading, his audiences have largely been poor and working—

Dyson: Absolutely, they have been present, although by no means exclusively. So that contradicts your characterization of them, Mr. Cosby! If the poor were all the stuff you said—not interested in self-help, not interested in becoming better, not interested in getting some help—why the hell are they coming out to see you? I'll tell you why. Because they are not who you say they are. As T. D. Jakes said in a sermon, years ago, before he became famous, "You might have done what they said you did, but you're not who they say you are." And Mr. Cosby is finding the fruitful, fleshly contradiction of his ideas about the poor at every stop he makes along his blame the poor tour. These people are hungry, even desperate, for a way out of their circumstances and conditions. They are already self-critical. They're critical of black-on-black crime. They're critical of people who don't take care of their children. They're critical of not having enough desire to become better educated. They're critical of the destructive consequences of drugs and other illicit behavior in their communities. That ain't nothing new to them. But they want a way out.

And here's the real tragedy—Mr. Cosby has little by way of intellectual substance and social analysis to offer them. Now, to his credit, he brings in people who have worked in communities, and some of whom have expertise in these areas, but not nearly enough, number one. And number two, he could use this as an opportunity to jump-start a more serious and substantive conversation and dialogue, which means you have to have people on stage who disagree with you. One of the great tragedies of Mr. Cosby's blame the poor tour is his willful ignorance of the lives of these people through study, through examination, through taking the time to listen and engage and to take a measure of their extraordinary diversity and their robust complexity.

Furthermore, on many of these stops of the tour, when people have tried to ask him questions about my book, he completely cuts them off. He doesn't want to engage them. And if your purpose, Mr. Cosby, is to have an open dialogue and exchange of ideas about helping poor black people, you and I, as prominent black people, want to achieve this. If you're talking about the need for black people to get rid of shameful habits, how about the inability to speak to one another? So in the process, his refusal to sit down together with me at the "table of brotherhood"—as Dr. King phrased it—is a mark of not only his analytical failure but at some level an ethical lapse and a philosophical fault in his own approach. And I think, at that level, it's utterly lamentable.

Now, I'm not saying that Mr. Cosby needs to debate me in public. I'm simply suggesting, "Why can't we come together and discuss our similarities of goal, perhaps, but also our different approaches in order to help the poor get better footing?" And we can even agree to disagree. We might conclude that he should carry on in his way and I should carry on in mine, as we both pursue the goal of helping poor black people. When the Apostle Paul and one of his evangelists had to split, the Bible says Paul went his way, the disciple went his way, but they were both trying to serve the kingdom of God. And so I think at that level, Mr. Cosby has been unwilling to become a partner in the process of helping poor black people. And that does say something.

Bruce: What is the benefit of this tour? Hasn't it been discontinued?

Dyson: No. Well, it's episodic. It goes on and it doesn't go on. I think that the benefit of the tour doesn't redound positively to those who are poor because they don't usually get much information. Because Cosby gets up, he rambles, he says some things, he gets things off of his chest, he repeats that black people should be responsible. And, of course, black people agree with that already. He says black people should take care of their kids. Well, they agree with that, but how? And can you tell us how that can occur? Don't simply tell us. Give us the means to achieve that. Give us some insight about the structural features of our existence that might be addressed even as we attempt to expand the narrative of personal responsibility. And, again, we've got to put personal responsibility in a broader context. And this is what Mr. Cosby especially fails to help people see—that even though personal responsibility is critical, it ain't sufficient to help poor people.

There are many other forms of responsibility—social, and political, and moral responsibility that must be brought into play. I think Mr. Cosby is beyond his depth. He's in over his head. And his refusal to even acknowledge that, on the one hand, makes it difficult to help him understand where he might do a better job. And on the other hand, his nearly untamed arrogance, as a black celebrity who has rarely been challenged, means that he's unwilling to hear. And so—

Bruce: I guess it depends on how you see things. Because I have to tell you, initially, when I first learned of Mr. Cosby's remarks, my visceral reaction was, right on. That's right. I felt like somebody needed to say it. But then, and mainly because of your book, and even before I read the book, I was seeing you on C-SPAN and elsewhere, and you were giving a much more analytical approach to what he had said. And it made me think more deeply about what he said and who he was talking about. It did make me feel—and I know the prerogatives of book selling. You have to have a title that's going to stand out. But do you think the black middle class has lost its mind, or do you just think Bill Cosby has lost his mind?

Dyson: Let me say something first before I answer that question. And that's the purpose of my book—it is to do exactly what you said: To bring a more edifying, insightful, complex, engaged analysis of the plight and predicament of the poor. And, furthermore, to represent them in all of their characteristic colorfulness, and beauty, and struggle, and strife, and horror, and, yes, at times, in all of their self-destruction. But with the interest, should I say, of trying to help poor black people overcome their difficulties while, at the same time, trying to argue in a public sphere that is already overgrown—saturated, brother—with vicious and narrow beliefs about poor black people.

Now, yes, the title of the book was deliberately provocative—some would say incendiary, some would say controversial. But it does express my attempt to try to put this debate in stark terms, and to mount a counteroffensive to Mr. Cosby's brutally dissatisfying remonstration against the poor and to figure out how we can come up with better insight about what he said. I don't just want to simply engage *him*; I want to engage the tradition from which he emerges. And I know that most people in America, including black people, didn't understand that what he said grew out of a tradition. It grew out of a tradition of what I have termed, in my book, the Afristocracy—the black blessed, the black gifted, the black fortunate. So it grows out of a tradition where well-to-do black people and wealthy elites have assaulted poor black people.

They were first caught, these elites, in the gaze of white society. And as a result of that—being surveyed and monitored by white society—they felt the ethical heat and moral pressure from white communities to clean up the detritus and the garbage of black life. Now here's the irony—black elites were trying to prove to white folk that they could become citizens of the American mainstream, but they're trying to prove it to people who held us in slavery for two hundred fifty, three hundred years. So the moral dimensions of the mainstream are already to be called into question because of their evil activity of enslaving black people. And yet, because whites had power and the ability to legitimate, or de-legitimate, us, elite black people sought to prove in part to white folk that we were worthy of being considered American citizens. And one of the things we had to do was to clean up the mess, morally and socially, of our communities. Now, the positive side of what is known as racial uplift—and that's how historians and social analysts have characterized this attempt of the black elite to address these problems historically—the upside of racial uplift is that even ordinary black people attempted to use their religion and their social philosophy in order to make the situation better for black people. "Lifting as we climb," was how the National Association of Colored Women put it. That was an edifying and even a noble incarnation of that belief.

On the other hand, the black elite took it in a different direction and began to beat up on poor black people from the convention hall, from the political floor, from the pulpit, from the political podium, and from the sororities and fraternities and so on. They began to just berate poor black people, and tried to make them assimilate and conform to this dominant white ideal and to the Victorian pressures that were implicit in elite black culture. So that's why, in my book, I spend so much time giving the historical context and the political circumstance from which black elite thinking has emerged. So by the time you hear what Cosby said in 2004, you get a sense of what preceded him and what was said before him and, as a result of that, you begin to understand how difficult and complex are the circumstances and situations that shape black life. And you better understand the history of the assault upon poor black people by their more elite black brothers and sisters.

Bruce: Is the notion of the Afristocracy and the Ghettocracy, as you call it, dynamic, or is it stagnant?

Dyson: Oh, no, it's definitely dynamic. In the sense that the Afristocracy is really a term to conjure the elite among African American people. These are not only stylistic definitions and distinctions but also class-based and moral distinctions. For me, for instance, the Afristocracy is a dynamic class that suggests that there are people who believe automatically that the black poor or the black elite are either cursed or blessed, respectively. Furthermore, what I mean by Afristocracy and Ghettocracy—those who are mired at the bottom, those who are stuck, those who are poor and working poor and who get up and work forty and fifty and sixty hours a week and yet can't make it above the poverty level—is my attempt to imagine the forces that keep people within an economic mainstream or excluded from it, and the sociological, moral, and theological justifications that are marshaled in order to defend the self-interests of a particular class of black people.